"LGBT" Politics

Asian Perspectives

"LGBT" Politics

Asian Perspectives

Edited by

Wataru Kusaka
Tsukasa Iga
Kaoru Aoyama
Keiko Tsuji Tamura

TRANS
PACIFIC
PRESS

"LGBT" politics: Asian perspectives
Translated by the first Japanese edition, *Tōnan Ajia to "LGBT" no seiji:*
Seiteki shōsūsha wo megutte nani ga arasowarete irunoka ["LGBT" politics in Southeast Asia:
What is being disputed regarding gender and sexual minorities?]
Published in 2021 by Akashi Shoten.

English edition ©2025 Wataru Kusaka, Tsukasa Iga, Kaoru Aoyama, Keiko Tsuji Tamura
Published in 2025 by Trans Pacific Press Co., Ltd.

Trans Pacific Press Co., Ltd.
[Editorial Office]
2-2-15-2F, Hamamatsu-cho, Minato-ku,
Tokyo, 1050013, JAPAN
[Registered Office]
PO Box 8547 #19682
Boston, MA, 02114, United States
Email: info@transpacificpress.com
Web: http://www.transpacificpress.com

Copyedited by Dr. Karl E. Smith, Melbourne, Australia
Layout designed and set by Ryo Kuroda, Tsukuba-city, Ibaraki, Japan

Distributors

World
Independent Publishers Group (IPG)
814 N. Franklin Street,
Chicago, IL 60610, USA
Email: frontdesk@ipgbook.com
Web: http://www.ipgbook.com

Japan
MHM Limited
3-2-3F, Kanda-Ogawamachi, Chiyoda-ku,
Tokyo 101-0052
Email: sales@mhmlimited.co.jp
Web: http://www.mhmlimited.co.jp

China
China Publishers Services Ltd.
718, 7/F., Fortune Commercial Building,
362 Sha Tsui Road, Tsuen Wan, N.T.
Hong Kong
Email: edwin@cps-hk.com

Southeast Asia
Alkem Company Pte Ltd.
1, Sunview Road #01-27,
Eco-Tech@Sunview
Singapore 627615
Email: enquiry@alkem.com.sg

The publication of this book was supported by a Grant-in-Aid for Publication of
Scientific Research Results (Grant Number 23HP6003), provided by the Japan Society
for the Promotion of Science, to which we express our sincere appreciation.

Library of Congress Control Number: 2024952450
ISBN 978-1-920850-49-4 (paperback)
ISBN 978-1-920850-50-0 (eBook)

"LGBT" Politics

Asian Perspectives

Edited by

Wataru Kusaka
Tsukasa Iga
Kaoru Aoyama
Keiko Tsuji Tamura

TRANS
PACIFIC
PRESS

"LGBT" politics: Asian perspectives
Translated by the first Japanese edition, *Tōnan Ajia to "LGBT" no seiji:*
Seiteki shōsūsha wo megutte nani ga arasowarete irunoka ["LGBT" politics in Southeast Asia:
What is being disputed regarding gender and sexual minorities?]
Published in 2021 by Akashi Shoten.

English edition ©2025 Wataru Kusaka, Tsukasa Iga, Kaoru Aoyama, Keiko Tsuji Tamura
Published in 2025 by Trans Pacific Press Co., Ltd.

Trans Pacific Press Co., Ltd.

[Editorial Office]
2-2-15-2F, Hamamatsu-cho, Minato-ku,
Tokyo, 1050013, JAPAN

[Registered Office]
PO Box 8547 #19682
Boston, MA, 02114, United States

Email: info@transpacificpress.com
Web: http://www.transpacificpress.com

Copyedited by Dr. Karl E. Smith, Melbourne, Australia
Layout designed and set by Ryo Kuroda, Tsukuba-city, Ibaraki, Japan

Distributors

World
Independent Publishers Group (IPG)
814 N. Franklin Street,
Chicago, IL 60610, USA
Email: frontdesk@ipgbook.com
Web: http://www.ipgbook.com

Japan
MHM Limited
3-2-3F, Kanda-Ogawamachi, Chiyoda-ku,
Tokyo 101-0052
Email: sales@mhmlimited.co.jp
Web: http://www.mhmlimited.co.jp

China
China Publishers Services Ltd.
718, 7/F., Fortune Commercial Building,
362 Sha Tsui Road, Tsuen Wan, N.T.
Hong Kong
Email: edwin@cps-hk.com

Southeast Asia
Alkem Company Pte Ltd.
1, Sunview Road #01-27,
Eco-Tech@Sunview
Singapore 627615
Email: enquiry@alkem.com.sg

The publication of this book was supported by a Grant-in-Aid for Publication of
Scientific Research Results (Grant Number 23HP6003), provided by the Japan Society
for the Promotion of Science, to which we express our sincere appreciation.

Library of Congress Control Number: 2024952450
ISBN 978-1-920850-49-4 (paperback)
ISBN 978-1-920850-50-0 (eBook)

Table of Contents

List of Figures

List of Photos

List of Tables

Notes on Naming conventions

This book draws on research and source materials from various countries in East and Southeast Asia, where naming customs and practices differ widely. To the maximum extent possible, the referencing and bibliography in this book follow the Harvard referencing conventions. Where references are cited from languages that do not follow the Western naming conventions of naming, we have attempted to respect the vernacular languages, while ensuring that the in-text reference directly correlates to the bibliographical listing. Transliteration of Chinese titles and names follows Mandarin pinyin spelling, except when an established alternative spelling was available.

About the authors (In alphabetical order)

Kaoru Aoyama (Conclusion) is a professor at the Graduate School of Intercultural Studies, Kobe University. She holds a PhD in sociology and specializes in gender/sexuality studies, gendered labor and cross-border migration. She is currently leading two corroborative pieces of research both as the PI: on migrant sex work and trafficking in the sex industry in nine countries in Europe and Asia; and challenging the notion of dichotomous sex/gender/sexuality from Asian perspectives, which is a successor project of this book. Her publications in English include *Thai Migrant Sex Workers from Modernisation to Globalisation*, Palgrave/Macmillan, 2009; *Asian Women and Intimate Work*, Brill Academic Publication, 2013, edited, with Emiko Ochiai (winner of the 2014 Choice Outstanding Academic Title Award); and 'Researchers, Gatekeepers and Participatory Action Research in Japan's Sex Industry,' in Susan Dewey, Isabel Crowhurst and Chimaraoke Izugbara eds., *International Handbook of Sex Industry Research: New Directions and Perspectives*, Routledge, 2018.

Genya Fukunaga (Introduction and Chapter 6) is an associate professor at Division of Diversity and Inclusion, Komaba Organization for Educational Excellence, the University of Tokyo. He specializes in feminist/queer studies, sociology, and East Asia area studies. He holds a PhD. Most of his works focus on the intersections of colonialism/imperialism, the Cold War regime, and gender and sexual politics in East Asia. He is the author of 'Queer politics and solidarity: Post–Cold War homonationalism in East Asia,' in Kazuyoshi Kawasaka and Stefan Würrer eds., *Beyond Diversity: Queer Politics, Activism, and Representation in Contemporary Japan*, Düsseldorf University Press, 2024; and *Sei/sei o meguru tōsō: Taiwan to Kankoku ni okeru seiteki mainoriti no undo to seiji* (The Struggle over Sexuality/Gender: Queer movements and politics in Taiwan and Korea), Akashi Shoten, 2025.

Naomi Hatsukano (Chapter 14) is an associate senior research fellow at the Southeast Asian Studies Group II, Area Studies Center, in IDE-JETRO, Japan. She holds a MA in International Studies. Her research focuses on international development and Cambodia. Recent research interests include the policy environment of Cambodian migrant workers and their situations in Thailand and Japan. She wrote 'Kanbojia no imin rōdōsha seisaku: Shinkō sōshutsukoku no seido dukuri to kadai (Cambodia's labor migration policies and laws: Institutional building and challenges as a newly emerging sending country)' in Miwa Yamada ed., *Higashi Ajia ni okeru imin rōdosha no hōseido:Sōshutsukoku to jyunyūkoku no kyōtsu kiban no kōchiku ni mukete* (Laws and labor migration policies in East Asia: Seeking a common platform of sending and receiving countries), IDE-JETRO, 2014; 'Kikoeru nowa dare no koe: Ratanakirishū no senjyūmin to tochi mondai o shien suru hitotachi (Whose voice can I hear?: Indigenous people of Ratanakiri and supporters of land issues)' in Waka Aoyama, Hiroyuki Ukeda and Takaaki Kobayashi eds. *Kaihatsu enjo ga tsukuru shakai seikatsu: Genba kara no purojekuto shindan (dai 2 han)* (Living with aid: Development projects observed from multiple perspectives), Daigaku kyoiku shuppan, 2017.

Shinsuke Hinata (Chapter 8) is an associate professor at the Graduate School of Humanities, Osaka University. He holds a PhD in area studies. His research focuses on the political and cultural history of modern Thailand. He is the author of 'A History of Thai Intellectuals' Perceptions of Khon, the Masked Dance of Ramayana, on the Modern World Stage,' in Madoka Fukuoka ed., *Ramayana Theater in Contemporary Southeast Asia*, Jenny Stanford Publishing, 2022; '1910 nen "Shamu koku no kyōiku ni kansuru chokugo" kōfu keikaku: Keii to shisōteki haikei ('Royal Rescript on Education of Siam' (1910): An unrealized plan and its ideological background),' *Studies of New Century Humanities*, 4, 2021 and 'Kindai Tai ni okeru kōkogaku gyōsei no dōnyū katei: Daiichiji sekai taisen to "kobutu chōsa, hozon ni kansuru fukoku" (1924) o keiki to shite (Introduction of archaeological administration in modern Thailand:

First World War and the "Decree of Investigation and Conservation of Antiquities" (1924))', *Asian and African Area Studies* 18(2), 2019.

Tsukasa Iga (Introduction and Chapter 3) is a designated associate professor at the Asian Satellite Campus Institute, Nagoya University, specializing in political science and area studies. He holds a PhD in political science. His publications include 'Marēshia ni okeru media tōsei to yotō UMNO no kigen: Datsu shokuminchiki no Marē go jānarizumu to seiji kenryoku (The Origins of Media Control and the United Malays National Organization (UMNO) in Malaysia: Malay Journalism and Political Power in the Decolonization Era),' *Tonan Asia Kenkyu*, 55(1), 2017; 'Gendai Marēshia ni okeru "sekushuariti poritikkusu" no tanjō: 1980 nendai ikō no kokka to LGBT undō (The birth of 'sexuality politics' in contemporary Malaysia: The state and the LGBT Movement since the 1980s),' *Asian and African Area Studies*, 17(1), 2017; 'Rôle des médias et montée de l'Internet dans la démocratisation de la Malaisie de l'après Mahathir 2003–2013 (Media and politics in post-Mahathir Malaysia: The political roles of media in a transitional society 2003–2013),' David Delfolie, Nathalie Fau, Elsa Lafaye de Micheaux eds., *Malaisie contemporaine*, Paris: Irasec et Les Indes Savantes, 2021.

Masao Imamura (Chapter 1) is a professor at the Faculty of Humanities and Social Sciences, Yamagata University. He holds a PhD from the National University of Singapore (geography). Most of his works examine majority-minority dynamics in mainland Southeast Asia, especially Myanmar. His recent publications include '"Shūkyō to kindai" to Tōnan Ajia kenkyū ('Religion and Modernity' and Southeast Asian Studies),' *Southeast Asia: History and Culture*, 48, 2019; "Henkyō kara miru Myanmā seihen: Naisenshi no nakano kūdeta (Myanmar's political change–seen from a periphery: A coup d'état in the context of the civil war)," *Sekai*, 948, 2021, and "Owariga mienai Myanmā no gunji seiken (Myanmar's resilient junta)," *Ajia Taiheiyou ronsou* 24, 2022.

Peter Anthony Jackson (Preface) is an emeritus professor of Thai history and cultural studies in the College of Asia and the Pacific, Australian National University, Canberra. He holds a PhD in Buddhist philosophy and has written extensively on modern Thai cultural history, with special interests in Buddhism, magical cults and gay, lesbian, and transgender cultures in Asia. His books include: *Queer Bangkok: 21st Century Markets, Media, and Rights*, Hong Kong University Press, 2011; *First Queer Voices From Thailand: Uncle Go's Advice Columns for Gays, Lesbians and Kathoeys,* Hong Kong University Press, 2016; and *Deities and Divas: Queer Ritual Specialists in Myanmar, Thailand and Beyond* with Benjamin Baumann, NIAS Press, 2022.

Yumi Kitamura (Chapter 15) is an associate professor at the Research and Development Laboratory, Kyoto University Library, specializing in Southeast Asian Studies and Library and Information Science. She holds a PhD. She is an author of 'Parallel Development: Southeast Asian Studies and Library Collections,' in Khoo Boo Teik and Jafar Suryomenggolo eds., *State and Society in Motion: Essays in Honor of Takashi Shiraishi*, NIAS Press, 2020; 'Long Way Home: The Life History of Chinese Indonesian Migrants in the Netherlands,' *Wacana: Journal of the Humanities of Indonesia*, 18(1), 2017; and is co-editor of *When East Asia Meets Southeast Asia: Presence And Connectedness In Transformation Revisited,* World Scientific, 2022.

Takahiro Kojima (Chapter 12) is a professor at the Department of International and Cultural Studies, Tsuda University, specializing in cultural anthropological studies of Theravada Buddhist practices. He holds a PhD in area studies. Most of his works examine Theravada Buddhist societies in Myanmar and Southwest China, and the history of cultural exchange between Japanese and Burmese Buddhists. He is the author of 'Tai Buddhist Practices in Dehong Prefecture, Yunnan, China,' *Southeast Asian Studies*, 1(3), 2012; 'From Tea to Temples and Texts: Transformation of the Interfaces of Upland-Lowland Interaction on the China-Myanmar Border,' *Southeast Asian Studies*, 2(1), 2013;

and *Kokkyō to Bukkyō jissen: Chūgoku/Myanmā kyōiki ni okeru Jōza Bukkyōto shakai no minzokushi* (Borderland Buddhism: An Ethnography of Theravada Buddhist practices across the China-Myanmar national boundary), Kyoto University Press, 2014.

Wataru Kusaka (Introduction and Chapter 13) is a professor at the Graduate School of Global Studies, Tokyo University of Foreign Studies, specializing in political science and Philippine studies. He holds a PhD in social and cultural studies. Most of his works examine Philippine politics from the perspectives of marginalized people using ethnography and discourse analysis. He is the author of *Moral Politics in the Philippines: Inequality, Democracy and the Urban Poor*, National University of Singapore Press and Kyoto University Press, 2017; 'Bandit Grabbed the State: Duterte's Moral Politics,' *Philippine Sociological Review*, 65, 2017; and 'Disaster, Discipline, Drugs and Duterte: Emergence of New Moral Subjectivities in Post-Yolanda Leyte,' in Koki Seki ed., *Ethnographies of Development and Globalization in the Philippines: Emergent Socialities and the Governing of Precarity,* Routledge, 2020.

Satoshi Miyawaki (Chapter 5) is a professor at the Graduate School of Humanities, Osaka University. He holds a PhD in International Social Sciences (the University of Tokyo), specializing in sociology of religion and Philippine area studies. Most of his works critically reevaluate the Catholic Church's involvement in politics in the Philippines by analyzing extensive public documents in their broader political and social contexts. He is the author of 'Discourse of the Catholic Church in the Philippines on the National Elections since 2009: An Analysis of CBCP Pastoral Statements,' *Studies in Language and Culture*, 49, 2023; *Firipin katorikku kyōkai no seiji kan'yo* (The political involvement of the Philippine Catholic Church), Osaka University Press, 2019; 'Gendai Firipin katorikku kyōkai ni okeru rekishi no kinen no shikata (Commmemoration of History by the Philippine Catholic Church),' *Studies in Language and Culture*, 42, 2016.

Nara Oda (Chapter 7) is a lecturer at the World Language and Society Education Centre, Tokyo University of Foreign Studies. She holds a PhD in area studies. Her recent research focuses on the modern history of Vietnam in the context of traditional medicine, healthcare, family and issues related to gender and sexual minorities. She is the author of 'Traditional Medicine in the Mekong Region' in Seiichi Igarashi ed., *From Mekong Commons to Mekong Community: An Interdisciplinary Approach to Transboundary Challenges*, Routledge, 2021; *"Dentō igaku" ga tsukurareru toki: Betonamu iryō seisaku shi* (The making of 'traditional medicine': A history of Vietnam's medical policies), Kyoto University Press, 2022; 'More Eastern than Traditional: The making of Đông y in the Republic of Vietnam during the Cold War' in Michele Thompson, Kathryn Sweet and Michitake Aso eds., *Fighting for Health: Medicine in Cold War Southeast Asia*, Singapore University Press, 2024.

Masaaki Okamoto (Chapter 4) is a professor and works at the Center for Southeast Asian Studies, Kyoto University, specializing in area studies. He holds a PhD in area studies. His research focuses on politics in Southeast Asia, mainly Indonesia, including dynasty politics, urban politics and social media politics. He is the author of *Mushrooming Smart Cities in ASEAN Countries and the Risk of Unhealthy Multi-actor Competition.* Roles Report No. 20, 2022; 'Non-state Violence and Political Order in Democratized Indonesia', in Atsushi Yasutomi, Rosalie Arcala Hall, and Saya Kiba eds. *Pathways for Irregular Forces in Southeast Asia: Mitigating Violence with the Nonstate Armed Groups,* Routledge, 2022; editor of *Local Governance of Peatland Restoration in Riau, Indonesia: A Transdisciplinary Analysis* (with Takamasa Osawa, Wahyu Prasetyawan and Akhwan Binawan), Springer, 2023; and *Indonesia at the Crossroads: Transformation and Challenges* (with Jafar Suryomenggolo), UGM Press, Kyoto University Press and Trans Pacific Press, 2023.

Yūsuke Ōmura (Chapter 11) is a research associate at the Research Institute for Languages and Cultures of Asia and Africa, Tokyo University of Foreign Studies, specializing in cultural anthropology. He holds a M.A. He has conducted anthropological fieldwork in Vientiane, Laos from 2019 until the present (including a long-term stay from 2019–2021). His research focuses on the urban networks of cisgender men who desire men in Vientiane, life history studies of an individual gay man, contemporary art (especially contemporary dance) in Laos. He is currently working on a PhD focused on an ethnographic study of a single gay person and examines ethical and aesthetic dimensions of his life.

Naoya Sakagawa (Chapter 2) is an affiliated researcher at the Center for Southeast Asian Studies, Kyoto University, specializing in area studies and film history. He holds a M.A. in area studies. He wrote a series of articles titled 'A Film Trip Around Asia in the Internet Age' for the Internet magazine *Tokion*. https://tokion.jp/en/series/a-film-trip-around-asia-in-the-internet-age/

Akitomo Shingae (Chapter 10) is a professor at the Research Center for Human Rights, and the Graduate School of Urban Management, both at Osaka Metropolitan University, specializing in cultural anthropology. He holds a PhD. Most of his works examine gender and sexual minorities in Japan from the perspectives of medical anthropology and queer studies. He is the author of *Nihon no 'gei' to eizu: Komyunitī, kokka, aidentiti* ('Gays' and AIDS in Japan: Community, state, identity), Seikyūsha, 2013; 'Relationships among lesbians involved in childbirth/parenting, sperm donors, and children in Japan,' *Journal of Lesbian Studies*, 25(4), 2021; and 'Daibāshiti suishin to LGBT/SOGI no yukue: Shijōka sareru shakai undō (The future direction of diversity promotion and LGBT/SOGI: Marketized social movements),' in Kōichi Iwabuchi, ed, *Nihon ni ikiru, Nihon o hiraku* (Living in Japan, opening up Japan), Seikyūsha, 2021.

Khanis Suvianita (Chapter 15) is a lecturer at Ledalero Institute of Philosophy and Creative Technology and a board trustee member of GAYa NUSANTARA, a pioneering NGO for gender and sexual minorities in Asia. She has been specializing in gender and sexual diversities and religious studies in Southeast Asia. She holds a Ph.D. in Interreligious Studies. She is an author of 'Human Rights and the LGBTI Movement in Indonesia,' *Asian Journal of Women's Studies*, 2013; co-author of '"Just Became a Love Slave": Shedding Light on Relationship Violence Against Males,' *ANIMA Indonesian Psychological Journal*, 2019; and 'The Tension and Synergy of Ethical Sources in The Relations of Lecturers and Students in Indonesian Universities,' *KARSA Journal of Social and Islamic Culture*, 2019.

Keiko Tsuji Tamura (Chapter 9) is an emeritus professor and research fellow at The University of Kitakyushu, specializing in international relations theory and Southeast Asian area studies, especially politics, society and gender in Singapore. She is also president of Japan Center for Borderlands Studies. She holds a PhD in law. Her major publications are 'Changing Family and Gender in Singapore,' in Yoko Hayami, Junko Koizumi, Chalidaporn Songsamphan and Ratana Tosakul eds., *The Family in Flux in Southeast Asia: Institution, Ideology, Practice*, Kyoto University Press and Silkworm Books, 2012; *Taminzoku kokka Shingapōru no seiji to gengo: 'Shōmetsu' shita Nanyō daigaku no 25nen* (Politics and language in Singapore, a multiethnic nation: 25 years of 'vanished' Nanyang University), Akashi Shoten, 2013; and 'Looking into States and Civil Societies in Taiwan and Singapore Through the Lens of Sexual Minorities,' in Khatharya Um and Chiharu Takenaka eds., *Globalization and Civil Society in East Asian Space*, Routledge, 2023.

Preface

Models of LGBT Activism Across Southeast and East Asia: Queer Thailand in Regional Perspective

Peter A. Jackson

Introduction

Island and mainland Southeast Asia and East Asia form some of the most culturally and linguistically diverse parts of the world and are home to peoples who speak languages from multiple distinct language families. In the premodern period, these two regions' complex geography of mainland river valleys separated by heavily forested mountains and thousands of islands spread across several archipelagos contributed to the emergence of many distinctive cultures and polities. In the classical and early modern eras, the diverse world religions of Hinduism, Buddhism, Confucianism, Islam and Christianity became established in different Asian societies, blending with vernacular spirit beliefs and local ritual forms to create stunning varieties of hybrid religious expression.

The diversity of the region was accentuated further during the era of European, Japanese and American imperialism, when different Asian kingdoms and polities respectively came under the colonial domination of Spain, the Netherlands, Britain, France, Japan and the United States. Siam, renamed Thailand in 1939, was the only Southeast Asian kingdom that avoided the fate of colonization, while in East Asia modernizing Japan became the only Asian society that transformed into an expansionist colonial power. In the colonial period, relations with the respective imperial metropoles often took priority over connections with neighboring Asian societies. Even independent Siam gave importance to enhancing its connections to imperial Japan and the European powers, as part of a concerted policy to ward off the threat of colonization. It has only been since post-World War II independence, often achieved after hard-fought wars against the different colonial regimes, that the many societies of the region have turned their attention to re-building connections with their immediate Asian neighbors. In Southeast Asia, the Association of Southeast Asian Nations or ASEAN, established in 1967, has been one of the notable frameworks for promoting political, economic and social cooperation.

This multidimensional diversity – in terms of geography, cultures, languages, religions and political histories – makes the study of Southeast and East Asia as regions particularly challenging. This is no less the case when it comes to understanding the cultures of gender and sexuality and the modern politics of gender and sexual diversity in these two regions. The impulse of the scholar is often to look for patterns and commonalities among the manifold empirical differences that are presented to the researcher in the field. And the fact that the countries of Southeast and East Asia are geographically near to each other can lead to a naïve view that their proximity should lead to similarity. However, the simplifying assumption that the societies of Asia share common patterns of life or culture can at times lead to generalizations that do not match the complex realities on the ground. It is indeed the case that many of the modern societies of Southeast Asia are based on foundations of negotiating the complexities, multiplicities and differences within this region. However, the ways in which these differences are addressed and managed often differ from one society to another. In studying homosexual and transgender identities, communities and human rights activism in Asia our academic impulse to look for shared patterns among the region's queer cultures needs to be tempered by an awareness that there are likely to be exceptions to any general statements or conclusions we propose.

The challenges presented by the empirical diversity of Southeast and East Asia can at times discourage attempts to present overall perspectives. However, the editors and authors of this excellent collection of studies have not been put off by the challenge. Recent decades have seen an increase in single-country studies of Southeast and East Asia's queer cultures and communities.[1] These studies have usually either taken Western societies and the histories and politics of LGBT communities in Europe, North America and Australia as their point of comparison or, alternatively, they have focused on local processes within each Asian society. However, there have been very few studies that compare the queer and trans cultures of countries within Southeast and East Asia and there have also been very limited numbers of synoptic accounts of gender and sexual diversity across these regions. This means that we have not been able to specify the actual commonalities that do exist across mainland and island Southeast Asia and East Asia. The focused studies of LGBT activism, cultural politics and modern history in this collection provide a much-welcomed corrective to the tendencies to focus on individual societies or to take the West as the default point of comparison. The Introduction by Wataru Kusaka, Tsukasa Iga and Genya Fukunaga presenting Southeast and East Asian perspectives on what is being contested in these regions and Kaoru Aoyama's concluding perspectives on the intersections of capitalism, the state, religion and human rights activism on gender and sexual politics reveal innovative insights that provide strong foundations for the projects of comparative Southeast and East Asian queer and trans studies. What is more, as scholars working from and within the Japanese academy, the contributors to this collection provide additional comparative dimensions by bringing the situation of gender and sexual minorities in Japan into conversation with studies of Southeast and East Asia. The inclusion of Genya Fukunaga's study of the intersections of feminist and queer politics in Taiwan further broadens the comparative scope of this book to an East Asian society that has had major colonial-era influences from Japan and whose legalization of same-sex marriage and gender and sexual rights has been held up as an inspiring beacon by queer people across Asia.

---

1   The titles published in Hong Kong University Press's *Queer Asia* monograph series are some notable examples of the growing number of single-country studies of modern queer cultures and communities across East and Southeast Asia.

Beyond the new information on LGBT communities in different Southeast and East Asian societies provided in each chapter, this collection makes two important contributions to the comparative study of gender and sexual diversity internationally. Firstly, it provides an empirical basis for deriving important new insights on the patterns of gender and sexual diversity across Southeast and East Asia today. And secondly, and just as importantly, this translated collection makes the research of Japanese scholars available to the international academic and activist communities. There are all too few translations of the excellent social, cultural and political research undertaken in Japanese universities and the series of studies in this book brings Japanese scholars into conversation with the rapidly emerging field of comparative international Asian queer studies.

This collection also materializes the critical approach that Kuan-Hsing Chen (2010) has called "Asia as Method," that is, to move beyond Euro-American perspectives by locating Asian discourses as the starting point of analysis and not merely as forms of local data to be fed into Western theories. This book also responds to Dipesh Chakrabarty's (2000) call to "provincialize Europe" in studies of Asian histories, cultures, societies and polities. That is, to regard Europe and North America as other provinces of knowledge alongside Asia, Africa, Latin America, the Pacific and other world regions, which all need to share equal epistemic status with the West.

Placing modern Southeast Asian cultures of gender and sexuality in conversation with the situation in Japan and Taiwan is not only important in decentering Western perspectives. It also gives recognition to the fact that since the 1960s and 1970s Japan and Taiwan have each had significant cultural influences across the Southeast Asian region. It is true that in terms of queer political activism, the West, and especially the United States, have often been held up as models in struggles to advance the rights of sexual and gender minorities. However, in the fields of media, fashion and popular culture – which together contribute to molding the social and cultural matrix within which queer struggles for recognition and respect take place in everyday life – Japan and Taiwan have had major influences in many Southeast Asia countries.

Thailand in queer Southeast Asia

This book poses two interrelated set of questions: what factors have determined the differences in the rights and welfare situations of sexual and gender minorities in the various Southeast and East Asian countries and how have these minorities resisted marginalization and discrimination, whether by activism on the model of LGBT movements in the West or by other means? In the remainder of this preface, I wish to highlight the major contributions of this book to exploring these questions, and to international studies of gender and sexual difference, by placing them in comparison with the situation of homosexual and transgender communities in Thailand. On the one hand, Thailand's lack of a colonial history might make it seem to be an exception that places this country outside accounts of the impact of imperialism on gender and sexual cultures in Southeast Asia and Taiwan. However, recent critical historiography has argued that while Siam/Thailand was not subjected to a direct form of colonialism, it nonetheless was an indirect colony or semicolony of Europe.[2] I have argued that the modern forms of Thailand's gender cultures emerged in response to the challenges presented by colonial-era European notions of "civilization," in particular, how a "civilized" man or woman should dress and act (Jackson 2003).

There are important reasons for using Thailand as a point of comparison in the broader study of queer Southeast and East Asia. While Western societies have often been taken as models of gay liberation and gender rights activism in the later decades of the 20th century, intra-Asian queer cultural and other exchanges have arguably become equally important influences in the development of LGBT activism and cultural change in the 21st century. Thailand plays an important role in contemporary intra-Asian queer connections and influences. As Aoyama observes in her concluding chapter, in some ways Thailand's influence on the phenomena, discourses and representations of sexual and gender minorities in Southeast and East Asia is on par with that of the West.

---

2   For discussion of Thailand as a semicolony see Jackson 2007 and Harrison and Jackson 2010.

Indeed, the study of Thailand's queer cultures is arguably the most extensive in Southeast Asia and the country has at times assumed an iconic place in studies of sexual and gender cultures in Asia and beyond. To an extent, this is because of Thailand's lack of a colonial history and the comparatively tolerant attitudes of the country's dominant religion of Theravada Buddhism towards gender and sexual diversity, which is discussed more below. The modern situation of gender and diversity in Thailand, as well as of Japan, which similarly avoided colonization and shares a Buddhist religious culture, raises the interesting question of what the modern forms of queer cultures in other Asian countries would be like today if they too had avoided colonization. Do Thailand and Japan perhaps present models of what a modern, never-colonized queer Southeast and East Asia might have looked like?

By taking Thailand as my point of comparison, I also aim to contribute to the critical projects of taking Asia as method and provincializing Europe. Since the 1970s, Thailand's large and vibrant commercial gay and trans scenes, together with the country's significant tourism infrastructure, have seen the country become a magnet, first, for Western gay tourists and, since the 1990s, for gay tourists from across Southeast and East Asia. Thailand has played an increasingly important role as a queer-friendly location of intra-regional gay tourism within ASEAN. In his chapter here, Shinsuke Hinata traces the central importance of international gay tourism in the urban and economic development of the Thai resort city of Pattaya.

The growth of gay tourism within Asia has followed from the economic development of the region, which has seen the rise of gay middle classes keen to travel and experience gay life in other countries. Since 2002, the ASEAN Tourism Agreement has facilitated gay tourism within the Southeast Asian region by instituting an open-borders policy that allows visa-free travel for citizens of ASEAN nations to travel to each other's countries. Bangkok has been chosen as the site for several regional queer organizations, such as APCOM, the Asia Pacific Coalition on Male Sexual Health. The United Nations' first Independent Expert on Protection Against Violence and Discrimination Based on Sexual

Orientation and Gender Identity (often shortened to the UN Independent Expert on Sexual Orientation and Gender Identity [UN IE SOGI]) was internationally recognized Thai human rights lawyer Vitit Muntarbhorn, who held the position from 2016 to 2017. In recent years, Thai queer media in the form of "boy love" or BL television series and movies have also become major queer cultural influences across Asia. While the BL genre of manga and young adult novels of romance between young men began in Japan, the development of this genre in Thailand has had major impacts internationally, including in Japan (see Baudinette 2023).

As Kusaka, Iga and Fukunaga note, in Southeast and East Asia the influences of colonialism in the 19th and early 20th centuries and international LGBT movements in the late 20th and early 21st centuries are layered on top of indigenous cultures that already included diverse forms of gender and sexual difference. The different indigenous and international cultures of gender and sexual difference now coexist and intersect in multiple layers. In the premodern period in Thailand, the term *kathoey* was used to label all forms of gender and sexual difference, but because of foreign influences over the past two centuries it now refers only to trans women (Jackson 2000). While some English terms have been borrowed into Thai, notably "gay" for male homosexuals, new local terminologies for sexual and gender diversity have also been invented in other settings. In their chapter here, Yūsuke Ōmura summarizes how the terms *kathoey* and *kee*, from "gay", are also key terms for trans women and male homosexuals in Laos, which shares many cultural, religious and linguistic similarities with neighboring Thailand.

The critical insights of Western queer theory have been adapted by some Thai scholars of gender and sexual diversity (see, for example, Narupon and Jackson 2021a, 2021b, 2023). However, the term "queer" has only a limited resonance in Thai, although it is increasingly well-known in Thai academic circles. Since the early 2000s, a local expression meaning "gender/sex diversity" (*khwam-lak-lai-thang-phet*) has been used by Thai LGBT groups and by sympathetic media, academics and bureaucrats as an accepted expression to refer collectively to all forms of same-sex, transgender and transsexual identity. This Thai expression has similarities to the Japanese notion of "sexual/gender (*sei-no*) diversity" noted by Aoyama in her chapter.

Historically, gender and sexual minorities in Thailand were tolerated but nonetheless suffered widespread discrimination and lacked legally recognized rights. The dominant religion of Theravada Buddhism did not condemn homosexuality or transgenderism as sins, but rather saw them as unfortunate conditions that, according to the law of karma, resulted from immoral deeds such as adultery committed in a previous life (Jackson 1995, 1998). Compared to the intense forms of religiously sanctioned and legally enforced homophobia experienced in many Western and other cultures, premodern Thailand had a comparatively open culture that can be characterized as tolerant but not genuinely accepting of sexual and gender minorities (Jackson 1999a). In the second half of the 20th century, Thailand became the home to large, vibrant communities of gay men, lesbians and trans women. From the 1970s, Thailand's gay and trans scenes of bars, saunas and commercial sex venues became popular destinations for large numbers of international gay tourists, from both Western and Asian countries.

Gay men from more repressive Asian societies have often been able to socialize more easily in the gay scenes in Bangkok and other Thai cities than in their home countries. Alex Au (2011) argues that in the 1990s socializing among Singaporean gay tourists in the more open environment of Bangkok's gay venues established networks that subsequently proved crucial to the development of gay community activism in the city state. Until this time, Singapore's more repressive legal and cultural environment had restricted the development of homosexual community organizations and identity politics, and as Asian economic growth saw the emergence of middle-class gay tourism within ASEAN and East Asia, Thailand's more open society proved important in the broader development of LGBT communities and activism across these regions.

In contrast to the experience in many Western countries, where from the 1970s homosexual rights movements emerged in parallel with commercial gay scenes, for several decades Thailand had a queer-tolerant (but not queer-accepting) culture that nurtured flourishing commercial gay and trans scenes but no real movement for LGBT political and human rights. Ironically, this lack of a political movement to advance the legal rights of queer people in part resulted from the country's comparatively tolerant sexual and gender culture and the fact that same-sex behavior was not criminalized. Never having been colonized, European anti-sodomy laws were not enforced in Thailand. In the West, homosexual rights movements often began as forms of political activism to overturn anti-sodomy laws that had been used to prosecute and often imprison homosexual men. In the absence of such discriminatory laws, Thai homosexual men had no need to organize to change their legal status. Instead, the forms of discrimination that they suffered emerged from antipathetic cultural attitudes that were often diffuse and hence more difficult to confront or challenge by the forms of direct political activism that characterized homosexual rights movements in the West.

In Thailand, sexual and gender minorities first became the focus of public attention and state policies in the 1960s and 1970s, when then newly introduced anti-prostitution laws led to trans women sex workers being arrested and sent to men's prisons (Jackson 2009a). In the 1960s, high profile crimes, including the murders of some prominent homosexual men, also led the country's sensationalist press to highlight the emergence of communities of men in Bangkok who identified with the then new identity category of "gay" (Jackson 1999b). At this time, the anti-gay views of state actors and the sensationalist media did not incite any gay organized political movement, although individual gay men did publicly challenge the negative stereotypes of homosexuality and transgenderism.

As was the case in a number of other Asian countries, the first time that sexual minorities in Thailand became the concerted focus of public policies was in the 1980s, when HIV spread among gay men and public health measures were introduced. It was in response to these state interventions in LGBT lives in the 1980s and 1990s that gay and trans activists working on HIV issues formed the first LGBT organizations. In addition to engaging in education to promote safe sexual practices among the homosexual men and trans women who were threatened by the HIV virus, these organizations took on community development roles with the aims of developing a sense of pride in gay and trans identity and promoting acceptance of gender and sexual difference in the mass media and among government agencies and the public. The 1990s also saw the emergence of the first lesbian community organization, which in the early 2000s often joined with gay and trans woman organizations in public education activities and calls to end discrimination in media reporting, work, education, access to health care and other fields.

While Thailand's queer communities emerged as the largest and most visible in Southeast Asia in the latter decades of the 20th century and were the focus of at times negative stereotyping as the HIV/AIDS epidemic impacted increasing numbers of people, at this time the country's political leaders largely regarded LGBT people and their issues to be unimportant and irrelevant to national political concerns. Exceptions were sections within the national health bureaucracy, which in the 1990s collaborated with gay community organizations in combating the HIV/AIDS epidemic, and the Tourism Authority of Thailand, which at times used the country's queer communities as advertising drawcards to promote international tourism.

However, from being regarded as politically irrelevant by national politicians throughout the 20th century, LGBT issues have rapidly moved center stage in Thailand in recent years. In 2021 and 2022, Thai queer groups for the first time joined with pro-democracy activists in public demonstrations against the military-led government. Nattapol Wisuttipat describes queer participation in a pro-democracy street rally in August 2021 as follows,

> LGBT rights activists [were] easily discernible among the pro-democracy protesters. They sported the rainbow-colored pride flags, dressed as drag queens, danced in the parade, and sometimes turned the street into a catwalk for a satirical fashion show aimed at the Thai monarchy. Their demands were inspired by the global gay rights movement, such as legalization of same-sex marriage and sex workers, and educating

about gender and sexuality diversity or *khwam-lak-lai-thang-phet.* (Nattapol 2022: 1–2)

When Pride Parades resumed in Bangkok in 2022 after the end of COVID-19 lockdowns, mainstream political leaders participated for the first time. In 2022, the mayor of Bangkok, Chadchart Sittipunt, who in the 2010s had been a Deputy Minister of Transport in the national government led by Thailand's first female Prime Minister, Yingluck Shinawatra, walked in the parade. In 2023, prominent members of both the Pheu Thai and Move Forward parties, which have the largest number of elected MPs in the national parliament, also walked in the Pride Parade in Bangkok. The Pheu Thai Party, which is now the main party in the ruling coalition government, appointed an LGBT policy officer during the lead up to the May 2023 general election and several major parties actively courted the pink vote by including the legalization of gay marriage in their policy platforms. The Move Forward Party, which won the most seats in the 2023 election, has four openly queer members in the current Thai parliament. In 2024, the Thai parliament voted to legalize same-sex marriage, making Thailand the third country in Asia, after Taiwan and Nepal, to recognize queer relationships.

Capitalism and imagined Southeast Asian queer communities

Citing Okano (2015), Kusaka, Iga and Fukunaga note that sexual and gender minorities who are forced to flee families and home environments because of homophobic and transphobic attitudes have often been able to build relationships and find safety in spaces provided by capitalism. Indeed, a notable commonality across Southeast and East Asia, as well as across the world, is that modern LGBT communities emerged outside the state and the family in spaces provided by the market in cities. The first modern queer communities in Asia typically formed in national capitals that were the centers of economic activity and education and where everyday life was most heavily impacted by the marketization of labor and the commodification of services. Over the past century and a half, capitalism and commercial media have permitted the emergence of imagined communities of sexually and gender diverse people in cities across the world, including in Asia. When state institutions, religion and heteronormative families provided no opportunities or safe spaces for the expression of sexual or gender difference, it was the urban domain of the market – often in the form of small bars and commercial venues catering to gay, lesbian and transgender customers – that enabled previously isolated homosexual and trans people to come together and begin to form the first modern queer communities.

The rise of urban market economies provided queer people with the opportunity to explore and establish collective forms of existence outside the restrictive laws of the state and the strictures of the heteronormative family. I have argued that imagined LGBT communities first came into being in Thailand because of processes mediated by the market and commercial media like those that Anderson (1983) contends led to the emergence of modern nations as "imagined communities" (Jackson 2009a, 2009b, 2011a, 2011b). However, the first queer communities often largely existed underground. This book relocates the focus of attention from the private spaces of the first underground communities of sexual and gender minorities to the public domain of the body politic in Southeast and East Asia, as previously excluded and minoritized communities have claimed a voice and the right to be heard in the political domain. This book moves analysis from the spaces of the market and commercial media, which nurtured Asia's first modern queer communities, to the domains of national politics and legal frameworks as these LGBT people seek to be recognized as rightful members of the nation deserving of equal treatment by the law and by the state.

Capitalism and queer gender exclusions

Following Richardson (1998), Kusaka, Iga and Fukunaga argue that sexual minorities find it easier to enjoy the rights of citizenship when the notion of being a "good citizen" is defined as someone who contributes to national economic development. Indeed, in Thailand, the country's commercial gay scene of bars, discos and other venues has been highlighted by state agencies such as the Tourism Authority of Thailand in international advertising programs that aim to support the country's economically important tourism industry. However, capitalism is a double-edged sword that not only provides opportunities for some gender and sexual minorities but also creates new forms of exclusion for others. Cisgendered gay men are often more privileged in terms of education, careers and income than homosexual women and transgendered people. In many Southeast and East Asian societies gender-based discrimination and wage gaps between men and women, as well as between cities and rural areas, mean that lesbians and minorities in rural areas often have lower incomes than urban gay men. Furthermore, while transgender people typically need to pay for the expensive private medical treatment required for gender transitioning – because Asian states do not include these procedures in national health programs – they nonetheless face discrimination in finding jobs and have restricted incomes.

As Aoyama mentions in her conclusion, there is much less research on lesbians in Southeast Asia compared to cisgendered gay men, which reflects the patriarchal social biases that restrict women's opportunities. This mirrors the under-representation, discrimination and marginalization of lesbians, trans women and women-assigned persons in general. While all gender and sexual minorities suffer from discrimination and stigmatization, patriarchal social structures may nonetheless provide more opportunities to queer people assigned male, notably cisgendered gay men, to engage in activism for their respective rights than people who are assigned female. Women, including trans women, suffer the same restricted opportunities in education, work and careers as heterosexual women and live in societies that privilege male sexuality and male sexual autonomy over female sexuality. This is as true in Thailand as in other Southeast and East Asian countries (see Harrison 2000). It is especially notable that despite the participation of small, and slowly increasing, numbers of women, politics and the field of power have historically been male dominated domains in Thailand. This is symbolized by the fact that the Thai monarchy has always been headed by a king, never a queen.

Religion and LGBT rights

In their Introduction to this book, Kusaka, Iga and Fukunaga note Finke and Adamczyk's (2008) argument that secularization was one of the prerequisites for the development of modern homosexual rights movements in many Western societies. However, secularization is only a necessary precondition for the emergence of modern LGBT communities and movements in societies in which the dominant religion condemns homosexuality and transgenderism as sins or immoral activities that contravene religious injunctions. When a society's dominant religion does not condemn sexual or gender difference – such as in the forms of Theravada Buddhism found in Thailand, Myanmar, Cambodia and Laos and the Mahayana Buddhism of Japan and Taiwan – then secularization is not necessary for queer identities, communities and political movements to emerge.

On the contrary, the growth of some forms of religious expression and ritual can provide spaces for greater queer autonomy and community development. Across the Theravada Buddhist societies of mainland Southeast Asia, and in Vietnam, new forms of spirit rituals have emerged in recent decades (see Brac de la Perrière and Jackson 2022). In these new movements, which have predominantly emerged outside or on the fringes of Buddhism, queer ritual specialists have become increasingly important religious figures (see Jackson and Baumann 2022). The new spirit ritual movements in Myanmar, Thailand and Vietnam are different from the premodern religions in parts of island Southeast Asia, such as the Bissu priests among the Bugis people of south Sulawesi, in which transgenders played important roles. Nonetheless, the new spirit ritual movements in several mainland Southeast Asian societies do point to the important fact that some of the diverse forms of religious expression across the region provide welcoming spaces for sexual and gender differences in which queer people can achieve honor and respect as ritual specialists.

Nonetheless, while some new religious movements in mainland Southeast Asia are contributing to the acceptance of queer people in respected roles, forms of doctrinal Islam in Malaysia, Indonesia and Brunei, as well as Christianity in the Philippines, are also restricting if not undermining queer rights. As Aoyama notes, religions can oppress sexual minorities through fundamentalist ideologies and societal sexual politics, constituting forms of cultural and political power that control individuals and work to construct sexuality and gender to conform to heterosexist and patriarchal norms. However, the common assumption among many Western homosexual and trans activists that religion as a whole is anti-queer is challenged by the situation in Southeast Asia.

Colonial-era anti-sodomy laws and queer rights

In examining the status of gender and sexual minorities in Southeast Asia in particular an important question is why several former colonies in the region have resisted removing colonial-era anti-sodomy laws and continued to use these laws to restrict and at times criminalize indigenous sexual and gender minorities. Even though regimes in these countries have often been strongly critical of their former colonial powers, they have nonetheless continued to use and at times enforce punitive anti-sodomy laws that have since been abolished in the old colonial powers themselves. As Kusaka, Iga and Fukunaga observe, in some Southeast Asian societies restrictions on sexual and gender minorities have at times increased since independence and the end of colonialism. In part, this is because local ruling elites have found outdated colonial-era anti-sodomy laws to be useful in their own projects of political legitimation. Rather than always producing a more liberal environment, the adoption and adaptation of Western models of modernization in some post-independence Southeast Asian nation-states have at times led to restrictions on the rights and liberties of gender and sexual minorities. Indeed, some of the modern forms of discrimination experienced by LGBT minorities have not resulted directly from colonialism. Rather, they have been enacted by local, usually male, political and bureaucratic elites since the end of colonialism. Kusaka, Iga and Fukunaga argue that this apparent contradiction emerges from the nationalist policies of modern nation-states that have been formed on the model of a heteronormative family that upholds so-called "traditional" Asian values.

"Good citizens" as members of national "families"

A key insight of the studies in this book is that across the region the politics of inclusion and exclusion is often based on definitions of the "good citizen." The history of LGBT activism in many Western countries, such as the politics of gay liberation, have sought radical change by confronting patriarchal and heteronormative laws and institutions. In contrast, in Asia queer people have more often sought inclusion by seeking to demonstrate that they contribute to the greater social good by conforming to notions of being "good citizens." In this, much LGBT activism in Asia is more similar to the homophile movement in the United States in the years before the Stonewall uprising in New York in June 1969.

The politics of the "good citizen" has been particularly notable in Thailand in recent decades. In the aftermath of the two most recent military coups in 2006 and 2014 that toppled democratically elected governments, conservative pro-monarchy political discourses in the country promoted the idea of rule by "good people" (*khon di*). The subtext of these conservative discourses was that the "good people" who were most qualified to rule Thailand were members of the traditional pro-military and pro-monarchy establishment, with the lesser-educated masses being implicitly defined as not conforming to notions of the good Thai citizen and hence not suitable to lead the country.

Kusaka, Iga and Fukunaga also argue that the ideology of being a "good citizen" in Asia has been closely related to a parallel political discourse that the community of the modern nation should be understood on the collective model of the family. Heteronormative notions of what constitutes a proper Asian national family of "good people" have at times contributed to the stigmatization and oppression of LGBT people in post-independence societies. Indeed, the ideology of the "national family" has long been central to conservative discourses of political legitimation in Thailand. Thai political leaders often address the populace as "siblings," *phi-norng khon Thai* or "Thai brothers and sisters." Thai kings have often been typified as "founding fathers," which is reflected in the titles of monarchs such as King Ramkhamhaeng (r. 1279–1298 CE) of the early kingdom of Sukhothai, who in Thai is called "Respected Father (*phor khun*) Ramkhamhaeng." When the custom of celebrating a national "Father's Day" and "Mother's Day" was introduced in recent decades, the birthdays of the late King Bhumibol (r. 1947–2016) and his wife, Queen Mother Sirikit (b. 1932), were chosen as the dates of these events. The late King Bhumibol's birthday of 5 December is now also often called Thailand's national day.

Authoritarian vs democratic regimes

Thailand is internationally well-known, if not notorious, for the large number of military coups that have been launched in the country's modern history and for the fragility of its democratic institutions. In some other parts of the world, such as Latin America, military governments have often been allied with conservative religious and moral figures and strongly repressed LGBT communities. However, Thailand's military governments have not had anti-queer agendas. Thai pro-democracy activists have often been jailed and subject to violence at the hands of successive of military governments. However, conservative politics has rarely been linked with conservative sexual or gender policies. On the contrary, Thailand's commercial gay scene has often continued to grow and flourish under military governments. This follows a broader pattern across modern Southeast Asia, where Kusaka, Iga and Fukunaga observe that authoritarian regimes in the region have not necessarily stigmatized or oppressed gender and sexual minorities. On the contrary, democratic governments have at times been more interventionist in pathologizing and oppressing LGBT groups. The transition to democracy in some parts of Asia does not necessarily improve the situation of sexual and gender minorities. In the early 2000s, Thailand's then democratically elected national government led by the Thai Rak Thai Party of billionaire Prime Minister Thaksin Shinawatra instituted a moral order campaign that led to police raids of gay venues and the temporary closing of some bars and gay saunas.

Why should democratic regimes and regimes transitioning to democracy oppress sexual minorities who do not present any threat to these governments, and, conversely, why do authoritarian regimes that oppress pro-democratic civil society groups nonetheless tolerate queer communities? Kusaka, Iga and Fukunaga propose that democratic governments in Asia may institute anti-LGBT policies when there is a renewed emphasis on conservative interpretations of religion as a basis of national cultural identity imagined in terms of a traditional heteronormative family. This is often part of a politics of opposition to a West whose contemporary support for LGBT minorities is represented as a neocolonial attempt to continue to exercise hegemonic dominance over former Asian colonies. This type of anti-LGBT nationalism has become more visible in parts of Southeast Asia as the influence of resurgent conservative Islam has grown internationally, and especially since the Asian economic crisis of 1997–98, when the imposition of stringent restructuring measures by the International Monetary Fund incited opposition to perceived Western interference.

In societies where the powers that be mobilize legitimating discourses that link the nation, family and religion in establishing notions of the "good citizen," sexual minorities are more likely to be excluded and oppressed as scapegoats. On the other hand, in societies where discourses of the national "family" are more linked to notions of economic progress, the ruling powers may grant limited rights to sexual minorities if they are viewed as contributing to national economic development. This is especially likely to be the case when sexual and gender minorities are not regarded as posing any threat to the state, or, as was the case in Thailand until recently, they are seen as largely irrelevant to contests over national political power. Situations where political elites do not use gender and sexual minorities as political resources but nonetheless do not actively advance LGBT rights can perhaps be regarded as forms of contained marginalization. In instances of contained marginalization LGBT communities do not face direct oppression but nonetheless do not see any expansion of their rights. Throughout most of the 20th century in Thailand, LGBT people did not come under state influence because they were regarded as being irrelevant to the issues that concern national politicians and bureaucrats and hence were seen as being outside the ambit and concern of the state.

Integrating institutional politics and the politics of everyday life

One of the most important insights of this book is that many sexual and gender minorities in Asia are not seeking to promote their welfare and dignity by engaging in official politics or participating in public forms of LGBT activism in formally constituted organizations or movements. Rather, many members of these communities are engaging in forms of "everyday politics," such as engaging in various niche occupations, leading religious rituals and building care relationships with their fellow sexual minorities to support each other's lives. Several chapters in this book deal with the cultural and social issues that are the field of the queer politics of everyday life in Southeast Asia today. Organized forms of LGBT activism are more likely to be pursued by educated, middle-class gay men, lesbians and trans people while a queer politics of everyday life is often more typical of working-class people who may lack the cultural and financial capital needed to establish and run organizations. Middle-class queer movements typically seek to engage and challenge state power, whether in the administration of the national or local bureaucracies or in the framing of laws. While the working-class queer politics of everyday life may not lead directly to changes in the legal status of gender and sexual minorities, it may nonetheless achieve genuine social change in fields outside the bureaucratic and administrative scope of the state. In Thailand, the politics of everyday life is especially visible in the ways that trans women have sought to claim positions of respect as specialists in feminine beauty and as ritual specialists in spirit cults.

The contrast between organized middle-class institutional politics and informal working-class everyday politics is an especially important result of this book's analyses that has broader relevance beyond the study of LGBT issues in Asia. This key contrast points to the fact that in comparative queer studies of movements for recognition of LGBT people we need an expanded notion of queer activism that recognizes the existence of socio-economic differences and multiple, class-based strategies of engaging with patriarchy and heteronormativity. In comparative international queer studies the notion of queer activism needs to include both organized political action as well as the politics of everyday life. An expanded account of queer activism needs to include all forms of LGBT engagement with and opposition to the diverse modalities of power that stigmatize and minoritize queer people. Perhaps the most important contribution and conclusion of this book is that international queer studies needs to develop integrated analyses that view the totality of the intersecting ways that LGBT people from diverse social, educational and socio-economic backgrounds actively engage the state, social arrangements and cultural forms in working to achieve the legal, institutional and local-level transformations that improve all dimensions of their lives.

Introduction

What Is Being Contested over Gender and Sexual Minorities? An Asian Perspective

Wataru Kusaka, Tsukasa Iga and Genya Fukunaga

Introduction

The purpose of this book is to explore the politics surrounding gender and sexual minorities known as "LGBT" (Lesbian, Gay, Bisexual and Transgender) from the perspectives and experiences of Southeast and East Asia. All societies have people with diverse and often fluid gender identities, sexual orientations and expressions of sexuality that deviate from dominant norms. Until now, however, the dominant discourses in the social sciences and humanities relating to these people have been mainly based on Western experiences and norms. Criticizing the trend to regard Western developments and cultures as universal models, pioneering studies have explored non-Western cultures and experiences and advocated for more diverse and postcolonial perspectives (Masaad 2007; Martin and Jackson et al. 2010; Luther and Loh 2019; Bosia and McEvoy et al. 2020). Yet, an analytical framework that explains diversities and changes in the situations of gender and sexual minorities in Asia remains absent. This volume aims to fill the gap by presenting an analytical framework on "LGBT" politics based on an in-depth analysis of wide-ranged Asian experiences.

In the West, the spread of the Reformation strengthened social and legal exclusion against individuals who deviated from strict Christian sexual norms. By the end of the 19th century, the development of sexology and policies based on it, economic growth and urbanization, and the efforts of gender and sexual minorities to detach themselves from moral deviance led to the creation of the categories of "heterosexuals" and "homosexuals" based on sexual orientation, which formed an individual's identity. The complex contestation between moral and scientific discourses on sexuality led to varied outcomes: decriminalization occurred in some countries, but criminalization in others. In the late 1960s, gender and sexual minorities formed active social movements, and secured victories in the 1970s in areas such as decriminalization, de-pathologization, and anti-discrimination. In the 1990s, the concept of "transgender" began to displace earlier ideas of gender inversion. Through the 1980s and 1990s, as HIV infection spread around the world, primarily among gay men and trans women, the rights movement spread with it (Altman 2004; 2008). As a result, while there was some progress towards decriminalization, anti-discrimination, and same-sex marriage, a severe backlash also erupted.

The various states' treatment of gender and sexual minorities differs significantly, ranging from oppression, pathologization, and neglect to support. To explain these differences, many researchers have focused on the extent to which the global LGBT movement has been able to counter local conservative norms and forces. They have argued that certain conditions are important for the success of LGBT movements: first, economic conditions of urbanization and modernization by means of capitalism (Boswell 1980; Florida 2002; Inglehart and Norris 2003); second, social conditions such as the majority no longer perceiving the granting of rights to gender and sexual minorities as a "threat" (Mucciaroni 2008), secularization (Finke and Adamczyk 2008), and a free civil society (Offord 2011); third, conditions for social movements, such as resource mobilization (Adam, Duyvendak, and Krouwel 1999) and the degree to which international norms are "visible" within a country (Ayoub 2016); and fourth, institutional conditions such as decentralized power and an independent judiciary (Tremblay et al. eds. 2011), and the strength of democracy (Encarnacion 2014).

These conditions or variables may explain, for example, the 2019 legalization of same-sex marriage in Taiwan. But there are many cases in Asia that are proof to the contrary. Korea, for one, meets the conditions of economic development, democracy, and a free civil society, but the movement to guarantee rights for gender and sexual minorities remains at a standstill. In contrast, Thailand and Vietnam are economically semi-developed countries with non-democratic regimes, but have expanded legal rights for gender and sexual minorities to some extent. In Asia, the development of democracy and capitalism have not necessarily played an emancipatory role, nor have they proven necessary to emancipation of gender and sexual minorities.

Moreover, one cannot assume that the LGBT culture and movement that originated from the West always liberates the oppressed in the non-Western world. In Asia, vernacular transgender people have long been active in religion, entertainment, and other fields, playing important roles in supporting the social order. It was rather Western colonial rule and the modernization and nation-state formation it introduced that marginalized and criminalized these people. Certainly, urban middle-class youth in Asia have actively accepted the LGBT culture and movement. However, many rural residents, the elderly, and the poor have embraced various vernacular identities and are uncomfortable with the Western concept of LGBT. Similarly, 'coming out' and being highly visible is an unattractive strategy for those fearing oppression in many societies.

Considering the Asian contexts, the following issues are yet to be sufficiently addressed. First, what factors determine the differing rights and situations of gender and sexual minorities in Asian countries? Second, how have Asian gender and sexual minorities resisted marginalization? Has their resistance been shaped by, or is it more or less independent from the West-derived LGBT movement?

This volume takes the following approaches to address these questions, while each chapter has varied emphases. First, it explores the lived experiences and agency of gender and sexual minority people. Second, it aims to clarify contested politics of inclusion and exclusion in which states, dominant social forces, the majority, and gender and sexual minorities themselves try to define "good citizens" for their own advantages. Third, it focuses on not only legislation and social movement in the public sphere but also "everyday politics," in which ordinary people, by utilizing vernacular cultures and resources, negotiate dominant norms and existing institutions to resist marginalization. Finally, the studies in this volume try to disclose the gendered and sexual characteristics of

Asian nation-states, which are not always obvious, by analyzing how they have treated gender and sexual minorities.

The significance of focusing on Asia is not limited to its rich history of various genders and sexualities. Asia has distinguished characteristics, such as a familism that takes priority over individualism, experiences of colonialism, catch-up nation-state formations, and rapid modernization. How Asian gender and sexual minorities have experienced these processes cannot be understood from a Western-centered perspective. In addition, the diversity of political systems, religions, economic conditions and experiences of colonialism in Asia is helpful to understand how such factors affect the circumstances of gender and sexual minorities from a comparative perspective, which the book uses to construct new hypotheses, not to demonstrate causal relationships. Furthermore, the abundant practices in everyday politics in Asia suggest a plethora of possibilities for building societies in which gender and sexual diversity are legitimately recognized.

In this volume, we use the term "gender and sexual minority" in principle to collectively refer to diverse people who tend to be marginalized for deviating from the norms of their society in their sexual orientation, gender identity, gender expression or sexual characteristics. This term also encompasses various vernacular Asian identities that do not fit into the contemporary Western concepts of gender and sexuality. Meanwhile, we generally use the term "LGBT" as a symbol constructed by discourses, rather than a substantial entity. We bracket the term in the book title to draw attention to the fact that various actors from the states, the market, and society have variously interpreted, misunderstood, celebrated, contested and exploited "LGBT" as a useful exogenous symbol, often regardless of the realities of gender and sexual minorities, causing significant impacts. We aim to clarify the dynamic and contested processes and outcomes of "LGBT" politics.[1] The choice of "LGBT," rather than "LGBTQIA+,"

---

1   We broadly define politics as dominance, resistance and cooperation over allocation of resources and definitions of values to create social order, which includes not only formal but also informal politics that occurs in everyday settings.

is a conscious one; not because we do not appreciate the effort to create a more inclusive umbrella term for gender and sexual minorities, but because the local politics that we investigate in contest the term "LGBT" and its meanings.

Gender and sexual minorities in Asia

Vernacular social orders

Looking into Asian contexts helps us realize that the fluid and ambiguous gender identities and relations, which have become more apparent recently in the West, have had a long history in the region. This fact suggests that the cis-hetero norm based on a rigid gender binary was a product of modernity only recently derived from the West.

Historians have unearthed general characteristics of gender and sexuality in pre-modern Southeast Asia to some extent (Peletz 2006; Andaya 2006; Reid 2015: 24–25). According to these scholars, most pre-modern Southeast Asian societies were organized by a system of bilateral descent in which women enjoyed relatively high status. The different roles and spheres of activity of "men and women"[2] were viewed as complementary. While men were concerned with political power and status, women were autonomously engaged in commercial activities and enjoyed inheritance rights. As the population was scarce, the economic value of women was high, and a man's family paid a bride price to the woman's family in marriage. Divorce was also common and relatively easy to conclude, either by returning the money received at the time of marriage if the wife requested the divorce, or by paying an additional sum if it was the husband's request. Moreover, people were broad-minded about sexuality; premarital sex and homosexual acts were not problematic, and women's sexual pleasure was not denied.

There was gender pluralism in which diverse genders were taken for granted and coexisted in pre-modern Southeast Asia. There were no major barriers to transcending what today are called gender differences,

---

2   The gendered categories may differ from today's concepts.

or to exploring different gender roles and experiences. Moreover, polytheism viewed the different roles and spheres of activity of men and women as complementary, and a union of the two as an ideal that would generate powerful forces. From such a perspective, "vernacular transgenders" symbolized the wholeness of the universe, and were highly valued for their abilities to protect kingship and the well-being of the universe through their sacred role as intermediaries between the human and spiritual/natural realms. They presided over important rituals related to kingship, childbirth, marriage, and agriculture, and were respected for supporting their local communities (Peletz 2006; Reid 2015: 98).

Meanwhile, in many parts of East Asia, as well, it has been argued that women's status was possibly relatively high, gender norms were not particularly strong, and vernacular transgender people also performed religious roles. One of Japan's foundational myths, for example, features the story of Yamato Takeru, a beautiful boy who adopted female attire. Many parts of Japan have rituals to access spiritual power by males dressing as women (Mitsuhashi 2022).

However, the influence of Confucianism, which considered families based on patrilineal system, patriarchy, and subordination of women as the fundamental unit of society gradually gained ground in East Asia. The trend started during the Song dynasty (960–1279) in China and from the middle of the Yi dynasty (1392–1897) on the Korean peninsula (Kohama 2023). In Vietnam (especially in the north), Confucianization progressed from the late 15th century, but vernacular culture that guaranteed certain economic and property rights of women remained (Nguyen 2013). In Japan, Confucianism became stronger during the Edo period (1603–1868) as an ideology to justify feudal rule, but its influence was limited compared to other East Asian societies.

In East Asia during this period, although Confucianism diminished the status of women, it did not erase the fluidity and diversity of sexualities and genders. In China, women were strictly segregated to maintain the patriarchal order, but this made same-sex relationships more intense, and homosexual behavior was not viewed as a problem unless it interfered with the reproduction of patrilineal families (Mann 2015; Kohama 2023).

In Korea, all-male itinerant troupes of entertainers called "*namsadang*," which included youths assigned female gender, traveled the country, performing and offering prayers for good health and prosperity. In Japan, the practice of "*nanshoku*" remained active, in which adult males who had become "men" after completing "*genpuku*" ceremonial rites (which involved "playing woman": shaving their eyebrows, blackening their teeth, and wearing their hair in the style of a newly-married woman) had sexual relations with younger men. Also, the culture has remained, which gives meaning and roles to gender transcendence in religion, entertainment, and child rearing (Mitsuhashi 2022).

Modernization

Modernization was hostile to sexual and gender fluidity in Asia. In Southeast Asia, modern states built under Western colonialism undermined vernacular social orders in pursuit of a what they believed to be a more rational social order. As mentioned, vernacular transgender people were closely associated with vernacular kingship, polytheism, and worldview, and were therefore stigmatized, marginalized, and criminalized by world religions and modern states seeking a new social order. Theravada Buddhism spread in the 14th and 15th centuries, and Sunni Islam and Catholicism arrived in Southeast Asia in the 17th and 18th centuries. Such world religions were androcentric, legalistic, and hierarchically organized, diminishing the status of women and eroding the sacred role of vernacular religious leaders who supported local kingship. Moreover, the development of modern systems such as bureaucratization and industrialization expanded "male" spheres (Peletz 2006: 315–18: 324; Andaya 2006: 75–103; Reid 2015: 314–318).

In the early 20th century, colonial officials from the West introduced a patriarchal puritanism that degraded the status of women and gender and sexual minorities in Southeast Asia.[3] In 19th century Europe, amid

---

3   Women were made to withdraw from public and economic activities, and were confined to the role of adorning an imagined "nation." As men in Southeast Asia were not accustomed to the economic activities women had performed, modern economic activities were almost entirely monopolized by ethnic Chinese (Reid 2014: 6).

rapid industrialization and urbanization, people who sought success in
highly competitive and dangerous cities adopted strict moral principles
such as thrift, diligence, discipline, sexual morality, and patriarchalism,
and believed in individual salvation through personal dialogue with
God (Reid 2014). Colonial officials who internalized this puritan code
marginalized vernacular gender and sexual minorities, redefining them as
criminals harmful to society. In particular, the British introduced Section
377 of the Penal Code (commonly known as the "sodomy law") which
prohibits sexual acts that are "against the order of nature" in its colonies,
including British Malaya (now Singapore and Malaysia), Burma (now
Myanmar) and others.[4] For the male elites of Southeast Asia, who strove
for independence and to build their own nation-states, the modern
patriarchalism of the West was attractive but too foreign to be accepted
as it was. They therefore turned to Buddhist, Confucian, Islamic,
and Christian scriptures to justify their new patriarchal cultures, and
promoted national unity as an analog of the patrilineal family. Religious
reformers also preached women's subordination, devotion to housework,
and avoidance of premarital sex. Their efforts institutionalized patriarchy
and heteronormativity in family and marriage laws (Reid 2014). However, despite all these hostile forces in the course of modernization, the
vernacular culture of gender and sexuality in Southeast Asia did not
totally disappear, retaining gender and sexual fluidity to some extent
and women's status relatively higher than in 19th-century Europe and
elsewhere in 20th-century Asia (Reid 2015: 316–318).

In East Asia, too, gender and sexual minorities were pathologized
and marginalized in the processes of top-down, catch-up style nation-
state building. Japan's Meiji government positioned patriarchy and
the heterosexual family as the foundations of society, and excluded
women from realms such as politics, bureaucracy, higher education, and
conscription. Being conscious of the Western gaze, it also introduced

---

4   The British initially codified the law in India and exported it to other colonies
    in Asia and Africa, settler societies such as New Zealand and Australia, and in
    Britain itself.

modern moralism, forbade cross-dressing, and, for a period of time, criminalized sexual intercourse between men. In Korea, patriarchy was reinforced first by the Japanese colonial rulers and then by its post-independence leaders who tried to restore supposedly pre-colonial traditions. The Communist Party of China, aiming to break with Confucian and feudal traditions, legislated gender equality in marriage, inheritance, education, welfare, and so forth, and encouraged women to engage in productive labor. However, this still meant that women had to bear the double burden of domestic labor.

Treatments by the state

Asian states have treated gender and sexual minorities in various ways. In communist China, homosexual acts between men were criminalized in 1979, and homosexuals became targeted for "treatment." Meanwhile, other Asian countries did not regard gender and sexual minorities as targets of policy intervention until the HIV/AIDS epidemic of the 1980s, when public health measures had to be mobilized. Since the 1990s, while the LGBT movement has expanded, states have responded in various ways, either: suppressing gender and sexual minorities, providing limited support, or ignoring the movement and leaving them alone.

There is a generally accepted assumption that democratic regimes are more likely to support the LGBT movement's demands for legal rights, while authoritarian regimes are more likely to repress, criminalize and pathologize gender and sexual minorities. However, a review of the situation in Southeast and East Asian countries as of 2024 reveals that while some cases do fit this assumption, many others do not (Table I.1). Moreover, if we measure by the number of participants in pride parades and rallies prior to the COVID-19 pandemic in 2020 we find that active civil society does not always draw state support for gender and sexual minorities (Table I.2).

Certainly, democracy can sometimes contribute to more rights for gender and sexual minorities. This appears to be the case in Taiwan, which became the first Asian country that succeeded in legislating anti-discrimination and same-sex marriage. Democracy, freedom and the

Table I.1: Rights situation of gender and sexual minorities by states in
Southeast and East Asia (as of 2024)

	Repression (Criminalization/ pathologization)	Neglect, or fail to support	Support (legal rights)
Democracy	Indonesia Korea (Military Criminal Code)	Philippines Japan	Taiwan Anti-discrimination law (2007) Same-sex marriage legalized (2019)
Transitional system Competitive authoritarian regime	Malaysia	Singapore Cambodia	Thailand Anti-discrimination law (2015)
Military regime and One-party regime		Vietnam Laos Myanmar China	

*   In the Philippines and Japan, although a number of local authorities have introduced Same-sex Partnership Ordinances, there has been no national legislation of the same kind.

**   Although the law that criminalizes sexual activities between persons of the same sex has not been repealed in Myanmar, neither has it been enforced.

*** Change of legal gender has been legalized in Vietnam, Singapore, Indonesia, China, Korea, and Japan. However, apart from Korea, it is conditional upon gender-reassignment surgery, and in practice, there is no access to such surgery in the first four countries listed.

defense of human rights became cornerstones of the national identity in Tawain amid democratization and the fierce competition with China over claims of sovereignty. In this context, guaranteeing the rights of gender and sexual minorities was positioned as a sign of successful democratization, which prompted both the ruling and opposition parties to claim to be "LGBT-friendly" (Fukunaga 2017c; Chapter 6).

But a transition to democracy does not necessarily improve the situation of gender and sexual minorities. Malaysia, where gender and sexual minorities have been oppressed since the 1980s, replaced its almost 40-year-old single party government with a multi-party government in 2018. However, while the new government has talked about "social inclusion," it has adopted policies to "correct" gender and sexual minorities and to "prevent" young people from engaging in non-conforming sexual and gender behaviors. In Myanmar, which transitioned from military to civilian rule in 2011, the National League for Democracy (NLD), which campaigned on democratization and the protection of human rights, was elected in 2015. However, the NLD administration's engagement on gender and sexual minority rights was limited. Since the military coup in 2021, the human rights situation of gender and sexual minority has deteriorated to its worst in Myanmar.

Even more consolidated democracies have failed to guarantee state support of gender and sexual minorities. In the Philippines, the LGBT movement has been campaigning for anti-discrimination laws since 1995, but no such legislation has yet passed Congress. In Korea, similarly, the LGBT movement has been growing since 2000, but has succeeded neither in passing anti-discrimination laws nor in repealing the military penal code that proscribes military personnel from engaging in homosexual acts (Kim 2016). In Japan, a series of same-sex partnership ordinances have been passed by local governments since 2015, but these have served to hinder rather than advance fundamental transformation of the situation of gender and sexual minorities (Khor, Tang, and Kamano 2020). In Indonesia, discrimination and violence against gender and sexual minorities have increased due to an Islamic backlash since the mid-2000s (Boellstorff 2007). By the mid-2010s government officials legitimized violence with statements such as "the LGBT movement is more dangerous than nuclear warfare" (Okamoto 2016a; 2016b).

Conversely, authoritarian regimes and dictatorships that severely repress civil society sometimes give limited recognition to LGBT movements. Pride parades have become common, for example, in Cambodia, Laos, and Vietnam, where anti-government protests are not allowed. Since 2009, the Singaporean state has allowed tens of thousands of people to participate in a "Pink Dot" event, albeit under surveillance.

Dictatorial regimes sometimes offer limited expansion of rights for gender and sexual minorities. In 2015, Vietnam's communist dictatorship permitted gender reassignment in the official family registers while continuing to ban gender reassignment surgery. It also revised the Marriage and Family Law, lifting the ban on same-sex marriage. China

Table I.2: Main Pride parades and rallies in Southeast and East Asia

	Location	Estimated participants[5]	Event name (first year held)
Support	Taiwan (Taipei)	30 (2019)	Taiwan Pride (2003)
	Thailand (Phuket)	100 (2017)	Phuket Pride (1999)
Non-involvement	Philippines (Manila)	52,000 (2019)	Metro Manila Pride March (1994)
	Myanmar (Yangon)	6,000 (2018)	&PROUD LGBT Festival (2014)
	Japan (Tokyo)	10,000 (2019)	Tokyo Rainbow Pride (2000)*
	Vietnam (Hanoi)	5,000 (2019)	Viet Pride Hanoi, later Hanoi Pride (2012)
	China (Shanghai)	3,000 (2009)	Shanghai Pride Festival (2009)
	Cambodia (Phnom Penh)	100 (2017)	Cambodia Pride (2004)
	Laos (Vientiane)	100 (2012)	Proud to be Us! (2012)
	Singapore	20,000 (2017)	Pink Dot SG (2009)
Suppression	Malaysia	None	none
	Indonesia	None	none
	Korea (Seoul)	70,000 (2019)	Seoul Queer Parade (1999)

*   In Thailand, Bangkok Pride was also held until 2006. In 2020, a Pride Parade with 1000 participants took part in an anti-government campaign calling for democratization.[6]

---

5   Brian Hioe, Over 30 Participate in Taiwan's 2019 Pride Parade, New Bloom, October 26, 2019. https://newbloommag.net/2019/10/26/2019-prideparade/; Watsamon June Tri-yasakda, "Thailand's Only Pride Parade Marched in Phuket," Coconuts Bangkok, May 11, 2016. https://coconuts.co/bangkok/features/thailands-only-pride-parade-marched-phuket-photo-essay-0/; "80,000 take part in 20th Seoul Queer Parade. Inaugural Pink Dot [event] also held on previous night," Out Japan, June 1, 2019. https://www.outjapan.co.jp/lgbtcolumn_news/news/2019/6/1.html; 'Tokyo Rainbow Pride' and 'Pride Festival' events held on grand scale: parade participants top 10,000 for the first time, recording mobilization of 200,000 over 2 days, Out Japan, April 30, 2019. https://www.outjapan.co.jp/lgbtcolumn_news/news/2019/4/19.html; Bonz Magsambol, Record-breaking: 70,000 Filipinos Join Metro Manila Pride 2019, Rappler, June 29, 2019. https://www.rappler.com/moveph/metro-manila-pride-2019-attendees-breaks-record; Tom Halford, "Myanmar Hosts First-ever Public LGBT Festival," Pink News, January 30, 2018. https://www.pinknews.co.uk/2018/01/30/myanmar-hosts-first-ever-

decriminalized homosexual acts in 1997 and has allowed limited scope for homosexual activist groups to address AIDS prevention (Guo 2020). Singapore repealed Section 377A of the Penal Code, which criminalized same-sex sexual activity, while emphasizing the legal protection of heterosexual marriage in 2022. Thailand's military junta passed an anti-discrimination law in 2015 and a same-sex partnership registration law in 2018, allowing partners the authority to inherit property and consent to surgical procedures. While holding elections in 2019, the military and royal family have continued to resist substantive democratization. In these circumstances, in 2024 the parliament, in which the military has great influence, passed a proposal to legalize same-sex marriage, and the king gave his approval.

From the above, the following questions emerge. Why do democratic regimes, including transitional ones, that require legitimacy from the electorate, reject the demands of – or oppress – gender and sexual minorities who pose no threat to the regime? And on the contrary, why do authoritarian regimes that severely suppress civil society allow limited LGBT movements or even improve the treatment of gender and sexual minorities?

Multi-layered cultures

In Asian societies, both vernacular and Western cultures have coexisted and interacted to produce new hybrid cultures. Western identity and

---

public-lgbt-festival/; Vietnam Net "Hanoi Pride Festival 2019 Welcomes 5,000 Participants" September 24, 2019. https://vietnamnet.vn/en/society/lively-hanoi-pride-festival-2019-welcomes-5-000-participants-570817.html; Shanghai Pride. https://alchetron.com/Shanghai-Pride; UN WOMEN, Asia and Pacific "Cambodia LGBTIQ People Celebrate Identity, Hope for Acceptance," June 14, 2017. https://asiapacific.unwomen.org/en/news-and-events/stories/2017/06/cambodia-lgbtiq-people-celebrate-identity; The Telegraph "Laos Holds First Gay Pride Event," June 27, 2012. https://www.telegraph.co.uk/news/worldnews/asia/laos/9359330/Laos-holds-first-gay-pride-event.html; Pink Dot SG. "Pink Dot2017 Official Statement," July 1, 2017. https://pinkdot.sg/2017/07/pink-dot-2017-official-statement/.

6 Reuters. "Thai LGBT and Anti-government Protesters Join in Pride Parade," November 7, 2020. https://www.reuters.com/article/us-thailand-protestspride-idUSKBN27N0G9.

rights movements have gradually spilled over into Asia. Homosexual culture arrived and spread among the urban middle class from the 1920s in Japan, and from the mid-1960s in the Philippines and Thailand (Garcia 1996; Jackson 1999a; Kazama and Kawaguchi 2010). In the 1980s, gay men and others working against HIV/AIDS organized themselves in various parts of Asia. Starting in Manila in 1994, pride parades spread to many countries, sometimes with the support of corporations, Western embassies, and UN agencies. Participants have been mainly young people who studied abroad and lived in urban areas. LGBT organizations increasingly cooperate with others in global networks, and proposing policies to their respective governments. Electoral politics are also changing: in the Philippines, a trans woman won a seat in the House of Representatives in the 2016 election, and in Thailand, four "LGBT members" were elected to parliament in 2019.

However, Asia does not simply follow the West. Due to rapid and compressed modernization, Western influences have piled upon vernacular cultures in waves; different cultures coexist in layers while mutually influencing one another. Even in East Asia, where top-down modernization and nation-building have drastically altered the social order, vernacular cultural norms and values around sexual and gender diversity have survived in areas such as religious rituals and entertainment industry (Mitsuhashi 2022).

In Southeast Asia, while the urban middle class has absorbed many Western concepts, many poor, elderly, and rural dwellers have cherished their vernacular identities. For example, "*kathoey*" in Laos and Thailand, "*achauk*" in Myanmar, "*bakla*" in the Philippines, "*bapok*" and "*pondan*" in Malaysia, and "*waria*" and "*banci*" in Indonesia are vernacular trans women. The Dao Mau spirit mediums of Vietnam, the "*bissu*" of the Bugis people, the "*nat kadaw*" of Myanmar, and so on, have passed down their vernacular religious roles and beliefs to the present day. The "*mak andam*" of Malaysia look after dresses and make-up at weddings. Although homosexuality is a widely recognized category, it is not always conceived purely in terms of sexual orientation, but is often understood within the vernacular culture that views men who love men as transitioning to women, and women who love women as transitioning to men (Garcia 1996; Jackson 2001).

Southeast Asian societies are often seen as "tolerant" of gender and sexual minorities because they have maintained rich vernacular cultures of sexual and gender diversity. However, in many cases this "tolerance" is granted only at the margins of society and only to those who play roles that conform to the majority's expectations of them under dominant heterosexual and cisgender norms. In contrast to the highly individualistic West, Asian gender and sexual minorities are embedded in communities. They are not excluded by dominant norms, but subsumed and marginalized within them. The situation can be termed as "marginalization within inclusion."

Trans women, for example, are expected to equip themselves with beautiful and elegant femininity and entertain people in an amusing manner (Tan 2001). While trans genders are at least familiar to the majority within the vernacular culture, homosexuals are less familiar and thus are often understood only as a type of gender transitioner by the majority. Moreover, to escape being regarded as dangerous foreign influences who destabilize the norms, many homosexuals have not "come out" and have been forced to marry (Jackson 1999; Boellstorff 2005; 2007). When gender and sexual minorities deviate from the understandings and expectations that the majority imposes on them and start demanding equal rights, they are subjected to backlash and oppression even in "tolerant" Southeast Asia. This is especially true for people who are economically marginalized and under oppressive states and societies.

To resist marginalization, LGBT activists have thus tried to expand the majority's understanding by conveying Western culture and models and translating them into local understanding (Offord 2013). Meanwhile, gender and sexual minorities who embrace vernacular identities have sought everyday well-being and dignity by earning their living through niche occupations such as beauty or entertainment, or by religious rituals, or by building mutually supportive care relationships with their peers. More recently, encounters and exchanges through social networking services (SNS) have supported these practices.

To understand various practices of gender and sexual minorities to resist marginalization in the Asian context, we must look beyond the LGBT movements that demand legal rights by lobbying the state, and pay attention to "everyday politics," as well as the interaction between the two. James C. Scott (1985) coined the term "everyday forms of resistance," which highlights how ordinary people discreetly engage in subtle forms of disobedience and resistance without formal organization and leadership outside of the legal system to gain practical benefits under authorities' radars. Benedict Kerkvliet (1990) then broadened this concept and renamed it "everyday politics" to refer to how ordinary people come to terms with and/or contest dominant norms and regulations. Some studies in this volume explore whether the everyday politics of gender and sexual minorities will form the basis for future legal rights, hinder the LGBT movements and reproduce the status quo, or create a new social order without new laws.

Hegemonic struggles for "good citizenship"

Sexual citizenship

As discussed, many studies focus on how LGBT movements have over-come conservative norms and forces, but such a narrow perspective would not provide a clear view of the state's various treatment of gender and sexual minorities in Asia and the diverse ways people resist marginalization. Thus, as an alternative approach, this volume analyzes the politics around gender and sexual minorities from the perspective of a hegemonic struggle over the definition of "good citizens."

We derived this approach from the theory of sexual citizenship, which argues that while proclaiming its own neutrality and universality, citizenship is in fact constituted by patriarchal heterosexual norms and has sustained unequal power relations over gender and sexuality (Richardson 1998; Brandzel 2005). This theory reminds that only those who are considered to be legitimate members of a community can enjoy citizenship. Of course, notions of legitimacy have changed dramatically over time; the earliest nation-states limited citizenship to men, founded on beliefs that while men could overcome their bodily desires and act with "reason," women were subject to the "natural" (in terms of the body, emotions, sex, and so forth). Gender and sexual minorities, in turn, were excluded due to their association with the "unnatural" (Lister 2002: 194).[7]

The bias in citizenship has limited gender and sexual minorities' civil rights (such as marriage, military service, and legal protection against discrimination), political rights (exercise of political power), and social rights (such as pensions, inheritance, and tax benefits) in many countries. Even if gender and sexual minorities are entitled to citizenship, homophobia substantially restricts their ability to exercise their rights (Lister 2002: 193). They are "tolerated" by the majority, as long as they keep their "differences" in the private sphere and do not seek recognition or rights in the public sphere (Richardson 1998: 89–90). In response to this marginalization and exclusion, sexual citizenship theory calls for the following rights: 1) Free expression of sexual identity, desire, and experience by women and sexual or gender minorities; 2) bodily autonomy, including reproduction and contraception, abortion, medical care, and gender conformation; 3) institutional inclusion around marriage, military service, education, parenting rights, health care, the labor market, housing, taxation, pensions and insurance, political representation, and so forth; and 4) participation in politics over access to space (Richardson 2000: 107; Hekma 2015).

However, sexual citizenship theory is permeated with Western liberalism, which idealizes the individual bearer of universal rights who exercises free self-determination. In Asia, though, citizenship is often based on communities imagined in terms of a common culture or family, rather than as a contract among independent, free individuals. The Western norm is not representative of citizenship in the Asian context as it denies the agency embedded in interpersonal relationships and the "common good" of local communities (Sabsay 2012). Furthermore, the individualist norm has colonialist connotations in the non-Western world. Indeed, the international LGBT movement has inadvertently harmed

---

7   Bisexual citizenship has not been given room to exist (Evans 1993: 148).

diverse local identities and practices by imposing Western norms in the name of "liberating" gender and sexual minorities (Masaad 2007).

Thus, a focus on non-Western gender and sexual minorities is an opportunity to de-Westernize and re-imagine sexual citizenship theory (Richardson 2017: 216–19). It can also enrich Western understanding of gender and sexual diversity by backlighting the extent to which "pre-gay identities" and "heterogendered same-sex desire" existed in the West, as well (Brown et al. 2010).

From this perspective, this book analyzes how states and social forces try to define and construct the "good citizens" entitled to citizenship through the inclusion and exclusion of gender and sexual minorities in Asian countries. Many states and dominant social forces have manipulated the symbolism of "LGBT" to enhance their own legitimacy both domestically and internationally. In countries such as Laos, Myanmar, and Cambodia, where the state has not yet made political use of gender and sexual minorities, "marginalization within inclusion" persists. Meanwhile, gender and sexual minorities have sought to redefine "good citizens" for their inclusion by demanding legal rights from the state through the LGBT movement, and by engaging dominant norms through everyday politics to negotiate roles that are acceptable to the majority. We hypothesize that such dynamic hegemonic struggles have defined the varied situations of gender and sexual minority rights in the respective countries and regions, as well as political opportunity structures to their diverse practices resisting marginalization and exclusion.

In this hegemonic struggle, the state and dominant social forces often invoke the nation, the family, religion, and the economy in their moral discourse to define "good citizens." These discourses sometimes reinforce each other to construct a "good citizen," excluding gender and sexual minorities. Yet, the discrepancies and tensions between the discourses sometimes create openings for minorities to negotiate or even subvert dominant discourses. Characteristics of these discourses are outlined below.

Imagined nations

Both in the West and in Asia, gender and sexual minorities have not been recognized as legitimate members of the "imagined communities" that constitute a nation (Anderson 2006), because they were considered to threaten the heterosexual family, the foundation of the nation-state (Richardson 1998: 90–92). In the 1950s in the US, homosexuals were defined as "anti-citizens" and were denied entry to the country, welfare benefits, and military service (Canaday 2009). In many countries, states and dominant social forces have invoked "political homophobia" that constructs gender and sexual minorities as "enemies of the people" and an "us" comprising the majority to strengthen their own legitimacy and control as leaders fighting against the enemy (Bosia and Weiss 2013).

In response to discrimination and exclusion, the LGBT movement in the US made marriage rights and equal participation in the military its main goals. The Asian LGBT movement has also tried to position gender and sexual minorities as "good citizens" who contribute to the well-being of the nation. In the 21st century, some states have begun to emphasize their initiatives to guarantee the rights of gender and sexual minorities as legitimate members of the nation.

However, claims to being "LGBT-friendly" by authoritarian states and states complicit in other human rights abuses often go no further than token efforts to legitimize the regime in the eyes of the West. Moreover, overtly including gender and sexual minorities in the nation can create new divisions and exclusions when combined with nationalism. After the simultaneous terrorist attacks in September 2001, there was an upswelling of "homonationalism" in the US that extolled the virtues of including homosexuals while othering Muslims for its perceived homophobia, calling them "uncivilized" and "barbaric" (Puar 2007). The Israeli government has similarly mobilized homonationalism against Muslims to "pinkwash" its settlement and human rights violations in Palestine (Yasui 2018). In Taiwan in the 2010s, too, homonationalism was mobilized in its conflict with China, othering the latter's "barbaric" policies as being incompatible with the values of "democracy" and "freedom" (Fukunaga 2024).

Furthermore, the discourses and practices of people who seek to be seen as "good citizens" tend to confirm the status quo. For example, under a one-party regime that does not allow free speech, LGBT organizations in Laos have stressed their contribution to the government. One of them celebrated the 100th birthday anniversary of the first prime minister by quoting his statement of "No matter what your gender is, if you have faith in peace, independence, freedom, democracy, and sovereignty you are friends of the party" (Proud To Be Us Laos 2020). In Indonesia, dominant discourses have emphasized national integration based on heteronormativity and the nuclear family, urging gay men to seek "good citizen" status by marrying women and having families (Boellstorff 2005; 2007).

In addition, gender and sexual minorities' demands for inclusion as "good citizens" can marginalize those who do not fit that mold. For example, in the 1990s, when HIV/AIDS countermeasures were introduced by the public health system, a distinction was made in Japan between "responsible gay men" who avoid risk and "irresponsible gay men" who engage in risky sexual behavior (Shingae 2013). Similarly, in the Philippines, middle-class gay men stressed their morality and responsibility to differentiate themselves from poverty-stricken "*bakla*" (Tan 1995).

Family ideology

Family ideologies based on heterosexual norms have also been used for national integration in many societies, which has excluded gender and sexual minorities from legitimate membership of the nation on the grounds that they violate the heterosexual norm of "good citizens," namely, bearing and raising children (Alexander 1994).

In Asia, patriarchy, rather than the fiction of the social contract, was used to legitimize the nation-state. In their catch-up style of nation-state-building, male national leaders emphasized nationalism imagining the state as "the home," themselves as "fathers," their wives as "mothers," and their people as "children," and have attempted to integrate diverse social groups into the "family"/nation. This patriarchalism strengthened the imagination conflating a nation with a family, which excluded women who did not conform to the norm of a "good wife/mother," and gender and sexual minorities, making all of them subjects of vigilance (Tiwon 1996; Wieringa 1998). Moreover, on these criteria, many people have been excluded not only from the imagined community of the nation, but also from their immediate families.

The Western LGBT movement has long viewed the family as an oppressive social unit. However, following the HIV/AIDS crisis and a lesbian baby boom in the 1990s, same-sex marriage legalization became the main goal of the movement (Okano 2015: 65). In Asia more recently, the LGBT movement has also begun calling for the right to form officially recognized families.

Yet, here, too, the dilemma of inclusion and exclusion persists. Middle-class homosexuals' demands for the right to marriage as "good citizens" marginalize those who do not meet the criteria (Brandzel 2002). Moreover, including same-sex couples in the institution of marriage not only reinforces state control of intimacy, but also perpetuates a family ideology that places the burden of care on women while denying public responsibility and expenses to support their care work. Family ideology grants tax and social security benefits to family members who maintain their own care relationships as "good citizens," while imposing disadvantages and social stigma on those who have difficulty in establishing stable care relationships and must rely on welfare (Okano 2015; Aoyama 2016).

In Asia, the states have exploited strong family ideologies, consolidating the idea that families are responsible for their care needs, and failed to develop adequate social welfare institutions. However, this condition has created an opportunity for people to build various forms of "new families" based on care relationships and to deconstruct existing family norms. Particularly in Southeast Asia, people have developed extensive care relationships based on networks of regional bonds, kinship, or religious beliefs. As the birthrate declines and the population ages rapidly, "care provided by society as a whole" has become activated (Hayami 2019). Many people from gender and sexual minorities who had left their biological families have established new families to care for each other. Such practices to expand the concept of family also affected discourses of social movements. In Malaysia, for example, the LGBT movement has adopted the slogan "We are family!" with the aim of expanding the diversity of the family (Iga 2017: 92).

Religious morality

In regions where world religions such as Christianity, Islam, and Buddhism are dominant, religious discourse often defines "good citizens." However, religions differ in how they regard gender and sexual minorities. In Theravada Buddhism, for example, men are believed to be more virtuous than women, and trans women are disfavored. Yet, it is generally understood that homosexuality is not included in the five precepts that lay Buddhists should observe, although some consider it to be a violation of the precept of abstaining from "sexual misconduct" (Kojima, Chapter 12). In contrast, many Christians and Muslims regard gender and sexual minorities as evil because they do not participate in God's work of creating life through marriage between a man and a woman.

However, even in regions where Christianity and Islam are dominant, there are significant differences and changes in the degree to which gender and sexual minorities are oppressed. Islamic dominant regions in Southeast Asia have a rich history in cultural diversity of gender and sexualities, and their oppression strengthened relatively recent years as politicians and religious leaders have stoked "political homophobia" (Bosia and Weiss 2013). In Malaysia, in the 1980s, under the patriarchal "Asian values" espoused by Prime Minister Mahathir, gender and sexual minorities were regarded as "regressive" or an "unacceptable kind of modernity" that reflected corrupt Western values (Peletz 2006; Iga 2017). In Indonesia, when the LGBT movement launched in the mid-2000s, some Muslim men perceived it as an invasion of the nation and used violence to disclaim gender and sexual minorities as members of the nation in the name of Islam (Boellstorff 2007: 161–180). Repression of gender and sexual minorities in the name of religion also intensified in the mid-2010s as the military sought to destabilize the Joko Widodo administration, by creating a moral panic about the threat homosexuality posed to the state (Okamoto 2016a).

In Taiwan and Korea, leaders of the Christian churches had allied with the military regimes to expand their base during the Cold War, but advancing democratization from the late 1980s provided openings for feminists and gender and sexual minorities to secure their rights from the state. Since the 2000s, however, there has been a backlash from the Christian right construing homosexuality as a threat to the nation and its traditions to mobilize conservatives. In Korea in the 2010s, the Christian right joined forces with trans-exclusionary radical feminists (TERFs) in claiming that respecting the rights of trans women threatened the safety of cisgender women (Fukunaga 2022c). This backlash gained ground as a reaction against the positioning of "LGBT" rights as a progressive agenda, while resonating with the transnational "anti-gender movement" (Pearce, Erikainen and Vincent 2020) that antagonizes homosexuality, transgender and reproductive rights.

Yet, while internalizing or being hurt by dominant religious discourses that stigmatize them, gender and sexual minorities also have agency to search for God in their lives, commit to their faith, and pursue a good life and death. Their spiritual struggles amid tensions between faith and sexuality create possibilities for new articulations of religious redemption (Cornelio and Dagle 2024).

Economic contributions

In a capitalist society, contributing to the economic development of the community through the production and consumption of wealth are prerequisites of being "good citizens." On this criterion, gender and sexual minorities are more likely to enjoy citizenship than others (Richardson 1998). Homosexual identity became a possibility after the capitalist development reduced the family's importance as a unit of production and created a large number of wage workers living in cities as consumers. Sexual citizenship, in effect, expanded along with capitalism (D'Emilio 1983; Evans 1993). Gender and sexual minorities who were excluded from their family homes could create new relationships and find belonging in consumer capitalism (Okano 2015).

More recently, Asian states and business communities have also recognized the economic value of gender and sexual minorities and have sought to capitalize on them. Thailand has promoted itself as "LGBT-friendly" to attract gay male couples with high disposable incomes as tourists to spend their "pink dollars." Japan attempted a similar approach with an advertising company during the 2020 Tokyo Olympics. In the Philippines, English-speaking gay men and trans women who work in the call centers of North American companies have been hailed as "new heroes" for their contributions to the nation earning foreign currencies (David 2016).

However, capitalism does not always benefit gender and sexual minorities because it treats those who do not produce wealth and depend on welfare as "second-class citizens." In most societies, lesbians and rural gender and sexual minorities tend to have lower incomes than urban gay men because of the large wage gap between men and women and between urban and rural areas. Also, urban gay men, whether single or coupled, without children requiring their financial support, have higher disposable incomes than others. In contrast, transgender people who incur high medical costs and are subject to employment discrimination tend to be economically disadvantaged. Hence, while a "new homonormativity" under capitalism creates opportunities for middle class urban gay males to be accepted as "good citizens", it also creates new divisions and exclusions (Duggan 2002). Moreover, "emancipation" through capitalism can be a fantasy, considering that gender and sexual minorities may achieve "success" within capitalism, but they only enjoy freedom to the extent that the majority can consume their lifestyle (Woods 1995).

Also, capitalism can work together with family ideology to sustain a notion of citizenship based on heterosexual gender norms, in which women bear the burden of unpaid care work and men devote themselves to wage labor, disparaging gender and sexual minorities who do not conform to those norms (Okano 2015: 138–9, 155). However, this setup for industrial capitalism, which had its prime in the 20th century, is now adapting to the new economic structure of the 21st century, accumulating from more diverse and neoliberal consumption. For the state, incorporating certain – middle class, urban and capitalist – sections of gender and sexual minorities works to go along and survive with this market. For instance, recognizing same-sex relationships, marriage, and partnerships can cater to new consumption without requiring financial resources. Hence, the "LGBT good citizens" can emerge, challenging the old gender-divided norms of capitalism while confirming homonormativity. In aging Asian countries in particular where reproduction by heterosexual couples can no longer sustain the working population, such policies could also be a means to increase the types of "families" responsible for care and to prevent welfare budget increases (Aoyama 2021).

The structure of this volume

Based on the findings of the research presented in this book and previous studies, the introduction has tried to outline an analytical framework for examining Asian LGBT politics, although it remains hypothetical, not a rigorously verified argument. The following chapters, in turn, do not necessarily attempt to verify the introduction's hypothetical framework, but rather to elucidate the politics surrounding sexuality and gender diversity in their own ways, based on each author's academic interests and political constraints. In this section, the chapters are summarized in terms of the framework, but it should be noted that the richness of the chapters' case studies cannot be fully conveyed here.

Part I focuses on the politics of the nomenclature and visual representations of gender and sexual minorities. Today, the Japanese terminology for understanding sexual diversity relies heavily on transliterations of English-derived expressions. The use of such terms contrasts with the fact that gender and sexual minorities in the United States have dared to embrace discriminatory slang terms to refer to themselves as a form of resistance. To surpass the confines of the English language and enrich the vocabulary of sexual diversity in Japan and Asia, it is necessary to focus on everyday speech, vernacular languages, and local history (Chapter 1, Masao Imamura).

Analyzing visual representations is an effective means of getting an overview of the situation of gender and sexual minorities in a country. In Southeast Asia, films and television programs featuring gender and sexual minorities are produced in Thailand, the Philippines, and Vietnam. Their representations of gender and sexual minorities have shifted from the caricatured "others" in comedies, to the "realistic imagery" in independent films made by sexual and gender minorities themselves, and the "friendly neighbors" of sitcoms. This transition indicates how people who were previously marginalized and othered have been re-imagined as a familiar part of "us" (Chapter 2, Naoya Sakagawa).

In Part II, we employ case studies from different countries to examine how various states and dominant social forces have mobilized moral discourses based on nation, family, religion, and the economy to define "good citizens," and how they have treated gender and sexual minorities.

First, we focus on cases in which, despite the progress of democratization, conservative religious forces and states have interwoven the moral discourses of nation, religion, and family to formulate a rigid vision of "good citizens" that excludes gender and sexual minorities. In Malaysia, after the first electoral victory of opposition parties in the nation's history in 2018, the new government denounced discrimination and hate speech under the banner of an "inclusive society." However, needing the support of the Malay Muslim majority, it denied the rights of gender and sexual minorities and provided so-called "correction" programs (Chapter 3, Tsukasa Iga). In Indonesia, the LGBT movement, which had been revitalized by the democratization of the late 1990s, has been faced with an "anti-LGBT" backlash in the name of Islam. Religious leaders and psychologists have pathologized gender and sexual minorities, with some religious practitioners attempting to "cure" homosexuality by "exorcism" (Chapter 4, Masaaki Okamoto).

The Catholic Church in the Philippines has also expressed alarm, warning that global forces are undermining the sanctity of the "family" that creates life and the "nation" based upon it by promoting gender and sexual minority rights and same-sex marriage. Furthermore, as the self-proclaimed moral leadership of the nation, the Church has called for the people to renounce any activity that affirms homosexual relations, while recognizing homosexual orientation as a disorder rather than a sin and calling for compassionate engagement with it. However, neither the state nor the people appear to be heeding those calls, suggesting that the Church's influence has declined (Chapter 5, Satoshi Miyawaki).

Second, we examine cases in which dominant moral discourses, on the contrary, create certain liberating opportunities while limiting other possibilities. In Taiwan, in the context of democratization and international conflict with China, a nationalism centered on a democratic identity has taken root, breaking down patriarchal family systems and norms, and actively promoting the rights of gender and sexual minorities, including the legalization of same-sex marriage in 2019. This has been underpinned by the deepening discourse of "gender equality" in civil society to include rights and protections for gender and sexual minorities, and solidarity between feminism and the LGBT movement. However, since the 2010s, there has been a growing backlash, especially among right-wing Catholics, against the rights of gender and sexual minorities (Chapter 6, Genya Fukunaga).

In Vietnam, under its family ideology, negotiations between the LGBT movement and the one-party state have led to some expansions of rights. The LGBT movement, primarily young people fluent in English, appealed to the one-party state for the right to same-sex marriage and gender reassignment as non-political issues of "love." Although the state has refused to recognize same-sex marriage, it has lifted the legal ban on gender reassignment. The state, reinforcing the norm of family as the foundation of the nation-state, regarded the "curing" of members of gender minorities into men and women who could constitute a family as a positive thing (Chapter 7, Nara Oda). This case shows that within the bounds of existing family ideology, even a one-party state can accept some of the rights demands of the LGBT movement.

Capitalism, too, has benefited gender and sexual minorities in some instances by including them as "good citizens." In Thailand since the

1960s, Western gay men attracted to Thailand as a place to be free from the gender and sexual norms of their home countries developed the sex industry in partnership with Thai businesspeople. As a result, urban spaces were created in which gender and sexual minorities enjoyed relative autonomy. In the process of developing Pattaya into such a space, trans women dancers achieved social recognition as legitimate members of the nation who attract foreign tourists and thus contribute to the economic development of the nation-state (Chapter 8, Shinsuke Hinata).

In Singapore, gender and sexual minorities were oppressed under its "Asian values" ideology in the 1980s. Since the 2000s, however, the state has promoted itself as a creative, intelligent city, tolerant of gender and sexual minorities to attract foreign professionals, and in 2022 it abolished Section 377A of the Penal Code. However, when religious groups expressed opposition to the Pink Dot movement, the government tightened its control, fearing that the situation would divide the nation, and foreclosed the courts' potential to recognize same-sex marriages by declaring that the parliament reserves the right to define the institution of marriage. When capitalist demands to exploit gender and sexual minorities appeared to threaten national unity, the state tightened its control on the former to preserve the latter (Chapter 9, Keiko Tsuji Tamura).

Moreover, granting rights to gender and sexual minorities under capitalism can entail another kind of exclusion. In Japan, under a mayor's initiative in 2011, Osaka City began promoting neoliberal "diversity management" to capitalize on more diverse "human resources" for financial reconstruction and economic growth. The resulting top-down enactment of a "same-sex partnership system" functioned as a "pinkwash," glossing over the abolition of other human rights programs that citizens had long advocated for – such as *burakumin* (a discriminated group), war victims and comfort women in neighboring countries – on the pretext of a financial burden (Chapter 10, Akitomo Shingae).

In Part III, we focus on the identity dynamics and everyday politics surrounding diverse sexualities and genders. In Laos, there has long been a vernacular identity called "*kathoey*" that includes both trans women and men who desire men, but since the early 2000s, the Western concept "*kee*" (gay) – appropriated via neighboring Thailand – has been adopted to distinguish men who desire men, mainly in urban areas. However, the distinction between *kathoey* and *kee* is neither definitive nor consistent. Rather, in online and face-to-face everyday communication, these categories appear to be ambiguous and fluid, with those adopting them moving between them rather than insisting on one over the other (Chapter 11, Yūsuke Ōmura).

Complex parallels between Western and vernacular cultures are also evident in gender and sexual minorities' resistance to marginalization, as seen in the class-differences between everyday politics and the organized LGBT movement. In Myanmar in 2011, after a long-awaited transition to civilian rule, the NLD party, which was in power from 2016 to 2021, made no significant progress on human rights issues for gender and sexual minorities. Although human rights activists outside Myanmar who were primarily educated urban middle class professionals had developed LGBT movements, their lobbying efforts were strongly opposed by conservative Buddhists. Meanwhile, many lower-socioeconomic status trans women, independently of those high-level political conflicts, improved their lives and dignity by filling the demand for spiritual mediums and makeup artists that grew with the transition to capitalism (Chapter 12, Takahiro Kojima).

In the Philippines, despite a relatively free civil society and vibrant democracy, the LGBT movement led by urban middle class activists has campaigned unsuccessfully for an anti-discrimination law. Part of the problem is that the LGBT movement has not sufficiently reached people who embrace vernacular identities in depressed or rural areas. The gap was created by the fact that many vernacular trans women were disinterested in legal rights, rather seeking to heal their intimate sorrow. Furthermore, the movement's emphasis on "moral decency" tends to marginalize gender and sexual minorities who do not conform. In these circumstances, vernacular trans women have worked to improve their personal well-being, not by political campaigning and advocacy, but by occupying niche jobs and creating new care relationships (Chapter 13, Wataru Kusaka).

Everyday politics focuses on narrow and immediate interests but has the potential to change prevailing family and religious norms, even where the organized LGBT movement has been unsuccessful in seeking legislation of rights. In this way, everyday politics and formal advocacy can be seen as complementary. In Cambodia, the ban on same-sex marriage was abolished in the Civil Code of 2007, but same-sex marriage has not been legally recognized. Under these circumstances, "traditional marriage ceremonies" celebrating same-sex relationships are increasingly common and are widely recognized by relatives and community members. Thus, despite significant barriers to legal change, social attitudes are changing through the complementary efforts of NGOs and everyday politics (Chapter 14, Naomi Hatsukano).

In Indonesia, where the "anti-LGBT" storm has been stirred-up in the name of Islam, a national Protestant organization issued a statement calling for the elimination of discrimination against LGBT people. Behind this call was a group of pastors who had studied queer theology in the West. However, for ordinary members of a sexual or gender minority who embrace a conservative Christian position, intimate care from a congregation who shares the same religious view is more important for feeling religious inclusion than abstract queer theology (Chapter 15, Yumi Kitamura and Khanis Suvianita).

Finally, the concluding chapter (Kaoru Aoyama), reviewing the case studies of each chapter, argues that the politicization of the term "LGBT" in various manners and the diverse ways and asymmetric outcomes of seeking and gaining recognition and rights among gender and sexual minorities show that the "solidarity" traditionally implied by the term is, in fact, becoming more divisive. As a step toward overcoming such contradictions and opening new understandings of gender and sexual diversity from non-Western perspectives, Aoyama suggests further research crossing the boundaries between area studies and gender and sexuality studies, such as in this book, focusing on a variety of societies, politics, histories, and everyday practices of people.

PART I

Nomenclature and Representations

1

How to Update the Names of Gender and Sexual Minorities: The Anti-Politics of Anglo-American Normativity in Japan

Masao Imamura

Introduction

Socially marginalized minorities are routinely subject to belittling and mocking names. The slurs – both blatant and nuanced – demonstrate the minorities' low social standing and that they are collectively looked down upon by the majority. Combating such names is for a minority group to gain social recognition. Such efforts in the English language are widely-known: gender and sexual minorities in the US, for example, have led efforts to destigmatize slurs such as "faggot," "dyke," and "queer." Scholars have referred to this linguistic tactic as "reappropriation" or "reclamation."

But do such linguistic tactics work in other places? Does it take place in other languages? Towards answering these questions, this chapter presents a case study of Japan and Japanese. Common stigmatizing slurs in Japanese referring to gender and sexual minorities have been contested over the past few decades, and as a result these old slurs are hardly used today. This change in language use, however, did not involve reappropriation. In Japan, the "solution" was to import and use English words. The acceptance of English names and categories has reinforced Anglo-American norms. This chapter seeks to draw critical attention to critical attention of the rise of this particular normativity.

What's in a name?

When a particular minority group is marginalized, their own self-referential names tend to be ignored. When they contest slurs, a minority group insists that their own self-referential name be publicly recognized. We can find examples of such contestation from ethnic minorities around the world. Many minority groups think that it is indispensable to have their endonyms widely used. The Romani people presents a good example. They have rejected the well-known exonym "Gypsies" and insisted that they be called by their endonym. The Rohingya, a Muslim minority group from western Myanmar, is another good example. The government of Myanmar has consistently refused to use the name "Rohingya," claiming that there are no such people in the country. Instead the government insists on using "Bengali," which usually refers to a far larger population including the ethnic majority of Bangladesh. Thus, in using "Bengali," the Myanmar authorities effectively argue that the Muslim minority group belongs not to Myanmar but to the neighboring country of Bangladesh. The Rohingya insist on their endonym, arguing that they have been living in Myanmar for generations (Oh 2012).

The Rohingya case shows that the politics of naming are not just a matter of legal formality but indeed a matter of life and death. In 2012, it was reported that thousands of Rohingya in Pauktaw Township in Arakan State refused to sign government-issued registration forms because the authorities erased the term "Rohingya" from completed forms, replacing it with "Bengali." According to the news article, the Rohingya feared that they would be declared illegal migrants and deported if they registered as Bengali. In response, the government removed the names of those refusing to register as Bengali from the residential lists; as a result, they were not recognized as legal residents of the area (Lawi Weng 2012).

Social and political recognition of self-referential terms is important for gender and sexual minorities too. If someone grows up in an environment in which gay people are commonly subject to derogatory or mocking names, it is only natural for that person to feel that there is something wrong about them. Autobiographical narratives by LGBT writers often describe a coming-of-age moment in which this doubt is overcome. For example, in *When We Rise: My Life in the Movement*, Clive Jones, a prominent gay activist, recalls encountering a magazine article mentioning "gay liberation" in his high school library in 1971. Jones explains that upon encountering this article, he realized that he was "gay" and that he was not alone. He writes: "that was the exact moment I stopped planning to kill myself" (Jones 2016: 68).

When a member of a minority group encounters a word that recognizes them with respect, that word is likely to enter their "final vocabulary," to use a concept proposed by Richard Rorty. Final vocabulary is, in Rorty's explanation, a set of words that a person:

> employ[s] to justify their actions, their beliefs, and their lives. These are the words in which we formulate praise of our friend and contempt for our enemies, our long-term projects, our deepest self-doubts and our highest hopes. They are the words in which we tell, sometimes prospectively and sometimes retrospectively, the story of our lives. (Rorty 1989: 73)

We can see that the word "gay" entered Clive Jones's "final vocabulary," for without this word it would be impossible for him to tell his life-story.

The English-language case: Linguistic reappropriation of slurs

How gender and sexual minorities around the world have fought slurs and struggled for social recognition of their endonyms has not been sufficiently studied. One reason is that exonyms and endonyms for gender and sexual minorities, unlike those for ethnic minorities, vary tremendously from one language to another. That is, for example, while the Rohingya demand is that they be recognized as "Rohingya" everywhere around the world, those who identify themselves as "queer" in the US are not making such a claim. Because each language has its own rich vocabulary, it is impossible to cover all the variations used around the world. In this chapter, we will focus on English and Japanese to ascertain how names have been updated.

The acceptance of "gay" was a historical watershed because it was the fist time the minority group's endonym was widely used. "Gay" was established as the major self-referential name by the 1960s; when a group was formed in New York City in 1968 after the Stonewall Riots was famously named the "Gay Liberation Front." This word was, however, not used by mainstream media for many years. Until 1987, the *New York Times* would not print the word "gay" (in the sense of sexual orientation); "homosexual" had to be used instead (Dunlap 2017).

The method of linguistic reappropriation is explained in the 2014 film *Pride*, which narrates the story of young gay activists in the UK in the mid-1980s. The film is based on the true story of gay activists supporting miners during a year-long strike, notably with a fundraising concert billed as "Pits and Perverts." In the scene, Mark, the group leader, tells his friends how to respond when they are verbally insulted:

> Bromley: They called us perverts.
>
> Mark: Bromley, it's time for an important part of your education. Hands up, in this room, if you've ever been called a name like that.
>
> *all guys raise their hands*
>
> Mark: Now, there is a long and honorable tradition in the gay community and it has stood us in good stead for a very long time. When somebody calls you a name ... am I right Jonathan?
>
> Jonathan: Dead right.
>
> Mark: You take it and own it. (*Pride* 2014)

Activists carried out a series of "take it and own it" campaigns, targeting a variety of words like "gay" and "dike." Although the pejorative senses of "gay" are no longer widely recognized, the word used to imply immoral pleasure as indicated by phrases like "gay houses" meaning brothels and "gaycats" meaning young prostitutes (Chauncey 2019: 17). In order to reclaim "dyke," activists in the US even fought long legal battles. In 1976, a lesbian motorcycle club in San Francisco coined the name "Dykes on Bikes." Although the United States government refused to register the name for decades, the group eventually won a prolonged legal case to have it registered in 2006 (Anten 2006; Ilyasova 2006).

Yet the word that best represents the activism of linguistic reappropriation is "queer." The rise of this word is associated with a lengthy manifesto titled "Queer Read This," distributed by Queer Nation and Act Up during the 1990 New York Gay Pride Day parade. The following passage from the section titled "Why Queer?" is worth quoting at length:

> Couldn't we just use "gay" instead? It's a much brighter word. And isn't it synonymous with "happy"? …

> Well, yes, "gay" is great. It has its place. But when a lot of lesbians and gay men wake up in the morning we feel angry and disgusted, not gay. So we've chosen to call ourselves queer. Using "queer" is a way of reminding us how we are perceived by the rest of the world. It's a way of telling ourselves we don't have to be witty and charming people who keep our lives discreet and marginalized in the straight world…

> And when spoken to other gays and lesbians it's a way of suggesting we close ranks, and forget (temporarily) our individual differences because we face a more insidious common enemy. Yeah, queer can be a rough word but it is also a sly and ironic weapon we can steal from the homophobe's hands and use against him. (Anon. 1990)

Here, "queer" is distinguished from "gay" as an explicitly angry and confrontational term. It is a "weapon" to be stolen from the "common enemy" and "used against him." This word functions to remind the speaker and the listener how painful it is to be looked down upon by the majority. During the 1990s, "queer" captured the imagination of academic scholars in ways that "gay" had never done. In 1990, an academic conference called "Queer Theory" was held at the University of California at Santa

Cruz. In 1993, Duke University Press launched Series Q, which proved to be influential for two decades.

When "queer" began to circulate as a self-referential term in the US a quarter-century ago, it was meant to surprise and disturb the listener. Reflecting on the time when Queer Nation was formed, Michael Warner, a queer theorist, says that the name "seemed, as I recall, mainly hilarious to all of us who heard it" (Warner 2012). Because the word was so unlikely to be widely accepted, it is all the more remarkable how quickly and widely it circulated, gaining prominence among both activists and academics.

The Japanese case

Removing old vernaculars altogether

In Japan too, the terms used to refer to gender and sexual minorities have changed significantly during the past few decades. Beginning in the 1990s, major publishers in Japan began to reconsider how to classify and name them. Back then, the words officially used by public institutions to refer to homosexuals were either medically or morally stigmatizing. The gay community in Japan used a great variety of different words for self-reference in different times and spaces. As recently as the late 1990s, there was no widely shared, common self-referential name for gender and sexual minorities in Japan.

This linguistic instability and fragmentation was acknowledged in a 1996 essay titled "We exist although there are no names for us," published as a postscript to an edited volume on sexual diversity. In this essay, Usagi Nakamura (1958-) presents the following self-affirmative declaration: "This is me. The is how I feel about myself. This is the kind of sex I like. This is how I get turned on. I don't know how you name it. Whatever you name it, I exist here!" (Nakamura 2003: 317). The volume was edited by Noriaki Fushimi (1963-), a leading gay activist-writer; it was published originally by a small company called Potto Shuppan, but it found broad readership and was eventually reprinted as an inexpensive paperback by a major publisher. Resonating with many readers across the country who were unsure of what to call their sexual orientations, the publication turned out to be a rare success.

In retrospect , we can identify a turning point in a 2001 debate, stirred by a magazine article using an old slang term "*okama*."[1] The weekly news magazine *Shukan Kinyoubi* (Weekly Friday) published a long article by a young writer named Kenji Oikawa, profiling Ken Togo (1932–2012). Togo was openly gay. He had a unique career. Since 1963, he had operated gay bars in various cities. In 1981, he founded a magazine titled *The Gay*, and actively campaigned to promote HIV/AIDS awareness. He organized a political party called "*Zatsumintou*" – which can be roughly translated as "the party of the unwanted peoples." He repeatedly – and unsuccessfully – ran for public offices, including the lower house of the National Diet and the Governor of Tokyo. He gained notoriety by giving public speeches that were sexually explicit, playful, and provocative. It was not entirely surprising that this eccentric figure was profiled by *Kinyoubi*, which was a well-known advocate for the rights of various minority groups.

The *Kinyoubi* article turned out to be exceptionally controversial for one simple reason: it printed the word *okama*. We do not know much about the history of the word, but we do know that in the latter half of the 20th century, it was the most widely used term for referring to men who were transvestite, homosexual and/or unusually feminine. Although it had never been used by a major newspaper, it was used widely in the popular media. Every native speaker, regardless of gender, age or orientation, was familiar with this slang.

As soon as *Kinyoubi* published the article, a gay advocacy organization called "Sukotan Kikaku" led by Satoru Ito (1953–) vehemently condemned the article, arguing that the word was discriminatory and harmful to gay people. In response, the magazine kowtowed and quickly published a didactic article titled "Sexuality and human rights" written by Ito and his colleague. This publication triggered a new round of

---

1   This debate has been admirably discussed by Mark McLelland (2009), but I approach it from a different perspective.

criticisms from other gay activists, who took issues not only with Ito and
his colleagues but also with the publisher. Notable among these critics
was the previously mentioned writer Noriaki Fushimi. The debate lasted
for months, dividing the magazine's editorial board, and resulting in
the resignations of a board member (a Korean-Japanese activist) and a
veteran editor (who had approved Oikawa's original article).

It is easier to see the importance of this debate in hindsight today.
It was the first public debate about what a gender and sexual minority
should be called in Japan. Fushimi recognized this importance from the
outset and, with colleagues, organized a public symposium that was
attended by many gay activists. After the event, he even published a book
titled "Is 'Okama' a Slur?" including the symposium proceedings and a
series of relevant articles (Fushimi 2002).

In retrospect it is not surprising that the *Kinyoubi* article used the
word simply because Togo insisted on calling himself *okama*. He even
titled his autobiography *Beyond Common Sense: The 70-year Journey of
an Okama* (Togo 2002). In the *Kinyoubi* article, Togo was directly asked
by Oikawa why he insisted on calling himself "*okama*." He replied:

> I very much like the word *okama* precisely because we have been
> oppressed in society. There is nothing to be embarrassed about a man
> loving a man or a woman loving a woman. It would be embarrassing not
> to be true to yourself. It would be embarrassing not to be able to love
> anyone. I believe that "okama" is etymologically related to the Sanskrit
> word "kama," which means "love." You see, "okama" is all about love.
> (cited in Fushimi 2002: 30)[2]

Although Togo's understanding of etymology is not supported by
academic scholarship, the point remains that *okama* was unambiguously
his choice. By using the vernacular *okama* as a self-affirming word, Togo
was arguably pursuing a tactic of linguistic reclamation.

---

2   This translation is mine. McLelland et al. 2007 presents a translation of the entire
    article.

This article was published at a time when young gay activists in Japan were trying to update the names for gender and sexual minorities. Dictionary entries began to be revised throughout the 1990s. In 1991, for example, *Kojien*, considered to be the most authoritative dictionary, redefined the entries for words like "abnorm *douseiai*" (meaning "homosexual love") in response to a letter from an advocacy group (Nagayasu 2017).

Linguistic reappropriation fails in Japan

Ito was a leading activist who challenged old vernaculars, seeking to replace them with "correct" ones. He effectively demanded that *okama* be censored and that "*gei*" (from the English "gay") be used instead. His website emphasizes the need for "correct information and knowledge" (*seikaku na jyouhou to seikaku na chishiki*).[3] He went to a very prestigious high school in Tokyo and graduated from the most prestigious university in the country (University of Tokyo). Upon graduation, he became an English language teacher and wrote several textbooks for learning the language. Since coming out as a gay man in the 1990s, he has tirelessly delivered awareness-raising lectures. His source for this "correct" information and knowledge was very often the English language.

It is safe to say that Ito lost the 2001 debate among gay intellectuals. He did not even attend the symposium; by then he likely knew that he was losing ground. Younger gay activists argued that if Togo wanted to call himself *okama* it was unnecessary to censor the word. While Togo purposefully used vulgar words to expose social taboos and prejudices, his style of activism, filled with provocation and irony, was entirely lost on Ito. Despite the heated debate in which an old vernacular was defended, the broader trend of importing English words and categories turned out to be unstoppable.

In Japan both activists and academics have, with remarkable consistency, preferred "correct" names and eschewed humorous, ironic

---

3   See the organization's website: https://sukotan.jp/qa-all (accessed October 22, 2024)

and emotional expressions. A consensus emerged in Japan among a wide range of stakeholders that gender and sexual minorities would benefit from using English words as common names and categories, used by both the majority and minorities. Hence a broad array of English concepts and categories – which were regarded as trendy, refreshing, and authoritative – have been incorporated into Japanese. Words like *jendaa* (gender), *sekushuariti* (sexuality), *gei* (gay), *rezubian* (lesbian), and LGBT have secured places in most Japanese dictionaries.

While the Queer Nation's manifesto emphasizes anger and hate, these emotive qualities have been largely neglected by academia. It has therefore proven difficult to translate "queer" into Japanese, for its "sly and ironic" inferences did not resonate with Japanese activism. Queer has therefore been simply phonetically transliterated into Japanese, rendered as "kuia." *Kuia* (queer) is not listed in a typical Japanese dictionary, however. Occasionally we find the word in a daily newspaper; typically in the arts and culture section. It is unlikely that *kuia* will ever gain popularity in Japan because very few people use it for self-reference. It is only used by intellectuals.

There were efforts to translate "queer" into a Japanese word. In 2003, Kazuko Takemura, a renowned feminist scholar known for highly-acclaimed translations of Judith Butler, suggested *"hentai"* (cited in Komori 2003: 146). The word *"hentai"* has a long understudied history, with multiple meanings including "transformed," "strange," and/or "pervert" (McLelland 2006). It could be used as a slur, but it could also be used affectionately. But this suggestion was not favorably received, and *"hentai"* has ended up on a very different journey globally as a referent to a particular genre of *anime* pornography.

Thus, linguistic reappropriation, a distinct tradition of the gay movement in places like the US and the UK, ultimately failed in Japan. Importantly, this failure did not become an issue in the country, because linguistic reappropriation or self-naming was never considered a noteworthy activist practice.

English words and Anglo-American norms prevail in Japan

English words have become the dominant referents to gender and sexual minorities in Japan. Since the 1990s, public events organized by and for these minorities have strongly favored transliterated words like *gei* and *rezubian*. The first film festival of its kind in Japan, held in Tokyo in 1992, was named *"resubian & gei firumu fesutibaru"* (lesbian and gay film festival). The first pride march in Japan, held in Tokyo in 1994, was named *"rezubian gei pareedo"* (lesbian gay parade). In 1997, an influential highbrow magazine, *Gendai Shisou*, had a special issue on *"rezubian gei sutadiizu"* (lesbian gay studies). For such events, English names were simply transliterated. An effort to find a Japanese word was, and remains, elusive.

This remains the case today. For example, *LGBT wo Yomitoku – Kuia Sutadiizu Nyuumon* (Reading LGBT: An Introduction to Queer Studies), is an affordable paperback that introduces five "basic concepts": *pafoomatibitii* (performativity), *homosoosyaru* (homo-social), *heteronoomatibitii* (heteronormativity), *homonoomatibiti* (homonorma-tivity), and *homonasyonarizumu* (homonationalism). Such an array of English words is not unusual for a book by a Japanese academic of *kuia sutadiizu* (queer studies). The English words "gender" and "sexuality," phonetically rendered as *jendaa* and *sekushuariti* have been established as names of academic fields. Today, "gei" and "LGBT" are found in most Japanese dictionaries and used by mainstream newspapers. LGBT has been officially endorsed as correct and authoritative, while most old vernacular terms, such as "homo" and *okama*, have been effectively removed from the public domain.

English expressions, as opposed to Japanese, have been preferred not only by academia but also by the commercial sectors. Japanese words are deemed rigid, serious, and old-fashioned, while English words sound fashionable and attractive. This tendency can be observed in recently published retrospective oral histories of gay activists in Japan such as *Yakudo-suru Gei Mubumento* (Dynamism of the Gay Movement). While the first generation of gay activists, unabashedly left-leaning, tended to focus on legal issues, the younger generation shifted the focus to entertainment, prioritizing events like dance parties to draw young gay people together. The new approach is highlighted in the oral history of a Sapporo-based activist called Kenta, who was a successful organizer of the city's annual pride parade (Saitō 2023: 426). In the late 1990s, Kenta decided that it was necessary to make the event far more entertaining and commercially successful. He had observed that the local gay bars in Sapporo were totally detached from, if not hostile to, the typical activist events, which were regarded as confrontational and above all boring. Kenta began to organize night-life events at trendy clubs with famous Tokyo-based Djs. What is important for our discussion is that advertisements for these events were predominantly in English. The entertainment industry and mass media in Japan quickly adopted English words like "gay" and "queer," in part because their meanings were unclear. English words were easier to use precisely because they were purposefully apolitical; they were disconnected from the familiar Japanese expressions and therefore uncontroversial and trouble-free.

At a deeper level, however, the ascendance of Anglo-American norms in the realm of gender and sexuality in Japan is not simply a matter of preferring non-confrontational language. The key function of Anglo-American normativity is transforming all sorts of political issues to technical issues of finding the "correct" – that is, Anglo-American – concepts and models. In this sense, Anglo-American normativity works as an anti-politics machine in Japan.

Why does linguistic reappropriation succeed in English?

Perhaps rather than asking why linguistic reappropriation has failed in Japan, we should ask instead why it has succeeded so well in English. Because this question has not been sufficiently pursued in the existing literature, I can only speculate and point to two factors: the vibrant culture of vernacular expression in US politics, and the self-sufficiency of the English language.

First, the exceptionally rich culture of vernacular expression in the US seems to make it easy for linguistic reappropriation to work in that country. The richest case of all reappropriated words in the history of English is perhaps "nigga," an unmistakably American term. Today this colloquial slang, deriving from the notorious slur "nigger," is used almost exclusively among African-Americans, often in an amicable and affectionate way. This term came into wide circulation in the 1990s with the rise of hip hop culture (Kennedy 2002). Given the history of the slur, it is truly remarkable that African-Americans have reappropriated this very word.

Words like "nigga" show that the US has an extraordinarily dynamic culture of vernacular expressions, which perhaps owes much to African Americans. In his 1970 essay "What America Would Be Like Without Blacks," Ralph Ellison identifies a "vernacular revolt" against authority as a quintessential American national quality (Ellison 1970: 585). If Ellison is right, a minority group using vernacular expressions in their revolt is an American national tradition. If that is so, linguistic reappropriation in the US belongs not just to queer and other minority groups but to politics in general. In other words, reappropriating slurs is a common and familiar political practice in the US.

Indeed, we can observe linguistic reappropriation at play at the highest level of political contest in the US: the presidential campaign. When, for example, in the 2016 presidential election Hilary Clinton referred to Donald Trump's supporters as a "basket of deplorables," the Trump campaign immediately made a meme celebrating "Les Deplorables" and adopted a Les Miserable song with the famous line "Do you hear the people sing, singing the song of angry men?" (Robinson 2016). In return, when Trump called Clinton a "nasty woman," many women supporting Clinton began wearing shirts and waving banners and sporting other merchandise identifying themselves as "nasty woman." Because of the combative style of politics and activism in the US, insults and slurs are frequently used – and rejected, reclaimed, and appropriated.

Second, the English language is so self-sufficient that it does not need to be deeply disturbed by a foreign language. The influence of English appears to be especially strong among gender and sexual minorities around the world, as shown by the global circulation of "gay men's English" (Leap and Boellstorff 2004: 2). Martel has reported the profound influence of the American model in the globalization of gay identity (Martel 2018). Even French-speaking peoples are no exception; the process has been described richly in *Queer Theory: The French Response* by Bruno Perreau.

While it is difficult for non-English speakers around the world to entirely avoid English words, the global supremacy of English effectively guarantees that its native speaker hardly ever need to rely on a foreign language for self-identification. It must be rare for a word of a foreign language to enter the final vocabulary of native English-speakers living in the US or the UK. Unsurprisingly, Rorty's examples of "final vocabulary" are all English words. But such an environment, where one's native tongue is sufficient for their final vocabulary, is in fact rare around the world.

Conclusion: Re-centering normativity

In Japan, the activism of linguistic reappropriation did not interest scholars of gender and sexuality. Nor did it interest LGBT activists. Today old Japanese vernaculars tend to be dismissed; once gone, they are not even missed. The Japanese scholarship on gender and sexuality has not paid critical attention to these linguistic changes. This is partly because it is extraordinarily difficult to trace the evolution of vernacular expressions but mainly because scholars have been the most eager proponents of these changes. Ironically, the Japanese case of embracing foreign words sharply contrasts with the Anglo-American "tradition" of revitalizing old slangs and slurs.

Scholars of gender and sexuality in Japan raise awareness about the domination of heteronormativity, but they hardly ever question that of European or Anglo-American normativity. They are not interested in "provincializing Europe," as Dipesh Chakrabarty put it. Writing of

India's premodern intellectual traditions, Chakrabarty has pointed out that "Indian social scientists or social scientists of India … treat these traditions as truly dead, as history" (Chakrabarty 2000: 6). The same can be said of the typical Japanese scholar's attitude on the country's premodern traditions of gender and sexuality. As a result, historiography of gender and sexuality remains very underdeveloped in the country. We can find many books written in Japanese on the history of the gay movement in the US or on the history of homosexuality in Europe, but when it comes to Japanese history, very few are available. While scholars of Japanese history and Japanese literature have been presenting relevant findings, they are rarely picked up by the scholars of gender and sexuality, who are more interested in the latest Euro-American norms.

Japan's endorsement of English vocabulary also sharply contrasts with other Asian countries. In the Philippines, the language spoken by gay men, known as *swardspeak* mixes different languages such as Tagalog, Cebuano, English and Spanish (Hart and Hart 1990; Manalansan 2003). In Chinese-speaking countries, old vernacular expressions, most famously "*tongzhi*" (meaning comrade), have been creatively reappropriated by gay communities (Bao 2018; Wong and Zhang 2001). The Thai case is striking in that the fundamental triangle of male, female, and the third gender called *kathoey* persists despite the onslaught of Americanization and globalization. As Peter Jackson points out. "Thailand's transgender and transsexual subcultures are largely uninfluenced by English borrowings and continue to use the long-established term *kathoey*" (Jackson 2004: 219). According to these studies, in China, Hong Kong, Taiwan, the Philippines, and Thailand, old vernaculars remain relevant and vibrant.

The hegemony of the Anglo-American in Japan does not mean that there are no vibrant vernacular expressions for gender and sexuality. In fact, low-brow cultural works such as *manga* and *anime* are filled with unique vernacular expressions. The genre of Boys Love has grown so much in the past two decades that it is easy to imagine that some of the vernacular expressions have entered the "final vocabulary" of youths in Japan.[4] Studies of Boys Love readers across Asia suggest that this is happening not only in Japan but also across Asia (Baudinette 2023; Welker 2022).

Understanding how final vocabularies are changing across Asia deserves more attention. For becoming familiar with other people's self-descriptions is a necessary first step towards regarding them as co-equals. As Rorty pointed out in *Contingency, Irony and Solidarity*, the

> process of coming to see other human beings as 'one of us' rather than as 'them' is a matter of detailed description of what unfamiliar people are like and of redescription of what we ourselves are like. This is a task not for theory but for genres such as ethnography, the journalist's report, the comic book, the docudrama, and, especially, the novel (Rorty 1989 xvi)

If we wish to understand better how norms of gender and sexuality are evolving in Asia, we will do well to study *manga, anime*, and TV dramas, filled with creative vernacular expressions.

---

4   Some of the genre-defining terminology such as "*yaoi*" and "*fujyoshi*" are expressions of self-deprecating humor. *Yaoi* comes from the phrase "*Yama nashi, ochi nashi, imi nasshi*" (no climax, no point, no meaning). *Fujoshi*, meaning "rotten girl," is a pun on an old word with the same pronunciation but a different *kanji* meaning "girl/lady." The best introductory article on the subject to my knowledge remains James 2016.

2 | Gender and Sexual Minorities in Contemporary Southeast Asia: An Attempt at Image Categorization

Naoya Sakagawa

Since around the time of the 2017 Academy Awards, there has been an increasingly explicit embrace of sexual diversity in visual image content in Western media. The 2017 Best Picture Oscar went to *Moonlight*, which tells the story of a young black man coming to terms with his sexuality; at the 2018 Academy Awards, *A Fantastic Woman* (Chile), which depicted the life of a trans woman, won Best Foreign Language Film; and James Ivory, director of *Call Me by Your Name* (an Italian-French-Brazilian-US co-production), took the award for Best Adapted Screenplay. Other films positively depicting gender and sexual minorities, such as *Bohemian Rhapsody*, *Green Book*, and *The Favorite*, also won their respective categories at the 2019 Academy Awards.

But how are gender and sexual minorities represented in contemporary Southeast Asian visual media? I will attempt to create a typology in this chapter. Of course, Southeast Asia is a wide area, and treatment of gender and sexual minorities differs from country to country. Naturally, even within Southeast Asia, there are regions where moving images related to gender and sexual minorities can be produced relatively openly, and others where they cannot. I employ the terms "moving images" and "visual media" rather than "films" to include video content on the Internet.

First, I will discuss the degree of "publicness" of images of gender and sexual minorities in contemporary Southeast Asia; then, I will explain the types and characteristics of gender and sexual minority images in regions where they are available. Finally, after summarizing and categorizing the characteristics of the representations of gender and sexual minorities in

contemporary Southeast Asian images, I will discuss future prospects
and further issues to be addressed.

The public nature of gender and
sexual minority images

One of the most influential film genres in Southeast Asia is "national
cinema," which presents national role models through heroes fighting
against foreign enemies, mythologizes national origins as glorious,
and confirms national identity (Yomota 2017). Examples include the
Philippines' *Noli Me Tangere* (Touch me not) (1961) and *Jose Riza*
(1998), Thailand's *The King of the White Elephant* (1940), Indonesia's
Darah dan Doa (Blood and Prayer, released in English as the Long
March, 1950), and Vietnam's *Chung Một Dòng Sông* (The Same River,
1959). As national cinema emphasizes a family romance grounded in
heroic masculinity and femininity, it does not depict gender and sexual
minorities who deviate from dominant norms. Still today, countries that
imagine "members of the nation" based on family configurations founded
in heterosexual norms continue to exclude and conceal representations of
gender and sexual minorities.

Images of gender and sexual minorities challenge the dominant
culture and "the nation" based on heterosexual norms by bringing into
the public space identities, relationships, issues, and practices that have
hitherto been confined to the individual and private space. This chapter
will examine the extent to which gender and sexual minority images have
created "publicness" or "a commonality that does not seek closedness and
homogeneity, a solidarity that resists exclusion and assimilation" (Saitō
2000) in Southeast Asian countries. However, degrees of publicness
are not easily measured, so I will examine the publicness of gender and
sexual minorities through moving images in Southeast Asian countries,
focusing on academic research, film festivals, and awards.

First, there have been numerous academic studies of gender and
sexual minority images in South East Asia, which is testament to the
prevalence of such images. There are monographs in English (Ünaldi

2011; Fuhrmann 2016) and papers in Japanese (Hiramatsu 2017) on Thailand and Indonesia (Murtagh 2013; Fukuoka 2016). The Philippines has yielded a doctoral dissertation in English (Inton 2017) and a book chapter and journal article in Japanese (Yamamoto 2018a; 2018b). Michael Nuñez Inton's doctoral dissertation examines the evolution of representations of *bakla* from 1945 to 2015,[1] indicating the long history of Filipino films on this subject. In Vietnam, where gender and sexual minority films have begun to be produced more recently, online articles have been published.

Second, let us consider the presence or absence of film festivals on gender and sexual minorities. Countries where gender and sexual minority images are publicly screened also have film festivals relating to gender and sexual minorities, and these are widely open to the public. These festivals attract images on gender and sexual minorities produced not only by professionals, but also by students and amateurs. For example, the Quezon City International Pink Film Festival, run by Quezon City in the Philippines, exclusively presents films on gender and sexual minorities, screening 64 works (including 42 short films) in FY 2018. This included a program of short films made by Filipino students and by local communities in the Philippines. Although some films from Thailand and Indonesia were screened by invitation, Filipino works comprised most of the festival program. In contrast, there are no gender and sexual minority film festivals in Malaysia, Brunei, or Laos at present. Other festivals on gender and sexual minorities in Southeast Asia include Singapore's Short Circuit (since 2006), which returned in 2023 after six years since its sixth edition in 2017, and Vietnam's Hanoi International Queer Film Week (HIQFW, since 2017).

However, while the number of such film festivals is growing, the "Q! Film Festival" (2002–17), which ran for fifteen years in the Indonesian capital of Jakarta, has gone on hiatus after receiving demands from Islamic organizations to cease and desist. John Badalu released a

---

1 On *bakla*, loosely characterized as male-to-female transgender individuals, see Kusaka, Ch. 13 of this volume.

statement[2] explaining that maintaining the "Q! Film Festival" was "a long struggle." He said: "All of us find it easier to create something new than to maintain it, and although we are suspending the festival for now, we will return one day when the right time comes." This case highlights the fragile environment in Southeast Asia for sustaining a film festival focusing on gender and sexual minorities.

Third, let us examine the awards received at national film festivals. The extent to which gender and sexual minority films are officially recognized as outstanding works in mainstream national film awards can be indicative of their public acceptance. In Thailand, for example, the 28th Suphannahong National Film Awards, the country's most prestigious film awards, held on March 2, 2019, awarded Best Film to *Malila: The Farewell Flower* (2017), about two gay male ex-lovers. It also received seven other awards, including Best Director (Anucha Boonyawatana, a trans woman), Best Actor (Sukollawat Kanarot), Best Supporting Actor (Anuchyd Sapanphong), Best Screenplay, Best Cinematography, and Best Art Direction. This was the first time in the history of Asian cinema that a trans woman had won both Best Film and Best Director at the most prestigious film awards in the country. Notably, one of the producers of *Malila: The Farewell Flower* was John Badalu, founder of the "Q! Film Festival;" perhaps we should consider this as a sublimation in Thailand of his bitter experience in Indonesia.

In addition, when award-winning films on gender and sexual minorities are screened outside of their country of origin, disparities in the public nature of such films can be exposed. The 2011 Vietnamese coming-of-age ensemble film, *Lost in Paradise* (*Hotboy nổi loạn và câu chuyện về thằng Cười, cô gái điếm và con vịt*), in which the main characters are two gay males, was recognized as the first Vietnamese film to address male homosexuality, and won the Silver Lotus Award (*Bông sen bạc*) at the 17th Vietnam Film Festival (2011), the most prestigious film festival in that country, where it also was named Runner-up to the Grand Prix for Best Film in the Drama category.

---

2   https://twitter.com/qfilmfestival accessed September 20, 2020.

According to an article in the Malaysian newspaper *Malay Mail*,[3] an attempt to screen *Lost in Paradise* on July 11, 2017 at the Performing Arts Center in Penang, Malaysia, was cancelled after pressure from several Islamist groups. In Vietnam, a sequel, *Lost in Paradise 2*, was released in cinemas in March 2017, but it too was not screened in Malaysia.

In sum, the countries with the greatest public acceptance of gender and sexual minority films in Southeast Asia are Thailand and the Philippines, with Vietnam surging to catch up. Indonesia has stagnated somewhat in recent years, but is gradually making a comeback. Even Laos and Malaysia, which have no gender and sexual minority film festivals, are showing signs of breaking out of the most laggardly group; a Malaysian/ Taiwanese co-production, *Miss Andy* (2020), was made in Malaysia, featuring a trans woman in the leading role. In contrast, Myanmar, which was beginning to open, has been in a steep decline following its 2021 coup d'état. Thus, there is a large disparity in the public acceptance of gender and sexual minority images between open societies such as Thailand and the Philippines, and Brunei, which in 2014 became the first Asian nation to introduce a criminal code based on Islamic law (*sharia*), which carries a penalty of up to ten years in prison for both male and female homosexuality.

Types and development of gender and sexual minority films

The "other" in local comedies

Next, I will explain the types and characteristics of gender and sexual minority images in contemporary Southeast Asia. Nations with high public acceptance, specifically Thailand, the Philippines, and, to a lesser extent, Vietnam, are creating new trends in gender and sexual minority images. Even in Indonesia, which had once been more accepting, one

---

3   https://www.malaymail.com/news/malaysia/2017/07/11/gay-film-screening-in-penang-cancelled-after-pressure-from-islamists/1418193. Accessed September 20, 2020.

can see glimpses of those new trends. In contrast, in times when and regions where gender and sexual minorities are excluded by censorship, gender and sexual minorities are erased from moving images, and are considered to never have existed. In other words, they are an invisible or "transparent" presence. The role subsequently given to gender and sexual minorities was that of the "heretic," not the main character in the film, but merely a diverting support role that complemented the main character.

However, comedies featuring cross-dressing, especially those with "heretics" in women's clothing playing lead roles, are popular in those parts of Southeast Asia where the public acceptance of gender and sexual minority films is high. These local comedies are rarely screened outside their country of origin, and have vernacular gender and sexual minorities as main characters who indiscriminately embrace such modern Western identities as male-to-female transvestites, transwomen, and gay men. They are called by different names in different regions: "*bakla*" in the Philippines, "*kathouey*" (กะเทย)[4] in Thailand, "*banci*" or "*waria*" in Indonesia[5] and "*pê-đê*" in Vietnam.[6] By contrast, I am unaware of any female-to-male cross-dresser comedies that have become hits. Male-to-female cross-dressing comedies are most popular in the Philippines and Thailand. In Philippine cinema, as of April 2019, three comedies with *bakla* protagonists ranked in the country's top five all-time locally produced box office hits.[7] Notably, all three of those *bakla* comedies, the second-ranked *The Super Parental Guardians* (2016), No. 3 *Fantastica* (2018), and No. 4 *Gandarrapiddo! The Revenger Squad* (2017, directed by Joyce Bernal), had the same lead performer, star comedian Vice Ganda,[8]

---

4   See Hinata, Ch. 8 of this volume.

5   See Okamoto, Ch. 4 of this volume.

6   See Oda, Ch. 7 of this volume.

7   https://wikivisually.com/wiki/List_of_highest-grossing_Philippine_films. Accessed September 20, 2020.

8   For more on Vice Ganda, see Yamamoto (2018a), which analyzes his starring role in the comedy "Beauty and Her Best Friend."

Photo 2.1: Poster of *Gandarrapiddo!*
The Revenger Squad (2017),
starring Filipino comedian Vice Ganda

who has come out as gay himself, but mainly plays *bakla*, as in the talk show he hosts on ABS-CBN, a major Filipino television station.[9]

Serhat Ünaldi writes on films about *kathoeys* in Thailand, and explains (Ünaldi 2011), that while such films are mainstream in Thailand, those about gay men are sidelined as independent art films. However, Ünaldi identifies a second wave of Thai queer cinema, represented by the *kathoey* comedy *The Iron Ladies* (2000). Modeled on the real-life *kathoey* volleyball team, *Satree Lek*, this sporty comedy about overcoming discrimination and prejudice to win a tournament was the second highest-grossing film of all time when it was released in Thailand, grossing 100 million baht (Ünaldi 2011). Ünaldi quotes Vitaya Saeng-aroon from CyberFish Media, an independent gay media company in Thailand, who explained: "*The Iron Ladies* represents a turning point in the history of gay-related cinema in Thailand, both locally and internationally, it being the first film to portray a positive image of gay people" (Ünaldi 2011).

---

9   For example, in "Barabara Quadruplets' Happiness Puzzle" (2016 Girl, Boy, *Bakla*, Tomboy), Vice Ganda played the quadruplets Girl (female), Boy (male), *Bakla*, and Tomboy (trans masc) in four roles apiece.

The Iron Ladies was also released internationally, including in Japan, and was well received. Thanks to its success at the box office, a sequel, *Iron Ladies II: All Together!* was produced, and in 2014, the third installment, *Iron Ladies Deluxe*. Many of the most popular *kathoey* comedies since *The Iron Ladies* have been made into series, a typical example being *Ho taew taek* (2007–), which combines *kathoey* comedy with horror. In 2018, the sixth installment of the series, *Ho taew taek 6*, directed by Poj Arnon, who also directed *The Iron Ladies Deluxe*, was released in cinemas. The fusion of *kathoey* comedy with horror may be unique to Thailand, the kingdom of the bizarre.

In Indonesia, also, comedies were once produced with cross-dressers, known as *banci* or *waria*. The most notable is *Madame X* (2010, Lucky Kuswandi), a superhero action comedy starring a *banci* or *waria* (Fukuoka 2012: 91–103). It is worth noting the parallels with the previously mentioned Filipino action-comedy *Gandarrapiddo: The Revenger Squad*, in which the lead character is a *bakla* superhero (or should I say superheroine?) fighting evil. As Fukuoka points out: "While the [*Madame X*] takes the approach of a comedy from start to finish, it is unique in that it concerns the struggles of gay men against homophobia, a serious issue in contemporary Indonesian society."[10] Directed by Lucky Kuswandi (1980–), the film deals with the struggles of gay men and homophobes in the Philippines and Thailand. Unlike the latter two countries, however, Indonesia has produced very few *banci* or *waria* comedies since *Madame X*. Its director, Kuswandi, has not made any more such comedies, but has continued to make films that address gender and sexual minority issues. As of the 2010s, such comedies had not become fixtures in Indonesia.

Comedies about cross-dressers, called *pê-đê*, are also increasingly popular in Vietnam. The comedy film *Let Hoi Decide* (*Để Mai tính 2*, 2014, directed by Charlie Nguyen), featuring a gay real estate magnate, broke the all-time box office record for Vietnamese films at the time. The main character, Hoi (played by Thai Hoa), was originally a sub-character

---

10 http://www.minpaku.ac.jp/sites/default/files/research/activity/publication/periodical/tsushin/pdf/tsushin144-12.pdf. Accessed September 20, 2020.

in Charlie Nguyen's previous film, *Fool for Love* (*Để Mai tính*, 2010), who was so popular that a spin-off featuring him was made.

However, the film was criticized by Vietnamese LGBT support groups for its exaggerated portrayal of Hoy as a gay man. According to the UK's *Guardian* newspaper,[11] the criticism stemmed from concerns that it might reinforce negative stereotypes of gender and sexual minorities. The director and producer of the film refuted these concerns, saying that neither such an intention nor such concerns applied to the film. Like *Let Hoi Decide*, cross-dressing (transvestite) comedy films tend to exaggerate or caricature, that is, to treat gender and sexual minorities as "others," to draw laughter from the audience. This tendency has been observed since before the cross-dressing film genre was established, when cross-dressers appeared in films as comic sub-characters. Their utilization as protagonists in comedies can be attributed to their conspicuous and flamboyant external appearance, and, furthermore, to their presence in value-reversing comedies, being both male and female, or neither male nor female, that shake up the gender norms of the audience by playfully inducing confusion. The roots of cross-dresser comedy can probably be traced back to vernacular popular theater that was prevalent in many regions before the advent of cinema.

The "realistic-image" in independent cinema

In recent years, in response to the global trend against homophobia and transphobia, cinematic works have more closely approximated the real-life experiences of gender and sexual minorities and others connected with them, in contrast to the local comedies of major film companies that portray gender and sexual minorities as "others." With few exceptions, these works are independent films funded by self-financing, domestic and international grants, and, more recently, crowd funding. Underpinning this trend is discomfort at the distortion or absence of representations of gender and sexual minorities in commercial entertainment films

---

11 https://www.theguardian.com/film/filmblog/2015/jan/30/with-de-mai-tinh-2-has-vietnam-finally-embraced-gay-film-making. Accessed September 20, 2020.

produced by major film companies. Since a lack of information promotes stereotypes of gender and sexual minorities, those independent filmmakers inform society by producing films that are closer to the real-life experiences of gender and sexual minorities. Thus, in this section, we will outline some of the recent trends in independent films in each country of Southeast Asia.

In Thailand, the most notable movement is the emergence and rapid advance of trans women filmmakers. As mentioned, *Farewell Flowers* (2017) by director Anucha Boonyawatana won seven awards at the 28th Suphannahong National Film Awards in 2019. In the 2019 election, four transgender people were elected to the House of Representatives for the first time, including the director Tanwarin Sukkhapisit, a member of the innovative, anti-military government Future Forward Party. Tanwarin is best known for directing *Insects in the Backyard* (2010), which was banned in Thailand, and *It Gets Better* (2012), which featured trans women. Tanwarin stated that her artistic work was insufficient to achieve change in the legal framework governing LGBT lives, saying: "We needed to get into politics."[12] Her first action as a member of congress was to propose revising the legal definition of a married couple from "man and woman" to "individual and individual." In 2024, Thailand became the second country in Asia, after Taiwan, to recognize same-sex marriage. In addition to Tanwarin's films, Thailand has also produced a short documentary *Screaming Goats* (2018), directed by Thunska Pansittivorakul (1973–),[13] depicting the southern border region through the conversations of a lesbian couple. One half of the couple is Anthicha Sangchai, founder of an LGBT organization in the predominantly Muslim region of Patani.[14]

A notable trend in the Philippines is the rise of female directors who realistically portray the love of adolescent lesbians. Even in the

---

12 https://www.afpbb.com/articles/-/3229973. Accessed September 20, 2020.

13 See Coda in Fuhrmann 2016 for director Thunska Pansittivorakul's work prior to *Screaming Goats*.

14 On her activities, see Fukutomi 2017, Section 2: "Local Authors and Bookstores," and Section 3: "Local Independent Bookstores."

Philippines, the Southeast Asian country considered the most tolerant of gender and sexual minorities, there were directors who made gay male films, but for a long time there were none who represented lesbian cinema. However, Manila-born director Samantha Lee, through her debut feature films *Maybe Tomorrow* (*Baka Bukas*, 2016), *Billie and Emma* (2018), and the volleyball film *Rookie* (2023), portrays lesbian love and coming-of-age, achieving further monumental advances in gender and sexual minority cinema not only in the Philippines but also in Southeast Asia.

As mentioned, there was a time when gender and sexual minority film making was vibrant in Indonesia. Director Teddy Surya Atmadja filmed a reunion between a *banci* or *waria*-turned father and his Muslim daughter in *Lovely Man* (2011), while *Madam X* director Lucky Kuswandi made *Losing the Sun* (*Selamat Pagi, Malam*, 2014), an ensemble drama that included a lesbian couple. Amid the growing storm of criticism against films dealing with gender and sexual minorities, master Indonesian director Garin Nugroho depicted the boyhood and adolescence of male dancers performing female roles in *lengger* (a traditional dance from the Banyumas region of Central Java) in *Memories of My Body* (*Kucumbu Tubuh Indahku*, 2014). In an interview, Nugroho stated:

> We focused on the LGBT traditions that are rooted in lesser-known rural areas. The truth is there are many, but no one frames them. LGBT cinema is regarded as something that mainly the middle class and above watch as a lifestyle choice. But LGBT has a place in traditional Indonesian culture. The film does not address LGBT directly, but rather the masculinity (masculine) and femininity (feminine) that comingle in one body.[15]

Memories of My Body won eight awards at the Indonesian Film Festival in 2019, including Best Film, Best Director, and Best Actor. Despite the later backlash against films featuring gender and sexual minorities,

---

15 https://jfac.jp/culture/features/f-ah-tiff2018-garin-nugroho/3/. Accessed September 20, 2020.

director Ismail Basbet's documentary *Her Soul* (2022), about Shinta Ratri, founder of the Islamic School for Trans Women (*waria*), who passed away in 2023, and *Sara* (2023), a play about a trans woman played by trans fashion designer Asha Smara Darra, are both attempts to breakthrough the tide of oppression. Asha Smara Darra, who stars in the latter, is the first trans woman in the history of the Indonesian Film Festival to be nominated for the Citra Award for Best Actress.

Finally, as mentioned, films about gender and sexual minorities have recently been produced in Vietnam, mainly by independent filmmakers, since *Lost in Paradise* turned the tide. The documentary *Madam Phung's Last Journey* (2014: *Chuyến đi cuối cùng của chị Phụng*), which focuses on a traveling troupe of transvestites and their leader, Madam Phung, was released theatrically and was much discussed. The film was later adapted as the play *Lô Tô* (2017). In 2015, the lesbian romance film *Love* (*Yêu*: 2015) was released in cinemas and became a hit. Since *Love*, however, only a few films have featured lesbians, including *The Third Wife* (*Vợ ba*: 2018), whose release was cancelled after four days. Furthermore, most Vietnamese films relating to gender and sexual minorities have been set in Ho Chi Minh City and its surroundings, or the Mekong Delta – that is, in southern Vietnam – with only a few, including *The Third Wife*, set in Hanoi or the northern part of the country. One plausible reason for films on gender and sexual minorities being biased toward the south is that Ho Chi Minh City has the most developed capitalist economy in Vietnam, and its visual culture has also arguably been enlivened by its attraction for gender and sexual minorities. Conversely, Southeast Asian independent films perhaps will not venture beyond the more sophisticated metropolitan areas (Bangkok, Manila, Ho Chi Minh City, and Jakarta in former days).

To sum up the situation regarding Southeast Asian independent cinema by LGBT individuals and those connected with them, the respective countries' film industries have increasingly recognized filmmakers who have come out as gay men, trans women, and lesbians. However, in some countries, such as Indonesia, it has become more difficult to produce and screen such films in recent years. Moreover, representations of lesbians,

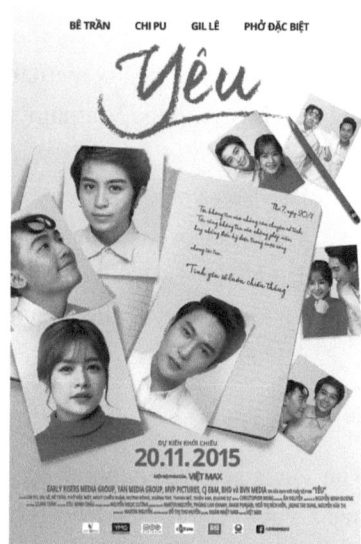

Photo 2.2: Poster of a Vietnamese film,
Love (*Yêu*, 2015)

trans men, and bisexuals are rare in contrast to the number of representations of gay men and trans women.

The "friendly neighbor" image in sitcoms

In Southeast Asia, the most popular genre of entertainment films is comedy, with many sitcoms being produced, principally on YouTube. Sitcoms are comedic dramas with fixed characters and settings that are broadcast as a series of complete episodes. A common trope in sitcoms is to inject comedic elements into "realistic" or "life-like" settings. The advantages of sitcoms are their accessibility (being free of charge) and ease of dissemination. Furthermore, as they can layer a broad array of scenes from everyday life, they can portray gender and sexual minority characters as likeable people with whom the audience can empathize. *My Best Gay Friends* (*Bộ ba đĩ thõa*: 2012–16), the first Vietnamese sitcom about gender and sexual minorities, was a huge hit. Directed by and starring Huỳnh Nguyễn Đăng Khoa, the series ran for thirteen episodes. Khoa was a film school student in Ho Chi Minh City at the time, and was only twenty-one years old when production began. The main characters are three gay men who, as the sitcom begins, are living together in an apartment. The series is available on YouTube with English subtitles. In an interview with the Vietnamese newspaper *Tuoi Tre*, Khoa commented:

> I have seen many films and comedies about the homosexual community. Their images of homosexuals are very negative and the audience has an ugly idea of the homosexual community. But that is not right. I am a gay man and my life seems very normal, so I want to convey the true image of homosexuals to everyone in order to change the audience's view of us.[16]

The series is not only about gay men, though. One of the main characters has a younger brother who is a cross-dresser, and one of the three main characters was inspired by that brother to take the opportunity to dress in women's clothing. One episode (no. 9) revolves around the protagonists helping their friends, a lesbian couple, to organize their wedding.

Indonesia also produced a sitcom featuring gender and sexual minorities before the most recent religious suppression: *CONQ* (2014) was directed by Lucky Kuswandi, who had previously directed *Madame X* and *Losing the Sun*.[17] *CONQ*'s main character is a gay, intellectual university faculty member living in Jakarta, and the series' nine episodes comically portray scenes from his daily life. It was restricted to viewing by adults eighteen years and older because of its frequent dirty jokes. Although there are no sex scenes, the protagonist talks to the audience about his sex life and HIV infection, which he had previously seldom discussed in his personal life as a gay man. The first episode is entitled *Unstereotype Me*, a comical depiction of gay stereotypes. The final episode, entitled *The Wedding*, is about the protagonist's best friend who marries a woman for his parents' sake.

---

16 https://tuoitrenews.vn/lifestyle/8433/vietnams-first-gay-sitcom-goes-viral. Accessed September 20, 2020.

17 https://www.viddsee.com/series/conq. Accessed September 20, 2020.

Thailand is where sitcoms about gender and sexual minorities enjoy their greatest popularity. One of the most popular series is *Diary of Tootsies* (2016–). According to the *Bangkok Post*, the thirteen-episode series[18] is the first in Thailand in which all the main characters are openly queer. It follows the daily lives and love adventures of four close friends, three gay men and a lesbian, in the form of the Facebook diary of Gus, the central character. Based on the real-life diary of Thachpacha Setthachai, a gay man who mainly wears women's clothes but sometimes men's clothes. The main characters, including their nicknames, were cast to recreate Thachpacha and her real-life best friends. The series is produced and streamed by the very popular Thai video company GDH559 (maker of *Bad Genius* and other films) and is available on YouTube's GDH559 channel. Due to popular demand, the video sequel *Diary of Tootsies 2* was released online in 2017, and a film version *Tootsies & the Fake* (2019) streamed on Netflix. This *Tootsies* series is characterized by extremely risqué jokes. But it also addressed serious issues; for example, in one episode a member of the gay trio is infected with HIV/AIDS and consults his friends about how to tell his mother; in another, the younger boy with whom Gus falls in love breaks it off because his parents oppose the relationship.

The common feature of the three sitcoms discussed in this section is that they do not have the picture-perfect happy endings of local comedies depicting "others," but instead try to portray gender and sexual minorities as "friendly neighbors" living forward-looking lives in situations where happiness slightly outweighs misfortune by a ratio of 7 to 3, or 6 to 4. The popularity of such sitcoms can be seen reflected in more mainstream local comedies that emphasize "otherness." In Vietnam, for example, when we compare *Let Hoi Decide*, and *Lô Tô* (2017), two films that provoked protests from LGBT groups, the latter presents cross-dressers more as "friendly neighbors." Another prime example is *Butterfly House* (2019: *Ngôi nhà bươm bướm*), by *Lô Tô* director Huỳnh Tuấn Anh. *Butterfly*

---

18 https://www.bangkokpost.com/life/social-and-lifestyle/903212/gender-bender. Accessed September 20, 2020.

Photo 2.3: Poster of a Thai sitcom, *Diary of Tootsies* (2016–)

House is a Vietnamese adaptation of the French slapstick comedy *La Cage au Folles* (The Birdcage), set around the marriage of the straight son of a gay couple. In a scene where the gay husband (living in Ho Chi Minh City) meets the parents of his son's fiancée (the father being vice-principal of a school in Hanoi) for the first time, the gay husband's love for his child is conveyed to the audience.

In the Philippines, the BL (boys' love) drama series *Gameboys* Season 1 (2020) can be positioned as a new post-COVID gender and sexual minority sitcom. The story revolves around video calls and social networking screens while the country was in lockdown due to the COVID pandemic. Its sequel, *Gameboys the Movie: The Shape of Our Love* (2021), was selected as the closing film of the 8th Taiwan International Queer Film Festival (TIQFF) in 2021. It came out of the production house, The IdeaFirst Company, which was founded in 2014 by directors Jun Robles Lana and Perci Intalan. An early film from The IdeaFirst Company is *Die Beautiful* (2016), a highly critical and excellent comedy that projects a "realistic" or "life-like" image, while borrowing from the *bakla* comedic trope of the "other" in home-grown comedy previously discussed. In addition to the *GameBoys* series, The IdeaFirst

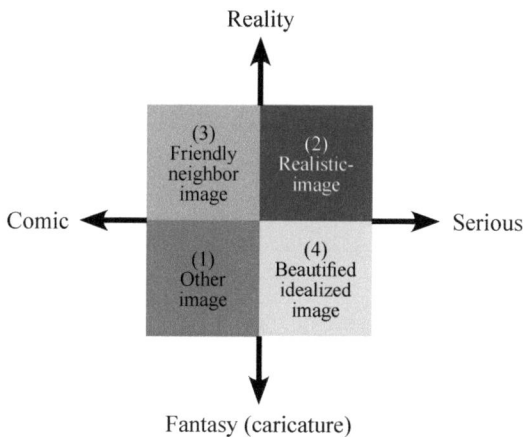

Figure 2.1: Cinematic representations of sexual minorities in Southeast Asia

Company has produced a number of moving images relating to gender and sexual minorities, both hard and soft, including *Big Night* (2021), a black comedy about a gay hairdresser who gets blacklisted for being a drug addict, and *About Us But Not About Us* (2022), a situational thriller in which *GameBoys*' star Elijah Canlas plays a character type quite at odds with his previous work. As a leading producer of gender and sexual minority films, The IdeaFirst Company's future moves will be worthy of attention.

The characteristics, future, and issues of gender and sexual minority films in contemporary Southeast Asia

As discussed, in Southeast Asia, various moving images of gender and sexual minorities have been produced despite the exclusion and concealment of those minorities in national films. Their representations include the "other" in local comedies from major film companies, the "realistic" or "life-like" image in independent films by the minorities themselves, and the "friendly neighbor image" in sitcoms. The "other" is gradually being displaced by these two emerging themes, especially the latter.

Figure 2.1 provides a four-quadrant classification of these three types, with the variables of reality/fantasy (caricature) on the vertical axis and comic/serious on the horizontal. In this classification, documentaries are categorized as works depicting "realistic-images" because these filmmakers seek to capture and portray reality and the minorities in their work. Also, the involvement of gender and sexual minorities, including staff and actors, in the "friendly neighbor image" is because of the emphasis on reality as a reaction against the "other." The vertical reality/fantasy (caricature) axis also relates to the controversy surrounding the playing of gender and sexual minority roles, especially transgender ones, by actors who are not themselves LGBT. While the "realistic-image" and the "friendly neighbor image" share the same emphasis on reality, the former leans toward the serious, as it often delves into conflicts between gender and sexual minorities and their relatives, and especially their partners' relatives. The latter deals less with relatives and focuses more on the bonds among gender and sexual minorities. Of course, this figure is only a typological schema; there have been innovative films that go beyond this figure in their individual productions, and we can anticipate seeing more of them in the future.

Although not a focus of this chapter, BL (boys' love) dramas are increasingly popular in Thailand, the Philippines, and Vietnam. As we can see in Japanese headlines such as: "Thai BL drama actors are too handsome. Thai language fever also rising"[19] and "(Photo feature) Thai BL was a bottomless swamp! Too-beautiful men,"[20] BL dramas portray a "beautified" and "juvenile" fantasy, featuring young, beautiful actors. In Figure 2.1, this could be hypothetically conceptualized as a "beautified idealized image" in reaction to the "other." The question is whether BL dramas, the latest trend in gender and sexual minority video images, will become ever more fantasy-ridden, or move away from fantasy and toward more realistic images, including using actors who are gender and

---

19 https://dot.asahi.com/wa/2020090200081.html. Accessed September 20, 2020.

20 https://dot.asahi.com/photogallery/archives/2020090300079.html. Accessed September 20, 2020.

sexual minorities. I wish to pursue this topic in future, keeping a close eye on whether comedic elements will intensify and shift towards the friendly neighbor image.

However, the recent developments summarized in this figure are limited to works produced in the Philippines, Thailand, Indonesia, and Vietnam. Furthermore, we must acknowledge disparities in the ways LGBT persons are featured in the gender and sexual minority films discussed here. The overwhelming majority of these individuals are gay men, with very few lesbians or bisexuals. In addition, there are far more transgender films dealing with trans women than trans men. When we include BL dramas, whose numbers have increased in recent years, only the number of works about gay men stands out in the LGBT field. One of the reasons for the scarcity of films about lesbians may be the gender imbalance in the film industry in each country. Notably, films about lesbians are beginning to appear in the Philippines, where female directors are producing hits, and in Vietnam, where female directors are becoming increasingly prominent.

Another question that is beyond the scope of this work is the strictures and regulations on sexual expression, especially film and broadcast ratings regarding nudity and genitalia. Regulations on sexual expression in the countries of Southeast Asia are more stringent than those in Japan or the West, with many more restrictions on expressing sexuality. The background and evolution of the regulation of sexual expression in Southeast Asian moving images, as well as the relationship between that regulation of sexual expression and that of the filmic expression of gender and sexual minorities, are topics for future study.

PART II

Inclusion and Exclusion through Defining "Good Citizens"

3 Sexual Politics after the Change of Government: No Progress in the "New Malaysia"

Tsukasa Iga

Introduction

In the Malaysian general election of May 2018, 60 years after independence, the country experienced its first change of government in history when Pakatan Harapan (PH), a coalition of political parties, defeated Barisan Nasional (BN). BN, where the United Malays National Organization (UMNO) had always been the dominant party, had ruled the country for decades. With the end of BN's long-standing rule, many Malaysians hoped for the emergence of a "New Malaysia," one that would be more politically and socially inclusive. However, the PH government collapsed in less than two years, falling short of these expectations. In the six years since the 2018 general election, there have been five prime ministers and at least three changes of government. In short, since the end of UMNO's dominance, Malaysia's political situation has remained in a state of flux, with both the ruling and opposition parties undergoing significant changes in composition.

The Japanese version of this chapter discussed the politics of sexuality surrounding gender and sexual minorities in Malaysia immediately after the 2018 change of government. In that version, I examined whether the political and social inclusion of gender and sexual minorities under the new PH government was progressing. I concluded that, although Malaysia had made progress in democratization in terms of competition between political parties, there had been no advances in the inclusion of gender and sexual minorities, which ran counter to the goal of deepening democratization.

This chapter is a revised version of the Japanese original, updating the analysis that focused on the change of government to cover the period from 2018 to 2023. Specifically, it examines the discourses and activities of state-linked political and religious leaders concerning gender and sexual minorities and the responses of the LGBT movement.

This chapter is organized as follows. The first section briefly summarizes the development of sexual politics in Malaysia and the state's position on gender and sexual minorities and the LGBT movement prior to the 2018 regime change. In the second section, an analysis of incidents that occurred after the change of government in 2018 reveals the stance of politicians on sexual minority issues in the public sphere and the rise of the LGBT movement. The third section focuses on the religious agencies and actors linked to the state to demonstrate how the Malaysian state deals with the minority sexual orientations and gender identities, which belong to the private sphere of individuals. The fourth section looks at trends in activism in the LGBT movement.

The state and the LGBT movement under the old regime

At the federal level, Section 377 of the Malaysian Penal Code criminalizes same-sex sexual activity as being against the order of nature. This statute, inherited from British colonial rule, has long been known to oppress gender and sexual minorities, though it was rarely enforced. Meanwhile, since the 1980s, Malaysian state governments have actively prosecuted homosexual acts and cross-dressing under state-enforced Shariah penal codes. That was when the oppression of gender and sexual minorities began to take serious hold.[1]

---

1   Section 377 of the criminal code is generally known as the "sodomy law." It proscribes sexual acts such as oral sex, anal intercourse, bestiality, etc. Note that while the *Shariah* penal codes of each Malaysian state vary slightly in wording and provisions, they are consistent in regulations prohibiting male-on-male sexual activity, female-on-female sexual activity, cross-dressing and cross-gender behavior, etc.

These state-based "crackdowns" on gender and sexual minorities were driven by competition between the ruling and opposition parties to win the support of the Muslim Malays, who constituted about 60% of the Malaysian population. After the 1978 Islamic Revolution in Iran, many Muslim countries around the world, including Malaysia, renewed their commitment to Islam. Rival political parties claimed to follow the "true Islam" in contrast to their opponents and competed to promote policies that were seen as more "Islamic." In the 1980s, the then opposition Pan-Malaysian Islamic Party (Parti Islam Se Malaysia: PAS) increasingly highlighted its Islamist credentials while intensifying its criticism of the ruling party.

To counter the criticism by PAS, the government, led by the ruling UMNO, introduced various Islamization policies, including outlawing homosexual acts and cross-dressing, through the various state-based Shariah penal codes.

The Asian values discourse of the first Mahathir regime in the 1980s and 1990s led to increasing discrimination towards and oppression of gender and sexual minorities. In criticizing Western colonialism and promoting East Asian superiority, then Prime Minister Mahathir identified homosexuality as a pathology stemming from Western individualism, hedonism, and materialism. The view that homosexuality originated in the West, and is incompatible with Malaysian tradition and society, is a discourse that has been and continues to be repeatedly asserted by politicians, religious figures and others in Malaysian society.

The climax to this was the 1998 case in which the then Deputy Prime Minister Anwar Ibrahim was expelled from the government and ruling party and, in an application of Article 377 of the penal code, was tried and convicted on charges of deviant sexuality (including homosexuality). This case can be traced directly to the confrontation between Deputy Prime Minister Anwar, who supported IMF-type structural reforms in response to the Asian economic crisis, and Prime Minister Mahathir, who feared that such structural reforms would radically change the nation's socioeconomic structure. Mahathir used accusations of deviant sexuality to eliminate Anwar, who had earned a strong reputation as a young Muslim leader during his rapid rise to prominence.

In 2008, Anwar was again arrested on allegations of sodomy and jailed. Although Anwar and his supporters claim that these two arrests and terms of imprisonment for homosexuality were political conspiracies, the veracity of the competing claims is irrelevant to this chapter. What is important here is that the sexuality of a top-level politician was employed to create a political scandal which was sufficient to oust him from power. In other words, the fact that the (alleged) sexuality of individuals was now reported in the mass media and broadcast to the general population as a scandal, regardless of its veracity, was a new development in the 1990s, prior to which, such claims would only spread as rumors within the elite circles of Malaysian politics.

While the state and national elites repressed gender and sexual minorities and politicized sexuality, gender and sexual minorities began to organize themselves in the 1980s. In 1987, for example, amid growing concern about the HIV/AIDS epidemic, Pink Triangle (later renamed the PT Foundation) was organized mainly by gay men. The PT Foundation initially focused its activities on HIV/AIDS prevention and empowering gender and sexual minorities within their communities. It later extended support to transgender people and sex workers, as well.

Anwar's expulsion from the government and ruling party in 1998 inspired the *Reformasi* movement, a political and social movement that called for change in the BN regime. The movement activated and strengthened the links between civil society organizations and opposition parties. Coalitions were formed to oppose the BN regime, and their demands were somewhat met by the government, resulting in moderate political and social liberalization. In these circumstances, seeking to guarantee the human rights of gender and sexual minorities on more solid grounds than the HIV/AIDS issue, various organizations formed in the 2000s to engage in both policy advocacy and connecting with the public. Seksualiti Merdeka, which means "sexual independence" in Malay, was representative of such organizations. Beginning in 2008, it hosted an annual festival to celebrate sexual diversity while calling for the public to recognize and guarantee the human rights of gender and sexual minorities. The festival was banned by the government in 2011, but its activists have continued to promote human rights to the public and the government. Seksualiti Merdeka has had significant influence on subsequent activism by gender and sexual minorities pursuing human rights, providing a means for sexual minority activists and organizations to engage in public advocacy for human rights in cooperation with other human rights NGOs and other organizations.

In summary, in the 1980s, the state and political elites politicized sexuality and gender and sexual minorities for political purposes. Then, from around 2000, community organizations that had formed to combat HIV/AIDS and to empower gender and sexual minorities began to directly engage in policy advocacy while also appealing to the public. The revitalization of the LGBT movement thus effectively consolidated sexuality as an issue of political and social contention.

The political discourse around gender and sexual minorities

Immediately after the May 2018 general election, in which the PH coalition defeated BN, the "New Malaysia" discourse emerged in the mass media and on the internet. The phrase "New Malaysia" expressed a hope that politics and society would become more inclusive of the diversity inherent in Malaysia. PH had pledged in its election manifesto to "create an inclusive, moderate, and globally respected Malaysia" (Pakatan Harapan 2018). However, PH was forced to backpedal significantly on this election promise in the face of political pressures when it took office. Among other things, gender and sexual minorities became a point of political contention immediately after the change of government, and PH leaders responded by continuing their exclusion.

The PH regime rapidly lost support due to infighting within the ruling party combined with a coordinated opposition attack emphasizing the symbols of Islam and Malay nationalism. It collapsed in February 2020. Subsequently, two successive conservative governments were formed by three parties based in the Malay Peninsula, namely the Parti Pribumi Bersatu Malaysia (United Malaysian Indigenous Party: BERSATU), which broke away from the PH, UMNO, which had governed Malysia from independence until 2018, and PAS, an Islamist party, with participation from regional parties in the states of Sabah and Sarawak. In November 2022, dissolution and general elections were held under the leadership of Prime Minister Ismail Sabri Yaakob from UMNO, and a PH-led administration formed the new government. As a result, PH leader Anwar Ibrahim who, as we have seen, had been ousted from the post of deputy prime minister in 1998 after accusations of deviant sexuality, became Malaysia's tenth prime minister.

The frequent changes of government since 2018 are evidence that Malaysia has become more democratic in the sense of increased competition between political parties. However, there has been little progress in the inclusion of gender and sexual minorities into Malaysian society. In the next section, we discuss four incidents that occurred under the PH-led government to examine politicians' discourses on gender and sexual minorities.

Removal of LGBT activists' portraits

From August 4 to September 2, 2018, an auxiliary organization of the Penang state government hosted the George Town Festival in its state capital, George Town. During the festival, portraits of LGBT activists on display were removed on the minister's instructions. Since 2008, when it was inscribed as a UNESCO World Heritage Site, the George Town Festival has hosted cultural events. In 2018 the feature exhibition displayed portraits of celebrities holding the Malaysian flag to celebrate Independence Day. Among the photos were two LGBT activists, Pang Khee Teik and Nisha Ayub. Over the years, the George Town Festival had become well-known among the general public, and was reported in the international media, but there had not been any exhibits prior to 2018 that featured LGBT activists. As we have seen, the government changed shortly before the 2018 festival and there was widespread anticipation of a new openness in "new Malaysia". In that context, the exhibition sponsors and photographers took the initiative to showcase photographs of LGBT activists at a high-profile public event that involved the state government.

However, the photographs of the two activists were removed at the direction of Minister of Religious Affairs Mujahid Yusof Rawa on the grounds that the spread of LGBT activities in a public arena was incompatible with the new government's policy.

Subsequently, transgender activist Nisha Ayub requested a direct meeting with Mujahid, and the two met privately. During this meeting, Nisha said that she had no problem with the removal of her photo, and the main topic of discussion was dealing with discrimination against transgender people. After this meeting, Mujahid said that hate speech and discrimination against transgender people in the workplace and in public places should be eradicated. At the same time, however, he warned that his meeting with Nisha did not mean that he agreed with all the demands of the LGBT movement, nor did he endorse LGBT practices (Pillay 2018). Indeed, Mujahid had explicitly stated on other occasions that the demands for LGBT rights should be curbed because it was an extreme idea and incompatible with Malaysian religion and tradition (Palansamy 2018). Deputy Prime Minister Wan Azizah, too, while expressing opposition to hate and discrimination against transgender people, shared Mujahid's view of the LGBT movement's rights-seeking activities. Although she acknowledged the existence of the LGBT community, she stated that its activities should be limited to private life, and that in the Federation of Malaysia, where Islam was the official religion, private life should not be "made into something seductive" (Shazwan 2018).

International Women's Day march

A clearer manifestation of the PH administration's leadership's negative attitude toward demands for sexual minority rights occurred on International Women's Day in March 2019. On that occasion, a small number of LGBT activists and their supporters joined a march organized by the women's movement. Minister of Religious Affairs Mujahid criticized this action as an abuse of democracy, and declared it unacceptable to the government (*Malaysiakini*, 2019). Similarly, Wan Saiful Wan Jan, an influential politician from BERSATU, then a constituent party of PH, said that the struggle for women's rights was a noble and respectful act deserving of support, but that combining it with the LGBT agenda was "extremely offensive" (*The Star Online* 2019).

In response, Marina Mahathir, an activist in the women's movement for many years, criticized them for focusing on just one of the many demands raised by the march, which she said distracted attention from women's serious demands. The march organizers, the Joint Action Group for Gender Equality (JAG), also responded, stating that in a democracy, all people (and groups of people) deserved the right to express their interests peacefully, and that they could voice their opinions on policies that affected them (*The Star Online* 2019).

Mujahid's and Wan Saiful's responses to the marches was to deny gender and sexual minorities the ability to assert their rights in the public sphere. What is noteworthy about this incident is that while most politicians in the PH administration were silent, some leaders, including Mujahid and Wan Saiful, loudly declaimed that even though they would allow women to march, they would not countenance the participation of even a few members of gender and sexual minorities. Why did they take the trouble publicly to insist on separation of the women's movement from the LGBT movement?

Compared to the women's movement, which began to be organized in the 1970s, the LGBT movement did not begin to organize in earnest until the 2000s, with smaller organizations and personnel, and scant influence on political parties. Given this premise, one might guess why Mujahid and Wan Saiful went out of their way to demand the separation of the women's and LGBT movements, and to criticize the latter. Mujahid, an influential politician in the PH administration at the time, belonged to the Parti Amanah Negara (AMANAH), a splinter party of the Islamist party PAS, while Wan Saiful was a member of BERSATU. These parties are unable to recognize public assertion of rights by gender and sexual minorities because their main support base comprises Malays who adhere to Sunni Islam, whose official doctrine rejects homosexuality and sexual minority rights claims. Indeed, there is a high likelihood that Mujahid and others sought to cement conservative Malay Muslims' support for their own party by condemning the LGBT movement. The support for PH that existed immediately after the change of government in 2018 was rapidly lost as the opposition parties, PAS and UMNO, formed an inter-party alliance and emphasized Malay nationalism and Islamism, criticizing the PH administration for being anti-Malay and anti-Muslim. Therefore, for AMANAH and BERSATU politicians, whose main support base was Malays, there was apparently a need to claim that their parties espoused "true Islam" by condemning the LGBT movement, thereby securing the support of the conservative base.

Caning Malay women in Terengganu

The reaction to canings of Malay women carried out in Terengganu,[2] a state with a population that is over 90% Muslim, highlighted the subtle differences in attitude between the federal and state governments. In August 2018, two Malay women in Terengganu each received six strokes of the cane and a fine of 3300 ringgits in accordance with the state *Shariah* criminal code for having sex in a car. The caning was executed in the presence of about 100 people, including members of the public, and made national and international headlines as the first ever caning of a woman in Malaysia.

In Malaysia, there are two penal codes that criminalize homosexual acts: Penal Code Section 377, discussed above, which applies in principle to the entire federation, and the *Shariah* penal codes, which are enacted in each state. Under constitutional provisions, the administration of Islamic affairs is basically the purview of the state governments. It was the state of Terengganu that enforced the *Shariah* penal code vis-à-vis the two women in this case. Since 2018, PAS had been the party in power in Terengganu, while at the federal level it was in opposition to PH, the

---

2   The state of Terengganu, situated on the east coast of the Malay Peninsula, notably lags in development compared to the peninsula's more economically developed and urbanized west coast states, and with Malays comprising the majority of the state's population, a conservative political climate prevails.

ruling party in the federal government. With the ruling and opposition parties reversed at the federal and state levels, there were differences of opinion between the federal and state governments on the execution of the caning sentences.

Prime Minister Mahathir expressed the federal government's disapproval of caning a first-time female offender on the grounds that it would increase non-Muslims' prejudice against Islam and could tarnish Malaysia's international image. Minister of Religious Affairs Mujahid agreed, saying there was room to amend the way the punishment was applied (Mahathir 2018). The federal government criticized the caning of women, not on the merits and demerits of the *Shariah* penal code or its application vis-à-vis gender and sexual minorities, but on consideration for women, concern for Islam and Malaysia's international reputation.

In response to domestic and international criticism, PAS president Abdul Hadi Awang, whose party ruled in the state government, said: "I am confident that a fair comparison of the caning penalty based on *Shariah* and whipping under civil law would lead even non-Muslims to opt for *Shariah* caning" (Hadi Awang 2018). However, there was significant opposition, at least among non-Muslims, to the application of the physical punishment of caning and the fact that the execution of the sentence was open to the public, albeit in limited numbers. In response to reports from the BBC, *The Guardian*, and other British media, the PAS Youth chief expressed alarm, stating that Malaysians should be reminded that they face challenges from enemies of Islam around the world (Choong 2018).

Concerns about Malaysia's international reputation and the attitudes of non-Muslims were secondary, though, to the competition between the federal and state governments for political support. Rivalry between political parties and coalitions to win the support of Malay Muslims, who constitute the majority in the country, has been fierce since the 1980s. PAS, the governing party in Terengganu, appealed to conservative Muslims by enforcing the *Shariah* penal code vis-à-vis Muslim women, although this had been effectively shelved in the past; while PH, in control of the federal government, appealed to the rest of the population by showing concern for women, in awareness of the domestic and international repercussions for Islam and Malaysia.

Banning and seizing Swatch's Pride watches

The three cases outlined above demonstrate the PH administration's stance against discrimination and harassment of gender and sexual minorities was based in concern for its public and international reputation as an inclusive government. At the same time, though, various politicians in the administration opposed public assertions of human rights by the LGBT movement, businesses, and others. They claimed that it was a political and social issue on the grounds of tradition and culture, while at the same time opportunistically scapegoating gender and sexual minorities in the hopes of increasing support from conservative Malays.

Although the PH government collapsed in February 2020, that discourse resumed under the Anwar-led PH government that formed in November 2022. We can see this at play in an incident in which rainbow-colored wristwatches sold worldwide by the Swiss watch company Swatch as part of its Pride Collection were seized by the Malaysian police. On May 13 and 14, 2023, the government raided eleven Swatch stores in Malaysia, seizing 172 watches. About three months later, on August 10, 2023, the government published a ban in an official gazette on the sale of the wristwatches under Section 7(1) of the Printing Presses and Publications Act (PPPA), as being harmful or potentially harmful to public order, morals, or public opinion. The police investigation and seizure of the watches drew criticism from Swatch, LGBT activists, lawyers, and others. When Prime Minister Anwar was asked about the seizure of watches in a CNN interview in September 2023, he effectively rubber-stamped the police action, stating that while he did not approve of the harassment of gender and sexual minorities, it was necessary to respect trends in public opinion that did not want to see public displays that incorporated LGBT symbolism (Kasinathan 2023).

In this interview, while invoking Malaysian tolerance, Prime Minister Anwar justified suppressing the public expression of minorities' views on the grounds of respect for the "will of the majority." This argument, however, drags out some of the logic of the "Asian values discourse" of which the then Prime Minister Mahathir was a major proponent in the 1990s. Mahathir had placed Malaysian "culture" and "traditions" at the forefront, and then linked homosexuality to Western materialism and hedonism, and condemned gays and lesbians for supposedly inducing incest (Mahathir and Ishihara 1994: 113). Politicians who condemned gender and sexual minorities under the pretext of opposing Westernization or asserting the uniqueness of their own cultural values almost disappeared after 2018, and references to gender and sexual minorities softened in tone. But despite the softer tone, the logic of suppressing minority expressions of opinion on the grounds of "tradition," "culture," and the "will of the majority" has not changed.

Notable in this case is that lawyers condemned the police seizure of watches under the PPPA on the grounds of Article 10 of the Constitution, which guarantees freedom of expression, but also declared it illegal on procedural grounds. Recall that the ban on the Swatch watches that justified the police search and seizure in May was only gazetted three months later. In other words, the search and seizure was illegal because the prohibition order had not yet been gazetted when the watches were seized (Alhadjri 2023). How do we explain this three-month delay between the police raid and seizure and the publication of the ban in the official gazette?

One plausible reason was the state elections held simultaneously in six states on August 12, 2023. PH had returned to power in the November 2022 general election in a coalition with BN, with its former nemesis UMNO as its core, but the most significant breakthrough in this election came from the formation of the National Alliance (Perikatan Nasional: PN), a coalition between PAS and BERSATU, whose support base was conservative Malays. PN had overwhelmingly strong support in the northern part of the Malay Peninsula and the east coast states with a high proportion Malay population, and was dubbed the "Green Wave" because of the apparent swing of the Malay population toward Islam. As the voting age was lowered from 21 to 18 in the 2022 general election, bringing in about 1.4 million new voters, the influence of Islam was seen to be growing among the younger generation, as well. The ruling party led by PH needed to retain the support of conservative Malays to prevent PN from scoring a breakthrough in the state elections in the six provinces scheduled for August. Therefore, they seized the watches in May as a sign of their commitment to Islam, but the momentum of PN remained undiminished, so the ruling party published the prohibition order two days before polling day, seemingly to clarify the position of the PH administration and appeal to conservative Malays.

Opinion among researchers is divided as to the extent to which commitment to Islam, considered a basic element of conservative Malays, has advanced in recent years: some studies attribute the PN's breakthrough in the 2022 general election not to the acceptance of PAS's Islamism by Malay voters, but to economic malcontent (Washida 2023). In certain areas, however, the influence of Islam is clear, and the issue of gender and sexual minorities is the prime example. In a survey conducted by Pew Research Center in 2023 in twelve Asian countries, 82% of Malaysians opposed same-sex marriage, second only to 92% of Indonesians. As for sexual minority rights, same-sex marriage is only part of the problem. Nevertheless, compared to Japan, with 26% opposed to same-sex marriage, and Vietnam, with 30%, it can be inferred that the average Malaysian has stricter views on sexual minority rights. The same survey by religion in Malaysia found that 59% of Buddhists, 49% of Hindus, 35% of Christians, and 8% of Muslims approved of same-sex marriage (Pew Research Center 2023).

As we have seen, the PH politicians' discourse basically suppresses public expression of opinion and demand for rights by gender and sexual minorities, while sometimes opportunistically attacking gender and sexual minorities to appeal to the Malay majority electorate. On the surface, this discourse focuses only on the demands of gender and sexual minorities in the public sphere, but this raises questions about the extent to which the state and political actors interfere in the private lives of gender and sexual minorities. In the next section, we will address the interference by federal and state religious affairs departments and their affiliated religious leaders with the intention of "correcting" or "preventing" the gender and sexuality of individual members of gender and sexual minorities.

Gender and sexual minorities subject to state correction and prevention

This section examines the programs for "correction" and "prevention" of sexuality that have been developed by the Department of Islamic Affairs (Jabatan Kemajuan Islam Malaysia: JAKIM), a federal agency that coordinates the various states' Islamic administration, and by the states' respective religious affairs departments. Activists in the LGBT movement have criticized these programs, describing them as "state-sponsored violence and discrimination." Attempts to "correct" the sexuality of gender and sexual minorities through rehabilitation and training began under the BN government before 2018. For example, the Department of Federal Territory Islamic Affairs (Jabatan Agama Wilayah Persekutuan: JAWI) began offering programs consisting of Koranic studies, faith enhancement, self-development and the like to gender and sexual minorities in 2005, relatively earlier than the other states (*Malay Mail Online* 2014). It was not until the 2010s that JAKIM introduced such programs on the national level. Programs aimed at "preventing" youth from "becoming" gender and sexual minorities also began in earnest around the same time: the *Mukhayyam* program[3] introduced by JAKIM in 2010 is a three-day camp program that provides Muslim members of gender and sexual minorities with basic knowledge about HIV/AIDS, and offers lectures on Islam, as well as professional occupational skill development talks and workshops. The camp features trekking and other physical activities as well as counseling and religious education. Moreover, through this program, JAKIM extends microcredit to some

---

3   In Arabic, *mukhayyam* means "camp."

participants, and works with other government agencies and private organizations to provide job placements for others (Zurairi 2014; Tilaga 2017: 154–155). One JAKIM staff member stated that as of October 2018: "1,450 individuals from LGBT groups have already recovered (from their LGBT illness) through *Mukhayyam* programs implemented in rehabilitation centers around the country" (Nambiar 2018). In principle, participation in the program is voluntary, with many people seemingly applying on their own initiative in pursuit of religious peace of mind and financial support. Although most participants appear to be trans women, gay men and cross-dressers also appear to have participated (Zurairi 2014). However, many who had participated in the program reported feeling that JAKIM was trying to forcefully brainwash them (Human Rights Watch 2014 59–60; Zurairi 2014).

In addition to providing so-called "therapeutic" and "rehabilitative" programs, JAKIM frequently holds seminars for students, their parents, school teachers, medical staff, Muslim NGO officials, and others to explain that LGBT is a pathology, and how home-based education and measures can prevent family members becoming gender and sexual minorities. JAKIM's ideas are presented in pamphlets distributed to the public, and are covered in Malay-language newspapers and other media. JAKIM has also turned to internet media, producing an LGBT conversion e-book called *Hijrah Diri: Homoseksualiti*, which it made available as a smartphone application. This e-book delivered daily anti-LGBT language based on *hadith*[4] chapters and verses, and at one time enabled users to search for counselors in their neighborhood. However, in 2022, Google Play Store, from which the app was downloaded, deemed the content to include pseudoscientific conversion therapy and ceased supplying it. JAKIM's conversion therapy approach can also be seen in YouTube videos targeting Muslims, where sexual orientation was

---

4   The Hadith is a report of the words, actions, or approvals of the Prophet Muhammad, used by Muslims to understand and apply Islamic teachings. It serves as an important source of guidance after the Quran.

likened to horseback riding, with the explanation that it could be changed through training and instruction.[5]

In July 2016, JAKIM published its "Action Plan to Address LGBT Practices as a Social Pathology" (*Pelan Tindakan Menangani Gejala Sosial Tindakan Perlakuan LGBT*), which summarizes the above measures. The three main objectives of this action plan were to "promote the diffusion of up-to-date information in relation to strategies to control social pathologies, especially gender confusion involving LGBT people," to "train personnel for the currently increasingly critical task of implementing programs for the effective control of gender confusion as a social pathology," and to "link JAKIM, state religious affairs offices, national institutions, higher education institutions, and NGO programs in cooperation in order to address issues related to gender confusion."[6]

In addition to the state religious affairs departments, the national government displayed a united stance for implementing the action plan, with twenty-two related ministries, including the Ministry of Women, Family, and Community Development, the Ministry of Education, the Ministry of Health, and the Ministry of Youth and Sports listed as agencies that would collaborate with JAKIM.

JAKIM has cited the rapid increase in the number of gender and sexual minorities in Malaysia as justification for expanding the "prevention" and "correction" programs it has advocated for in recent years. According to figures released by JAKIM, there were 173,000 gay men in Malaysia in 2013, increasing to about 310,000 in 2018. Similarly, they claim that the number of transgender people in the country had increased from 10,000 in 1988 to about 300,000 (Nambiar 2018). JAKIM's recent discourse on "correction" and "prevention" programs in recognition of the burgeoning number of gender and sexual minorities does not advocate the strict exclusion of gender and sexual minorities, but rather seems to emphasize tolerance. The head of JAKIM's Family, Society, and Com-

---

5   https://www.youtube.com/watch?v=IM9Z1zyYTDs.

6   http://www.islam.gov.my/berita-semasa/34-bahagian-keluarga-sosial-komuniti/48-pelan-tindakan-menangani-gejala-sosial-kecelaruan-gender.

munity Department preaches the following approach vis-à-vis gender and sexual minorities:

> Do not scorn [gender and sexual minorities]. Be close to them, talk to them, and pray for them. As Muslims, we do not hate the sinner, we hate the sin. We do not agree with the act of sinning, we want to advise them. In Islam, there is no room for the forgiveness of homosexual acts. That is why in JAKIM we seek measures that will reconcile those who have deviated with the Islamic faith and help bring them back to the right path. (Nambiar 2018)

Thus, the series of programs offered to gender and sexual minorities by religious institutions, including state religious affairs departments, led by JAKIM, in the name of controlling HIV/AIDS, religion, and sometimes well-being, regards any sexuality other than heterosexual norms to be pathological and a deviation from the legitimate teachings of Islam, and takes a "preventative" or "corrective" approach. Such perceptions or approaches have been criticized by activists in the LGBT movement in Malaysia as diverging significantly from the recognition of sexual and gender diversity, which is becoming mainstream in the world, and notably, among international organizations.

Furthermore, as quoted above, although JAKIM and the various state religious affairs departments express their commitment to be close to gender and sexual minorities, there is much room to doubt their under-standing of the genders of gender and sexual minorities. For example, transgender people, whom JAKIM considers "confused," can be sexually attracted to someone of the same sex from the perspective of biological sex, while having feelings consistent with heterosexual norms from a gender perspective. Thus, it seems there is a high likelihood that JAKIM is formulating and implementing policies without understanding the gender of gender and sexual minorities.

LGBT activists

This section will examine how the LGBT movement reacted to the political changes since 2018 and the discourse and activities of politicians, religious leaders, and other actors connected to the state. We will focus on the activities of two activists of different generations who have developed different approaches.

Pang Khee Teik

The first of the two LGBT activists is Pang Khee Teik, who was involved in the portrait removal incident and founded *Seksualiti Merdeka*. Pang, a gay activist with Chinese ancestry, is of an age to have experienced firsthand the *Reformasi* movement that rose to prominence with the expulsion of Anwar in the late 1990s and has worked closely with anti-BN opposition parties and civil society organizations. However, he has never personally been a member of a political party, and the *Seksualiti Merdeka* events were strictly nonpartisan. Even after *Seksualiti Merdeka* was banned, Pang continued to regularly organize events[7] and speak out in newspapers and online news sites about topical sexual minority issues. In March 2018, just before the change of government, Pang, along with other LGBT movement activists, launched *Queer Lapis*, an online sexual minority community and website for disseminating information, with funding from the Canadian government.

After the change of government in 2018, Pang published a short essay titled "Political Suicide vs. LGBT Suicide," aimed at politicians in the PH administration and activists who participated in the government. In the piece, Pang criticizes PH politicians and former activists who remain silent because they see speaking out against bullying and the suicide of young gender and sexual minorities as political suicide. At the same time, he criticizes the government for continuing to channel funding towards "LGBT treatment" instead of towards mental health and

---

7 Pang organized the "Arts for Grabs" event which continued from 2007. These events encompassed a range of content, such as lectures in shopping complexes in Kuala Lumpur and its outskirts, as well as seminars, mini bazaars, stage performances, etc.

suicide prevention measures for gender and sexual minorities. He says that politicians who remain silent pretend to allow gender and sexual minorities to do what they want in the private sphere, but they are in fact socially marginalizing those minorities by stigmatizing them. Pang calls for dialogue with the PH administration, writing:

> We [gender and sexual minorities] are the experts in our own lives. Stop misrepresenting us and perpetuating harmful stereotypes about who we are and what we want. This government wants to dialogue. Let's dialogue. We have ideas on how to work together. How to find a way to create more channels, more discourse, more platforms for the public to hear our stories and empathise. More empathy in Malaysia can go a long way not just for LGBT people, but for everyone in Malaysia living at the margins and struggling just to exist. (Pang 2018)

We discussed the meeting between Minister of Religious Affairs Mujahid and transgender activist Nisha after the August 2018 portrait removal incident and note that six years later there has still been no space in which gender and sexual minorities can interact with the government and autonomous actors, as Pang has asked. Rather than recognizing gender and sexual minorities' autonomy, JAKIM and the various state religious affairs departments have deemed them to be deviates from "true Islam," or pathological, and have targeted them for "correction" and "prevention."

Numan Afifi

The other LGBT activists is Numan Afifi. Younger than Pang Khee Teik, who became an activist in the wake of the *Reformasi* movement, Numan is of the generation that became social activists after the BN had failed for the first time to win two-thirds of the Lower House seats in the Federal Assembly in the 2008 general election. Numan was involved in founding the Pelangi campaign in the LGBT movement and has been involved in various other social movements for youth empowerment, voter education, and interfaith dialogue. He became known to the public in June 2017, when he organized and implemented "Gay Iftar" as a district-level youth leader in the Democratic Action Party (DAP), then an opposition party that later formed the PH and became the ruling party. Iftar is the evening meal Muslims eat when fasting and is a time of joy and sharing with family, friends, neighbors, and colleagues. The purpose of planning the first Gay Iftar, Numan said, was to return to our roots and deepen our love for each other by facilitating dialogue as we recognize our respective beliefs, culture, and identity (Aedi 2017). However, the event was harshly condemned by religious figures and experienced a huge online backlash, which led Numan to leave the DAP and focus on social activism.

He nevertheless maintained ties with politicians, and before the change of government, Numan was involved in Syed Saddiq Syed Abdul Rahman's public relations activities in BERSATU, which was chaired by Mahathir. Syed Saddiq, who had become the face of BERSATU to the younger generation while still in his mid-twenties, was appointed Minister of Sports and Youth upon the change of government. When it became known that Numan would also join the government as the minister's press officer, there was widespread opposition, especially on the internet. Some online posts included serious threats, and ultimately Numan declined the appointment as press officer. PH politicians and their officials, including Syed Saddiq himself, never properly addressed the case and various civil society organizations, particularly those led by LGBT activists, called PH's silence a betrayal of its election manifesto to "create an inclusive, moderate, and globally respected Malaysia." Syed Saddiq was singled out for particularly harsh criticism for his failure to protect Numan (Chu 2018).

The incident sparked a reaction that reached far wider than just politicians. Yu Ren-Chung, one of the activists in the Women's Aid Organization (WAO), a leader in the women's movement, said that those who express the view that "I do not support LGBT but I am against discrimination" deserve criticism for "perpetuat[ing] a culture where hiring an LGBT person (i.e. not discriminating [against] that person) is scandalous and seen as 'supporting LGBT'" (Yu 2018). Yu criticized the current Malaysian society, where rejection of and discrimination against gender and sexual minorities was strong even among those seen as progressive, such as PH supporters and social movement activists.

Less than a year later, Numan was back in the public gaze. At the UN Human Rights Commission's Universal Periodic Review (UPR) in March 2019 he, along with activists from several civil society organizations, critically reported on the situation of gender and sexual minorities in Malaysia. In April, the police issued an order for Numan to appear before them, citing what he had said at UPR. Foreign Minister Saifuddin Abdullah expressed concern on Twitter about the order to call Numan in for questioning, publicly declaring that there was no taboo on discussing human rights issues, including LGBT (Weiss 2019). While there were glimpses of differing opinions within the government, Saifuddin's views represented only a small minority within the government, and most PH politicians remained silent even on this occasion.

Some Islamic civil society organizations, however, accused Numan of spreading lies in his speech at the UPR. For example, the Center for Human Rights Research and Advocacy (CENTHRA) and the International Women's Alliance for Family Institution and Quality Education (WAFIQ) retorted that Numan's claim that the *Mukhayyam* program was a form of "conversion therapy" and "state-sponsored violence" was untrue (MACSA 2019). Both CENTHRA and WAFIQ are relatively new conservative Islamic organizations that became fully active in the 2010s and have close ties to JAKIM through participation in seminars and lectures. As such, they can be seen as non-government organizations that represent JAKIM's views and ideas to a significant degree.

By comparing Numan, who became a public figure around the change of government in 2018, with Pang, who was very active in the early 2010s, several changes within the LGBT movement become apparent. First, the fact that an openly gay activist like Numan came to the forefront of the movement is a new development in the Malaysian LGBT movement. Second, Numan differs from Pang in that he had direct ties to political parties while engaging in a wide range of activities aimed not only at the LGBT movement, but also at young people. In Pang's case, although he had networks with opposition party members and activists critical of the government, his activism was non-partisan and expressed through his art. In contrast, in the more recent case of Numan, various opinions, including opposition to his activities, have erupted, resulting in a lively debate about sexuality. Sexual politics is on its way to taking root in society.

Conclusion

This chapter has examined the political and social inclusion of gender and sexual minorities amid expectations of a "New Malaysia" following the nation's first ever change of government in 2018. The results were as follows.

Compared to the BN regime politicians who had held power for more than sixty years, PH politicians showed a slightly more favorable attitude towards gender and sexual minorities, declaring opposition to discrimination and hate speech against gender and sexual minorities. At the same time, however, they have also opportunistically exploited the issue of gender and sexual minorities in their pursuit of support from conservative Malays, maintaining that the state would not become involved as long as gender and sexual minorities kept their private lives private, but would not allow them to demand their rights in the public domain through demonstrations and other means. However, contrary to the politicians' proclamations of non-interference in the private lives of gender and sexual minorities, the Department of Islamic Development Malaysia (JAKIM) and the various states' religious affairs departments deems any sexuality that deviates from heterosexual norms as being pathological, and a departure from legitimate Islamic teachings; and has developed a series of programs to "prevent" and "rectify" sexual "deviance." These perceptions and approaches have been condemned by LGBT activists in Malaysia, as they fail to recognize sexual and gender diversity, contrary to the prevailing view around the world, especially among international organizations. Thus, even after the 2018 change of government, there is little evidence that the political and social inclusion of gender and sexual minorities has advanced. It is clear, however, as our spotlight on the activists Pang Khee Teik and Numan Afifi has shown, that the LGBT movement has become more active since the 2000s.

There are, of course, other issues that were not covered in this chapter. While a politics of sexuality focused on gender and sexual minorities has been developed by politicians, religious figures and LGBT activists, the public has also become increasingly involved through social networks. Some of these activities have incited discriminatory posts and flame wars against gender and sexual minorities, courting responses from politicians. For example, the personal information of trans woman Nur Sajat was exposed during a flame war in 2020–2021,[8] resulting in abusive posts and harassment. The online furor surrounding gender and sexual minorities, which sometimes causes serious human rights and privacy violations, will be discussed at another time.

---

8   The case against Nur Sajat, a trans woman, began when she posted a photo of herself on Instagram wearing female prayer robes to Umrah (a pilgrimage to Mecca which can be undertaken at any time of year), which caused an online firestorm and sparked intervention from politicians and religious officials. Accused of wearing an inappropriate outfit while visiting a religious school for donation purposes, Sajat was ordered to appear before the Islamic Religious Department (JAIS) in Selangor for trial in 2018; but after fleeing to Thailand, she was granted refugee status by the United Nations High Commissioner for Refugees (UNHCR) and granted asylum in Australia.

4 Conflicts between Globalism and Localism in Psychiatry over LGBT in Indonesia

Masaaki Okamoto

Introduction

While there have been moves to recognize same-sex marriage not only in the West, but also in some parts of Asia, such as in Taiwan and Thailand, moral and legal discrimination against gender and sexual minorities remains intense in the Islamic world, including in Arab countries, due to the tenacious idea that Islam does not recognize homosexuality. An anti-LGBT stance is also clearly apparent in the Southeast Asian sultanate of Brunei, and in Malaysia, where Islam is the state religion. More than 80% of the population of Indonesia, the country discussed in this chapter, is Muslim, and there is growing influence of conservative Islam, which strictly interprets the Qur'an and takes a negative attitude towards co-existence with other religions. When Indonesia's 32-year-long authoritarian regime collapsed in 1998, marking the beginning of democracy and decentralization of power, local governments in conservative provinces with a majority Muslim population began to draft ordinances that discriminated against gender and sexual minorities, and there were incidents such as attacks on transgender beauty pageants by conservative Islamic organizations.

Meanwhile, in concert with the expansion of political freedoms, the demands of gender and sexual minorities began to surface: in 2006, 29 international human rights experts gathered in Indonesia's ancient capital of Yogyakarta to establish the landmark Yogyakarta Principles, which called for the elimination of discrimination based on sexual orientation and gender identity; and in the 2014 direct presidential election, various

LGBT organizations campaigned around the country in support of the populist presidential candidate Joko Widodo, or "Jokowi" as he is known. As a result of Jokowi's election, some LGBT activists expressed hope that Indonesia could be an exception in the Islamic world and publicly tolerate the rights of gender and sexual minorities. However, quite the opposite occurred: as I will elaborate later, in 2016, for the first time in Indonesian history, discrimination against gender and sexual minorities by state and social actors surfaced rapidly, and nationwide. The discourses justifying this growing discrimination were diverse, ranging from the moral, religious and legal, to those of psychiatry.

Considerable research on gender and sexual minorities in Indonesia has already emerged, and numerous reports have been published on the post-2016 changes relating to gender and sexual minorities.[1] In this context, this chapter focuses on moves towards the psycho-pathologization of gender and sexual minorities by the state and society that have been little addressed by existing research. From the perspective of gender and sexual minorities, it must cause considerable spiritual anguish not only to be deemed ill because of one's sexual orientation or gender identity, but also to have that diagnosis justified by religious and moral norms. In the West and in global terms, psychiatry has progressively de-pathologized gender and sexual minorities, now taking the stance that to be LGBT is natural to the persons in question and that the social discrimination they face is a very real problem. In Indonesia, by contrast, the outdated psychiatric connection between gender and sexual minorities and mental disorders in the form of sexual deviance has been reinforced. As conservative opposition to LGBT became more outspoken from 2016, some Indonesian psychiatrists rejected the prevailing evidence-based positions of the Diagnostic and Statistical Manual of Mental Disorders (DSM) and the

---

1   Studies on gay men in Indonesia are represented by Boellstorff (2005); lesbian studies by Blackwood (2010) and Ōgata (2019); the development of the LGBT movement in Indonesia and the rise of anti-LGBT movements by Wijaya (2020); discussions on LGBT human rights by Oetomo and Suvianita (2014), among others; and on the moral panic against LGBTs that began in 2016 in the report by Human Rights Watch (2018).

International Classification of Diseases (ICD) and defended the religious and moral pathologization of gender and sexual minorities. Thus, against the global movement towards de-pathologizing LGBT people, Indonesia continues to associate LGBT people with mental disorders. This, in turn, has sparked a conflict in psychiatry between globalism and localism on the issue of sexual and gender minorities. In this chapter, I will first explain how the LGBT concept emerged in Indonesia and how the anti-LGBT movement responded. Then, after outlining changes in global psychiatric norms, I will examine the dynamics of localism in which Indonesian psychiatry continues to link sexual and gender minority status to mental disorders as it plays a part in the anti-LGBT movement.

The birth of the LGBT concept: Subjectivity and organization

In pre-modern Indonesia, diverse sexual orientations and gender identities were considered natural; for example, sexual activity between males was not uncommon.[2] However, from the 17th century, Dutch colonial rule promoted the spread of Christian values, and the understanding began to prevail that only heterosexuality and heterosexual marriage were morally right. Then the Islamic revival movement of the early 20th century began to extend into Southeast Asia, spreading strict Islamist interpretations of sexuality that prohibited homosexuality, and sexual diversity was officially frowned upon. With the formation of the nation-state in the mid-20th century, sexual diversity was publicly rejected on the grounds of national morality as well as religious value systems. A particular patriarchal view of the family became the norm under Suharto's authoritarian regime, which took power in 1966 and endured for 32 years (Suryakusuma 2011). The norm of heterosexual marriage was so prevalent that so-called gay men and lesbians often entered heterosexual

---

2   Diverse sexual orientations and gender identities prior to the colonial state have been noted and studied (Anderson 1990: 278; Oetomo 2001; Boellstorff 2005: 35–57; Itō 2000; 2003; Andaya 2000).

marriages, often while continuing to engage in same-sex sexual relations (Boellstorff 2007: 116–120).

When, then, did gay, lesbian, bisexual and transgender subjectivity in the current sense emerge?[3] The pejorative terms *bencong* and *banci* had begun to be used in the mid-19th century to refer to male-to-female (M to F) transgender individuals whose gender was deemed to be female. Such people were ridiculed from childhood because they were physically male but behaved in feminine manners and so forth; in terms of their self-identification, they arguably developed an awareness from an early stage that they were different than normative males and females. It was not until the late 1970s and into the 1980s that "gay" and "lesbian" subjectivities emerged, a decade or two later than other Southeast Asian countries such as Thailand (Boellstorff 2007: 60).[4]

Naturally, transgender, gay and lesbian people only began to organize themselves after such identities had been recognized both by self and others, with M to F transwomen, or *waria* in Indonesian,[5] being the first gender and sexual minority group to organize as such. *Waria* were often publicly conspicuous, frequently dressed in women's clothing, and many

---

3   The terms "gay" and "lesbian" are not necessarily used in the West with the same connotations as in the Indonesian context, and mutual misalignment has been pointed out by gender researchers, but we will not explore this in depth here. I refer the reader to the work of Boellstorff and Blackwood.

4   Rather than being positioned as an extension of pre-colonial gender diversity, gay and lesbian consciousness is better regarded as a new self-identification mediated through the mass media (Boellstorff 2007). The first public mass media coverage of gays and lesbians was a lesbian wedding reception in Jakarta in May 1981, which marked the beginning of gender and sexual minority self-identification.

5   *Waria*, a term coined in 1980, is an abbreviation of *wanita pria* (*wanita* meaning woman, and *pria* man, so the literal translation is "[both] man and woman." The expressions "*bencong*" and "*banci*" are still used, but often harbor discriminatory or pejorative nuances. This is partly why the term *wadam* began to be used in the late 1960s. However, *wadam* is an abbreviation of *hawa adam*, where *hawa* means female and *adam* male. respectively. Adam was the first prophet in Islam, and the application of that prophet's name to transgender people was unacceptable for conservative Islamic forces. With then President Suharto's consent, the term *waria* was applied to transgender (M to F).

struggled to make a living as beggars or streetwalkers. But being highly visible targets for discrimination, also made them easily identifiable targets for support and highlighted the need for self-organization among fellow *waria*.

Ali Sadikin, who had been governor of the capital city of Jakarta since the 1960s, understood the hardships endured by *waria* and encouraged the formation of the Jakarta *Waria* Union (*Himpunan Waria Djakarta*, or Hiwad) in 1973 as a mutual support organization, the first organization of gender and sexual minorities in Indonesia. Later, a series of self-help *waria* groups emerged (Okamoto 2016b: 236). Closeted gay men were able to lead their daily lives without much hindrance, but Dede Oetomo and others who had learned about gay life while studying in the US and had decided to live openly as gay men established the first gay men's organization, Ramda Indonesia, which was inaugurated in 1982. Then, in 1986, the first lesbian organization, Persatuan Lesbian Indonesia (Perselin), was formed.

The spread of HIV/AIDS spurred further organization of gender and sexual minorities. As the number of patients with HIV/AIDS among gay men and transgender people increased and the death toll began to rise, donors began to extend support along with the Indonesian central and local governments to the gender and sexual minority organizations that had emerged in various parts of Indonesia. In this sense, while the spread of HIV/AIDs was a serious problem for LGBT people, it also provided a valuable opportunity to organize mutual support organizations (Suvianita 2016).

Such self-organizing was primarily a survival strategy, aimed at increasing unity and mutual interaction within each of the gay, lesbian and transgender populations, not to promote themselves to the general public or demand rights. Hence, they did not attract a lot of social interest, and there was neither any discourse about gay men or lesbians being a threat to society, nor any thorough efforts to eliminate the *waria* who begged or stood around on the streets. Research analyzing LGBT from a psychiatric perspective was therefore not of interest to anyone other than the individuals in question.

However, a major change followed the collapse of the Suharto regime in 1998 and the onset of democratization: the term LGBT came into use in Indonesia, and there were active moves to encourage collaboration among gay, lesbian and transgender people. LGBT activists in Indonesia started demanding their rights in the context of intensifying LGBT activism across Asia. Activists became more assertive political participants, with individual activists running for political and public office, and LGBT organizations supporting presidential and parliamentary candidates. Perhaps their most groundbreaking activity was their political participation in the direct presidential elections of 2014. Not only did LGBT organizations across Indonesia openly express support for presidential candidate Joko Widodo, who had shown an understanding of pluralism, but transgender and similar organizations worked directly with Jokowi's party in the election campaigns in various parts of the country (Okamoto 2016a).

Jokowi's narrow victory over a rival candidate with strong support from Islamic conservatives led some LGBT activists to anticipate that Jokowi would initiate LGBT-tolerant policies. However, the new president remained silent on LGBT issues, fearing criticism from increasingly influential Islamic conservatives. In addition, as the majority of Indonesians were intolerant of LGBT individuals, demonstrating understanding of LGBT people risked provoking a backlash from the greater part of the population. In a poll of 1,000 people conducted in March 2013 by the US Pew Research Center, 93% of respondents indicated that society should not accept homosexuality, with only 3% saying it should (Pew Research Center 2013). In February 2016, the Indonesian online media site Tempo.co asked 3209 of its readers: "Do you agree with the position that lesbian, gay, bisexual and transgender people have a deviant sexual orientation?" In response, 86.6% agreed, with only 12.4% disagreeing (*Tempo* 2016: 10).

One source of the extreme intolerance towards LGBT people is the tenacious view that they violate religious norms: both the Biblical Old Testament and the Qur'an have passages that have been interpreted as meaning that the city of Sodom was destroyed by the wrath of God because of its immoral homosexual practices.[6]

The wave of anti-LGBT movements

Despite the admittedly general climate of intolerance towards LGBT people in Indonesian society, by the mid-2010s, domestic LGBT activists had forged stronger links with the global movement and initiated attempts at active political participation within Indonesia, and gay and transgender people began to be visible in the media. Then, in 2014, alarmed at the emergence of these LGBT movements, the Majelis Ulama Indonesia (MUI), a semi-governmental body with strong Islamic conservative influence, issued a *fatwa* (Islamic legal opinion) clarifying its anti-LGBT stance, namely "*Fatwa* No. 57 of 2014 on Lesbianism, Gay Men, Sodomy and Indecency." The *fatwa* warned of the risk of disrupting the social order and endangering the institution of marriage due to an increase in the number of gay and lesbian couples, an insistence on equal rights and same-sex marriage by the gay and lesbian communities, and growing social unrest due to an increase in anal intercourse. MUI further stated that sexual activity was only permissible between heterosexual married couples, that same-sex sexual orientation was abnormal and should be cured, that deviations had to be corrected and that homosexuality was not acceptable.[7]

This *fatwa* clearly regarded lesbians and gay men as mentally ill and set the tone for the subsequent anti-LGBT discourse by Islamic conservatives. However, this did not trigger a wave of anti-LGBT movements, as MUI was well known to be an Islamic conservative organization and it had issued fatwa against religious pluralism, liberalism and secularism.

6   Among Muslims, who account for a minority in the West, some have begun to argue that LGBT is not rejected by Islamic religious norms (Kugle 2014). However, such a position is not widespread in Indonesia.

7   The MUI issued a *fatwa* on *waria* in 1997, in which *waria* were declared to be male and could not be seen as a group with its own gender; any *waria* behavior was deemed deviant and contrary to Islamic law; and such individuals must make efforts to return to their true nature (Majelis Ulama Indonesia 1997).

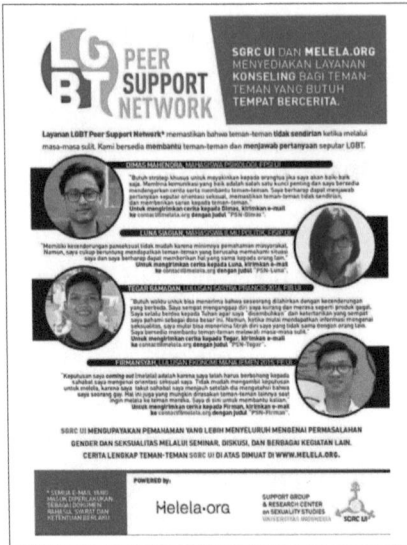

Photo 4.1: SGRC poster offering counselling to LGBT people

The anti-LGBT movement would only become a hot topic in Indonesia after same-sex marriage was declared constitutional in the US in 2015. In November 2015, Diponegoro University in Semarang became the first university to ban a debate on LGBT, saying that LGBT was against religious doctrine. In December, the rector of the University of Lampung warned that he would purge the campus of LGBT elements by sacking faculty members and admonishing LGBT students; and in January 2016, the prestigious University of Indonesia followed suit. When its Support Group and Resource Centre on Sexuality Studies (SGRC-UI), with a membership of 222 students, disseminated a poster online advertising that it would begin counselling to support LGBT people, the University's rector posted a notice online saying that SGRC was by no means permitted to use the University of Indonesia's name or logo in any of its activities to support LGBT (Sakinah 2016).

This response by the University of Indonesia was highly controversial: a series of ministerial level anti-LGBT statements were issued, and the anti-LGBT movement began to spread nationwide. The Minister of Research, Technology and Higher Education, who had jurisdiction over universities, and the Minister of Education and Culture, with jurisdiction over primary and secondary schools, stated that the LGBT community corrupts the morals of the Indonesian people, while the Chair of the National Council also stated that LGBT was a new phenomenon and did not fit with Indonesian culture. The Minister of Defense went so far as to regard LGBT people as enemies of the state and tools in a proxy war for control of Indonesia.[8]

The Chair of Nahdlatul Ulama, an Islamic organization with the largest following in Indonesia, and considered to be moderate, also declared that LGBT activities were not only counter to religious doctrine but also were against humanity, and that the "LGBT phenomenon" in Indonesia was too dangerous. The MUI, the Catholic Bishops' Conference of Indonesia, the Indonesian Buddhists' Representative (WALUBI), and the Supreme Council for the Confucian Religion in Indonesia issued a joint statement which, while acknowledging the need to guarantee LGBT people's rights as citizens and protect them, rejected any propaganda calling for legalization of LGBT or supporting their movement (Imanuel 2016).

The Indonesian Clinical Psychologist Association (IPK) issued a statement that the people of Indonesia rely on the Indonesian National Principles, one of which is belief in one Almighty God, and that humanity has been created as male and female. While showing an understanding and supporting a humanitarian response towards LGBT persons as individuals searching for themselves, it advocated for prevention and treatment and refused to recognize LGBT-support organizations and communities (Ikatan Psikologi Klinis 2016).

At the regional level, in turn, various ordinances were introduced in the 2000s seeking to eradicate homosexual acts, equating them with immoral prostitution. According to Riska Carolina, an activist from an LGBT-supporting NGO, there has been a surge in anti-LGBT local ordinances and other measures since 2015, with 22 ordinances explicitly outlawing homosexuals and transgender people, and another 45 seeking

---

8   The National Human Rights Commission, an independent government committee, has been highly critical of the homophobia movement and strongly criticized anti-LGBT statements by public officials as violating human rights and inciting acts of violence against LGBT people, but to little effect.

indirectly to crack down on LGBT people with the goal of eradicating social pathologies (Muthmainnah 2016; BBC Indonesia 2018).

Furthermore, anti-LGBT action has become more visible at the national political level. A parliamentarian from the conservative Islamic party, the Prosperous Justice Party (PKS), stated that LGBT people were a serious threat to the nation, while a former party leader said that communists and LGBT people endangered the state and national principles. The National Awakening Party (PKB), whose parent organization is the nation's largest Islamic social organization, Nahdlatul Ulama, recognized the rights of LGBT people as ordinary citizens, but did not allow same-sex marriage campaigns and other activities; it also emphasized Asian and religious values while showing an understanding of pluralism (Nursyahbani and Wieringa 2016: 98). The Prosperous Justice Party and other groups began to explore drafting anti-LGBT legislation around February 2016; and in 2018, a crackdown on same-sex sexual activity was included in a parliamentary debate on proposed amendments to the criminal code. Under the existing code, punishable indecent acts were limited to actions by males involving violence or threats against females under the age of eighteen. In contrast, the proposal would make obscenity in public a punishable offence, regardless of age or sex, even if the act involves persons of the same sex, and even if it is consensual and without threat or coercion (Ōgata 2019: 67–70).

In February 2019, feeling threatened by the perceived weakening of the family system, five members of parliament submitted a Family Maintenance Bill containing provisions on sexual deviance, which included homosexuality alongside sadism, masochism and incest, and prescribed social, psychological and medical rehabilitation and spiritual guidance for such sexual deviants.

In this manner, anti-LGBT discourse overflowed both politically and socially, and the association of LGBT with the sexually deviant mentally ill became widespread. At that point, the Indonesian psychiatric community began to sympathize with this growing anti-LGBT movement, in direct contrast to the de-pathologization of LGBT persons in the US and by the World Health Organization (WHO). The next section highlights this contrast by examining developments in Indonesia in contrast to those in the US and WHO.

LGBT in Western and WHO psychiatry

In the West, secular authority started to take precedence over religious authority in the 19th century, and the process of psychiatrically patholo- gizing same-sex sexual orientation and atypical gender identities in transgender persons as sexual perversions and mental illnesses based on a scientific perspective began to displace views of religious or moral sins. Moreover, because homosexuality and transgenderism were deemed to be disorders, attempts were made to treat and correct them. In the early 1940s, Hungarian-born American psychoanalyst Sándor Radó began to use aversion therapy such as morphine administration and electroshock, which had been used to address alcoholism, to treat sexual deviance. Blaming patients' anxiety about heterosexuality on unwholesome parenting, he employed aversion therapy to overcome it. Although this therapy did nothing but cause serious psychological damage to the patients concerned and did not lead to a cure, it continued to be prescribed (Rizzo 2009: 197–202; Drescher 2015).

In accordance with this pathologization of gender and sexual minorities in the West, the Diagnostic and Statistical Manual of Mental Disorders (DSM) compiled by the American Psychiatric Association and the WHO's International Classification of Diseases (ICD), which are used worldwide as the diagnostic criteria for psychiatry, long classified homosexuality and transgenderism as mental disorders. Indeed, one of the gay liberation movement's great successes in the US and elsewhere was the de-pathologization of gender and sexual minorities, supported by various psychiatric research findings: in the case of the DSM, first compiled in 1952, homosexuality ceased being associated with mental disorders in the 3rd edition in 1987 (Drescher 2015: 388; Lieberman 2018: 118–119; Hirata 2016: 985–990; Shiino 2017: 42–43).

In the 10th edition of the WHO's ICD, issued in 1990, in the annotation for code name F66 "Psychological and behavioral disorders associated with sexual maturation and sexual orientation," a note was included for the first time stating that sexual orientation by itself was not to be regarded as a disorder.[9] Furthermore, the WHO declared in 1993 that homosexuality was not in any sense to be a target for treatment. However, there were three categories in F66 – sexual maturity disorder, egodystonic sexual orientation and sexual relationship disorder – which were clearly mental disorders uniquely linking sexual orientation and gender expression. As for the ICD, it was only in the 11th edition, published in 2018, that sexual orientation such as homosexuality was declared to be unrelated to any mental disorders (Cochran et al. 2014).

It has taken even longer for transgenderism to cease being considered a mental disorder. The World Professional Association for Transgender Health (WPATH) defines transgender as an adjective "to describe a diverse group of individuals who cross or transcend culturally defined categories of gender. The gender identity of transgender people differs to varying degrees from the sex they were assigned at birth" (2012: Appendix A). It was a term brought to prominence by trans individual activists who aimed to de-pathologize their status. Until the 2000s, both the DSM and the ICD classified transgender people as having a mental disorder, namely a gender identity disorder. The fifth edition of the DSM in 2013 included transgender people in the category of mental disorders, but replaced the term "gender identity disorder" with a diagnosis of "gender dysphoria." Meanwhile, the ICD continued to use the diagnosis of "gender identity disorder" and considered it a mental disorder up to and including its 10th edition in 2010; but the 11th edition of the ICD in 2018 finally began to use the diagnosis of "gender dysphoria," and being transgender was no longer deemed a mental disorder (Davy 2015; Soll et al. 2018).

---

9   The 8th edition's cluster on sexual deviance included fetishism, pedophilia, dress perversion and exhibitionism as well as homosexuality.

The pathologization of LGBT persons in Indonesia

While the WHO was de-pathologizing LGBT people, though, the anti-LGBT movement in Indonesia was gaining momentum, and notably, among Indonesian psychiatrists where the backlash was spearheaded by a televised statement in February 2016 from Fidiansjah Mursjid, a senior official in the Ministry of Health, who had just been appointed as its Director of Prevention and Control for Mental Problems and Illegal Drugs. Whereas his predecessor had been sympathetic to the WHO's position, Fidiansjah's views on psychiatry were informed by his Islamic values, rather than clinical experiments or research findings. His position as head of the Religion, Spirituality and Psychiatry section of the Indonesia Psychiatrists Association (PDSKJI) granted him great influence in both the public and academic spheres.

In a television program, Fidiansjah stated that the Indonesian Mental Disorders Classification and Diagnostic Guidelines, 3rd edition (*Pedoman Penggolongan dan Diagnosis Gangguan Jiwa III; PPDGJ-III*), a literal translation into Indonesian of the section on mental disorders in the 10th edition of the IDC (1992), did not dichotomize science and religion, but was grounded in both perspectives. He added that the references to homosexuals and bisexuals in the above-mentioned code F66 indicated that they do have mental disorders, and that the same applies to transsexuals. Fidiansjah also opined that these mental disorders were treatable and there were many cases of successful treatment, and that these disorders could be transmitted through behavior and habits.

However, as mentioned earlier, a footnote to F66 in the 10th edition of the IDC, which Fidiansjah obviously misread, states that homosexuality in itself is not considered a mental disorder. LGBT activists who had appeared on the same television program therefore asked Fidiansjah to apologize for his misreading in March, through the Jakarta Legal Aid Society. Although Fidiansjah apologized at a press conference in response to that request, in his seven-point apology, he maintained his position that LGBT is a sexual deviation and did not even mention F66 (Sri 2016). Four days after his television appearance, he stated that homosexuals and bisexuals were people with mental problems who needed medical attention as soon as possible as they were extremely likely to become mentally disturbed. He expressed alarm at the LGBT movement, likening it to a fire that would have dire consequences if not dealt with early, and claimed that there were already signs of an increase in homosexuals and bisexuals (Hasanul 2016;).

The view that homosexuals and bisexuals have mental problems was not limited to Fidiansjah. The then Minister of Health declared that LGBT people as a group were not mentally disabled, but did have mental problems (*Merdeka.*2016). The Indonesia Psychiatrists Association issued a statement in the name of its president in February 2016, based on suggestions from Fidiansjah and others. The statement described LGBT persons in two categories in the Mental Health Act 2014, namely as "persons with mental problems" and "persons with mental disorders," as follows:

> In the Act, a person with mental problems is a person who is at risk of becoming mentally disabled due to physical, psychological or social problems, growth or development problems and/or quality of life issues. Persons who are homosexual and bisexual are categorized as persons with psychiatric problems… A person with a mental disorder is disturbed in terms of thinking, behavior and emotions, manifested in a clear series of signs and changes in behavior, which can give rise to distress and limitations in fulfilling their role as a human being. Thus, according to the PPDGJ-III, … a person who is transsexual is classified as a person with a mental disorder. (Perhimpunan Dokter Spesialis Kedokteran Jiwa Indonesia (PDSKJI) 2016)

Later, the Indonesia Psychiatrists Association added that it would support the exercise of the rights and obligations of people with psychiatric problems and mental disorders, and would provide integrated, comprehensive and sustainable health services, including mental health promotion, prevention of deterioration of mental health, and treatment and rehabilitation.

In my reading of the Mental Health Act, there was no wording that portrayed lesbian, gay and bisexual people as having psychological problems or transgender people as having mental disorders, but the above pronouncement by the Psychiatrists Association on LGBT persons linked LGBT to mental disorders. This invited heightened criticism from the West. The British Psychological Society, for one, posted condemnations on Facebook and Twitter (Jowett 2016). The American Psychiatric Association subsequently stated that the latest and best scientific research demonstrated that different sexual orientations and gender expressions occurred naturally and were not harmful to society. A letter of protest was sent to the President of the Indonesia Psychiatrists Association, saying that the latest edition of the DSM stipulated that LGBT people were not innately disabled (American Psychiatric Association 2016). Human Rights Watch also expressed its deep concern to the Indonesian Minister of Health about the statements from Fidiansjah and the Indonesia Psychiatrists Association. It also called upon the Ministry of Health to accept the international scientific standards and to reject the Indonesia Psychiatrists Association's attributing homosexual and transgender identities to mental health issues (Human Rights Watch 2016a).

In reply to the American Psychiatric Association's protest, the President of the Indonesia Psychiatrists Association explained that rather than the DSM, Indonesia used the WHO's ICD 10th edition, which stipulated that if LGB persons had psychological or behavioral disorders, they were eligible for treatment and deemed the gender identity of transgender persons to be a mental disorder.

The response also claimed that the reason for categorization of lesbians, gays and bisexuals as people with mental health problems in the Mental Health Act was that although they were not mentally disordered, they were at higher risk of being so. It further claimed that, as a professional principle, psychiatrists spoke on the basis of science, not of religion; and while some psychiatrists' personal view was that treating LGB persons meant changing them back into heterosexuals, the official stance of the Indonesia Psychiatrists Association was not to force people to be heterosexual, this being a matter of individual choice (Agus 2016).

This statement suggests that the president was against the treatments seeking to "revert" lesbians and homosexuals to heterosexuality, although he does link gender and sexual minorities to mental disorders. However, some psychiatrists, such as Fidiansjah, stand out for their emphasis on treatment. Suzy Yusna Dewi, a senior member of the Psychiatrists Association, for one, argues that lesbians, gays and bisexuals have mental problems and should make efforts to become heterosexual to avoid becoming mentally ill:

> What must be remembered is that nobody wants to be born "sick," nor does anybody want to be born "different." If you believe that it is your destiny and it cannot be helped, then don't let that destiny carry you away. All life requires "effort:" effort to heal and effort to change are indispensable. There is no need for all of us to follow you who are ill, nor to follow you who are different. (Dewi 2016)

With these words, Suzy Yusna Dewi advocated that lesbians and gay men should be cured and that they should not spread propaganda in Indonesia demanding rights as lesbians and gays. She also stated that Indonesia had its own culture and need not bow to Western values, and she expressed appreciation for the newly launched Perilaku Hidup Normal (Normal Life Behavior) (PHN) movement (Dewi 2016; Irawan 2016). The PHN movement aimed to popularize the term PHN and deflect attention away from the term LGBT, fearing that normalization of the latter term would be dangerous, both stimulating interest in LGBT people and issues and increasing the number of people who became LGBT.

As some psychiatrists in Indonesia began to emphasize the kind of psychiatry that took religion and morality into account, there were moves to amend the PPDGJ-III. In February 2016, the Religion, Spirituality and Psychiatry section of the Indonesia Psychiatrists Association, headed by Fidiansjah, asked the Ministry of Health to compile the PPDGJ-IV from the religious and spiritual perspective of the Indonesian people, as more than a decade had elapsed since the institution of the PPDGJ-III.[10] Fidiansjah was dissatisfied that the PPDGJ-III excluded homosexuality from the category of mental disorders, and by defining lesbians, gay men and bisexuals as persons with psychiatric problems and transgender persons as having mental disorders in line with the 2014 Mental Health Act, this new guideline would enable psychiatrists to help such persons "revert" to heterosexuality. Although the PPDGJ-III was a literal translation of the WHO's 10th edition of the ICD, Fidiansjah argued that it could be amended because the WHO recognized variation in approach according to local spiritual values and intelligence (Achmad 2016; Reja 2016).

According to Eka Viora, then vice-president of the Indonesia Psychiatrists Association, the board did not accept Fidiansjah's proposal. Subsequently, according to Fidiansjah, in 2017 the Ministry of Health produced new guidelines on mental health that dealt with LGBT people in accordance with the Mental Health Act. However, this did not culminate in amendment of PPDGJ-III as the Indonesia Psychiatrists Association did not agree with those guidelines. Overtly frustrated by the Association's position, in the 2019 elections to elect new board members, Fidiansjah aimed to drum up support for the new guidelines by increasing the forces endorsing the pathologization of LGBT people, but he failed.[11] However, the Ministry of Health has not made any moves to adopt the latest WHO ICD, 11th edition or create the PPDGJ-IV, because the 11th edition's complete rejection of any link between LGBT and mental disorders is incompatible with the stance of the Ministry of Health. This has given rise to a strange situation in which the government is continuing to follow 30-year-old guidelines in an effort to maintain the local value system

---

10 Based on Fidiansjah's statements on the request for revision of PPDGJ-III, although he declared on television that the PPDGJ-III classified homosexuality as a mental disorder, he knew that this was untrue (Tonny 2016). Fidiansjah's religious mission was to convert LGBT people to heterosexuals, and these narrative contradictions do not seem to concern him.

11 Interview with Eka Viora, October 1, 2018.

in Indonesia, relying on obsolete global guidelines while defying the current global trend and ignoring the latest evidence.

Fidiansjah himself became active not only in government circles and academia, but also in social movements. He was one of the founders of an organization called the Civilized Indonesia Movement (*Gerakan Indonesia Beradab*), a network of various organizations that took a conservative Islamic position launched in March 2016 and chaired by a specialist in Islamic psychology from the Faculty of Psychology at Gadjah Mada University (*Panjimas* 2017). It warned of the moral decline and loosening of family ties in Indonesia and criticized the prevalence of pornography and the LGBT phenomenon which arose from too much freedom, alongside social problems such as drugs, corruption, crime and poverty (Hafidz 2016).

Pathologization and Islamization

This series of attempts at psychological pathologization of LGBT people endeavors to transform Western-style psychiatry into one that upholds Islamic values, bringing to the fore the Indonesian national principle of belief in the One God, as conservative Islam became increasingly influential throughout Indonesian society. The discipline of Islamic psychology began in the 1960s and began to gain currency in Indonesia in the 1980s. Islamic psychology departments have been established in Islamic universities, and various books and journals have been published. Unlike Western psychology, Islamic psychology aims to construct a psychology in line with the teachings of Allah. Most books and journals on Islamic psychology argue, as far as I can see, that LGBT behavior is contrary to Allah's teachings and can be cured if treated. Islamic conservatives such as Fidiansjah seek to have this position reflected in psychiatry. The problem is that it emphasizes the religious dimension and disregards scientific research findings while asserting the compatibility of religion and science.

The position, reflecting Islamic doctrine, that LGBT people can revert to heterosexuality through treatment has been extremely influential, with

Photo 4.2: Poster for the national seminar "Generation of healthy minds without LGBT and HIV/AIDS" in Padang

Islamic leaders publicly speaking about it in sermons at Friday prayers. Abdul Somad, for example, an Islamic leader popular for his easy-to-understand sermons, advised a woman who had recently discovered that her spouse was gay that she should urge her husband to go to prayer; and he also recommended that Islamic exorcism (*ruqyah*) be performed because the husband was possessed by evil LGBT spirits called "djinn," and had tumors in his brain (Alfred 2019).

From 2016, as the anti-LGBT movement intensified, there has been a marked trend of treating LGBT people with Islamic exorcism, an approach that has been adopted by local authorities (Adam 2019; Evan 2020).

For example, the mayor of the city of Padang in West Sumatra takes a radical anti-LGBT position, arguing that "LGBT attitudes are totally incompatible both with Islam and the culture of the citizens of Padang, and need to be eradicated" and that it is caused when "female spirits enter the bodies of men so they like men, or vice versa." On that basis, municipal staff responsible for public order arrested LGBT couples and performed exorcisms upon them on the advice of Islamic leaders

(Adam 2019). The mayor boasts that these exorcisms were successful in expelling LGBT.

Conclusion

Particularly since 2016, an anti-LGBT movement has spread through both state and society in Indonesia, where LGBT persons' own subjectivity is completely ignored and moves have arisen to criminalize and pathologize them and make them enemies of the state because they ostensibly do not align with religious doctrine, Indonesian national principles or the morals of the Indonesian people. The LGBT rights movement has been deemed a Western-led human rights movement and demands that it not be permitted in Indonesia have become overwhelming. This chapter has focused on the development of the psychiatric discourse that pathologizes LGBT people by classifying them as sexually deviant persons with mental illness. If, for argument's sake, psychiatry is going to link sexual orientation and gender identity with psychopathology, then it should rely on clinical experiments and research to justify such pathologization rather than categorically denigrating gender and sexual minorities. However, amid the intensifying position of Islamic conservatives that sexual diversity is contrary both to divine providence and Indonesian national principles, there appear to be conspicuous moves by psychiatrists to associate LGBT status with psychiatric disorders and to make it the target of treatment without taking into account LGBT individuals' circumstances. This contrasts markedly with the prevailing view around the world, particularly in Europe and the US, and in the WHO, that in psychiatric terms, members of sexual and gender minorities are not mentally disordered.

Perhaps more concerning in this social context is the rise of the association of the term "LGBT" with "non-pious" as well as "mentally disabled." The aforementioned comment by Abdul Somad, urging a parishioner to encourage her gay husband to attend prayer more often was premised on the idea that if LGBT individuals only prayed sincerely, they would no longer be LGBT. In a different example, a leader of a schizophrenia-support NGO said that schizophrenia patients experience dual suffering: they suffer because of their schizophrenia and also from being told by Islamic leaders that they have schizophrenia because they do not pray enough. One cannot help seeing this same logic in the anti-LGBT movement.[12] At present, although there have been noticeable moves towards LGBT pathologization by some municipalities and Islamic organizations, this does not mean that the Psychiatrists Association and the Ministry of Health have normalized the overt pathologization and therapeutic exorcism of LGBT people. The last Joko Widodo government, in power from 2014 to 2024, was open to interfaith dialogue and continued efforts to curb the rise of conservative Islam by emphasizing moderate Islam. This has not, however, led to national and social acceptance of LGBT people, and blatant anti-LGBT discourse became pervasive in 2016, although there have been calls for LGBT acceptance by a small number of Islamic leaders, and there have even been attempts to justify their position in terms of Islamic law, relying on the Qur'an and other texts. Although such attempts have only just begun, and the voices to support them remain small, they might lead to LGBT de-pathologization and non-deviancy from religious and moral norms in the context of medium- and long-term social change, as happened in Taiwan and Thailand.

---

12 Interview with Anta Samsara (Chairperson of Chhaya Jiwa, Schizophrenia Patient Support Group), August 21, 2018.

5 | The Philippine Catholic Church Battling "Invaders:" Nationalism Surrounding Sex, Reproduction, and the Family

Satoshi Miyawaki

Introduction

In 2015, the United States Supreme Court issued a ruling allowing same-sex marriage in all states, based on "equality under the law," triggering a global debate over protection of the rights of gender and sexual minorities. This debate was particularly heated in the Philippines.

The scene was already fraught following the 2012 passage of the Reproductive Health Law (hereafter RH Law), which aimed to encourage family planning and promote sex education and contraception to youth, despite longstanding opposition and resistance from the Catholic Church, the majority religion in the Philippines. The Church continued its efforts to obstruct the implementation of the law, but Duterte's inauguration as President in 2016, with his anti-Church position and pledge to promote the law's implementation, made the Church's position untenable. The current president elected in 2022, Ferdinand Marcos Jr., is expected to basically continue the Duterte administration's policies.

The Church considers the "Filipino family" to be a Christian couple or family united by the sacraments of the Church. The "complementarity" of the couple (deemed possible only between heterosexuals) and the "sexual relationship always open to the possibility of childbearing" that should spring from it, as well as the "wholesome raising of children" (deemed achievable basically only by their parents) are considered to constitute a "little church" which provides the foundations upon which the Church is built. Therefore, the Church sees trends such as the promotion of gender and sexual minorities' rights, the legalization of public support for family planning and contraception, the legalization of divorce, and the promotion of education about these issues as a threat to the Church and the nation.

What is intriguing about this "threat" is that the Church has repeatedly condemned it as an international or imperialist plot. This rings very hollow when one considers that the Church, originally a foreign institution itself, has long sought to strictly police vernacular Filipino sexual customs and ethics according to the norm: "sex for procreation" (Brewer 2001). That is, the Church was originally introduced by an invader imposing a transnational colonial ideology of sex and reproductive health, and still today is an outpost of a global hierarchy based in the Vatican. But now, in the guise of a kind of nationalism dubbed "defensive sacralization" (Chow 2011), the Church is taking a stance against the "invasion of foreign ideology." Taking this paradox into consideration, this chapter seeks to understand the characteristics of the Church's involvement in the politics of gender and sexual minority rights. I will approach this in two ways.

First, I present an overview of the Philippine Catholic Church's activities relating to sex, reproduction, and the family, showing the intersection of the global and national positionings of "the family" in the Philippine Church.

Second, through discourse analysis of the Church's official documents, I reveal how the Church evokes a global colonialist plot against which to consolidate its position, as well as outlining its opposition to gender and sexual minority rights. This analysis highlights the nationalistic dimensions of what appears to be a global conflict.

Through this analysis, I confirm that the foundation of "the family" which sustains the identity of Catholicism as the majority religion in the Philippines is being shaken, and that this has further intensified the Church's attitude.

The Church in the Philippines and globally

Establishment of the global structure of the Catholic Church

The pre-modern Catholic Church was fragmented by the many states and religious orders vying for control, and thus lacked unity. However, the abandonment of church protection by various kingdoms amid the formation of nation-states in Europe in the 19th century led to the gradual restoration of the Vatican's control of the Church (Bolasco 1994). This reintegrated World Church consolidated in the early 20th century. The Second Vatican Council (1962–65) was a global plenary council of the Catholic Church that further consolidated this integration, while also affecting a major change of direction in opening a dialogue with the various branches of modern science and other religious thoughts. The documents of this council would become the premise for subsequent Catholic Church doctrine, controversies, and movements (Holy See 1965; Aberigo 2005/7).

Since the 1970s, the Church has held a series of world and Asian conferences, seeking to build consensus for the worldwide renewal and social involvement of the Catholic Church. Different currents – such as traditionalism, which focused on preserving the pre-council traditions and hierarchical authority of the Church; progressivism, which sought reform to enable the active participation of the laity; and radicalism, which aimed for radical social change through liberation theology – all came together vying for international collaboration.

From the 1980s, Pope John Paul II was successful in marginalizing radicalism in favor of moderation of the Church as a whole, and his extensive foreign travels fostered strong recognition of the Church's global presence. Under John Paul II and his successor, Benedict XVI, standard texts on Church doctrine and rules for the world at large were developed, including a new Code of Canon Law (1983), as well as the publication of the Catechism of the Catholic Church (1993) and the Compendium of the Social Doctrine of the Church (2004).

Strengthening ties to the global structures in the Philippine Church

The Philippines became a US territory at the beginning of the 20th century, dissolving the "Royal Patronage of the Church (*Patronato Real*)" that had been concluded with Spain. Under an agreement between the Vatican and the colonial suzerain, the US, the Catholic Church established itself as the church governing the majority of the population through training and promoting local clergy and connecting its religious orders with multinational networks (Bolasco 1994).

Although policy conflicts among the leadership surfaced under martial law after 1972, the Church eventually settled on a moderate reformist line and made its presence felt during the 1986 EDSA People Power Revolution, giving full play to its leadership powers. In the 1990s, the domestic Church produced a number of important texts, including publication of the documents of the Second Plenary Council of the Philippines (1991), the Catechism for Filipino Catholics (1997), and a series of pastoral statements (made by church leaders, aimed primarily at congregations under their jurisdiction to care for their souls) that summarized social doctrine (Miyawaki 2019; Youngblood 1990).

Meanwhile, the Catholic Charismatic Renewal Movement, which emphasized works of the Holy Spirit and miracles and the active partici-pation of the laity, rapidly expanded in the Philippines from the 1980s. In particular, the lay organization El Shaddai, though seriously conflicting with the Catholic Church leadership at one time, came to support and promote the Church's doctrines on sex, reproduction, and the family in the 2000s (Wiegele 2004).

The 2000s saw a generational shift resulting in the permeation of a system based on the currents of modernization and renewal of the World Church that had occurred since the Second Vatican Council. This period saw the translations into local languages of the Catechism (introductory manuals explaining the criteria of teachings to the congregation) and key pastoral statements, which had previously been mostly in English.

In this manner, the Catholic Church in the Philippines moved towards the renewal and standardization of institutions and norms in line with the global Church, with increased dialogue and sharing of activities. At the same time, the Church in the Philippines was progressively accumulating its own history and discourses within that context.

The Church's stance on sex and reproduction

Vatican standards on sexuality, reproduction, and the family

In this context, the Church's position on sex, reproduction, and the family has been a topic of debate. In dialogue with the various branches of contemporary science, the Second Vatican Council was responsible for launching a re-examination of the patriarchal traditions of sexuality and the family. In the wake of worldwide moves towards sexual liberation, lively expressions of various positions on sex, reproduction, and the family was heard both within and outside of the Church, and discussions were increasingly shared among religious orders and lay movements, and through networks of Christian intellectuals, theologians, and the like.

However, Pope Paul VI's 1968 encyclical, *Humane Vitae*, circumvented the various arguments within the Church and expressed a prudential position, declaring not only abortion but also population control through contraception to be grave sins. John Paul II upheld the conservative orthodox principle view that sexual intercourse was only permissible within heterosexual marriage, and that childbearing was its central goal. He deemed other forms of sex as being contrary to "life" and condemned homosexual acts, in particular, as grave sins while at the same time strongly opposing divorce and same-sex marriage. In short, contraception, divorce, and homosexuality came to be understood collectively as common violations against the "life" that the Church valued.

In response to these teachings, religious orders' and lay movements' defense of the family, campaigns against population control policies, promotion of "regulating" pregnancy via natural methods, and acceptance of homosexual people while rejecting homosexual acts have collaborated both nationally and internationally with parishes, dioceses, and the National Conference of Bishops.

Thus, the "modernization" of the Church's position on sex, reproduction, and the family was idiosyncratic, driven by restructured institutions and networks within the Church, while taking account of and sometimes objecting to modern medical knowledge.

Developments surrounding sex, reproduction, and the family in the Philippines

Each time a legislative proposal on sexuality, reproduction, or marriage has been mentioned, the Catholic Bishops' Conference of the Philippines (CBCP) has responded by issuing a pastoral statement. It has issued similar statements since the 1960s in response to basic policies on development and population from international development agencies and corresponding governmental population control policies.

In the 1990s, especially in response to the "Declaration on Sexual and Reproductive Health and Rights" adopted by the World Population Conference in 1994, the CBCP issued a pastoral statement calling for the protection of marriage and the family, and held various events such as public forums and prayer rallies. In the 2000s, the Church lobbied against increased pressure for "sexual and reproductive legislation" in the Philippines. In 2012, when the Reproductive Health (RH) Law was passed, Church efforts shifted to resisting its implementation. Moreover, when attention shifted to deliberations over an anti-discrimination bill which would protect gender and sexual minorities' rights, the Church took a strong stance against this, as well.

In response, lay movements – especially those of Filipino origin – began to be mobilized by the family defense movement. In the Catholic Charismatic Renewal Movement-affiliated Couples for Christ, anti-RH law hardliners complying with the wishes of Church leadership took control, sidelining the Gawad Kalinga Community Development Foundation, a more liberal civic movement. El-Shaddai, meanwhile, expressed its support for Church leaders by forming the Life Party (Buhay Partylist) and entering parliament. By contrast, Courage Philippines, introduced by an international Catholic organization, is an apostolate that "encourages same-sex-attracted lay people to avoid homosexual *acts* and to live a chaste life in accordance with Church teachings." The CBCP has conducted seminars and other activities in collaboration with Courage Philippines in churches.

The Philippine Church facing troubles at home and abroad

The Church's positions triggered various internal and external conflicts in political, economic, social, and ideological terms. In particular, despite the Church's opposition, the public was increasingly supportive of family planning and contraception, which facilitated the passage of the RH law. This highlighted a serious problem for the Church, given that 80% of the population is ostensibly Catholic. Although public support for abortion, divorce, and same-sex marriage is not particularly strong by world standards, understanding of these issues is growing. Local governments have adopted anti-discrimination ordinances in defense of the rights of gender and sexual minorities, the Ladlad Party was formed representing gender and sexual minorities, a transgender person was elected to congress, and President Duterte declared support for the protection of gender and sexual minority rights and appointed members of gender and sexual minorities to important positions.

Church leaders, however, are staunchly conservative in their views on sex, reproduction, and the family. Their fixation on this issue was such that, contrary to Church strictures against clergy engaging in partisan politics, some bishops have campaigned to unseat politicians with opposing views. They repeatedly demonstrated against the 2012 legislation, including a strongly worded statement that "contraception is corruption" (Bayoran 2013). Importantly, these campaigns were met with numerous objections from *within* the Church. Most notably, faculty, students, and staff at the Jesuit-run Ateneo de Manila University raised a series of objections to the Church leadership's unquestioning opposition to the RH bill, although the president of the university was eventually forced to yield to CBCP pressure (Alave 2012). Nevertheless, Claretian Publications, the largest Church-owned publishing house in the Philippines, published a book written primarily by church officials who were supportive of the RH law (Carvajal 2014).

Despite the Catholic Church leadership's refusal to compromise with RH proponents, and its full mobilization of the Church's resources, its political effectiveness was limited in these circumstances. Church leaders realized that they were on the defensive and moved toward a more reactionary and antagonistic response. The "defensive sacralization" noted in studies on sex and reproduction refers to this situation. Below, we will look at how Church leaders' pastoral statements portray the "global enemy" that threatened their position on sex and reproduction. In the process, we will uncover a local situation resulting from the collision of two global discourses on sexuality and reproduction (a medical discourse and a church discourse) in a specific location, namely the Philippines.

"Global enemies" in Philippine Church's discourse

This section outlines the "enemies" and "allies" identified in pastoral statements and the "frayed edges" within the Church, as seen in documents.

Enemies

The Church's condemnation of a "contraceptive mentality" has been consistent since 1990. This is deemed to be "an irresponsible attitude that seeks to avoid the responsibilities that come with having children" (Catholic Bishops' Conference of the Philippines (henceforth: CBCP) 1990b). The Church views contraception as the epitome of evil and opposes its promotion.

The Church argues that, along with the Philippine government's population control programs, "local and foreign non-government organizations have renewed their efforts to manipulate family size by... distributing drugs and devices which artificially prevent conception of and even abort human life already conceived in the womb" (CBCP 1990a), and declares that this is not harmonious with the Christian families' way of life.

We must not become the slaves of lending institutions. Through programs of population control, we became both collaborators and victims of

> contraceptive imperialism... Contraceptive technology entered the
> lifestyle of our people. It has produced an anti-life mentality... We are
> unwittingly caught in a systematic campaign against childbearing. It
> is a world-wide drive that undermines the value of life. (CBCP 1990a)

A pastoral letter issued prior to the 1994 United Nations International
Year of the Family stated: "We can thank God that our people as a whole
can still discern the TRUTH about family from deviations. But a growing
minority is already challenging this truth by the lifestyles they flaunt"
(CBCP 1993, emphasis original). It warned that government-supported
actions such as contraception, abortion and sterilization "work towards
the destruction of the Filipino family" (CBCP 1993). A pastoral letter
in 1994 responded to the International Conference on Population and
Development in Cairo, opposing the promotion of (economic) development through population control policies using contraception and abortion,
calling this a "type of imperialism which subjugates and determines the
future of peoples by money" (CBCP 1994). A later text says: "Finally,
so-called modern ideas from supposedly developed countries penetrate
our culture through mass media and insidiously deform family values
and degrade our traditional esteem for marriage, family, and human life"
(CBCP 2001).

It reiterated that once people have accepted mistaken teaching, there
will be no going back.

> We know the difficult situations that face many married couples, and
> we deeply sympathize with them. But dissolving the marriage bond
> as a form of relief from marital difficulties as a license to remarry
> goes against the very nature of the marriage covenant and will only
> undermine the very institution of marriage. The *legalization of absolute*
> *divorce* will violate the rights of other married couples to contract
> an indissoluble marriage and will, in practice, add difficulties to the
> obligation of marital fidelity. The ones most severely affected by the
> irreversible breakdown of a family, as brought about by divorce and
> remarriage, will be the children. (CBCP 2000b, emphasis original)

Pastoral statements describe the threats to the "Filipino Christian family" as follows.

> Materialist and consumerist values are also gaining inroads even among the poor. Mass media and entertainment are filled with subliminal secularist, sometimes erotic, images and explicitly materialistic messages that inflict heavy damage on Gospel values. (CBCP 2002)

> Divorce, artificial contraception, abortion, broken families, live-in partners, queridas, neglected children, and the onset of a materialistic, consumerist, and secularist culture are eating away at the biblical and ecclesial core values of the Christian family as God has planned it from the beginning of time. (CBCP 2002)

> The condom business is a multi-million-dollar industry that heavily targets the adolescent market, at the expense of morality and family life. Condom advertisements should be banned in television, radio, movies, newspapers, magazines, and public places, as they desensitize the youth's delicate conscience and weaken their moral fibers as future parents. (CBCP 2010a)

> A contraceptive-oriented population control program is not the moral way. Even if powerful organizations in the world might imperiously and ideologically promote and fund such programs we would still object. (CBCP 2010b)

Allies must be protected

The Church's pastoral statements defend and rely upon the "Filipino family," its values, the Christian faith of the majority, the Constitution and family law. The Church utilizes ideas derived not only from theology, but also from its dialogue with the various sciences, and advocates universal norms based on traditional natural law. Some characteristic examples include:

The Filipino family is a "church of the home where young Christians are formed to take their place later as adult Christians in the larger church"

(CBCP 1993), and any attack on it is a threat to the Church and Filipino society. However, there is no mention of the tangible problems facing families, people's concrete voices, dialogue vis-à-vis these, or specific measures the Church ought to take.

The Church claims that population suppression programs "go against the teachings of the Church to which 80% of the nation belongs" (CBCP 2000a), yet this refers not to what 80% of the people think, but what is authorized by the teachings of the church to which they belong. At the same time, it mentions the existence of numerous organizations and activities within the Church that support family values. Examples are given not only of local bodies but Philippine chapters of international organizations, as well (CBCP 2001).

As for reliance on Philippine law, quite frequent reference is made to the 1987 Constitution, in which the Church was specifically involved in the creation of family-related provisions. The following portions of the Constitution are quoted at the beginning of one statement (CBCP 2011a).

> The State values the dignity of every human person and guarantees full respect for human rights (Article 2, Section 11). The State recognizes the sanctity of family life and shall protect and strengthen the family as a basic autonomous social institution. It shall equally protect the life of the mother and the life of the unborn from conception. (Philippine Constitution, Article 2, Section 12)

From the perspective of women's rights, the second clause cited above is inherently problematic.

The claim of God's sovereignty is founded on various arguments, such as: "[C]ivil laws should be based on the Divine Law as its expression or application" (CBCP 2000); and "[T]he Bill if enacted into law will separate our nation from Almighty God" (CBCP 2008), who is also referred to as the "Supreme Lawgiver" (CBCP 2009).

Frayed edges

Internal fraying is apparent within the seemingly strong stance of the Church to which the greater part of the population belongs. A 1990 statement both contained an exchange of views between the government and CBCP officials on plans for population control (CBCP 1990c), and a warning that such dialogue should by no means be understood as implying support for government policies. There is an interesting contrast between the somewhat dialogical tone of the statement and the non-compromising tone of the preface, which was added later.

As well as condemning four bills, namely: a bill legalizing divorce; one legalizing abortion; one recognizing same-sex unions; and one promoting population control, the CBCP adds: "[W]e remind all Filipino Catholics of their duty to influence society by working for true human and Christian values" (CBCP 2000b). This reads as if the Church is identifying an underlying social trend unaligned with the Church, and warning that if people are Catholic, they are expected to listen to the Church.

The following wording suggests a similar intent: "All Catholics are moral agents of the Church," and "It is the duty of every Catholic faithful to form and conform their consciences to the moral teaching of the Church. We call for a more widespread dialogue on this [RH] Bill." While these words suggest widespread dissent within the Church that would require "dialogue," the "dialogue" called for here is directed toward yielding results that are amenable to the Church's teachings (CBCP 2008b).

In 2011, when the RH bill was on the brink of passing due to the support of President Benigno Aquino III and the ruling party in the National Assembly, the CBCP expressed total opposition. "This is our unanimous collective moral judgment. We strongly reject the RH bill," clearly illustrating the Church's treatment of internal dissent as if it did not exist. What follows is also very interesting: "The RH Bill, never more than a mere Catholic issue, is an outrageous attack on the orthodox human values of human life and the cultural values of the Filipino people that we have all cherished from all eternity. Simply put, the RH law lacks respect for a sense of morality that is central to Filipino culture" (CBCP 2011a).

However, opinion polls in recent years have repeatedly indicated that a national majority is in favor of contraception, population control policy, and the RH bill (SWS 2008), and so the above is yet further evidence of the Church discounting the voices of the public, the majority of whom are supposedly Catholics.

The Church's familial nationalism in the age of globalization, and its consequences

Catholic Church leaders claim that they have been waging a civilized and patriotic battle in the name of the Constitution and other laws, that their position is representative of the majority religion and universal morality against the deceitful and cowardly schemes of "evil imperialistic forces worldwide" against the "beautiful family of the Christian Philippines," and seeks to protect the nation's enduring Christian culture and Church.

The Catholic Church has consistently taken a hardline position against proposed legal reforms concerning sex, reproduction, and the family, but the Church's edifice is starting to waver. Church leaders claiming to represent the majority are now at odds with the popularly elected congress, and public opinion polls are more closely aligned with the congressional position. Since the RH Bill's passage in 2012, the Church has taken its battle to the courts, succeeding in preventing enforcement of part of the law, but their situation has become increasingly difficult due to the further measures introduced by the Duterte administration from 2016, and the solidity of public support for those measures. Moreover, the forceful suppression of the internal dissent to the leaders' opposition to the RH Bill generated considerable dissatisfaction with the leadership within the Church.

On same-sex love

What about gender and sexual minorities, then, which the Church has long understood within the common ethical category of "sex, reproduction, and family," but which have come into the spotlight in recent years? Here, I will discuss homosexuality as hitherto discussed by the Church.

Homosexuality in pastoral statements of the Church
of the Philippines

A basic doctrine on homosexuality had already been clearly stated in the
Catechism of the Catholic Church in the 1990s. The 1997 Catechism
of Filipino Catholics confirms the basic human rights of homosexuals,
opposes discrimination against them, and tolerates homosexual *orientation*
on the one hand; but on the other, it also clearly condemns homosexual
practices and denies legal privileges for same-sex marriage and same-
sex relationships. However, it is only recently that homosexuality has
been specifically addressed in pastoral statements by CBCP, particularly
in three documents issued around the time of the June 26, 2015 Supreme
Court decision in the United States that legalized same-sex marriage.

The first of these is the "Pastoral Moral Guidelines on the Anti-Discrimination Bill," dated March 3, 2015; the second "On the US Supreme
Court Ruling on Same Sex Marriage," dated June 27; and the third "The
Dignity and Vocation of Homosexual Persons: A Pastoral Response to
the Acceptance of Homosexual Lifestyle and the Legalization of Homosexual Unions," dated August 28 (CBCP 2015a, b, c). Although the three
were issued on separate occasions, their basic position is largely consistent. Here I shall examine the third, which is the most systematic and
extensive.

The first section of the document, "The Nature of Marriage in the
Divine Plan," cites complementarity and procreation as the true character
of marriage. Use of the term "complementarity" indicates the necessity
of heterosexuality. The word "procreation" also implies the assumption
that homosexual relationships are not permissible, especially between
men who cannot procreate.

The next section, "The Nature of Homosexuality in the Created
Order," defines sexual attraction towards the same sex as "disordered,"
not as a sin. It deems the affection between persons of the same sex to
be "genuine affection," but says it is "not ordered to the [sexual] union
of the two persons and to the procreation of children." On this basis,
homosexual practices are deemed "sins gravely contrary to chastity" by
being "gravely disordered." What ought not have been a sin at the start of

the discussion is seen to be transformed into a "grave sin" in one stroke due to homosexual "practices." Ultimately, this leads to the confusing explanation that same-sex-attracted people are called to "witness the life-giving nature of virtue-based friendships not ordered to sexual acts."

The ascetic virtues once supposedly required by Catholic teaching only of clergy and members of religious orders are now for some reason being demanded of homosexuals as well, even though they should not fall into such categories. Moreover, despite being unrelated to procreation or the raising of children, the nature of their relationships is declared to be potentially "life-giving." While taking the form of a series of seemingly reasonable arguments, the plot is distorted to impose harsh demands on homosexuals. Here, the message that "the Church loves homosexuals" is forcibly reconciled by a logic and sensibility of a clergy that endorses asceticism with one saying that "the Church will not change its traditional rules on gender and reproduction." This is extremely difficult for those unaccustomed to clerical logic to understand.

The following section, "The Social Reality of Homosexual Unions," based on documents from the Congregation for the Doctrine of the Faith, a bastion of Vatican conservative forces, forbids engagement in activities or gatherings that affirm homosexual relationships. However, it calls for the families of homosexuals to be "charitable" towards those who "struggle with homosexuality." It deems the ideology of tolerance to be biased, and says that young people should be taught about the immoral nature of same-sex unions, and kept away from such movements. It warns that laws legalizing same-sex marriage are "gravely unjust" and "pervert and undermine the common good." Families of homosexuals are urged to love them unconditionally, but never to affirm their "homosexual lifestyle" in any way. Here, "homosexual lifestyle" is used in the singular to essentialize the diverse ways of life of homosexuals as an ideologically single entity. The text warns "Catholic politicians" that "to vote in favor of a law so harmful to the common good is gravely immoral."

Claiming a basis in natural law, biology, and anthropology, the next section, "Arguments Against the Legalization of Homosexual Unions," argues that the homosexual family cannot function in a sound manner because children cannot be raised wholesomely without both a father and a mother.

The following section, "Responding to Arguments for the Legalization of Homosexual Unions," claims that since homosexual relationships ultimately cannot contribute as much to society as heterosexual marriage, it is not justifiable to grant them the same privileges as marriage. Furthermore, the Church condemns same-sex couples, saying that they will be unable to attain "salvation and … eternal beatitude."

Finally, "A Pastoral Response to the Legalization of Homosexual Unions," deems that young people should be catechized (in effect, taught a set doctrine) about the "true nature of … marriage." And it continues: "to homosexual individuals who are tempted either to pride" – a catchphrase in the pro-gender and sexual minorities movement – "or to despair, the Catholic Church is called to preach the power of grace through prayer and Holy Communion, and the mercy of Jesus Christ through the sacrament of penance."

Thus we can see how the points already made in the doctrine on sex, reproduction, and marriage are also made clear in various forms in regard to homosexuality. In one stroke, the discussion of homosexuality, which should have begun with "pastoral care," which is supposed to care for the individual, has culminated in a frame consisting of confrontation with the forces of evil. This stigmatization or demonization of homosexuals proceeds without acknowledging that it is discriminatory. Such treatment overlaps with that directed at believers who are exposed to divorce, contraception, or abortion. Although issues surrounding gender and sexual minorities are comparatively new for the Church, they arguably share similar properties to the politicization of other issues surrounding sex, reproduction, marriage, and the family.

Trends relating to gender and sexual minorities and the Church

Following the enactment of the RH law and the heightened focus on gender and sexual minorities, the Church's main battleground shifted to the defense of gender and sexual minority rights and the institutionalization of same-sex marriage or same-sex partnerships.

At the same time, the Church is likely to continue this "civilized and patriotic battle." Even though the Church has pulled together in the common purpose of criticizing the Duterte administration's war on drugs and its human rights abuses, its divisions over family planning and the RH law will continue to smolder within the Church. As for homosexuality, while the Philippine Church's policy to encourage people to avoid homosexual acts is clearcut, the widespread dissent both within and outside the Church is undeniable, including among the clergy.

In this context, Pope Francis has been perplexing. While he has not called for doctrinal revision, he has demonstrated acceptance of believers who have divorced, remarried, had abortions, or are homosexual, all of whom have long been considered incompatible with the Church's position. This is a clear departure from previous popes with whom the Philippine Church leadership was familiar and supportive. A statement issued in 2015 entitled "Understanding Pope Francis' Gesture Rightly" criticizes the mass media for spreading the message that "the Church's understanding of abortion has moved forward" after the Pope allowed priests to absolve women who have had abortions, previously the preserve of bishops, and stresses that the doctrine has not changed (CBCP 2015c). However, the CBCP's statement as a matter of doctrine clearly misses the point of the Pope's practical intentions.

At the same time, there was growing concern about the spread of HIV-AIDS, and a new basic law (Philippine HIV and AIDS Policy Act) was passed in 2018, but the Church's cooperation with the government on HIV-AIDS had been established since the 1990s, and this new law was not a particular problem in church–state relations (Apilado 2009). With young gay males comprising the great majority of persons with HIV-AIDS, the core purpose of the law is to consider the human rights of those affected, disseminate accurate information, prevent the spread of infection, and provide support for affected persons. In that regard, there has been real progress made in terms of policies regarding gender and sexual minorities.

There is quite widespread perception that the general public still has trust in the Church, and its political influence cannot be ignored, either. It remains to be seen how Church leaders, who remain politically influential, will move regarding the rights of gender and sexual minorities.

Changing views of the family in the Philippines

Central to the Church's discourse has been the "preservation of Filipino family values," which it has framed in terms of pastoral care, that is to say, care of the soul, but what does this signify for actual families in the Philippines, especially amid the changes they are now undergoing? To consider this point, I will highlight findings from a recent study on the sociology of the family.

Medina's 2015 *The Filipino Family* is the third edition of a textbook on family sociology in the Philippines. In discussing changes in the family, this textbook touches particularly upon the more open attitudes among adolescents toward premarital sex and homosexuality, as well as changes in family structure due to increasing numbers of migrant workers. It also points out that the roles of men and women have become gradually more equal, and shows changes in the thinking, attitudes, and relationships of people situated in the vortex of social change brought by globalization.

Based on various survey reports, Medina also points out that there has been no great change, but rather a continuum, in regard to the family. There were, for example, not the significant changes in perceptions of the importance of the family like those observed in postwar Japan (Iwama et al. 2015). Medina argues that the perceived importance of marriage to Filipino family relationships has not changed significantly, either. Additionally, in regard to gender roles in a couple or family, though there are increasing numbers of mothers assuming the fathers' role due to the fathers' absence, conversely, fathers do not fill the mothers' role when the mothers are absent. Instead, in many cases, grandmothers, aunts, or eldest daughters assume the mothering roles related to household chores, etc. This indicates that changes in gender norms have not progressed much. Even as social mobility increases and social relationships change, horizontal social relationships, which are in a sense bilineal, continue to be favored as a safety net; and heterosexual marriage continues to function as a cornerstone of social relationships.

Duterte promised same-sex marriage or same-sex partnerships when he ran for president in 2016. After taking office, however, despite showing some consideration for the rights of gender and sexual minorities, he eventually backed-away from this commitment (Tubeza 2017; Corrales 2018). It is worth noting that a survey by Social Weather Stations (SWS 2018) found that support for same-sex partnerships remains low.

Thus, on the one hand, there obviously have been huge changes in attitude about sexuality and the nature of family relationships, as illustrated by the broad support for the RH law and the open-minded position vis-à-vis gender and sexual minorities. On the other hand, the unit known as "the family" and its connections remain stable, and marriage, too, is still strongly bound to the context of family relationships that extend beyond the love and contractual relationship between individuals. This may be the basis for the not insignificant resistance to any configuration other than heterosexual marriage. In future, a large-scale survey on this point would be desirable, but assuming it to be the case, even if anti-discrimination laws protecting gender and sexual minorities were easy to accept, same-sex partnerships and same-sex marriage would likely face great hurdles. In this respect, the Church's position against same-sex marriage would be consistent with a substantial proportion of the general public, leaving the Church positioned to continue to act as the "guardian of the Christian family."

Gender Mainstreaming, Paradigm Shift, and Gender and Sexual Minority Human Rights: Intersectionality in Feminist and Queer Politics in Taiwan[1]

Genya Fukunaga

Introduction

One of the outcomes of the UN's Fourth World Conference on Women held in Beijing in 1995 was the adoption of "gender mainstreaming" into its platform for action. As a guiding principle that stipulates the introduction of a gender perspective into all policies, measures, programs, strategies and research, regardless of domain or sector, gender mainstreaming has since influenced politics in various countries and regions.

In modern societies, "being female or male" has been essentialized in relation to biological traits, and discrimination and oppression against women have long been justified. Feminism has persistently questioned the manner and extent to which human experience has been gendered and has critically discussed how knowledge around gender has been produced (Scott 1988; Butler 1990). The approach of gender mainstreaming has been to bring to light the fact that existing policies, measures, programs, strategies, research, and even the framework of "human rights," have been disguised as being gender neutral; and to aim for gender equality by foregrounding the gender perspective. In response, the gender perspective was incorporated into all activities of UN human rights bodies. The

---

1   This chapter is a reconstruction of the discussion in Fukunaga (2017a), written in Japanese, from the perspective of a paradigm shift in gender mainstreaming. The writing of this paper was supported by a Grant-in-Aid for Scientific Research (JP23K18828).

establishment and enhancement of "national machinery" in each country was advocated as an umbrella organization to promote gender equality, and gender mainstreaming was promoted in many countries and regions from the late 1990s to the 2000s.

The now-familiar slogan "women's rights are human rights" diffused throughout the Beijing Women's Conference. At the conference, there was also focus upon women's differences and diversity, with emphasis on the intersectionality between gender and other influences such as race, disability and age. The introduction of intersectionality was an important achievement by marginalized feminists representing Black feminism, vernacular feminism, and the like (Crenshaw 1989; Taylor 2017; Collins and Bilge 2020; Kumamoto 2020). Placing the issue of homosexuality on the agenda, lesbian activists, who comprised a composite minority in terms of gender and sexuality, tried to hold various activities during the conference, including demonstrations and networking, but in the face of opposition from various national governments, "lesbian rights" were not recognized as "women's rights." As a result, eliminating discrimination based on sexual orientation was excluded from the goals of "gender mainstreaming" and "gender equality" (Zhao Jing and Shi Tou 2015).[2]

Feminists from various nations in East Asia brought home the achievements of the Beijing Women's Conference and promoted gender mainstreaming, but gender and sexual minorities' human rights were not on the agenda. Among East Asian countries, South Korea promoted gender mainstreaming more strongly than others by establishing a Ministry of Women's Affairs as a central ministry in 2001, but the rights of gender and sexual minorities have remained outside its purview to this day. The situation in Japan is similar, with measures promoted within the framework of "gender equality" consistently developed independently of the human rights agenda of gender and sexual minorities.[3]

---

2   Nevertheless, the activities of queer women from various countries who participated in the Beijing Women's Conference gave a huge impetus to the queer women's movement in China (Zhao Jing and Shi Tou 2015).

3   An exceptional case in Japan is an ordinance on gender equality passed in Miyakonojō City in Miyazaki Prefecture in 2003, which addressed the human

Taiwan was an exception in this respect, as the human rights of gender and sexual minorities were included in the process of gender mainstreaming. This chapter examines the paradigm shift of gender mainstreaming in Taiwan that included the human rights agenda of gender and sexual minorities, and highlights the Gender Equity Education Act passed in 2004 which was conducive to this shift. This legislation, emphasizing the human rights of gender and sexual minorities, opened a new direction of gender mainstreaming in Taiwan: both marriage equality, achieved in 2019, and the transgender rights movement have been propelled under the discourses of "gender equality" and "gender mainstreaming" in Taiwan.

However, when the Gender Equity Education Act was first drafted, its name was *Liangxing pingdeng jiaoyu fa* (literally, "Equity between the Two Sexes [in] Education Act"), which did not acknowledge the existence of gender and sexual minorities. What, then, was the background and trajectory for the law's rejection of the concept of "equity" (*pingdeng*) between the "two sexes" (*liangxing*) in favor of a "gender equity" (*xingbie pingdeng*) approach? And why did the legislative approach to "equity between the two sexes" culminate in a "gender equity" that also encompassed gender and sexual minorities?

This chapter focuses on the development of Taiwanese feminism, which championed "equity between the two sexes," and its intersection with queer movements that developed under its influence. It then argues that the burgeoning of these movements against the backdrop of democratization led to the unique approach of "gender equity."

In what follows, we begin by focusing on the drafting of the original Gender Equity Education Act, with the meeting minutes and publications

---

rights of gender and sexual minorities by including the words "sexual orientation." However, it has been noted that this was possible because those involved in drafting the ordinance did not share a network with feminists or gender researchers who were only concerned with "gender" issues related to cisgender heterosexual women, and they lacked any notion of emulating some "model ordinance." In other words, paradoxically, the human rights issues of gender and sexual minorities could be included precisely because they lay outside the feminist network (Saitō and Yamaguchi 2012).

of the drafting team, as well as the public records of Legislative Yuan (Taiwan's supreme legislative organ) as our targets of investigation, examining them in the context of Taiwanese feminism and queer politics of the time. Next, we will investigate the marriage equality and transgender rights movements in relation to the discourse of "gender equity." Using Taiwan as a case study, this project focuses on the intersectionality of feminist and queer politics and attempts to elucidate its potential.

From the "Equity between the Two Sexes in Education Act" to the "Gender Equity Education Act"

In this section, the passage of the legislation called the Gender Equity Education Act is positioned as the result of feminist intervention in the education sector. It points out that during the legislative process, there was a shift from "equity between the two sexes" which refers to the safety of female students and the elimination of discrimination against women, to a new approach of "gender equity," which also encompasses the human rights issues of gender and sexual minorities, and discusses the background to this shift.

Feminist interventions in education

The passage of the Gender Equity Education Act was a feminist achievement. In fact, the four people engaged in drafting the bill were all feminists engaged in the women's movement or gender studies. So, how did Taiwanese feminists advance their intervention in the education sector?

From the late 1980s into the 1990s, against a background of macro-political structural changes such as democratization and political liberalization, groundbreaking reforms were proposed in the education sector. Educational reform was positioned as one of five major reforms, alongside judicial, administrative, fiscal and constitutional reforms. A common feature of such reforms was the creation of institutional conditions that expanded the role of "society" (the people) in contrast to "the state" (the government) (Yamazaki 2002). In fact, following the democratization of elections, education policy also came to be shaped by the will of the people, and the civic groups and social movements that arose following the end of martial law in 1987 emerged as important actors in directing education policy. Moreover, the educational reforms that encouraged citizens to become involved in politics also had a significant influence on the shaping of the Gender Equity Education Law.

The women's movement which developed in the 1980s began to focus on eliminating discrimination against women and achieving gender equity in the education sector. Su Chien-Ling (2001: 3), who drafted the Gender Equity Education Act, observed: "The promotion of gender equity education in countries around the world is a product of the women's movement and feminism, and Taiwan has been no exception."

A comprehensive review of textbooks by the Awakening Foundation (*Funü xin zhi jijin hui*, literally "Women's new knowledge foundation") in 1988 is regarded as the first intervention of Taiwanese feminists in the education sector (Su 2001; Hung 2007). These women investigated gender representations in primary, junior high and senior high school textbooks. They revealed that less than 10% of the people appearing in textbooks were women, and that women were predominantly portrayed as subordinate to men. The Awakening Foundation argued that school education had reproduced discrimination against women and proposed revising textbooks and education in accordance with the principle of gender equity. "Educational equity for both sexes" was then adopted as a key theme of education reform (Su 2001).

When equal education for both sexes was proposed in the 1990s, sexual harassment and sexual violence against women were coming to be recognized as a social problem. This was triggered by activism to recognize and compensate the so-called "comfort women" of the Japanese colonial period, as well as numerous incidents of sexual harassment, sexual violence and the like. As feminists called for action to stop violence against women, the murder in 1996 of a feminist politician named Peng Wan-Ru from the Democratic Progressive Party (DPP), a strong advocate of equal education for both sexes, was widely reported in the media, highlighting the issues and amplifying public calls to improve women's safety. The government hastily convened a Women's Safety Council and, with strong public support, passed the Sexual Assault Crime Prevention Act in 1997 (Hung 2007; Lee 2013). This law stipulated the introduction of "equal education for both sexes" in primary and secondary schools, and a Committee on Education for Equity of Both Sexes (*Liangxing pingdeng jiaoyu weiyuan hui*) was established under the Ministry of Education as an umbrella body to oversee this.

From an "Education for Equity of Both Sexes" Act to a "Gender Equity Education" Act

The Committee on Education for Equity of Both Sexes, established in March 1997, consisted of twenty-one members. The committee included two employees of the Ministry of Education and a mixture of gender studies scholars and feminist activists, in keeping with the previously mentioned shift towards educational reform focused on public opinion.

In 1999, the Committee began researching ways to promote gender-equity education aimed at drafting legislation. The Ministry of Education had identified legal obstacles to expanding equity education (Su 2001). The Sexual Assault Crime Prevention Act, which formed the legal basis for equity education, only mandated four hours per year of sex education in primary and secondary schools, which was deemed inadequate for related education, training teachers in the prevention of sexual assault and sexual harassment in schools, and conducting surveys and other research. Thus, investigation began into legislation specific to the education sector with the goal of "full promotion of education for equity of both sexes" (Su 2001: 16).

On December 3, 1999, the Committee announced that it had commissioned four members – Su Chien-Ling, Shen Mei-Zhen, Hsieh Shao-Fen and Chen Hwei-Syin; all feminists – to draft the Act on Education for Equity of Both Sexes bill. However, at this point, neither the Ministry of Education nor these four women had fully grasped the abstract idea of "education for equity of both sexes." They sought relevant laws in other countries to examine, only to discover that few countries have such laws. Thus, a decision was made to proceed with the drafting process based on the views of a wide range of citizens, including school teachers and feminist experts.

Over a period of one year from December 3, 1999, thirty-five meetings were held to discuss the draft. Teachers, as well as experts and activists from various fields were invited to the meetings, and public hearings were held in various parts of the country. Furthermore, a quarterly magazine published to inform the general population about the purpose of the legislation printed the draft in full, and a wide variety of opinions was collected. Queer scholars and activists intervened in this public process (Fukunaga 2017a) and soon the committee sought their advice. The quarterly magazine received numerous submissions from teachers expressing perplexity about how to deal with homosexual children in their classrooms, and the committee members sought expert advice on how to respond to these queries. Thus, in their research into practical ways to implement education to promote sexual equity, the feminists preparing the draft bill stumbled into awareness of the human rights challenges facing gender and sexual minorities.

Furthermore, as the draft was under consideration, an incident occurred that shook the "equity for both sexes" approach: on April 20, 2000, Yeh Yung-Chih, a junior high school student in Pingtung County, who had been bullied and sexually assaulted by classmates who called them "faggot," died in a boys' toilet at their school.[4] According to later revelations, in primary school, Yeh was ordered by a homeroom teacher to attend a psychiatric clinic for "not developing normally as a boy." In junior high school, they were sexually assaulted, including being made to remove their underpants in the boys' toilet by boys in their class as part of a "physical examination" to see if Yeh was a "real man." Yeh was eventually found collapsed and bleeding in the boys' toilet during a music class. Yeh was immediately taken to hospital in a critical condition, but never regained consciousness and was pronounced dead in the early hours of the next morning. The direct cause of death was deemed to be

---

4   To emphasize the ambiguity of Yeh's gender identity, the third-person pronouns they/their/them are used in this English version in reference to this person.

a contusion to the head; the judiciary concluded that Yeh Yung-Chih had slipped and fallen in the toilet.[5] Although Yeh had not disclosed their sexual orientation or gender identity before their death, the news reports of bullying and sexual assault because Yeh was regarded as "fruity" were a major shock to the queer community that was emerging in Taiwan at the time. It was a tragedy for "transgender" or queer youth in Taiwan (Bih 2000c).

The Committee on Education for Equity of Both Sexes was subsequently tasked with investigating incidents of sexual assault and sexual harassment that occurred in schools. In the course of investigating the Yeh incident, the committee "discovered" that same-sex-attracted and transgender children, and children who deviated from heterosexual norms even if they did not identify as gender and sexual minorities, were just as vulnerable as cisgender, heterosexual girls vis-a-vis sexual assault and various forms of violence.

In fact, Bih Herng-Dar, a member of the Committee on Education for Equity of Both Sexes, discusses homophobia and misogyny in relation to the death of Yeh Yung-Chih as follows:

> Until boys develop into adult men through a process of socialization, they experience a series of processes such as being compelled to be heterosexual under patriarchal pressure, being constantly forced to discriminate against women, to cloak themselves in homophobia, to "correctly" learn masculinity, and to denigrate femininity. Social exclusion and violence against women, effeminate boys and homosexuality are the result of different manifestations of masculinity. Hostility towards effeminate men is fundamentally linked with oppression against women. (Bih 2000a: 44–46)

---

5   Yeh Yung-Chih's mother pursued the school's responsibility and won a judicial decision in 2006 that found the school liable for "failing to create an environment consistent with hygiene to protect the safety of the students" (Taiwan Gender Equity Education Association 2006).

Su Chien-Ling, who was engaged in drafting the Act on Education for Equity of Both Sexes at the time of the incident, came to the same conclusion. In her words:

> From a gender perspective, women are a minority in the sense that they are disempowered. From the perspective of gender disposition, effeminate men and masculine women are subject to discrimination. From the perspective of sexual orientation, homosexuals are subject to discrimination. Perhaps we can be in solidarity in that we are all subject to gender discrimination? (cited in Bih 2000b: 78–79)

Thus, they highlighted the fact that by imposing heteronormativity, patriarchy not only oppresses (cisgender, heterosexual) women, but gender and sexual minorities as well.

It should be pointed out, however, that the Committee had a predisposition to "discover" the vulnerability of gender and sexual minority children. In reviewing the Act on Education for Equity of Both Sexes, it had learned that toilets and swimming pools were dangerous spaces in schools where girls were vulnerable to sexual violence. Yeh Yung-Chih's death in a toilet made it clear that attention needed to be directed at the diversity and vulnerability among children who are perceived as boys.

The tragedy of Yeh's death was a direct impetus for the Committee to advocate a new approach to "gender equity education" to the Ministry of Education (Bih 2000c). In response, the Ministry of Education set forth a change of policy to "diverse gender equity education" (*duoyuan xingbie pingdeng jiaoyu*) in December 2000, declaring:

> Calling for respect *not only for the traditional two sexes of male and female*, but for different sexual orientations and gender temperaments, the Ministry of Education ... has renamed the "Committee on Equal Education for Both Sexes" the "Gender Equity Committee" on December 16; and will shift the focus of educational policy from education for both sexes to education for diverse gender equity. (Bih 2000c: 132, emphasis added)

Thus, a policy of "gender equity" aiming to eliminate "gender discrim-ination" based not only upon gender, but also on sexual orientation and gender identity, was finalized. As a result, the Gender Equity Education Act, passed in 2004, brought this policy into practical realization. As will be discussed below, in Taiwan, as elsewhere in East Asia, a gender backlash mobilized by Christian conservatives arose around 2010, but when the Act was passed in 2004, it was yet to begin. In fact, the passage of this law received little attention from liberals and conservatives alike, and perhaps ironically, it may be that the lack of public interest facilitated the progressive nature of this legislation (Fukunaga 2017a).[6]

The initiation of gender equity education

The Gender Equity Education Act stated that "no person shall be subjected to discriminatory treatment on the basis of his or her biological sex, sexual orientation, gender disposition, gender identity or other differences." When recruiting or admitting students, and assessing or dealing with staff or students, schools were prohibited from discriminating on the basis of sex, sexual orientation or gender identity. Measures for pregnant students stipulated that reasonable accommodation was obligatory to guarantee their right to education.

Additionally, the Act made it mandatory for the central government, as well as local authorities and all schools, to establish a Gender Equity Education Committee responsible for implementing gender equity education. The committee in each school would investigate and handle any incidents of gender-based violence. Cross-examination of the victim and disclosure of information were prohibited, while in cases where the victim was a student, their right to continue learning was guaranteed and disciplinary punishments for the perpetrator (such as counselling by a specialist or attendance at gender equity education classes) were stipulated. The Act's guiding definition of gender violence assumed that anyone, regardless of gender, could be either victim or perpetrator.

---

6   In the 2010s, along with "marriage equality," a right-wing backlash began vigor-ously attacking the phrases "sexual orientation" and "gender identity" as defined by the Gender Equity Education Act (Fukunaga 2022b).

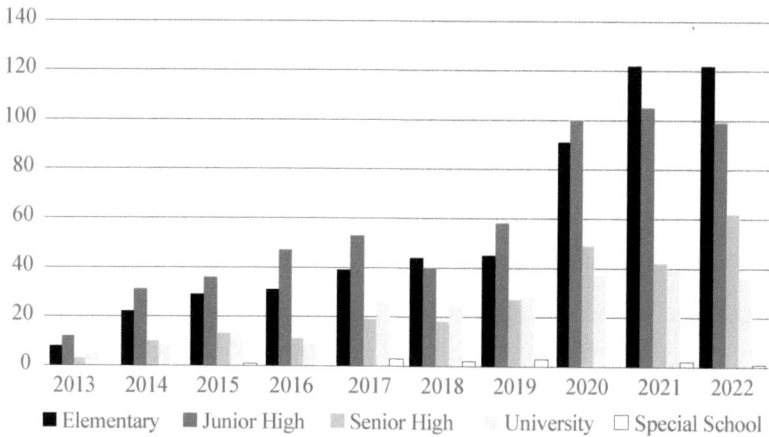

Figure 6.1: Incidence of sexual bullying in Taiwan by educational institution
(Compiled by the author based on Fig. 404-13, Statistics Bureau, Taiwan Ministry of Education, 2003)

The Ministry of Education launched a fact-finding survey on gender violence with the aim of achieving gender equity in schools. When the survey began in 2006, it addressed two types of violence, "sexual violence" and "sexual harassment;" in 2013 the concept of "sexual bullying" was introduced. According to the Ministry of Education's definition, "sexual bullying" refers to "verbal, physical or other violence that demeans, attacks or threatens the gendered characteristics or temperament, sexual orientation or gender identity of another person, but excluding sexual harassment" (Statistics Bureau, Ministry of Education 2023). Figure 6.1 shows changes by academic year in the number of incidents of "sexual bullying" in different educational institutions and indicates that the number of reports of sexual bullying increased dramatically in primary and secondary schools between 2013 and 2021. This should probably be interpreted as resulting from growing social recognition of the hitherto overlooked gender violence dubbed "sexual bullying," rather than a dramatic deterioration in school security.

Gender equity education, which has been in full swing in Taiwan since 2004, is an ongoing project that aims to reveal the various forms of gender-based violence and eliminate them through the involvement of various actors.

"Gender equity" and the politics of sexuality

This section will discuss how the new approach of "gender equity" became the nexus between queer and feminist politics, linking issues such as marriage equality and the promotion of transgender rights, and how solidarity between the two led to an "LGBT-friendly Taiwan."

A paradigm shift in gender mainstreaming

The passage of the Gender Equity Education Act by the Democratic Progressive Party (DPP) government in 2004 was positioned as a major achievement for gender mainstreaming in Taiwan, and was highly praised by the voting public. On this impetus, policies and measures aimed at gender mainstreaming were pushed forward, with "gender equity," encompassing the human rights of gender and sexual minorities, as established policy.

The Equality between Both Sexes in Employment Act (*Liangxing gongzuo pingdeng fa*) passed in 2001 was amended in 2007 to become the Act of Gender Equality in Employment (AGEE), "aligning it with gender mainstreaming principles." It prohibits discrimination based on sexual orientation or gender identity. The following debate on this amendment to the Act was observed in the Legislative Yuan:

> "Gender mainstreaming" has become a common perception in the global community as well as a prioritized measure of governments around the world ... The amendment from the "Equality between Both Sexes in Employment Act" to the "Act of Gender Equality in Employment" is intended to be in line with the principle of ensuring the gender diversity and difference [instituted by gender mainstreaming]. (Legislative Yuan 2009: 15)

The "gender diversity" mentioned here is of course an expression that assumes the existence of gender and sexual minorities. Similar moves can also be seen in the measures of local governments, such as the Gender Mainstreaming Plan announced by Kaohsiung City in December 2004, which also promoted the human rights of "gender and sexual minorities."

Gender mainstreaming in the Beijing Women's Conference's platform for action excluded discussion of gender and sexual minorities' human rights, but in Taiwan a paradigm shift in gender mainstreaming lead to the inclusion of gender and sexual minority rights.

Marriage equality and transgender rights

The Taiwanese women's movement and feminists led the new approach of "gender equality," providing a vital underpinning for propelling Taiwan towards becoming what the *New York Times* called "the most LGBT-friendly society in Asia" (October 29, 2014). Indeed, as the Gender Equity Education Law indicates, the rights of gender and sexual minorities in Taiwan have been guaranteed through the women's movement, which had acquired significant resources and legitimacy following democratization. Sharing the "gender equality" discourse has helped to create solidarity between feminist and queer movements, which eventually brought about marriage equality and the recognition of transgender rights.

The queer movement in Taiwan developed in the 1990s, influenced by the women's movement, and significantly expanded in the 2000s (Ho 2017; Shen 2019; Fukunaga 2017a, 2017b, 2022b, 2025). The Taiwan Alliance to Promote Civil Partnership Rights (TAPCPR), a key actor in bringing about marriage equality, is a prime example. TAPCPR is an offshoot of the Awakening Foundation, which had been a driving force for feminism in Taiwan and provided the alliance with financial and material resources such as offices, personnel and funds, as well as its ideological resources and goals.

The women's movement of the 1980s into the 1990s had prioritized revising the kinship chapter of the Civil Code, which strongly reflected misogynistic Confucian norms. Feminists considered that chapter to be the "root of patriarchy" (TAPCPR 2013); and saw the Awakening Foundation's amendment of the Civil Code as a means for realizing "gender equality" and "democratization" of the traditional household system (Shen 2019). The broad campaign to amend the Civil Code lost some steam in the mid-1990s after some degree of "gender equality" had been achieved through incremental legal reforms, but lesbian feminists affiliated with the Awakening Foundation continued their investigations, viewing the lingering heteronormativity in the kinship section of the Civil Code as a lingering problematic.

In 2006, the Awakening Foundation formed the Diverse Families Team (*Duoyuan de jiating xiaozu*) to research laws and regulations on same-sex partnership guarantees in other countries. In 2009, it established the Taiwan Alliance to Promote Civil Partnership Rights (TAPCPR) and sought solidarity with other queer organizations; and in 2013, TAPCPR published its draft of "Diverse Families" (*Duo yuan cheng jia*) and advocated a campaign for marriage equality. The subsequent achievement of marriage equality through amendment of the Civil Code was thus a direct inheritance of Taiwanese feminism. In fact, feminist legislators from DPP and women's movement organizations made significant contributions to realizing marriage equality both inside and outside of the Legislative Yuan.

The protection of transgender rights has also been positioned as a human rights issue to promote "gender equality," and various campaigns are underway: on September 23, 2021, the Taipei High Administrative Court ruled to allow a transgender woman who had not undergone gender affirmation surgery to change her legal gender. Furthermore, in December 2021, the Court requested a constitutional interpretation of a 2008 Ministry of the Interior Administrative Notice (*Neizhengbu xingzheng tongda*), which stipulated the removal of genitalia (penis and testicles, breasts, ovaries and/or uterus) as one of the requirements for changing legal gender, as it was suspected to be "unconstitutional."[7] The rationale was that "gender identity or attribution" is "the basis for maintaining human dignity and respecting the free development of the personality," and that "the right to determine one's gender based on the autonomy of the personality should be guaranteed by the Constitution" (Taipei High

---

7   Taiwan has no laws governing legal gender transition, and so the 2008 Ministry of the Interior Administrative Notice has been utilized instead. This notice requires that a doctor provide proof by means of a medical certificate that the genital organs (penis, testicles, breasts, ovaries, or uterus) have been surgically removed for a person to have completed gender transition.

Administrative Court 2021). Importantly, TAPCPR was the driving force behind these campaigns.

It is also worth noting that the transgender movement in Taiwan invoked the Convention on the Elimination of All Forms of Discrimination against Women (CEDAW) as a basis for eliminating the surgical prerequisites for changing legal gender.[8] Article 5(a) of the Convention requires parties to take all appropriate measures to:

> modify the social and cultural patterns of conduct of men and women, with a view to achieving the elimination of prejudices and customary and all other practices which are based on the idea of the inferiority or the superiority of either of the sexes or on stereotyped roles for men and women.

The transgender movement in Taiwan argued that forcing genital reassignment surgery at the time of legal gender transition violates this Article (Transgender Punk Activist 2014). In addition, in 2010 the Committee on the Elimination of Discrimination against Women published *Core Obligations of States Parties under Article 2 of the Convention on the Elimination of All Forms of Discrimination against Women*, No. 18, which identified "gender identity" as one of the elements of compound discrimination suffered by women. Taiwanese activists emphasize this point, arguing strongly that transwomen simultaneously experience not only discrimination against women but also homophobia and transphobia, and that despite this, transgender people have been excluded from all policy understandings and guarantees because they constitute a minority group (Transgender Punk Activist 2014). In this manner, transgender rights advocacy movements in Taiwan have mobilized the international

---

8   The Convention on the Elimination of All Forms of Discrimination against Women was adopted by the 34th UN General Assembly in 1979 and came into force in 1981. However, as Taiwan is not a member of the UN, it has not been allowed to ratify the Convention; it adopted the international human rights discourse of the Convention into domestic law in 2011.

human rights discourse of feminism and the women's movement, to great success.

The religious right and gender backlash

"Gender equality" in Taiwan developed by encompassing the human rights agenda of gender and sexual minorities, and precisely because of this, a backlash, mainly from the Protestant right, proceeded to mobilize in earnest around 2010.

While taking a pro-KMT (*Kuomintang*: Nationalist Party of China) stance during the Cold War, the Protestant right maintained a position of non-involvement in political activities, but in the late 2000s it began to organize the conservative movement on an "anti-homosexuality" platform. Huang (2017) points to three factors underpinning the Protestant right's promotion of political intervention: first, the state, which extolled anti-communist ideology and Confucian morality with the support of the United States during the Cold War, changed its role following the end of the Cold War and the formation of democratic political structures. The role of the state in the Republic of China – as the guardian of moral culture, symbolizing "orthodox China" – shifted to maintaining Taiwan's membership and standing in the international community, leading the way with liberal values such as "democracy" and "human rights." Ma Ying-jeou (KMT), who came to prominence in the late 1990s as a member of the political elite driving the new-era KMT, focused on "rights for homosexuals" among numerous human rights issues, exploiting this as a discursive resource to distance himself from the authoritarian KMT past and "barbaric" China (Fukunaga, 2025). Stigmatized during the Cold War through Confucian morality and male conscription, homosexuality was redefined by the state as a progressive human rights issue symbolizing the advent of a democratic era. This infuriated the Protestant right.

Second was the influence of religious networks within East Asia: in the 2000s, the impact of globalization led to increased Protestant interaction within the East Asia region, including South Korea, Hong Kong and Singapore. The influence of South Korea, internationally acclaimed as a successful example of Christian evangelicalism, was particularly significant, and the Protestant right in Taiwan emulated South Korea in adopting a unified worldview with "leading and transforming the nation" (*guodu zhuanhua*) as its mission. "Anti-homosexuality" was viewed as a movement to put this into practice.

Third, the 2010s saw the rise of religious entrepreneurs who integrated the secular and the religious. By exploiting secular discourses based on Chinese traditions and Confucian ideology, they contributed to the formation of a conservative civil coalition across religious and denominational lines.

Thus, the struggle over "gender equality" has intensified through feminist and queer politics, which has argued for gender-based justice, and conservative politics, which has rejected it. This tension is evident not only in Taiwan but in many other countries and regions, as well, and it will become increasingly necessary to consider discourses around gender equality from the perspective of transnational politics in future research.

Conclusion

The purpose of this chapter has been to elucidate how gender mainstreaming in Taiwan underwent a paradigm shift to define "gender equality" as inclusive of the human rights of gender and sexual minorities. Three important points stand out from an examination of the process of establishing the Gender Equity Education Act.

The first is that the period in which the Taiwanese women's movement and feminists burgeoned as actors intervening in the legislative process coincided with that in which social movements of gender and sexual minorities began to develop. Importantly, beyond the mere overlap in timing, it was already obvious by that stage that mainstream feminists, also, could not ignore the growing concern among teachers working in schools about homosexuality, or the findings of queer studies.

The second was the "discovery" of the vulnerability of young people deviating from heteronormativity by the feminists who drafted the Gender Equity Education Act. The impact on feminists of the death in 2000 of a junior high school student, Yeh Yung-Chih, was particularly strong, problematizing the fact that the existing concept of "equity between the two sexes" overlooked the "violence towards persons of diverse gender" and victimization of non-conforming children. As a result, the new approach of "gender equity" sought the elimination of discrimination based on sexual orientation or gender identity.

Finally, it was also noted that changes in macro-political structures, such as democratization and educational reforms, not only supported feminist interventions in the education sector, but also provided a drafting process widely accessible to a diverse range of researchers, activists and other citizens.

Starting with the Gender Equity Education Act passed in 2004, discrimination based on gender, sexual orientation and gender identity in the workplace was prohibited by the amended Act of Gender Equality in Employment (AGEE) in 2007. Then, in 2019, same-sex marriage became legal under the liberal government of President Tsai Ing-wen; and the surgical requirement for change of gender in legal status is expected soon to be abolished. Taiwan is now exercising a presence in terms of guaranteeing the rights of gender and sexual minorities, to the extent of being hailed at home and abroad as the most LGBT-friendly society in Asia. As a result, the discourse of homonationalism (Puar 2007), which *touts its national superiority and tolerance* to the international community, became mainstream in Taiwanese society in the 2010s, in contrast to Mainland China, which is considered reluctant to guarantee the rights of gender and sexual minorities (Ho 2017; Ning 2018; Fukunaga 2025).

While the guarantee of human rights for gender and sexual minorities was promoted in Taiwan through party politics, Taiwan's marginalized position in the international community facilitated it. The DPP government, established in 2000, has attempted to catch up with the international human rights discourse by promoting a "human rights state" and "human rights diplomacy."[9] In the context of China's rise in the international

---

9   It is also significant that for the DPP, which succeeded in overthrowing the KMT's
     authoritarian regime and expanding its support base by championing "democracy"

community since the 1970s, Taiwan has gradually lost political and legal recognition as a state through its experience of expulsion from the UN and severance of diplomatic relations with major nations, and thus has been unavoidably marginalized among the international community. For the DPP government, which sought to expand its survival space in the international community, the politics around "human rights nationhood" and "human rights diplomacy" was also a soft power strategy premised on differentiating itself from China while sharing the values of the UN, the US and other developed countries (Satō 2007). In this kind of DPP politics, the human rights of gender and sexual minorities were positioned as an issue to be resolved politically. For post-Cold War Taiwan, the self-image of being an LGBT-friendly nation became fuel for Taiwanese nationalism that extolled its membership in the global developed world while othering itself vis-à-vis China, its counterpart in a divided nation (Fukunaga 2025).

More recently, alarmist claims "radical LGBT education is progressing in schools overseas" and "problems are occurring in transgender education" have been spreading both nationally and internationally. The growing transnational anti-gender movement is intensifying, especially in its increasing attacks on homosexuality and transgender people, as well as on inclusive sexuality education that recognizes the human rights of gender and sexual minorities. At present, as some feminists are actively participating in the campaign against gender and sexual minorities (Shimizu 2021; 2022), I conclude this chapter, which has highlighted the significance of the intersection of feminist and queer politics based on empirical research, by arguing that this can constitute a critical intervention against the backlash.

---

and "human rights," women's rights and the progressive issue of gender and sexual minority rights were highly compatible with party's platform (Fukunaga 2017a).

7 Is Vietnam "Tolerant of Gender and Sexual Minorities"? Changing Policies and Norms around Same-sex Marriage and Gender Reassignment

Nara Oda

Introduction

In 2015, reports began to appear in the Japanese and European mainstream media that "Vietnam is a gay-friendly country." For example, "Vietnam opens up to same-sex marriage, 'de facto acceptance' of repeal of regulations" (Sasaki 2015) and "Vietnam takes gay-rights lead in SE Asia" (Bloomberg 2015). Furthermore, the relaxation of requirements for registering a change of gender in resident identification in 2015 was reported as "Vietnamese law change introduces transgender rights" (Agence France-Presse 2015) and in 2016 Vietnam was identified as one of "Six countries making progress on LGBT rights" (Banning-Lover and Clarke 2016).

Vietnam's high profile in these and similar reports can perhaps be attributed at least in part to surprise that the country's repressive one-party system, which allows no political diversity, had been receptive to lobbying by the gender and sexual minorities community and supporters' groups, and that minority rights (appeared to) have been guaranteed. Since the beginning of the Đổi mới (meaning "renovation," hereafter: Doi Moi) policy in 1986, restrictions on various aspects of life in Vietnam had been eased to varying degrees. Press reports of a country that is "friendly" to gender and sexual minorities can be seen as part of this trend.

Indeed, the legalization of same-sex marriage and gender reassignment (gender reassignment surgery and changing registered gender) were openly debated in Vietnam, for the first time in its history, several years before these reports appeared. In both debates, awareness-raising campaigns targeting both the government and the public were conducted by gender and sexual minorities and advocacy groups.

However, so far, these campaigns have not fully achieved their objectives. The legal ban on same-sex marriage was lifted, but same-sex marriage has not been legalized. Furthermore, there is no legal right to change gender without undergoing gender reassignment surgery, and no specific procedures or standards have been established for gender reassignment procedures. Importantly, these two debates are not proceeding hand-in-hand, or following parallel trajectories towards legalization, and thus it is hard to argue collectively that Vietnam is "making progress on LGBT rights." Examining the debates about legal reform of these two issues may provide insight into how gender and sexual minorities and advocacy groups seek to transform society in a context of limited political change and will contribute to better understanding family and gender norms in Vietnam.

Normative marriage and illegal marriage

The "desirable" family as defined by the law

In Vietnam, the Law on Marriage and Family and the Civil Code govern legal marriage. Same-sex marriage was not prohibited by these laws until an amendment to the Law on Marriage and Family in 2000.

The original Law on Marriage and Family was adopted by the National Assembly of the Democratic Republic of Vietnam (DRV) in 1959 (promulgated in 1960) and remained in force until 1986, when the Doi Moi reforms were adopted.[1] This Law was consistent with the policies of the socialist nationalist movement in Vietnam at the time, which rejected feudal customs, set a minimum age for marriage, and advocated for the liberation of women and gender equality (Thư Viện Pháp Luật a).

---

1   The Law on Marriage and Family presented in this chapter is drawn from an online database containing Vietnamese legislation (thuvienphapluat.com), unless otherwise noted.

Nevertheless, while it was consistent with certain "women's liberation" values, such as outlawing bigamy, it also sustained some conventional family norms, such as the stipulation of marriage as being between one husband and one wife, assuming this to mean between one male and one female.

Following Doi Moi in 1986, various social spheres enjoyed varying degrees of liberalization, but the new family policy tightened family norms: both the amended Law on Marriage and Family of 1986 and the 1992 Constitution deemed the family to be a fundamental "cell" of society (Thư Viện Pháp Luật b and c). These changes reflected the state's view that society is constituted by "family" units recognized by the state.

As Phinney points out, as the state dismantled its collectivized economic and social systems after Doi Moi reform, it appears that the state shifted its focus and expectations to sustain the society onto the remaining social unit: the family. For Vietnam to survive in the global market, the state focuses on the family unit as a resource as entities capable of bearing responsibility for nation-building (Phinney 2008: 330). The state's idea of the ideal family in the Law on Marriage and Family and Constitution reflects that the state will no longer guarantee economic and social systems as before, but instead expects each family unit to bear that responsibility.

Despite numerous amendments, the image of the family as a single unit consisting of one man, one woman, and their children remains unchanged. In addition to the "one husband, one wife" provision in the Law on Marriage and Family, the 2013 Constitution also states that "men and women have the right to marry and divorce each other" (Article 36) (Thư Viện Pháp Luật e).

Furthermore, although amendments to the Law on Marriage and Family in 2014 made Vietnam the first country in South-East Asia to authorize surrogate motherhood, this should be understood in the context of the image of the traditional family. Only a married couple – a man and a woman in a marital relationship – can engage a surrogate mother (Thư Viện Pháp Luật f). Here, again, the government has endorsed a family configuration that consists of a married heterosexual couple and children.

While a spouse and children has long been important in Vietnamese culture, these laws indicate that the state also prioritizes the family unit of a married man and woman and their children, and thus reinforces the norm of the heterosexual couple.

The prohibition of same-sex marriage and the popularity of same-sex weddings

Nevertheless, same-sex marriage was not prohibited by the Law on Marriage and Family or any other laws until 2000, when amendments to the Law on Marriage and Family specified same-sex marriage, bigamy, and marriage between immediate relatives as "cases in which marriage is prohibited" (Article 10, Thư Viện Pháp Luật d; Bui 2015).

One of the triggers for explicitly banning same-sex marriage at the time was a number of weddings of high-profile same-sex couples reported in the media. The earliest case that I can confirm was a wedding held in 1997 at a restaurant in Ho Chi Minh City with over 100 guests.[2] Although the administration did not recognize the marriage, the authorities did not prevent the wedding ceremony or reception. In 1998, a female couple wed in Vinh Long Province in the southern Mekong Delta, but the marriage was also declared invalid (Yomiuri Shimbun 1998; UNDP, USAID 2014). By this time, a proposal to amend the Marriage and Family Law to prohibit same-sex marriages had already been debated at the National Assembly, and in 2000, same-sex marriages were explicitly prohibited.

Furthermore, in 2001, a Government Protocol (87/2001/NĐ-CP) imposed a fine of between VND100,000 and VND500,000 for "same-sex marriages." In addition, a 2005 Ministerial Decree (09/2005/TT-BCA) detailing regulations in the "Protocol on Assembly"[3] (38/2005/NĐ-CP) issued by the Ministry of Public Security (*Công an Nhân dân*, the

---

2   The Immigration and Refugee Board of Canada Report, available on the UNHCR website, provides further details (Immigration and Refugee Board of Canada 2010).

3   This states that prior application to the People's Committee is required for gatherings and demonstrations of five or more people in public places (*Viet-Jo* 2005).

public security force, which provides both national security and regular policing), subjected weddings to police crackdowns.

Nevertheless, same-sex weddings continued to be held in Ho Chi Minh City and Hanoi,[4] and by 2010, the couples involved were publishing videos and photos online. The absence of news headlines reporting that the authorities had intervened suggests that the decision to apply penalties was at the discretion of the authorities.

In 2012, however, local authorities intervened in the weddings of three same-sex couples. One of these weddings was widely reported in the Vietnamese national media,[5] and was a major shock to the gender and sexual minority communities. The reported case was a male couple[6] in Ha Tien in the southern Kien Giang province.[7] Although local authorities had tacitly approved the wedding reception, they later fined the couple 200,000VND (approximately USD9.60 at the time) (Thiên Kim, 2012).

Interestingly, most of the same-sex weddings reported have been in the south. Vietnamese studies have found that patriarchal-based family norms appear to be stronger in the north than in the south of the country. Furthermore, the south, which had been integrated into Vietnamese society later than the northern region, appears to be a more open society than the north; and these findings may reflect regional differences in the acceptability of same-sex weddings. Many of the same-sex weddings in the south reported in the press appear to have included family members in the ceremonies. The intervention of local authorities in these weddings appear to have been particularly shocking in southern society and

---

4   A lesbian couple who wed in Hanoi in 2010 drew attention after posting their wedding photos on the internet, as did a male couple who wed in the same year at a luxury hotel in Ho Chi Minh City.

5   The event was reported with photos in the online media vietnam.net and the *Tuổi trẻ* newspaper, which has the largest circulation in the country.

6   The reported photograph of a man and two women – presumably parents or relatives – standing next to a male couple in tuxedos toasting in front of a champagne tower suggests that they were being congratulated by the people around them.

7   Ha Tien, Kien Giang Province, is a port city in the Mekong Delta bordering Cambodia with a population of fewer than 50,000.

mobilized an anti-discrimination movement to campaign for official recognition of same-sex marriages.

The campaign for recognition of same-sex marriage

A movement by gender and sexual minorities

Although the movement for the legalization of same-sex marriage did not take off until 2012, it built on previous consciousness-raising campaigns for the legalization and social acceptance of same-sex marriage.

There are places in Hanoi and Ho Chi Minh City where, reputedly, "gay men used to gather in the old days," but these men did not agitate to change the status quo. Sexual and gender minorities had to live either as members of special occupational categories or by keeping their sexual orientation secret, and it was taken for granted that they would conform to the norms of the majority.[8]

It was only after Vietnam introduced internet services in late 1997 (Endō 2012: 387) that gender and sexual communities in Vietnam began to mobilize. An online bulletin board ("The Forum") was created, becoming a place for both personal encounters and for forming personal networks for activism.[9] From 2004 to 2006, large numbers of

---

8   An article on the life of 73-year-old Mr. Hung (Trâm Anh 2012), "The story of the oldest homosexual person who came out in Vietnam," shows examples of how gay men were forced to follow the norms of the majority. Mr. Hung, born in Hanoi, hid his sexual orientation from others and thought that it was caused by a disease he had when he was young. Despite his efforts to avoid it, he ended up married to a woman and they had a child. After family life failed, he had relations with dozens of men. Although he once had a long relationship with a man who he supported financially, the partner was also unwillingly married to a woman and had children. Around the age of 73, he came out publicly as homosexual after meeting a leader of an HIV prevention organization, who had explained that homosexuality is not a disease and should be respected. After coming out he joined an HIV prevention organization. His life story highlights family values and norms in modern Vietnam and how the mainstream population views homosexual people.

9   The above flow of information is based on an interview with P.K.B. on September 18, 2018. According to Nguyen Hai Yen, a long-term activist for sexual and gender minorities rights in Vietnam, representative forums include Bangai.net, founded in 2003 by overseas Vietnamese; and omoi.org, founded by a lesbian in the Vietnamese community in the US in the 1990s (Hanoi Pride 2018).

homosexuals, particularly gay men, began posting on the forum, with some forming groups and developing consciousness-raising campaigns against discrimination in conjunction with overseas activists.[10] Since then, the internet, particularly social networking services, has been an influential platform not only for creating individual connections among gender and sexual minorities but also for campaigning and advocating for their human rights.

The first civic organization in Vietnam seeking gender and sexual minorities' rights was ICS (Information Connecting and Sharing), established in 2008, created by the new non-governmental organization, iSEE (Institute for Studies of Society, Economics, and Environment). Subsequently, CCIHP (Center for Creative Initiatives in Health and Population), CSAGA (Center for Studies and Applied Sciences in Gender, Family, Women and Adolescents), and other campaigning organizations were established by gender and sexual minorities and their supporters.

These organizations conducted activities such as seminars for media professionals to raise awareness about discrimination against gender and sexual minorities, an art exhibition featuring homosexuality (2009), and the production and screening of a documentary film about a lesbian couple (2011) (Kim Anh 2018). Furthermore, since 2013, six organizations have grown from ICS. Among these groups, the pioneering ICS and iSEE led the movement towards legalizing same-sex marriage (see Phạm 2022).

The movement's outreach

In May 2012, the Ministry of Justice began working on an amendment to the Law on Marriage and Family. In the process, it sought input from relevant organizations, including the United Nations Development Program (UNDP), which was developing a project to bring the law in Vietnam up to "international standards" (Ủy ban Quốc gia phòng chống

---

10 Leading rights and consciousness-raising organizations included ILGA ASIA (International Lesbian, Gay, Bisexual, Transgender and Intersex Association), a coalition of organizations from the Middle East, West and South-East Asia, and the Asia-Pacific. Some of its local members have participated in campaigns of APTN (Asia Pacific Transgender Network), which works in the region (Hanoi Pride 2018).

AIDS, ma túy, mại dâm 2012). iSEE took the lead in advocating to the Ministry of Justice, in collaboration with UNDP (Oosterhoff et al. 2014: 31–32). In 2009 ICS and iSEE organized consciousness-raising seminars for media and photographic exhibitions for public viewing, followed by several events organized by other groups within Vietnam (Phan 2018). This advocacy lead to, in October 2012, the National Assembly's Committee inviting researchers on same-sex marriage from the Netherlands and the USA to a workshop on social affairs organized in conjunction with the Vietnamese Government and UNDP (Sanders 2015b). These efforts, backed by international organizations, were influential within the Ministries of Justice and Health.

Aside from these events targeting policy makers, the influence of cultural events and art exhibitions is notable. Maika Elan's series of photographs titled Pink Choice was exhibited at the Goethe Institute in Hanoi in 2012 and later won the World Press Photo first prize for stories of Contemporary Issues in 2013.[11] The CCIHP also created an online exhibition on its website titled "The Moments in Life," archiving gender and sexual minorities' personal materials including pre-2000s printed materials. These cultural events directly impacted the mainstream population, especially in the cities.

By July 2013, the Minister of Justice announced that same-sex couples needed a legal framework for marriage, and the same-sex marriage debate began to accelerate. Notably, specific issues for consideration included legal rights to cohabitation, assets and child support.[12]

Around the same time, the Ministry of Health also recommended legalization. The Ministry stated that:

---

11 See Maika Elan's website https://maikaelan.com and https://www.worldpressphoto. org/collection/photo-contest/2013/maika-elan/1. Her photographs include one of Mr. Hung, the 73- year-old whose coming out story was mentioned above.

12 The Ministry stated that the first step was to create a framework for protecting the legal rights of same-sex couples who were already living together, and the next step would be to license same-sex marriages (Võ et al. 2013).

...medical science considers homosexuality and bisexuality not to be diseases, nor as targets for treatment. The law prohibits same-sex marriage in light of its defiance of social traditions and customs, and its impact on childbirth and upbringing... however, homosexuals, too, have the right to live normally and pursue happiness just like any other persons, and also have obligations towards the government and society. (Lan Anh 2013)

In this manner, the Ministries of Justice and Health announced their official support for the legalization of same-sex marriage. However, these announcements were not without controversy: there was a conservative faction within the Ministry of Justice that insisted that the current Marriage and Family Law should remain unchanged. Furthermore, opinion was divided in the National Assembly's Committee on Social Affairs between those in favor of legalization, such as the Minister of Justice, and those who opposed it in the belief that marriage should be between a man and a woman and "same-sex marriage goes against social morality and Vietnamese family traditions, and cannot maintain the species" (Kim Thanh 2013).

Social outreach: The "I do" campaign

After the wedding receptions in Kien Giang Province were cancelled, calls for the legalization of same-sex marriage grew louder and more widespread. From October 2013, iSEE and other advocacy groups launched the "I do" (*Tôi đồng ý*) campaign to further raise awareness among the mainstream population and bring public opinion to the National Assembly through a petition to legalize same-sex marriage and develop associated institutions.

The 8300 signatures collected on the petition (Tuoi Tre News 2013) were sent to all 500 National Assembly members along with campaign pamphlets, but only four or five responded.[13] In a society where it is rare

---

13 According to an interview with P.K.B., Hanoi Pride 2018 Secretariat, September 18, 2018.

to publicly challenge official views and policies, it would be reasonable for advocacy groups to expect a sluggish response to the petition drive, but the widely reported wedding interventions had brought the issue to the attention of a broad domestic audience, as evidenced by the 70,000 "likes" on the campaign's Facebook page.

Nevertheless, the parliamentary sitting in November 2013 did not endorse the legalization of same-sex marriage. It did, however, pass a new Government Protocol (110/2013/NĐ-CP) which removed the provisions that subjected same-sex weddings to fines. This removed one of the grounds for public authorities to intervene in same-sex wedding ceremonies, even though such marriages were still not legally recognized. Subsequently, further debate on the pros and cons of legalizing same-sex marriage lead to amendments to the Law on Marriage and Family.

The 2014 amendments to the Law on Marriage and Family (effective January 1, 2016) (Thư Viện Pháp Luật f) abolished a clause prohibiting same-sex marriage by the removal of "between people of the same sex" (paragraph 5) from the list of "cases where marriage is prohibited" (Article 10). At the same time, however, the new Law on Marriage and Family included a clause stating that "the State shall not recognize marriages between persons of the same sex" (Article 8, paragraph 2). Thus, contrary to the reports in the international media cited at the beginning of this chapter, the law reiterated that same-sex marriages were still not officially recognized. Although same-sex weddings were no longer prohibited, such ceremonies did not result in a legally recognized "marriage." Instead, these amendments simply returned Vietnam to a time when holding a wedding ceremony *per se* was not prohibited or punishable. However, the growing visibility of those seeking legal recognition of such marriages on a par with heterosexual marriages, and the growing momentum towards social recognition is markedly different. In this respect, it is fair to say that there has been some, albeit limited, progress towards legalizing same-sex marriage.

The question of "love" vis-à-vis the political arena

As discussed, the various associations of gender and sexual minorities and their supporters grew more active and diversified from the mid-2000s. The relationships between these organizations and the government appear to be cordial, with few tensions between them. Analysis has shown that this was an intentional strategy that the organizations adopted (Oosterhoff et al. 2014; Phạm 2022). Challenging the status quo in a one-party state that does not legally recognize the basic human rights of certain people could be seen as constituting political criticism of the party. However, these groups were careful to not employ critical language about the political situation, instead promoting an attitude that can be summed up in the phrase "love is fair," which, as Phạm (2022) observes, successfully avoided criticizing the government by appealing to emotions rather than political issues.

Consequently, the government tolerated the activities of gender and sexual minorities groups. "In Vietnam, as long as it doesn't touch on 'politics,' it's okay; LGBT issues are not considered political issues."[14] In the political arena, including in the Ministry of Justice, this position arguably enabled the Vietnamese government to dodge international criticism for repressing political activity. For conservatives, too, allowing "marriage" in a ceremonial capacity, but not recognizing marriage rights, could be viewed as an attempt to circumvent criticism while protecting their view of the family.

Achievements and limitations of the consciousness-raising campaign

Vietnam's first pride parade

It was under such circumstances that the first pride parade was held in Vietnam in 2012. Notice of the Hanoi Pride event was posted on Facebook and the event took place in August.[15] After some coordination with the

---

14 Interview with a journalist from a newspaper company, September 2017.
15 See Oosterhoff et al. (2014) for further details.

authorities in Hanoi, rather than marching in the streets, approximately 100 people pedaled around Hanoi city center on bicycles. The following year, around 1,000 people gathered in Ho Chi Minh City for a pride event that was publicized on social networking sites. Since then, pride events have continued to be held in ever increasing numbers of locations and attract more participants throughout Vietnam, especially among young LGBTIQ+ people or their allies. Unlike the "I do" campaign, Pride events are not focused on a single-issue but involve many gender and sexual minorities and their supporters and have been held annually since 2012.

The inaugural pride event was organized by a volunteer for an advocacy organization who had studied in the United States and wanted to make the "pride parade" a reality in Vietnam. Importantly, it seems that official permission has never been given for these parades. The bicycle rally appears to have offered the organizers another way to hold a "pride parade." Either way, in Ho Chi Minh City, the Viet Pride event has become an annual fixture, with participants gathering on the largest pedestrian street in the city center.

In both Hanoi Pride and Viet Pride, exhibitions and lectures were held in small venues in the city throughout the event. In 2013, Hanoi Pride became a three-day event, and on its final day in 2014, the Hanoi bicycle rally attracted 300 participants. In 2017, the event ran for a full week, and reportedly drew about 2000 participants. Foreign organizations were conspicuous sponsors of the series of programs, with the German Goethe-Institute, the American Club and the Embassy of Sweden providing sponsorship and venues.[16]

For example, in Hanoi Pride 2018, each venue hosted a diverse program that, unlike the campaign to legalize same-sex marriage, was not just about "the question of love." In addition to an exhibition on the heritage of the movement, there was also a workshop on AIDS prevention drugs sponsored by the US Centers for Disease Control and Prevention (CDC), a talk show featuring the parents of people who had come out as

---

16 In 2014, US Ambassador Osius was posted to Hanoi with his same-sex partner and adopted child. The family was positively depicted in the press (Dương Ngọc 2016).

Photo 7.1: 'Pride' event in Long An Province in southern Vietnam, projected in an exhibition hall in Hanoi. (photo by author, September 17, 2018)

gender and sexual minorities, and Hanoi's first drag show in conjunction with an art exhibition introducing international drag culture (rather than Vietnamese cross-dressing).

Internet-driven developments were also prominent in Hanoi Pride. In 2018, there were pride events in more provinces than ever before (Interview with P.K.B., September 18, 2018). In provinces where there were few participants, photographs were taken of individuals or small groups holding rainbow flags, and slides of these were projected in an exhibition hall in Hanoi.

At these events, the core staff and participants were born in the 1990s and 2000s and spoke English fluently. The generation born and raised after the Doi Moi reforms (those born in the 1990s, sometimes referred to as the "9X" generation)[17] lead the movement. After a hiatus of three years due to the COVID-19 pandemic, Pride Week was held on-site again

---

17 In Vietnam, the 9X generation refers to a cohort born after the Doi Moi reforms who grew up with information technology as Vietnam was becoming a more open society. The term is sometimes used derogatorily, but it generally refers to their proficiency with technology and openness to the broader world. They are seen as more rebellious and progressive than older generations, and more willing to question traditions and authorities (Muc Tim 2008).

in 2022. In Hanoi, the final day featured the cyclo (*xích lô*), Vietnamese pedicab and bicycle ride around the city, as well as a "parade" sponsored and joined by UN, European, and US embassy officials that wended its way through a weekend pedestrian precinct. Moving through crowds of people enjoying their day off was a strategic way for the Vietnamese gender and sexual minorities rights movement to maintain good relations with the government, and to continue organizing Hanoi Pride events.

The "visibility of existence" and the generation gap

A member of the Hanoi Pride secretariat noted that one of the achievements of the movement to date has been to "shift the conversation." Whereas in the past, when people talked about gender and sexual minorities, the focus was on health issues (HIV/AIDS) or the bullying of students, more recently they have become "ordinary topics." However, he also identified a "lack of solidarity with the older generation" as a major issue.

The "older generation" was apparently those "in their mid-thirties" and above (as of 2018). He speculated that because the movement was new and had a "youthful atmosphere," and due to fears that they might suffer from discrimination if their sexuality were made public, the older generation seemed to find it difficult to participate.

My informant added that compared to other countries where social oppression of gender and sexual minorities could be life-threatening, Vietnam's "non-threatening atmosphere" may have contributed to the movement's lack of appeal to the "older" generation. He explained that people were able to marry heterosexually at a young age and have children (or give birth) in line with family norms, and then either engage in homosexual activities or cross-dressing secretly outside their marriage (Interview with P.K.B., September 18, 2018). However, this kind of "escape" may have only been available to gay men. For married lesbians or bisexual women, the pressure to reproduce within the family, such as to raise children or grandchildren, was likely much greater than for men.

Another factor cited as hindering the "older generation's" participation is their respective relationships with the rest of the world. The younger people at the heart of the movement have strong links with international organizations and are intent on promoting their activities abroad in English. Thus, there seems to be a difference in the degree of penetration of "international standards" between those who are fluent in English and those who are not (especially those educated before Doi Moi, when there were strong ties with socialist countries), which may make it difficult to find common ground. In recent years, with the introduction of HIV prevention programs funded by international organizations, gender and sexual minorities involved in the movement have much greater consciousness of "international standards." Regarding the debate on legalizing same-sex marriage, there is arguably a sizeable gap in awareness between the generations that advocates legalization as a personal freedom and a right, and the generations that have matured in an environment in which seeking social recognition of their sexual orientation was unimaginable.

Reasons for differences in enthusiasm

Ms. A, a lesbian born in 1985, says that if she had a partner, she would "proudly introduce her as a partner and want her to be acknowledged by others" (interview, September 17, 2018), but explains that she could not ride the wave of seeking social recognition and legalized marriage. Her lack of interest in activism confirms the analysis above. Ms. A had been aware of her attraction to women for as long as she could remember, but throughout her life from elementary school to university, she was never particularly questioned about her sexual orientation. However, she did suffer from her family's lack of understanding and their pressure to marry a man.

However, recently, her brother, who had lived in the US for a time, has reportedly come to understand her sexual orientation and has encouraged her mother to understand it, as well. Although she has not told her father, Ms. A is no longer as uncomfortable in the family home. Despite strong social pressure to get married, she intends to stay unmarried. But, as noted, she is not interested in the campaign for same-sex marriage rights because if she became involved in the movement, it "would mean coming to confront that issue, and that would be painful for me to think only about it." Thus, although she expresses understanding of the campaign to legalize same-sex marriage, she keeps her distance from the community.

How should Ms. A's attitude be understood? The gender and sexual minorities and supporter groups we have seen earlier were energetically trying to address the inequalities suffered by homosexuals by making the legalization of same-sex marriage a point of contention. The presence of couples parading the phrase "Love is marriage" ("*Yêu là cưới*") in the "I do" campaign (RFI 2013) strategically appeals to emotions while confirming the institution of marriage as a robust social norm.

This slogan leaves room for questioning whether love that is not based in the institution of marriage is unacceptable. If one does not particularly wish to construct a relationship through marriage, then legalizing same-sex marriage will not confer any new rights for oneself. Moreover, as the "older generation" have experienced, it is not necessary to be legally married for lovers to build a relationship with one another. If unofficial same-sex weddings and marriages are merely about social recognition, then agitating for same-sex marriage may not have much appeal to such people.

Advocacy organizations have sought to change the legal system concerning marriage. By calling for legal marriage between people who love each other, asking, for example: "How can the law forbid two people to love each other?" (Thiên Kim 2012), they have advanced their cause by garnering increasing support from the mainstream population. However, the same-sex marriage debate stalled. It seems that trying to put love at the center of the campaign was not effective at shifting the government's position on same-sex marriage. As we have seen, for the government, the family is the basic unit of economic production and intergenerational security; and this is their basis for choosing to restrict marriage to the conventional family unit of a heterosexual couple and children. That said, the campaign appears to have had some success in shifting the government's attitude, as can be seen in the lifting of the prohibition on same-sex weddings, resulting in gaining better reputation from overseas.[18]

Debates on gender reassignment

Fixed gender classifications

By contrast, in 2015, legal reforms concerning change of gender after gender reassignment surgery progressed smoothly. This difference might be attributable to the historical development of gender norms in Vietnamese society.

Along with the debate on same-sex marriage, a point of contention for gender and sexual minorities and their allies concerns gender reassignment treatment. Such treatment, including surgery and hormone injections, was not legal in Vietnam, and transgender people sought surgery outside the country (mostly in Thailand), or received hormone treatment on the black market. However, following reforms of the Civil Code in 2015, gender reassignment treatment is no longer illegal, and transgender people are allowed to change their gender in the family register (*hộ tịch*) and newly introduced Identity card from 2016 (*Căn cước*) after reassignment.[19] In Vietnam, the family register and identity cards contain information relating to administrative procedures, from details of place of residence, registration of births, deaths and marriages, to property ownership. This lead to various forms of discrimination against transgender and cross-dressing people, especially in employment, because their gender according to the family register differed from their

---

18 In 2023, the "I do" campaign was rekindled after 10 years by a coalition of advocacy groups including iSEE. The campaign this time seems to be emphasizing the economic effects of legalizing same-sex marriage. The strategy was outlined in a 2021 report titled "Report on the Economic Impact Assessment of Same-sex Marriage in Vietnam" (Trung tâm Nghiên cứu Kinh tế và Chiến lược Việt Nam (VESS) and Viện nghiên cứu Xã hội, Kinh tế và Môi trường (iSEE) 2021) and presented at a Viet Pride event organized by ICS in September 2024.

19 Before 2015, in the southeastern province of Binh Phuoc, there were cases of local authorities approving gender changes on household registers, only to later revoke them; and the cadres who had approved them were punished (Phước Hiệp 2013).

presentation, and those affected sought a resolution to these issues (Hanoi Pride 2018).[20]

This issue highlights how Vietnamese society has regarded those who have "strayed" from the two orthodox genders, and how gender and sexual minorities have established their identities while reconciling with the prevailing social gaze.

According to Tran, who studied representations of Vietnamese gender and sexual minorities, the first dictionary to include the word "gender" (*giới tính*) as used today was a Spanish–Vietnamese dictionary published in Cuba in 1971 (Tran 2011: 51). The Vietnamese term next appears in a 1977 Vietnamese dictionary, which defines it as "a physical or psychological characteristic that distinguishes between men and women, or between females and males." (Tran 2011: 51).

Tran also points out that French–Vietnamese dictionaries published during the French colonial period from 1887 translate *sexe* as three words (*loại, giống, thứ*), each meaning "(biological) category," and *sexuelle* as "belonging to a category (of man or woman, male or female)," based on the biological classification into two sexes, and is not exclusive to humans.

Thus, it can be assumed that *giới tính*, which corresponds to "sex/gender" as used today, was not much used during the French colonial period and only became widespread after the re-unification of North and South Vietnam in the mid-1970s. What is certain is that the definition matching physical and psychological characteristics to one of the two sexes was the prevailing definition.

Similarly, male homosexuals were referred to colloquially as *pe-de* (*be-de*), a pejorative term derived from the French *pédérastie* (male

---

20 Some transgender people, or cross-dressers, make a living by performing in singing and dancing troupes in theaters, at funerals, or in local towns, particularly in the south. The documentary film *Madame Phung's Last Journey* (2014) shows the daily life of a traveling singing group, capturing both the fascination and the hostility of the locals. In the early the 2010s a group of cross-dressers (transvestites) or MTFs pooled their resources to open a restaurant to support themselves. Starting very modestly, it soon became locally popular, and as they expanded they were able to help other people in similar situations (see Châu Mỹ 2022).

homosexuality),[21] which was commonly used in overseas Vietnamese communities and in South Vietnam from around the 1960s and 1970s (Tran 2011: 79). According to Tran, it first appeared in print in Vietnam in a four-part report in the Ho Chi Minh City Public Security Newspaper called "Pede Love" (1987). It portrayed men who have sex with men as "real *pede*," a sickness, and those who dress as the opposite sex (women) as "false *pede*," which was not a sickness. Thus, this series pathologized male homosexual relations. It also linked them to HIV infection, which was beginning to emerge at the time (Tran 2011: 84–86). A similarly nuanced designation, *ô-môi*, was established for female homosexuals. This is believed to be derived from *homosexuelle*, or from the name of a fruit that resembles female genitalia. Other names used, such as *bóng*, meaning "shadow," were associated with illness, gloom and something to be hidden (Tran 2011: 82–83).

Neutral designations include the entries "homosexual: same-sex sexual relationship" and "lesbian: a woman who likes a woman of the same sex" (Đào ed. 1950), found in a 1950 French–Vietnamese dictionary, and "*Đồng tính luyên ái* (same-sex love)" (Đào ed. 1957) in a 1957 Chinese–Vietnamese dictionary, with the added note: "*amour homosexual.*" However, no word indicating bisexuality is found in either.

Currently, the designations *người đồng tính nam/nữ*, *người song tính* and *người chuyển giới*, which can be directly translated as "male/female homosexual," "bisexual" or "transsexual," are common in official documents and in the media. The terms "LGBT," "gay," "les," "bi," and "*Cộng đồng* LGBT (LGBT community)" are also frequently used by gender and sexual minorities activists and the support groups mentioned above.

We can find no evidence of nomenclature for a "third gender" in Vietnam. The phrase *ái nam ái nữ*, which can be written in Chinese characters as "love man, love woman," means "androgynous," or "hermaphroditic," and both concepts are based on a male-female-dichotomy. Sometimes

---

21 A 1936 French-Vietnamese dictionary refers to *pederastie* as "雞姦" (Đào ed. 1936).

this term is applied to individuals, implying an effeminate man (for example, in the case of the spiritual mediums described below) (Norton 2006: 68), but it does not directly refer to transgender people. People who waver between female and male genders do not have a vernacular name that is shared by society, or else are not assumed to be situated as a specific group.

Gender fluctuations and gender norms in places of faith

These norms that assume the two genders of male and female are also apparent in spaces of faith where gender or sexual fluctuations were recognized and accepted.

In Vietnam, spiritual mediums of the *Đạo Mẫu* (Mother Goddess Worship), a folk belief to worship the goddess as a mother of the world for good health and prosperity, still attracts many local people. During rituals mediums change costumes and gestures in accordance with the deities who possess them, while dancing to music played by a band. The practice was banned as a superstition during the strict socialist era, but after the Doi Moi reforms, the ban was lifted and increasing numbers of people have begun to participate.

Many *Đạo Mẫu* mediums are women, who perform rituals in the guise of a goddess. However, there are also male mediums who dress in women's clothing and make up, and it is understood that many male mediums are homosexuals, transsexuals or cross dressers.[22] Recently, the number of mediums has been steadily increasing, especially among the young males of the 9X generation. Through practices of *Đạo Mẫu* and its rituals, they are finding empowerment through expressing emotions and identity within modern Vietnamese society (Vũ 2016: 20–27).

---

22 A 1975 psychiatric study explained that male "witch doctors" who behaved like women were called *bong cái* in the south and *đồng cô* in the north (Heiman and Cao 1975), but it does not explain how these spirit mediums defined their gender and sexual identities. However, in the documentary film *Love Man Love Woman* (2007) by Nguyễn Trinh Thi, a male spirit medium defines himself as homosexual. The film shows how homosexuals and those who were regarded as effeminate practice *Đạo Mẫu* in modern Vietnam under the influence of Confucianism.

Mediums are believed to transcend gender during rituals when they can be possessed by a personality with a different gender from their own. However, their vacillation between the two genders does not disrupt so-called masculine and feminine gender norms (Norton 2006: 68). The shamans behave as "feminine" or "masculine" depending on the personality who has possessed them.

Đạo Mẫu was added to the World Intangible Cultural Heritage List in 2016.[23] Once suppressed by the state, the mediums of Đạo Mẫu have gradually incorporated into the "good citizens" who make up the Vietnamese state, while maintaining gender norms, as discussed in the Introduction.

Gender norms and sexuality

Even if Đạo Mẫu revives, that does not resolve the issues surrounding gender reassignment surgery. Similar to the campaign for legalizing same-sex marriage, the gender and sexual minorities and advocacy groups aimed to institutionalize gender reassignment and thereby change society through the legal system.

In 2015, alongside the debate about legalizing same-sex marriage, there were discussions about amending the Civil Code to allow people to register their preferred gender after reassignment surgery in the family register. The National Assembly debated the bill in November 2015, with 282 out of 336 members in favor (Human Rights Watch 2015), and the bill came into force in 2017. The amended Civil Code was, on the one hand, lauded as paving the way for gender reassignment surgery, which remained illegal in Vietnam. On the other hand, it was criticized for requiring surgery as a condition for gender reassignment, which constituted a restriction and a violation of human rights (Vu 2015: 45). The new Civil Code highlights the National Assembly's limited understanding of gender reassignment, as it primarily only refers to sex

---

23 For the history of Đạo Mẫu and its inclusion on the World Intangible Cultural Heritage List, see Norton (2006), Fjelstad et al. (2012) and Ōizumi (2019).

reassignment surgery aimed at aligning one's physical sex with their gender identity.

Curiously, the legislation on gender reassignment gained support from most National Assembly members whereas same-sex marriage received very little support. A female member of a healthcare advocacy organization that provided support to gender and sexual minorities in Vietnam, declared that it was far easier to garner support for this issue than for same-sex marriage. She explained that the mainstream population tends to view legal gender change as "treating" a person to match the gender they identify with. In other words, many people see the mismatch between one's physical sex and gender identity as a kind of illness. With this understanding, gender change is regarded as a necessary form of treatment. Changing into a man or woman by medical treatment who conforms to family norms is thus understood as a "treatment," and has their sympathy.[24] Moreover, the word "treatment" in Vietnamese, "*chữa*," also means to "cure" or "correct." Although cross-dressing has long been documented and such individuals are taken to have been common in literature and local beliefs (Tran 2011; Vu 2015), it was not always accepted. Indeed, a case of a cross-dresser from a rural area being taken to a psychiatry department in Saigon (now Ho Chi Minh City) may show that it was not accepted by all families (Heiman and Cao 1975). Until now, the mainstream population and the National Assembly seem to see gender reassignment on official documents in terms of "curing" an affliction.

On this basis, too, the amended Civil Code made it possible for a person to marry someone of the opposite sex after their sexual reassignment, as it grants them rights and obligations consistent with their new sexuality. However, since the amendment to the Civil Code, no specific criteria have been defined for allowing sexual reassignment surgery or licensing standards for medical institutions, nor specific procedures for changing registered gender. Thus, as of 2019, despite several applications for gender re-registration after gender reassignment

---

24 Interview with T.A.H., September 8, 2017.

surgery, no such registrations have been completed due to the authority's refusal to act (Tâm Lụa 2019).[25]

In the amendments to the Civil Code, the Vietnamese government appears to have responded to the demands of gender and sexual minorities groups and their supporters. However, the reality is that it is not immediately operational and there is no prospect of gender and sexual minorities being able to enforce their rights. Nevertheless, it appears that the government succeeded in convincing domestic and international audiences that it has a track record of creating something that meets social needs and that it is tolerant enough to respond to the requests of minorities.

Conclusion

In Vietnam, same-sex marriage and gender reassignment have been discussed from the 2010s at the national level, thanks to a successful grassroots movement since the mid-1990s. In these discussions, the state has given "tacit approval" but has not taken any concrete measures. Nevertheless, we cannot overlook moves from above by the state to correct misperceptions of gender and sexual minorities, such as the Ministry of Health issuing an official document in August 2022 stating that lesbian, gay, bisexual and transgender persons should not be regarded as mentally ill, a truly groundbreaking change in position.

The debates surrounding the recognition of gender and sexual minorities rights have also been seen as opening possibilities for further changes in a political situation where freedom is restricted by the one-

---

25 As of 2023, several cases have been reported in which transgender people were refused by authorities when attempting to change their gender on identity cards. Furthermore, in some cases where they were successful in changing the gender on their identity cards, they were denied changes to their birth certificates, leading to difficulties in administrative procedures in daily life (Vietnam Law & Legal Forum 2023). Currently, advocates are calling for more specific laws for gender reassignment surgery and hormone treatment in Vietnam and for changes in the law to allow people to change their gender without undergoing surgery (AFP 2018). However, discussions have not progressed beyond this.

party system, as well as in traditional gender and family norms. Although the movement to achieve such rights may have evaded political repression by making it a "love issue," or "economic issue" for the next step, the aims of these debates are still shadowed by repressive norms that are generally accepted in Vietnamese society.

In a survey of same-sex couples by iSEE (LeDoan 2017), 20% of 7,000 respondents said that relationships were unequal between couples. In couples where the relationship was reportedly unequal, one party was forced to take on the role of "wife" and was in a more vulnerable position, "having to do what he (*anh*) says." Both the legalization of gender registration after gender reassignment surgery and the official recognition of same-sex marriage are undeniably reproductions of gender norms that have categorized individuals into one of two genders, and, furthermore, have forced them to assume roles according to their gender.

Moreover, the ongoing movement and government action on gender reassignment represents a social context in which surgery is more likely to be encouraged and tolerated in order to "treat" an individual into one of the two genders that conforms to prevailing norms, rather than politically to defend the rights of the individual. Further research is necessary to determine what will be required to shift the government's position from tacit approval to concrete reforms of the legal system.

8 | The Pattaya Entertainment District: A History of Urban Space and Sexual Diversity during the Cold War

Shinsuke Hinata

Introduction

Thailand began to emerge as a world-class tourist destination during the Cold War period, especially after the Sarit Thanarat regime (1959–1963). Apart from a mere three years from 1973 to 1976, allied with the capitalist and liberal nations, Thailand actively encouraged foreign investment and promoted infrastructure development even while consistently being governed by a military dictatorship. At the same time, especially after 1965, Thailand became a crucial hub for bombing North Vietnam,[1] and strengthened its role as a recreation area for US troops. Although US troops stationed in Thailand began to withdraw following the October 1968 announcement of the cessation of bombing, as of 1969, there were as many as 46,277 US troops stationed in Thailand (Comptroller General of the United States 1977: 1). In February 1969, the Grand Prix Bar & Restaurant, reportedly the first successful go-go bar in Thailand, opened on Patpong Road in Bangkok which is today one of the world's most popular entertainment districts (Morledge 2008).[2] It was in this period that the original landscape of Bangkok as a tourist city was born, with its

---

1 As of December 1964, there were approximately 6,000 US Air Force personnel stationed in Thailand at bases at Udon Thani, Korat, and Ubon Ratchathani in northeastern Thailand (near Vietnam) and Takhli and Don Mueang in central Thailand (CHECO/ CORONA 1973: 1–2).

2 Luang Phatphongwanit, a Hainanese Thai commenced construction of Patpong Road in Bangkok's Bang Rak District in 1946, shortly after the end of World War II.

sex-related establishments typified by go-go bars jostling with restaurants and hotels catering to foreigners.

The American writer Tennessee Williams (1911–1983) visited Thailand in 1970 via Japan and Hong Kong. His memoirs published five years later record his impressions of his sojourn: "[M]y stay in Bangkok was a dream which I hope to have again someday. I wish that I had space to extol its exotic delights!" (Williams 1975: 237). This passage does not reveal much about what fascinated Williams so much, but Eddie Woods (1940–), an American reporter for the *Bangkok Post* at the time, who was close to Williams during his stay in Thailand, has provided details of those "exotic delights." To cite one example, Williams' favorite gay bar in Bangkok was called Eden and, apparently not content with just Bangkok, he also went to Pattaya with a friend, looking for fun (Woods 2013: 53–57).

Woods, himself a gay man, describes what Bangkok meant to gay Western men in the 1970s:

> So many western restaurant owners, managers, and maître d's in Bangkok were [homosexual]. It was a gay-friendly city, at a time when most gay European and American professional people felt unable to come out of the closet at home. In Bangkok they could relax, be themselves. Openly. The owner of a certain hotel in Pattaya was very gay. They had three restaurants and he wanted me to review them all. Invited me [to Pattaya] for a long weekend so that I could. (Woods 2013: 40)

It appears that the urban spaces of Bangkok, where the heterosexual sex industry was concentrated, and Pattaya, which was rapidly developing as a beach resort, were at the time perceived as providing a kind of asylum for gay men from the West.[3]

---

3   For more information on the social positioning of Western gay men in Thailand, especially in Bangkok, in the post-World War II and Cold War periods, see Jackson (1999b), which discusses the acceptance of the concept of "gay" in Thailand, focusing on English and Thai language newspaper reports on the murder of an American man in 1965.

However, this does not mean that such urban spaces in Thailand have been exclusively used by Western tourists and hotel owners as places for escaping the sexual norms of their own countries. According to Peter Jackson, who has conducted extensive research on sexuality in Thailand, particularly the social positioning of gay men, international tourist cities such as Pattaya, which provide jobs and communities that accept gender and sexual minorities, have also provided refuge for Thai gender and sexual minorities to escape the dominant heterosexual norms of their own country. He argues:

> The market is indeed a zone of both queer autonomy and subordination, providing a means to resist and establish freedom from heteronormative state controls and family expectations at the same time that it subordinates queer people to the vagaries of unpredictable market forces. Nonetheless, the market provides a space upon which queer rights are being built. (Jackson 2011c: 201–204; cf. the Preface to this volume)

A typical example of such queer spaces is the world-famous cabaret show and beauty pageant featuring transgender women in Pattaya, "Miss International Queen," which was widely covered in the Japanese media in 2009 when Japan's Ai Haruna won.

As such, Pattaya can be seen as an important case study for considering the development of the tourism industry and the spatial formation of gender and sexual minorities in Thailand. However, its history is surprisingly little known,[4] except for its prominence as a recreation area

---

4 Of the few extant studies of Pattaya, Russell Arthur Smith clarifies the parallels between beach resort evolution and urbanization in Pattaya by focusing on physical, environmental, social, economic, and political factors, based on the hypothesis that the general development of beach resorts can be classified into eight stages. According to Smith, while on the one hand Pattaya's rapid development in the 1970s contributed greatly to foreign exchange earnings, government revenue, and job creation, it also had negative environmental and social impacts, such as ocean pollution and child prostitution, that cannot be overlooked. The main causes were policy failures and a lack of physically and socially realistic resort development

for the US military during the Vietnam War. This chapter examines the Pattaya that was spawned by Bangkok's interpersonal connections and capital during the Cold War, and seeks to unravel how its entertainment district and spaces for gender and sexual minorities were formed, to produce a contemporary history of the city.

The beginning of Pattaya land development (1948–1950s)

Pattaya, located in Chonburi Province, about 150 kilometers southeast of Bangkok, the capital of Thailand, is an international tourist city with two faces: one as a beach resort; and another as an entertainment district (Japan International Cooperation Agency 1976: 12). In 2018, its foreign visitor numbers reached 8.67 million, making it the 18th most-visited city in the world (Mastercard 2018). Until the 1940s, however, it was a quiet fishing village and almost unknown to Thais, let alone foreign tourists. One of the first individuals to purchase and develop large tracts of land on the beach at Pattaya was Parin'ya Chawalitthamrong (1917–2005), a Chinese-Thai from Bangkok. Parin'ya was an administrative bureaucrat

---

plans (Smith 1992: 318–319). In contrast to Smith's study, which focused on the structural development of the city from the perspective of tourism studies, Kwankaew Udomboonyanuparp's master's thesis (2003) provides a more detailed analysis of Pattaya's relationship with US military bases, the Thai government's tourism policy during the Cold War, tourism promotion activities by local private organizations, especially the hotel industry, and the history of Pattaya up to its inauguration as a municipality in 1978. In addition to the specific trends related to the urban development of Pattaya, Kwankaew also provides a clear picture of the entertainment districts in Bangkok and around US military bases during the Vietnam War. In its concluding section, as with Smith, Kwankaew argues that although Pattaya developed into an internationally known resort through public efforts to lure tourists, it lacked long-term urban planning, which led to environmental and social problems (Kwankaew 2003: 152).

The Japan International Cooperation Agency also produced a series of reports in the late 1970s at the request of the Thai government for formulation of a basic plan for tourism development in Pattaya and an infrastructure improvement plan (Japan International Cooperation Agency 1976; 1977, and others). These reports, although not academic studies, comprise the most comprehensive and detailed basic data of land use and the tourism situation in Pattaya at that time.

as well as a businessman who ran a real estate business with his wife on Sukhumvit Road.[5] After purchasing the land, he took advantage of his position as an active bureaucrat and worked with the county mayor and the head of the Public Works Department to equip it with roads and electricity (Jonathan n.d.: 23).

In the 1950s, while Parin'ya was building infrastructure, Pattaya gradually became known to expatriates and the Thai elite in Bangkok. A YMCA (Young Men's Christian Association) branch was established in Chonburi Province in 1953 and a YMCA hostel in Pattaya the following year, and the locality began to be recognized as a marine sports destination (Kwankaew 2003: 48). The Varuna Marine Club was established in South Pattaya on February 15, 1958, spearheaded by Walter Meyer. One of the founding members was Prince Phisadet Ratchani (or Bhisadej Rajani) (1922–2022), a royal known as the "father of sailing" in Thailand. Prince Phisadet was a mentor to King Rama IX (reigned 1946–2016), a sailing enthusiast (*Bangkok Post* 2007). The prototype of Pattaya as a beach resort appears to have been formed during this period.

---

5   Sukhumvit Road is another name for National Highway 3, which extends from central Bangkok along the eastern shore of the Gulf of Thailand, passing through Pattaya to the Cambodian border at Trat Province. Parin'ya first visited Pattaya in 1948 with his wife to purchase land. At that time, Sukhumvit Road was still largely unpaved, and the Bang Pakon River had to be crossed by ferry. Leaving Bangkok at 8:00 in the morning, Parin'ya arrived at the Bang Lamung district around noon, and since there was not even a road leading to the coast until 1955 (when Pattaya was still covered with forest), it reportedly took another hour to finally reach the sea (Jonathan n.d.: 19–20). Parin'ya's explanation for purchasing approximately 800,000 square meters of land along the coast (Jonathan n.d.: 41–42) was simple: "Land in Pattaya was cheap at the time. I was able to exchange one Rai (1600 square meters) of land on Sukhumvit Road in Bangkok for 100 Rai (160,000 square meters) of land in Pattaya. And this was the only place close to Bangkok with such a long sandy beach" (Jonathan n.d.: 23). It may be significant that in 1951, only three years after Parin'ya first visited Pattaya, Thephassadin Bridge was built across the Bang Pakon River, which previously could only be crossed by boat, thus greatly improving access from Bangkok to Chonburi Province (Umpika 2015: 26). In pace with the development of Sukhumvit Road, originally a real estate endeavor, Parin'ya ended up in Pattaya with its still-pristine beaches (Jonathan n.d.: 38).

The military basification of Thailand and the creation of entertainment districts for the US military (1960s)

The connection between Pattaya's development and the US military is well known. The first time a group of US troops visited Pattaya appears to have been on June 29, 1959, when about 500 soldiers stationed in Korat in northeastern Thailand arrived for Rest and Recreation (R&R) leave (Empower Foundation 2015: 23; Harborne 2017; *Pattaya Mail* 2019).[6] Bear in mind that it was not until 1965 that the U-Tapao Royal Thai Navy Airfield in Rayong Province, adjacent to Chonburi Province, was expanded for use by the US military.

In 1960, Thawi Chunlasap (1914–1996), an Air Force general who served as Supreme Commander of the Armed Forces and President of the Thai National Olympic Committee, opened the Nautical Inn for US soldiers (Nautical Inn 2011; Empower Foundation 2015: 24). While small, with only 33 rooms, it was the first modern lodging facility for the general public in Pattaya, which until then consisted of only private villas and simple bungalows.

The Nipa Lodge Hotel (now Basaya Beach) opened in 1964 as Pattaya's first full-fledged resort hotel. Its manager was a German, Kurt Wachtveitl, who moved to the Oriental Hotel (now Mandarin Oriental, Bangkok) in 1967, and is renowned for having served as its general manager for more than forty years (Augustin 2007).

By the end of 1966, there were around 24,000 US Air Force personnel stationed in Thailand (CHECO/CORONA 1973: 1–2), quadrupling in just two years. The established clubhouses for Americans such as the Villa

---

6   A music festival and other commemorative events were held in June 2019, the 60th year since 1959 (*Pattaya Mail* 2019). Note that the *Pattaya Mail* article cited here gives March 29, 1959 as the date of the first visit to Pattaya by US soldiers, but considering the accounts in EMPOWER Foundation (2015: 23) and Harborne (2017), and the month in which the commemorative events were held, it is more likely that June was correct, so this chapter has employed the latter. Also, according to Parin'ya, it was Phra Yotsunthon, the father of Prachit Yotsunthon, first director of the Bank of Thai Commerce, that prepared a place for the soldiers to stay (Jonathan n.d.: 69).

Club and the Ers (NCO) Club in Bangkok could not meet the demand, and Patpong Road began to turn into America Town. Furthermore, from 1967, Phetchaburi Tat Mai Road also became a popular nightspot for US soldiers and Thais (Kwankaew 2003: 56). Other entertainment districts for the US military in 1967 included New Land in the vicinity of U-Tapao Air Base, about 40 kilometers from Pattaya, and Kilo 10 in Sattahip District, Chonburi Province, where many personnel connected to the military resided (Kwankaew 2003: 99).

In Pattaya in the same period, Ed Headley, an American, and Sumet Phattharasathon, a Thai, opened The Outrigger, the first restaurant with a bar, in 1967, followed the next year by its sister restaurant Coral Reef. Headley and Sumet were colleagues working for a US military company in Bangkok. Having been sent to its U-Tapao branch as an engineer, Headley noticed the lack of entertainment facilities in Pattaya and decided to run his own restaurant. When it first opened, it was an upscale bar and restaurant for Bangkok's elite (Burchall 2008: 15). According to Dolf Riks (1929–1999), a Dutchman who was a close friend of Headley's, there were two other restaurants in Pattaya in 1969: the Nipa Hut, a Mexican restaurant owned by Colonel George, and Charlie's Hideaway, owned by Charlie Cattanach, a US Army veteran.

In sum, resort hotels and restaurants began to proliferate in Pattaya in the late 1960s when entertainment quarters for the US military began to form in Bangkok and around the bases, although the kind of sex-centered entertainment district that we see today did not yet exist.

Pattaya's gradual transformation into a lively place can also be gathered from developments at the Varuna Marine Club mentioned above. Originally associated with the royal family, the club was the scene of royal diplomacy, having hosted a yacht race in March 1965 with Prince Philip, Duke of Edinburgh (husband of Britain's Queen Elizabeth II) as its invited guest, and so on; and in April of the same year, under the patronage of King Rama IX, the club was renamed the Royal Varuna Yacht Club (*Bangkok Post* 2007). It was subsequently relocated from near Bali Hai Pier to the rear side of the cape in October 1967 because of the increasing development of Pattaya, and remains there to this day (*Pattaya Mail* 2017). The prestigious club's relocation to a quieter environment well conveys the changes in Pattaya in the late 1960s.

The US military withdrawal and germination of the Pattaya entertainment district (1970s)

During the same period in Pattaya, the Royal Pattaya Palace hotel opened in 1970, with Swiss national Allois X. Fassbind,[7] later known as "Mr. Pattaya," as general manager (*Pattaya Blatt* 2003a; 2003b).[8] Fassbind had come to Thailand in 1966 and had worked as a resident manager at the Oriental Hotel and Narai Hotel (Glanzberg 2003: 59). According to Suttham Phanthusak (1947–2016), a former employee of Fassbind's at the Narai Hotel, who served as accounts manager of the Royal Pattaya Palace and later would become the owner of a world-famous cabaret show, Fassbind actively promoted Pattaya to Europeans and Japanese who had not previously visited the city,[9] and Pattaya's tourism industry grew rapidly in the two years from 1970 to 1972 (Arun 2017: 71–72; cf. Japan International Cooperation Agency 1976: 9).

Moreover, Eddie Woods, mentioned above, was invited to open a gay bar called Camelot, probably around 1971, by another friend who suggested: "Eddie, what say we open a gay bar in Pattaya? The place is ripe for it, but there isn't one yet" (Woods 2013: 90).[10] According to

---

7   Allois X. Fassbind is also known as Louis Fassbind.

8   In 1973, the Royal Pattaya Palace hotel was acquired by the Hyatt Group, a global hotel chain, and became the Hyatt Pattaya Palace (*Pattaya Blatt* 2003a; 2003b). Currently, the building is being used in its original form as Hotel Selection. It was designed by Dan Wongprasat (Pattayaone n.d.), a Thai architect known for the Siri Apartment in Bangkok. Note that upon its acquisition by Hyatt, Fassbind moved to Royal Cliff Beach Terrace, which opened in 1973, again as general manager (Arun 2017: 72).

9   According to Ricks's record, Fassbind promoted Pattaya at the Pacific Area Tourist Association's (PATA) meetings in 1971 at the Sheraton Hotel in Bangkok (*Pattaya Mail* 1998a).

10 This bar, which Woods and Rolnick ran in addition to their day jobs in Bangkok, closed soon after due to the two being too busy, problems with the manager, and the fact that the male staff Woods chose did not fit in with the gay scene in Pattaya.

Bill Jones, who worked for a man named Bill S. around 1971 at Ohm's Law, a bar in Pattaya: "It was called Ohm's Law, since we all worked as Electronic Techs, but came to be known in the end as Ohm's Law Gay Bar. The adjacent street, in turn, was nicknamed *Soi Katoey*"[11] (Ladyboy Street) (*Pattaya Mail* 1998b). It was reportedly because one of the bartenders was gay that gay men began to gather at the bar, and so it eventually became known as a gay bar (interviewed by the author, February 15, 2019). Thus, the early 1970s appears to have been the period of the burgeoning of gay bars in Pattaya. Incidentally, Jones opened BJ Bar, said to be the first pub in Pattaya, in 1974. Although that pub no longer exists, its name is etched in the memory of the city as "*Soi BJ*" (BJ Street).

At the same time that the tourists visiting Pattaya and its forms of entertainment were diversifying in this way, a student movement campaigning against the military dictatorship developed into a large-scale demonstration in Bangkok. This 1973 popular uprising resulted in the resignation of the Thanom Kittikachorn cabinet and led to a decline in foreign tourists (Kwankaew 2003: 102). Thailand, which had been under military dictatorship since the 1957 coup, had a brief period of democratization between the October 14, 1973 event which resulted in the end of the military dictatorship and the October 6 massacre in 1976. On March 19, 1975, between those two dates, the Thai government requested the withdrawal of all US troops from the country by 1976. Saigon fell on April 30, just over a month after this request. The U-Tapao Naval Air Station, the closest base to Pattaya, was completely returned to Thailand on June 13, 1976. The departure of the 27,000 US military

---

Also, the manager, a black man, was apparently a deserter from the US Army (Woods 2013: 90).

11 *Kathoey* (also spelled *krathoei*, *kratoey* or *katoey*) is a Thai word that refers to a sex other than male or female. The term has a long history, being also found in the *Three Seals Law*, a collection of laws compiled in the early 19th century. Before the spread of English-influenced expressions such as "gay" and "tom" to refer to homosexuals, *kathoey* had a wide range of meanings, including intersex, transgender, cross-dresser, and homosexual (Chonwilai 2012: 109–111), but today it generally connotes transgender women.

personnel that had been stationed in Thailand as of 1975 (Comptroller General of the United States 1977: 1) must have been a painful blow to the business people that had invested in satisfying the troops' demands.

Subsequently, however, from 1978 to the 1980s, employees of Middle Eastern oil companies and US Navy SEALs began to visit Pattaya, and the BJ Bar prospered (*Pattaya Mail* 1998b). The late 1970s was a time of the rapid popularization of Pattaya as evidenced by the declining proportion of first-class hotels, which had accounted for 85% in 1976, and had dropped to 56% in 1979 (Smith 1992: 310). Pattaya's first go-go bar, Tahitian Queen,[12] which is still in operation today, opened in 1978. The Tahitian Queen was partly financed by Luang Phatphongphanit, the well-known developer of Bangkok's Patpong Road, and the reliefs on its inside walls were created by his daughter (interviewed by the author, September 11, 2017). As in the hotel business, Bangkok's capital and connections played an important role in sex industry establishments such as go-go bars.

The birth of Tiffany's Show

The history of Tiffany's Show, a cabaret show featuring transgender women that has become a highlight of Pattaya tourism, dates to a show launched by Wichai Loetritrueangsin in South Pattaya (Tiffany's Show Pattaya n.d.) in 1974, around the time that Bill Jones opened BJ Bar. The show became the huge attraction that it is today when Wichai met Sutham Phanthusak, who had quit his hotel job to run a currency exchange business.

At the time of their acquaintance, Wichai, who was running a small bungalow-like hotel, was putting on a cabaret show there with about seven or eight transgender women performers, which was said to be very

---

12 One of the co-owners of Tahitian Queen had reportedly been a contractor for an oil company who had spent about a year in Saudi Arabia. In the course of that job, they came to know Pattaya and, in search of freedom, chose to manage the bar instead of renewing their contract with the oil company (interviewed by the author, September 11, 2017).

popular. However, Wichai was having trouble due to its inconvenient location for parking, and Sutham was considering what to do with the 2,800 square meters of land he had leased from Parin'ya Chawalitthamrong. Sutham approached Wichai and they decided to build a new theater. The 400-seat theater was completed in 1980, thanks to a 12-million-baht loan from Bangkok Bank (Arun 2017: 83–85).

Wichai oversaw production at the new theater, and Suphap Saengkhamchu, a dancer who had been the sole performer when the show began in 1974, was the director (Arun 2017: 85).

However, when the new establishment opened, it did not attract many customers, and Wichai was soon asking Sutham to quit. Sutham explains why he continued with the show, saying:

> If we had quit the business, what would have happened to the lives of the eighty dancers? Would that mean that we did not have to have responsibility for them? Those dancers are artists. But they are called a second type of women, or people of a third sex, and society is not yet tolerant enough to accept (their existence). They are people with fewer opportunities than ordinary people. Their profession of dancing does no harm, but merely entertains the hearts of others. My feeling is that people with limited opportunities should enjoy those opportunities, and should gain equality and sympathy from others. Although each of them is as involved in the development of the nation-state as anyone else, it's just that their role is different from that of the general public. Theirs is a livelihood that is honest and does no harm to anyone. As well, it captures the hearts of the tourists who come to our country. My new idea is that they should rather be applauded by their fellow citizens, shouldn't they? It is those very dancers that are introducing Thailand to the world. (Arun 2017: 85–86)

This is a later recollection, and it is not certain whether Sutham was running his business on such principles at the time of its opening in 1980. However, even if it is a post hoc fabrication, it is a valuable testimony about the position of gender and sexual minorities in Thai society, as a businessman with no prior involvement with the third sex or show business advocating for the rights and social status of transgender women while appealing to the value of developing the nation-state and raising Thailand's international visibility through tourism is laid out in readily understandable terms.

Parin'ya, who had leased the land to Sutham, recalled that he had never been interested in the show because he thought the *kathoeys*[13] were ill-behaved people; but when he finally saw the show after repeated invitations from the Mayor of Pattaya, he found it very entertaining and worth seeing, and was impressed by the *kathoeys'* performance (Jonathan n.d.: 73). Later, a man named Somphan Phettrakun came to Parin'ya, asking to rent a plot of land to build a theater for a similar show featuring transgender women, and it became a great success. This theater, called Alcazar, which opened on November 8, 1981, still boasts similar popularity to Tiffany's Show.

The birth of Gaytown

Next, I will outline the process leading up to the birth of Boyztown, the first gay town in Pattaya, based on an autobiography (Burchall 2008) which was privately published by Michael J. Burchall (1946–), a central figure in the town's creation.

Burchall was from London and had majored in genealogy at the University of Chichester. He worked as a teacher after graduation. His first visit to Thailand, via Hong Kong, was in February 1985, and he stayed in Bangkok and Pattaya. After returning to the United Kingdom, he could not stop thinking about Thailand, so he made a second visit to the country in November of the same year, and the following year he bought and reopened a bar that had been struggling to keep afloat.

Burchall purchased a place called the Cockpit Bar, a gay male go-go bar and restaurant. Founded by Ed Headley, owner of the Outrigger, who set up a company named Yarang with four associates, Cockpit Bar was

---

13 See Note 11 above.

established to cater to demand from the growing number of gay male tourists in Pattaya (Burchall 2008: 16).

As mentioned, Pattaya already had Ohm's Law Gay Bar and, albeit for a short time, Camelot, opened by Eddie Woods for gay men. However, in a list of gay bars in Pattaya from 1982–2008, Burchall cites Tiffany's as the only place that opened in the 1970s, identifying it as the first gay/mixed bar in Pattaya (Burchall 2008: 232). A gay/mixed bar is a bar that is aimed at gay men but is open to customers of other sexual orientations. It is speculated that Ohm's Law Gay Bar, too, which was not initially a gay bar, may have been of a similar nature. Woods' Camelot failed to take off and soon shut its doors, and before Burchall bought it, Cockpit Bar had also closed on and off, so although there were some establishments for gay men in Pattaya from the 1970s until the early 1980s, the number was very small, and their businesses were unstable.

During his first visit to Pattaya in February 1985, Burchall set out to enjoy himself at a total of five gay bars: the Why Not Bar, Gentleman's Bar, Number One Club, and Hercules Bar on Pattayaland Soi 1 (Pattaya Soi 13/3) in South Pattaya, as well as Adam and Eve, located at the northern end of the beach (Burchall 2008: 100). On his return visit in November that year, Burchall had a fateful encounter with Narong, who was working at a new bar called Club 69. He re-opened the Cockpit Bar a year later, on December 1, 1986, with Narong as his partner (Burchall 2008: 105, 118). The Cockpit Bar was located on Pattayaland Soi 3 (the second alley west of Pattayaland Soi 1 along Pattaya Sai 2 Street), where Boyztown, later known as Gaytown, took shape.

The impetus for the birth of Boyztown was the opening by Britons Gordon May and James Lumsden of Boys, Boys, Boys, a gay bar in Pattayaland Soi 3, following Burchall's lead, on December 6, 1988. Frequent visitors to Thailand since 1984, May and Lumsden first visited the Cockpit Bar around 1986–87, where they became acquainted with Burchall. They bought Gentlemen's Club in 1987, and upon its reopening the following year, it became Pattaya's most popular and successful go-go bar. Boys, Boys, Boys was a new place the two opened to expand their business (Burchall 2008: 132–135). One afternoon, all the bar owners in Pattayaland Soi 3 got together to discuss how they should work together in the future. During this meeting, they decided to name the street "Boystown." May reportedly proposed the name (Burchall 2008: 168). Although Burchall does not record when the meeting was held, the fact that the inaugural "Mr. Boystown Contest" was held in August 1989 (Burchall 2008: 151) suggests that the community dubbed Boystown (later renamed Boyztown)[14] had already been established by 1989.

In the previous section, we discussed cabaret shows by transgender women, but cabaret shows were also held in Boyztown. The first show seems to have been held around April 1987 at the Cockpit Bar with an invited troupe of dancers consisting mostly of transgender women. However, the show was mediocre, so Burchall's partner Narong decided to put on their own show, and shows by bar staff began a year later. The high caliber of the shows made them the talk of the town, so managers from Tiffany's Show and Alcazar came to see them, and some performers were scouted to become professional dancers. In addition, they were sometimes invited to local hotels and parties, and even to Thai-style funerals as entertainment (Burchall 2008: 121, 153–156).

Based on Burchall's recollections, the above is a basic summary of the events leading up to the birth of Boyztown. The author being a genealogy major, his record is meticulous, and other fascinating details are scattered throughout. Examples include his description of his close relationship with Dolf Ricks, a well-known restaurateur (Burchall 2008: 119), and his noting that the Pattaya Gay Festival, a gay parade in 2001 spearheaded by Ramsden from Boyz, Boyz, Boyz, was originally the idea of "Mr. Pattaya," Louis Fassbind (Burchall 2008: 223). Also of interest is the fact that Ed Headley, who had opened the first proper restaurant in Pattaya in 1967, had attempted to run a gay bar in the 1980s. Burchall's records

---

14 When first established, the name was spelt Boystown, but as it was soon realized that 'boys' was inappropriate due to its strong nuance of underage boys, the spelling was amended to Boyztown. The May and Ramsden bars were also initially called Boys, Boys, Boys, but changed nomenclature at the same time to Boyz, Boyz, Boyz for similar reasons (Burchall 2008: 142, 168).

provide a glimpse into the development of Pattaya's urban space amid a magnetic field of diverse nationalities and sexualities.

Conclusion

This chapter has summarized the events leading to the emergence of a city and entertainment district in Pattaya, and has further traced how spaces for gender and sexual minorities have been formed in that city. Here, I wish to conclude with a few additional observations, despite the very limited examples of cabaret shows by transgender women and Gaytown.

First, in regard to the establishment of spaces for gender and sexual minorities, we have confirmed that the germination of such spaces can be seen from the very first stage of urban development in Pattaya, as evidenced by the existence of bars where gay men congregated and the popularity of transgender shows in the early 1970s when there were still only a handful of hotels and restaurants in the city. Conversely, as we saw in the previous section, from records showing that the owner of the first restaurant later came to run a gay bar, and that "Mr. Pattaya," the key figure in Pattaya's development from an American military R&R resort to an international tourist city, organized a gay parade on his own initiative, it might be no exaggeration to say that rather than spaces for gender and sexual minorities having been spawned within Pattaya, it was gender and sexual minority networks that created the prototype for Pattaya's urban space.

As for relations with the local community, the show performed in Gaytown was so well received that its performers were invited to local funerals, which conveys how accepting the local Buddhist community was of gender and sexual minorities. Moreover, the anecdote about Parin'ya, whose negative views of transgender women shifted after he was impressed by the Tiffany show is an example of how Pattaya's tourism culture was not only incorporated into society, but also affected people's attitudes toward gender and sexual minorities.

Finally, looking back at this chapter from the perspective of the inclusion and exclusion of gender and sexual minorities and who comprises a "good citizen," as discussed in the Introduction of this book, Sutham Pantusak, the owner of the Tiffany Show, is perhaps the most illuminating. Sutham argued that given Thai society was not yet tolerant enough to accept people of a "third sex," such people "should be applauded by their fellow citizens" because they participate in society through the tourism industry, and further because they enhance the nation's reputation. This testimony concerns the definition and inclusion of "good citizens." Let us recall Jackson's observation that "[t]he market ... subordinates queer people to the vagaries of unpredictable market forces. Nonetheless, the market provides a space upon which queer rights are being built." The tourist market and the rights of gender and sexual minorities as "good citizens" are inextricably linked according to Sutham.

The lack of fixed spaces such as Pattaya's entertainment district for gender and sexual minorities other than gay men and transgender people is likely also attributable to the market, or the lack thereof. Like Pattaya, many of these so-called "entertainment districts" are basically market constructs of and for the "male gaze" structured around masculinity. I suggest that the reason gay bars and transgender shows were integrated into Pattaya's urban space from an early stage, whereas lesbian towns, for example, are less uncommon, can be found in the structure of such markets.

9 Looking into State and Civil Society in Singapore through the Lens of Gender and Sexual Minorities

Keiko Tsuji Tamura

Introduction

In 2022, the population of Singapore was approximately 4.07 million (citizens and permanent residents), with an ethnic composition of 74.2% Chinese, 13.5% Malay, 9.1% Indian, and 3.2% Others (CMIO categorization). Singapore is also home to some 1.57 million foreigners who are either long-term workers, students or trainees, and their families. As the city-state has already achieved economic development on par with developed countries, and because almost all public education from elementary school to university is conducted in English, the literacy rate in English is extremely high among Singaporeans, especially the young who are constantly exposed to the ideas and life-styles of Western English-speaking cultures.

Although Singapore appears in many respects to be a mature, liberal society, this appearance is belied by its treatment of gender and sexual minorities. In fact, sexual intercourse between men was illegal until January 2023, and, as will be elaborated below, until 2007 violators were subject to prison sentences.[1] Until quite recently, there was scant discussion of partnership systems, let alone of same-sex marriage.

However, a social movement demanding gender and sexual minority rights burgeoned in the 2000s, focusing on internet sites, and in 2007

---

1   However, even after 2007, when incidents of sexual intercourse between men were discovered in locations such as shopping centers, minor charges of indecent assault were often applied and fines imposed.

Photo 9.1: 2017 Pink Dot rally (photo by author, 1 July 2017)

a lively debate unfolded in Parliament over the criminal law banning homosexual activity. From 2009, an annual rally was organized by Pink Dot to demand rights for sexual minorities. Foreigners had been free to attend until 2016, and many non-citizens working for foreign companies and international students were in the crowd of 28,000 participants overflowing the Speakers' Corner section of Hong Lim Park. However, following the government's introduction of new regulations banning foreigners and foreign-affiliated companies from being involved, there were fears that the 2017 rally would be considerably smaller, but these fears proved unfounded, as 20,000 citizens and permanent residents attended the rally. We will discuss the 2017 rally in detail below.

In Singapore, as increasing numbers of people are beginning to demand greater tolerance of gender and sexual minorities, conflict is increasing with conservatives, especially Christians, who seek to preserve the "traditional family."

This chapter analyzes and discusses factors that promote or hinder protection of the rights of gender and sexual minorities and the legalization of those rights in Singapore, with an eye to political struggles over civil liberties, the political system, and democracy.

Section 377 of the Penal Code and booming Bugis Street

Most of the population are descendants of immigrants who arrived in Singapore in the late 19th and early 20th centuries The overwhelming majority of the first wave of immigrants were young males. According to Turnbull, "In 1884, there were 60,000 Chinese men but only 6,600 Chinese women, of whom at least 2,000 were prostitutes" (2009: 101). Homosexual prostitution was popular at the time, fueled for many years by an influx of boys from Hainan, an island in southern China. Sexual relations between men were viewed as normal in colonial Singapore.

The British, however, imposed Section 377 of the UK Penal Code to Singapore when they brought this small island under their colony. It banned sexual intercourse between persons of the same sex, stating that: "Whoever voluntarily has carnal intercourse against the order of nature with any man, woman or animal, shall be punished with imprisonment for life, or with imprisonment for a term which may extend to 10 years, and shall be liable for a fine." This is also referred to as the "Anti-natural (not for reproduction)" Sex Law, or more commonly, the "sodomy law." Section 377A states: "Any male person who, in public or private, commits or abets the commission of or procures the commission by any male person of, any act of gross indecency with another male person, shall be punished with imprisonment for a term which may extend to 2 years."

When Singapore separated from the Federation of Malaysia and became an independent republic in August 1965, Sections 377 and 377A remained on the books. Soon after independence, the fledgling Singapore government established a relationship with the US that would offer economic benefits and security. Singapore permitted the US armed forces stationed in South Vietnam to use Singaporean military facilities to repair damaged ships and planes as well as providing amusement facilities for US soldiers.

Bugis Street, a busy area near Singapore's city center, was a popular destination for American soldiers on furlough. In response to the influx of US soldiers to the area, a number of gay bars and gay saunas soon opened. Policemen were almost never on patrol because most individuals who frequented the area were foreign nationals, including US soldiers. A small number of local gender and sexual minorities also frequented the quarter, but they were seldom arrested for violation of 377A (C.K.K. Tan 2012: 128). It is worth noting that the UK abolished Section 377 and 377A of the Penal Code in 1967.

It should also be noted that it was not until the 1970s that the term "gay," defined by sexual orientation, became socially recognized in Singapore (R. Tan 2012: 118). Until then, there had been no set denomination or gender-specific terminology, apart from references in English-language newspapers to male-to-female cross-dressing dancers and prostitutes as "transvestites." For this reason, in Singapore, the term "gay" is often used almost synonymously with homosexuals, including lesbians. In this chapter, "gay" is used to distinguish male homosexuals from their female counterparts, except where a verbatim quote uses it more broadly.

Control and monitoring by the nation

The government's control and monitoring of gender and sexual minorities became more stringent when it felt uneasy about the risk of HIV/AIDS infection. When the first Singaporean AIDS patient was reported in 1985, most gay bars and gay saunas disappeared almost immediately, and the few that remained open were under police control (Chan 2015: 13).

Even more importantly, the government began to encourage women to have more babies, stressing a return to Confucian values. In the late-1980s, faced with a labor shortage, the government launched a pro-natalist policy with the slogan, "Have three or more if you can afford it." The government also announced five core Confucian values (nation before community and society above self; family as the basic unit of society; community support and respect for the individual; consensus not conflict; and racial and religious harmony) as the "National Ideology" that should be shared by all Singaporeans. The ruling People's Action Party (PAP), which had dominated Singaporean politics since independence in 1965, attributed a drop in its approval rating in the 1980s not to its authoritarian style, but to an irresponsible younger generation influenced by European and American liberal values and anti-government ideas.

Of the five values, the idea of family as the basic unit of society was considered to be the most important, and in 1994 the government announced the centrality of "Singapore Family Values," which highlighted love, care, and filial responsibility. The government also made it obligatory for adult children to provide financial support to their parents. The proposed bill became the Maintenance of Parents Act in 1994.

Furthermore, the government announced a range of incentives to encourage more births and promote "family values," such as tax breaks for married couples who had three or more children, although only legally married couples were eligible for these incentives. In contrast, for example, for a same-sex couple to purchase public housing, each party had to be more than 35 years old and they could only buy secondhand flats as "friends."[2]

The government regarded same-sex couples as incapable of natural procreation and deemed that allowing them to marry could contribute to social instability because they would not share the same "family values." Gender and sexual minorities were not employed as civil servants and the government severely censured print publications, public performances and media broadcasts that featured homosexuality, except for films shown at an international film festival.

The government's media regulation standards clearly state that, in order to protect "public morals and social values," "information on homosexuality, lesbianism, bisexuality, transsexuality, cross-dressing,

---

2   Around 80% of Singaporeans and permanent residents live in government-controlled public housing estates. Unless they purchase a higher-priced condominium (private apartment) or a detached house with land, residents have no other option but to live in public housing. Furthermore, purchase is the rule, and only those below a certain income can rent a property. Therefore, buying a new flat in a public housing complex or replacing an existing one, and making it as spacious and conveniently located as possible, is one of the most important choices a person can make in his or her life.

incest, and pedophilia, and anything related to those subjects or lifestyles should be given the most scrutiny" (Media Development Authority n.d.). Police frequently conducted sting operations against male homosexuals, and those arrested were widely reported with their names, ages, occupations, and photographs (Au 2009: 400). A lesbian woman recalling the 1980s, said:

> The eighties were not an easy time for any of us. Gay and lesbian books were banned in libraries and bookshops. Girls were getting raped for holding hands, boys were getting arrested and having their pictures put in the newspaper for being gay. You had to just grin and bear it. (Ng 2006: 69–71)

Gender and sexual minorities hid themselves to survive at that time. All male citizens must serve in the military for 2 or 2-1/2 years. If a man makes it known that he is gay, he is typically posted at a desk and assigned administrative functions because homosexuality and transsexuality are viewed as a threat to military life. Military laws protect their privacy, but rumors circulate that those who "come out" face discrimination and may receive a record that precludes them from later working in the government (C.K.K. Tan 2012: 77). As a result, almost all gay men finish their military service without coming out.

Toward an open and inclusive society

A "kinder, gentler society" under Prime Minister Goh and the Nation Party

When Singapore's first prime minister, Lee Kuan Yew, stepped aside in November 1990, Goh Chok Tong became the country's second prime minister. Goh launched his administration with a call for a kinder and gentler society and promised to create an open and inclusive society. Many Singaporeans welcomed this change in the government's position, feeling hopeful of a new era where they could speak freely after Lee's long and strong authoritarian rule.

Soon after Goh's inauguration, gay bars and saunas started opening again. A group called "People Like Us," formed in 1993 to promote awareness of issues concerning gender and sexual minorities and started organizing meetings with 80–200 participants (Khng 2001: 82–86). A gay church and a print library also opened (Chua 2014: 67, 100). Communities of sexual minorities were emerging in Singapore. The Nation Party, an event proposed by a government officer who had lived in the US for many years, was held to coincide with Singapore's National Day on August 9, 2002, with the participation of around 1,500 gay men. This party was held again in 2003 and 2004. As many as 8,000 gay men, including 2,500 foreign visitors, joined the party in 2004, which, as one journalist reported, seemingly "hailed Singapore as the gay capital of Asia" (Fairclough 2004: 53). "Many gender and sexual minorities applauded Prime Minister Goh's words that 'gays are like all of us and should not face discrimination in civil service" (C.K.K. Tan 2009).

The driving force behind this liberation was a campaign to protect the rights of gender and sexual minorities, which had begun in the 1970s in Europe and America and was spreading throughout the world in the 1990s. The Goh administration could not ignore this trend. The government also needed to retain foreign professionals to keep its economy developing. The Nation Party was organized to appeal to foreign professionals and demonstrate that Singapore was a creative, intelligent, and ideas-driven city. Earning "pink money," a reference to the purchasing power of the gay and lesbian community, was also a consideration. Organizers estimated that the party and related events pulled in nearly six million Singapore dollars (Fairclough 2004: 53).

In other words, Prime Minister Goh chose sexual minorities out of numerous possible issues because he thought it would be the most appealing and economically profitable way to call attention to the change of government, and not because he intended to change the authoritarian style of governing. Pro-government coverage in the major government-affiliated media hardly changed, and when the opposition won four seats in the 1991 general election (there were 81 seats in Parliament at the time) and the ruling PAP's share of the vote fell to 61%, Goh returned to the strict style of his predecessor, ruling both lawmakers and critics with an iron fist (Tamura-Tsuji 2016: 199).

Conservative Christian groups, however, opposed these liberal movements. The influential National Council of Churches of Singapore, composed of 150 churches including Methodist and Presbyterian, stated in 2004 that homosexual or bisexual practices were contrary to the teachings of the Bible and that the government should keep the present penal code to punish homosexuals (Tan and Lee 2007: 196). Some churches actively sought to change people's sexual orientation, hanging banners saying, "Homosexuals can Change" from the ceilings of their churches (Tan and Lee 2007: 188).

The government, acknowledging that the issue of sexual minorities might divide society, banned the Nation Party in 2005, so the 2006 party was held in Thailand. The group, People Like Us, which had not been permitted to register as a legal group before 1998 was once again denied registration in 2004 on the grounds that "the proposed group is likely to be used for unlawful purposes prejudicial to public peace, welfare or good order in Singapore" (Chong 2017: 156).

Repeal 377A: Petitioning for legal reform in Parliament

The Repeal 377A campaign of 2007 was the first time that an activist from a gender and sexual minority openly challenged legal reform in parliament. The campaign started when the Ministry of Home Affairs proposed a review of Section 377 of the Penal Code, deeming it to be outdated for heterosexual relations after former British colonies, such as Hong Kong and Australia, had repealed 377A in 1991 and 1997, respectively.

Section 377 was revised but 377A remained. Activists from gender and sexual minorities took action against the discrepancy associated with revising Section 377 (in the clause forbidding sexual penetration of a corpse) and retaining 377A. A petition to repeal 377A was submitted to the parliament with 8,120 signatures in October 2007 (Peh 2007: 3). It was a historic moment: the first time in Singapore that a petition backed by popular support was submitted to parliament. According to Singapore's Constitution, a member of parliament may present a signed parliamentary petition, but for activists it was very difficult to find a sponsor in the parliament, someone to present the petition, and to collect thousands of signatures under the country's strong authoritarian rule. So, the fact that activists did find a sponsor and collected thousands of signatures indicated that sexual minorities had created a "space" in society.

At the same time, however, supporters of 377A set up a website to collect signatures to request that the government retain 377A. The conflict made its way to the parliament floor where an unusually heated discussion took place in October 2007. For the first time in Singapore's independent history, the presence of homosexuality in society was openly acknowledged in parliament. A nominated member of parliament[3] who became a supporter and submitted the petition to repeal 377A said:

> The law is discriminatory and unconstitutional. The repeal of 377A is not just about fighting for gay rights. There are bigger issues like tolerance, understanding and inclusiveness. It is about upholding the fundamental protections afforded by the Constitution, the basic pillars underpinning our country. These are surely issues for all Singaporeans. (Peh 2007: 3)

The majority of parliamentarians, however, were in support of retaining Section 377A because it reflected "the moral and social values of the majority of Singaporeans" (Peh 2007: 3). In a speech, the third Prime Minister Lee Hsien Loong (inaugurated in 2004) highlighted that

---

3 The NMP (Nominated Members of Parliament) system of appointing parliamentarians was initiated in 1990. Under this scheme, parliament directly nominates not more than six non-elected members of parliament in order to secure a wide range of talented people from various sectors of society. This system asserts that the ruling People's Action Party (PAP) is receptive to the views of the people, but critics see it as a means of camouflaging PAP's one-party rule. In this case, however, it seems that the petition was easier to submit because the appointee belonged to neither the ruling nor the opposition party.

Singapore was "basically a conservative society with many [people being] uncomfortable with homosexuals, more so with public display of homosexual behavior. However, as recognition that homosexuals are often responsible, invaluable, and highly respected contributing members of society, the government would not proactively enforce Section 377A." He added, however, that "the government would not allow or encourage activists to champion gay rights as they do in the West." He also mentioned that "when it comes to issues like the economy, technology, [or] education, we'd better stay ahead of the game and adapt faster than others. But on moral values, we will stay one step behind the frontline of change, watch how things work out elsewhere before we make any irrevocable moves" (H.L. Lee 2007). Thus, to bring the heated discussion to an end, he asserted that the government would not proactively enforce 377A but would keep the law on the books.

Moreover, members of the Workers' Party, the main opposition, seldom expressed their views in the parliamentary debate. The Workers' Party has maintained the seat that its general secretary won in the 1991 general election, and won six seats in the 2011 general election, four years after the parliamentary debate on Section 377A. The party probably did not express its opinion because many of its supporters were people with relatively low incomes, whose main concerns were day-to-day life issues.

It is difficult to assess the veracity of claims that Singapore is a conservative society uncomfortable with the idea of homosexuality because very few opinion polls have been conducted on the topic. One of the few polls was a national survey in 2013 by Our Singapore Conversation, a government outreach program with a sample size of 4,000, which found that 47% of Singaporeans rejected "gay lifestyles," versus 26% who were in support and 27% who were undecided. There was even less acceptance of same-sex marriage, with 55% rejecting the idea, 21% in agreement and 24% undecided (Institute of Policy Studies 2013: 9–10). Views differed across age groups and educational levels, with the younger and more educated segments of the population being relatively more accepting of gay lifestyles and same-sex marriage.

However, there was much criticism of the government's intentional use of the words "gay lifestyle" in the survey without any definition, which suggested deviancy and quite likely skewed the survey (Chong 2017: 151).

The AWARE saga and Pink Dot

While Prime Minister Lee Hsien Loong seemed to support the status quo, he effectively set the stage for both advocates and opponents of gender and sexual minorities to compete in leading the public discourse.

In May 2009, a group of women from the Anglican Church of Our Savior, a new Christian group, joined the Association of Women for Action and Research (AWARE) a few weeks before the latter's executive committee election, capturing a majority of seats on the committee (Chong 2011: 1–6). AWARE is the most prominent NGO in Singapore advocating for and defending the rights of women. These new members insisted that AWARE had been too tolerant of gender and sexual minorities: for example, it had initiated sex education in schools where pupils were taught to accept homosexuality as something neutral rather than negative. Angry at this turn of events, older members created an online petition to "Save AWARE" that was in direct opposition to the association's new leadership. Membership of AWARE soared from 700 to 3,000. An extraordinary general meeting was called for a vote of no confidence in the new committee members and the latter were ousted. This ended the "AWARE saga," as it is generally known in local parlance (Loh 2011: 98–103), but the Ministry of Education stopped contracting AWARE to provide sex education and announced new rules a year later stipulating that providers of sex education inform students that homosexual acts were illegal (Chua 2014: 124).

In this sense, it can be said that conservative Christians were the clear winners in the AWARE saga. The AWARE saga sent several signals to activists supporting the rights of gender and sexual minorities, however. The setback on sex education reaffirmed the activists' assessment that they must build a stronger movement through closer partnership with allies. A gay activist proposed a public rally named Pink Dot for sexual minorities organized around the slogan "Freedom to Love" (Chua 2014: 124). In May 2009, about 2,500 people – gender and sexual minorities and their allies – flocked to the Speakers' Corner in Hong Lim Park, the only place where open-air events are permitted (after prior notification to police). Attendees brought pink things to celebrate "Love for All: Love between couples, lovers, brothers, sisters and friends." They noted that pink is the product of what happens when Singapore's national flag colors of red and white are mixed. The protesters also pointed out that the color, the result of accepting diversity, was already part of what it meant to be Singaporean because it was the color of the identity cards issued to citizens. Pink Dot turned out to be a family-friendly and patriotic parade aimed at cultivating familial ties, friendship and national feeling, which appealed to a wide audience.[4]

Beginning in 2009, Pink Dot has been an annual event, with the number of participants increasing each year. In 2016, Pink Dot organizers decided to focus on more active participation rather than simply on the number of attendees. They distributed plastic boards to the first 5,000 participants to write messages or draw pictures on, and they set up desks to provide legal advice and counseling (Pink Dot 2016). Foreign companies such as JP Morgan and Google provided financial support to Pink Dot and encouraged their staff to join the event. Fifteen companies became corporate sponsors in 2015, growing to eighteen in 2016 (Pink Dot 2016).

Other participating organizations included Sayoni, Singapore's most prominent lesbian exchange, information, and research organization. While small in scale, with the help of international women's human rights organizations, Sayoni submitted a report in 2011 entitled "Report on Discrimination against Women in Singapore based on Sexual Orientation and Gender Identity" to the UN Committee on the Elimination of Discrimination against Women, complaining of discrimination against gender and sexual minorities in Singapore (Sayoni 2011). Although the Singapore government was asked to explain in an international forum

---

4   Interview with a staff member of the 2017 Pink Dot, 30 June 2017.

for the first time, it went no further than to state that gender and sexual orientation were protected under Article 12 of the Constitution, which guarantees "All persons are equal before the law and entitled to the equal protection of the law," and "[T]here shall be no discrimination against citizens of Singapore on the ground only of religion, race, descent or place of birth."

While there are several active gay-male-oriented groups in Singapore, there are few focused on women. The Singapore government does not see the latter, including Sayoni, as posing a threat because they are unlikely to congregate in parks and shopping centers, and are therefore less visible. Female homosexuals generally lack economic power in comparison with their male counterparts, and thus cannot afford to campaign for their rights, meaning that they are more "docile" than gay male groups.

However, Pink Dot's rapid growth was not only due to the desire for "gender and sexual minorities being accepted," but also because its policy of "celebrating the diversity of love" made it difficult for its opponents to object and be hostile to, and so confrontation ceased to be a feature of its events. In addition, precisely because Pink Dot's insistence that "pink is the color of the Singaporean flag" made it a patriotic event rather than an anti-government one, many people felt comfortable attending.

As increasing numbers of people began to congregate at Pink Dot, some began to object to the way it was run. Noted Malay playwright and poet Alfian Sa'at, initially an ardent Pink Dot supporter and participant, announced that he would boycott the event from 2011. He criticized Pink Dot for turning into a mere "colour-coordinated picnic," claiming that people [we]re "going enthu [*sic*] apeshit as if they just repealed 377A [and] legalized same-sex marriage" (cited in Tang 2017: 109). He also referred to an Indian friend's comment that the (religious and ethnic) diversity of gender and sexual minorities had been lost and Pink Dot had become "as much a celebration of the LGBT community to love as it is a display of the self-love of Chinese, middle-class, English-educated liberals" (Tang 2017: 109). However, Sa'at fell silent in the wake of numerous online criticisms, such as: "No, you can't have a gathering of 10,000 people calling for repeal of 377A. So ... do nothing?" One critic,

Alex Au, commented: "[I]t should … be totally expected that the more privileged segments of our society are over-represented in the Pink Dot movement" (cited in Tang 2017: 110). Ultimately, the issues Sa'at raised were never discussed (Tang 2017: 110–112).

Indeed, most of the organizers of Pink Dot are of Chinese ethnicity, and there appear to have been very few non-Chinese among the participants. Yet if religious debate were involved, such as how Islamic or Christian doctrines regard gender and sexual minorities, people would probably shy away from Pink Dot. It is unclear how, while attracting large numbers of participants and supporters, the movement will translate its energy into expanded rights for gender and sexual minorities in Singapore, which remains under authoritarian rule. The organizers' distribution of message boards and setting up booths for legal advice at the rallies since 2016 could be seen as attempts to raise public awareness of sexual minorities.

Counter-movements, however, also intensified. A Muslim group organized the "Wear White Movement" and joined with the "Love Singapore Network" of more than 100 Christian churches to hold a big event opposing Pink Dot. They attracted 8,000 participants. The day after the 2016 Pink Dot event, Christian churches held a meeting with 3,000 participants to promote traditional "family values." The National Council of Churches of Singapore, meanwhile, adopted a wait-and-see attitude, stating that while it does not condone homosexual or bisexual practices, it also does not condemn those who are struggling with their gender identity and sexual orientation (R.M. Lee 2016).

Government countermeasures

With sharp spikes in both support for and opposition to Pink Dot rallies, the government decided that the best move was to suppress both sides in order to avoid a rift in society. According to the Singapore Census of Population in 2010, Christians made up 18.3% of the population and Muslims 14.7%. Over the previous ten years, the percentage of Christians had increased by 3.7% (Department of Statistics, Singapore 2010: ix). Both religious groups generally do not accept gender and sexual minorities.

However, Pink Dot is the only organization able to host an event large enough to pack a corner of the only park in Singapore where open-air gatherings are allowed, and it potentially constitutes a major threat to a government that views childless same-sex couples as a destabilizing factor in society because they do not share the same "family values." For this reason, the government wanted to suppress the Pink Dot movement.

Two children's books depicting families of same-sex parents were pulled off the shelves of the National Library after complaints that these books did not promote family values (Poh 2014). One of the two books has been selected as a "Notable Children's Book" in the US. The National Library's move sparked concern among civil society activists. The library stated: "Young children are among our libraries' most frequent visitors. Many of them browse books in our children's section on their own. As such, we take a profamily and cautious approach in identifying titles for our young visitors" (Poh 2014). This statement reflects the government's intention.

In June 2016, the government announced a new law that "foreign entities (foreign companies and foreign nationals) should not fund, support or influence such events held at the Speakers' Corner" (Sin 2016). Human Rights Watch, a New York-based group, criticized the new law, stating: "This is an outrageous interference in the right to freedom of association and a clear continuation of Singapore's anti-LGBT bias. Foreign companies with regional headquarters in Singapore should reconsider the city state's suitability as a business location" (Human Rights Watch 2016b). The organizers of Pink Dot said that they were disappointed with the new law but hoped that "more local companies would share our idea of 'Freedom to Love' regardless of sexuality or gender identity and would support us" (ibid.).

The 2017 Pink Dot and the "culture war"

Many worried that the 2017 Pink Dot rally would be smaller in scale because thirteen out of the eighteen companies that had sponsored the 2016 event were foreign companies. In the end, however, 120 local and

Photo 9.2: Security point at entrance (photo by author, 1 July 2017)

small companies offered their support to the 2017 event, realizing Pink Dot's goal of "collecting 150,000 Singapore dollars from 100 local firms and individuals" (Pink Dot 2017).

The atmosphere at the start of the 2017 Pink Dot rally on 1 July was bewildering. Speakers' Corner was surrounded by a long fence with seven makeshift gates watched over by security guards who checked identity cards and belongings so that only citizens and permanent residents would be able to enter. It took a long time for participants to enter the area, with seemingly endless queues at each entrance. Foreign media representatives with name cards identifying them as press were frisked and checked for official media passes at the gate.

Participants wearing pink arrived in a steady stream. People could hardly move when they all raised their pink light devices at 8:00 PM, at the climax of the event. Representatives from various organizations distributed information about their groups and activities. Booths offered legal advice and counseling. There were 500 volunteers helping to manage the event, double the number from the previous year.[5] Some advised

---

5   Interview with a staff member of Pink Dot, 30 June 2017.

visitors waiting to enter the area to stay calm because future events might be canceled if there was a disturbance. After its climax, the organizers reported that the event was a great success, with 20,000 participants,[6] although the mainstream media reported the event only briefly and did not mention the rigorous security.

The government's restrictions on the 2017 Pink Dot rally, as well as indifference by government-affiliated media outlets, was based in its concerns that conflict over gender and sexual minorities' rights would intensify and divide society. Regardless of government restrictions, however, large numbers of people attended Pink Dot events. Not held for two years due to the COVID-19 pandemic, Pink Dot was held again in June 2022, albeit on a smaller scale, and members of the ruling PAP and opposition Workers' Party could be seen among the several thousand participants (Singapore CNN 2022). An increasing number of cases were filed with the courts, claiming that Section 377A, which stipulates that sexual acts between males are illegal, is unconstitutional because it violates Article 12 of the Singapore Constitution.

In January 2023, amid an escalating battle over morals, dubbed a "culture war" (Bin Abdul Aziz et al. 2016: 7) waged during the COVID-19 pandemic, the government repealed Article 377A. Prime Minister Lee Hsien Loong explained that "many Singaporeans now consider sexual orientation and sexual behavior to be personal matters, and accept gay people." However, he added: "The repeal of the Act will not affect family traditions and social norms. [Norms relating to] schooling, media content such as television, and behavior in public places, will remain the same." He also announced that the constitutional provision on marriage, which did not explicitly stipulate that it must be between persons of opposite sexes, would be amended to say that "marriage must be between a man and a woman" (Goh 2022). This amendment prevents same-sex marriage cases from being heard in the courts, and reveals that the Singapore government's position remains hetero-normative.

---

6   The 2017 Pink Dot event is described in detail on the Pink Dot homepage: https:// pinkdot.sg/.

Conclusion

Although Singapore has surpassed Japan's per capita GDP, as well as having increasingly westernized its society, there has been little progress towards guaranteeing the rights of gender and sexual minorities.

The family is understood to be the basic unit of society in the PAP's "family values" orientation, which continues its long-term, authoritarian one-party rule. The family conceived here comprises a heterosexual couple (namely, a man and a woman) and their children. Same-sex couples who do not bear children are regarded as a destabilizing factor in society because they do not share those family values. Furthermore, there is little pressure for change of the authoritarian regime from the West: Singapore's corporate tax rate is the second lowest in Asia after Hong Kong, there are no restrictions on the economic activities of foreign companies, and it is easy to hire foreign workers. Which is why, when the Security Law was invoked in May–June 1987 and twenty-two people – including activists and lawyers – were arrested, and several Western NGOs condemned the action, the government felt no need to respond (Tamura-Tsuji 2016: 116–118).

However, due to the tolerant and liberal political atmosphere that emerged in the early 1990s and international trends towards recognizing the rights of gender and sexual minorities, the Nation Party was allowed and homosexuals began to be employed as public officials, Article 377 of the Penal Code was amended and Paragraph 377A was repealed in January 2023. At the same time, however, the Constitution was changed to clearly state that "marriage shall be between a man and a woman," thus eliminating the possibility of a court deciding to recognize same-sex marriage.

Nevertheless, while many people will continue to attend Pink Dot rallies celebrating the diversity of sexuality and love, and advocating for same-sex marriage, the activities of opposition forces are also likely to continue. Christians and Muslims account for 26% of the Singaporean population (Department of Statistics 2010: ix), and most of them do not accept gender and sexual minorities or same-sex marriage. Those that do accept gender and sexual minorities as members, such as the Free

Community Church, cannot join the National Federation of Churches of Singapore, and their influence remains extremely limited.[7]

Going forward, gender and sexual minorities and their supporters are expected to continue working within the bounds of government permissibility, growing the number of supporters and interested parties through annual Pink Dots, websites and suchlike, and endeavoring to translate that power into expanded legal rights for sexual minorities, including acceptance of same-sex marriage. However, if the heterosexual norm that the government staunchly upholds is to change, it will be due either to a political party that supports same-sex marriage winning the general election, or the authoritarian regime transforming by means of 'democratization from above,' but there seems little probability of either happening in the near future.

---

7   Interview with Reverend Miak Siew from the Free Community Church, 21 August 2018.

10 | Excluded "Human Rights"/ Included "Diversity": Establishing the "Same-sex Partnership Declaration System" in Osaka City

Akitomo Shingae

Introduction

This chapter analyzes how human rights policies for gender and sexual minorities are being institutionalized in Japan. In concrete terms, it examines the establishment of the so-called "same-sex partnership system" in which some Japanese local governments have recognized the partnerships of gays, lesbians, and other gender and sexual minorities.

In Japan, a proposed law on the protection of the human rights of gender and sexual minorities (hereafter, the "LGBT Law") has been debated repeatedly among Diet members since 2016. While opposition parties submitted so-called "anti-discrimination bills" to the Diet in order to prohibit discriminatory treatment by administrative agencies and businesses on the basis of people's sexual orientation and gender identity, as well as to promote the elimination of discrimination in employment and at schools, the ruling parties submitted a "Promotion of Understanding Bill" to the Diet which stated that rather than prohibiting discrimination against gender and sexual minorities, it was necessary first to create a society that recognized the diversity of sexual orientations and gender identities (in other words, to promote understanding), and that gender and sexual minorities themselves should first work to resolve the difficulties they face. The first draft of the understanding bill was shelved due to opposition from the conservative wing of the ruling party, but a revised version passed in June 2023.

Meanwhile, the Diet has made no progress on legislation regarding same-sex marriage: in 2019, thirteen same-sex couples in Tokyo, Osaka,

Nagoya, Sapporo, and Fukuoka simultaneously filed lawsuits against the state, demanding the right to marry. The plaintiffs claimed that the state's ban on same-sex marriage violated the rights guaranteed by the Constitution, such as "freedom of marriage" and "equality under the law." As of 2023, three district courts had ruled against the state's refusal to recognize same-sex marriage, with one ruling it unconstitutional, one constitutional, and one not in violation of the Constitution, but having "unconstitutional status." The deliberations continue in the High Court and Supreme Court.

While deliberations in the Diet had thus not progressed, local governments were quick to implement measures for same-sex couples: in March 2015, Tokyo's Shibuya City enacted the "Shibuya City Ordinance to Promote a Society in which Members Respect Gender Equality and Diversity," declaring that the city would recognize and certify same-sex partner relationships, and since then, various issues surrounding so-called "gender and sexual minorities" have attracted attention in Japan. Since the passage of this ordinance by Shibuya City, as of September 2020, fifty-nine local governments throughout Japan have introduced this system, and local governments' interest in issues concerning gender and sexual minorities has been growing rapidly.[1]

Here, we focus on the process of establishing the "Same-sex Partnership Oath System" in Osaka City which was enacted in July 2018. In Osaka, a new regional political party, the Osaka Restoration Association (*Ōsaka ishin no kai*, also known as One Osaka), was formed in 2010. In 2011, candidates from Osaka Restoration Association were elected governor of Osaka Prefecture and mayor of Osaka City, respectively. Subsequent human rights policies in Osaka City have strongly reflected the Osaka Restoration Association's corporate management approach. This chapter will analyze why the same-sex partnership system was introduced, and what kind of people were involved in its establishment,

---

1   For a discussion of changes in local government efforts to address policies concerning gender and sexual minorities, see "Nihon ni okeru kuia sutadīzu no kōchiku" kenkyū gurūpu ("Construction of Queer Studies in Japan" Research Group) ed., 2017.

while human rights measures that had been in place for many years since the end of the Second World War (WWII) were successively eliminated under the mayoralty of the Osaka Restoration Association. Here, we will analyze how the "Same-sex Partnership Oath System" in Osaka City was institutionalized through the politics of city council members, city officials, and the gender and sexual minority members involved who needed that system, and we will consider the system's symbolic meaning.

Background to the study

Prior research

In recent years, various studies on gender and sexual minorities have been conducted in Japan. A survey conducted in Osaka City in 2019 that mailed questionnaires to 15,000 people aged 18–59 randomly selected from the Basic Resident Registers of Osaka City, found that of the 4,285 valid responses (valid response rate: 28.6%), 352 respondents (8.2%) indicated they were "gay/lesbian," "bisexual," "asexual," "undecided/prefer not to decide," or "transgender" (Hiramori and Kamano 2020). It is hoped that human rights measures will be implemented by authorities based on these data.

Until now, legal scholars have often discussed the legal and social significance of a "same-sex partnership system" in Japan, but their discussions have focused on the legal implications of this system (Ninomiya 2019; Shin Ajia kazoku hō sangoku kaigi ed. 2018; Ninomiya ed. 2017; Kamikawa 2016; Taniguchi 2016). There have been few systematic studies of the process of institutional establishment from a political perspective. In analyzing why local governments came to implement the same-sex partnership system, various actors must be recognized. Several publications specifically describe who was involved in establishing this system, and in what manner, but most of these concentrate on efforts in Tokyo (Ninomiya 2017; LGBT Law Federation 2016; Shinohara 2016; Esumuraruda and Kira 2015).

While this partnership system was welcomed by the parties who needed a system, various problems have been pointed out. For example, use of this system does not enable gender and sexual minorities to equally enjoy the benefits guaranteed by legal marriage between heterosexuals (Taniguchi 2016; Sugiura 2019; Sugiura et al. 2016); the system was established using neoliberal market logic, and risks sidelining human rights issues (Kawasaka 2015; Shimizu 2017; Shingae 2021); and a "new homonormativity" by gender and sexual minorities is underway (Duggan 2002) which may reduce the ability of such people to criticize the exclusivity and power of the institution of marriage itself (Masaki 2015; Horie 2015; Okano 2015). These issues have often been discussed in the context of Tokyo's Shibuya and Setagaya Cities, the pioneers in enacting the partnership system.

So, do local governments in regions other than Tokyo face similar problems to those described above? Taking account of the previous research, this chapter will broaden understanding of this measure by focusing on the establishment of the Same-sex Partnership Oath System in Osaka City.

Methodology

The data for this survey is based primarily on interviews with administrative officials and politicians who were involved in establishing the Same-sex Partnership Oath System in Osaka City, as well as with gay men, lesbians, and other gender and sexual minorities residing in Osaka City. Interviews with officials from the Osaka City department in charge were conducted at Osaka City Hall on September 6, 2018. Before conducting the interviews, the minutes of Osaka City Council meetings were reviewed to learn what councilors had said about the Same-sex Partnership Oath System.

I also interviewed the councilors who spoke at the Osaka City Council about the Same-sex Partnership Oath System and other measures for gender and sexual minorities. I interviewed Tomoko Yamamoto, a member of the New Komeito Party, on December 3, 2018; Yoshika Itō, a member of the Osaka Restoration Association, on December 5,

2018; and Makoto Umezono, a former member of the Osaka Restoration Association, on November 28, 2018, each in Osaka City.

Outline of the survey area

The city of Osaka, the target area of the survey, had a population of 2.77 million as of January 1, 2024. Osaka City's Same-sex Partnership Oath System came into effect on July 9, 2018, and as of June 30, 2020, 200 couples had applied and registered. This was the largest number of applicants among local governments nationwide that had implemented similar programs. Incidentally, Osaka Prefecture (in which Osaka City is located) launched the "Osaka Prefecture Same-Sex Partnership Oath Certification System" on January 22, 2020, and made all residents in Osaka Prefecture eligible to use it.

Human rights policies and "pinkwashing" in Osaka City

From the Human Rights Office to the Diversity Promotion Office

First, we will examine the establishment of the Same-sex Partnership Oath System in Osaka City, starting with the administrative department in charge of managing the system. Currently, the department in charge of this system is the Diversity Promotion Office of the Osaka City Citizens Bureau. The department was given the name "Diversity" in October 2013, which offers a glimpse of how Osaka City's policies for gender and sexual minorities were positioned within the city government.

Osaka City is a metropolis inhabited by diverse minorities, and its administration has made enthusiastic efforts to address human rights issues. Osaka City's human rights measures began with the establishment in 1955 of the "Osaka City *Dōwa* 'social integration' Issue Research Office" in the Welfare Division of the Civil Affairs Bureau, which marked the beginning of the city's current human rights policies focusing on institutionalized discrimination against *Buraku* communities, made outcasts in feudal Japan and still disadvantaged in terms of education, employment and housing. Since then, the city has actively engaged in human rights education activities for its citizens. The Osaka Museum

of Human Rights History (Liberty Osaka)[2] was established in 1985;
the Osaka International Peace Center (Peace Osaka) in 1991; and the
Asia-Pacific Human Rights Information Center (Hurights Osaka) in
1994, as bases for these educational activities. These facilities were
funded by private foundations and subsidized by the Osaka prefectural
and municipal governments. At the time of its opening, Liberty Osaka,
in particular, was the only museum in Japan that exhibited materials
dedicated to human rights.

Along with the *Buraku* residents' social integration issue, the city's
human rights policies expanded to encompass other minority issues.
The city of Osaka was originally dotted with neighborhoods with
concentrations of residents in low socioeconomic circumstances, such
as resident Koreans, *Burakumin*, and day laborers. The city's human
rights policies for LGBT and other gender and sexual minorities have
been part of this system since the 2010s. The "Osaka City Ordinance for
Creating a Society that Respects Human Rights," which forms the basis
for the city's current human rights policies, was enacted in April 2000,
and the "Osaka City Human Rights Administration Headquarters" was
established in 2008. February 2009 saw the enactment of the "Osaka City
Human Rights Administration Promotion Plan," the city's action plan for
addressing human rights issues.

Promoting diversity in city management

However, a notable change in Osaka City's human rights policies
occurred after Tōru Hashimoto became mayor in 2011. After assuming
the mayoralty, Hashimoto – a member of the Osaka Restoration
Association – incorporated corporate management methods into his
administrative operations. Hashimoto's guide was Shinichi Ueyama,
a management consultant and academic who introduced corporate
management approaches to public administration (Ueyama and Osaka
2008). Accordingly, it was within that set of managerial logics that the
human rights measures of the past were transformed into new diversity

---

2   Renamed Osaka Human Rights Museum in 1995.

Table 10.1: The structure of Osaka City Citizens' Affairs Bureau

Until 2013	From 2013
Citizens' Affairs Bureau	Citizens' Affairs Bureau
Citizens' Affairs Department	Citizens' Affairs Department
General Affairs Section Municipal Administration Section Community Activities Section Employment & Labor Policy Section Gender Equality Section Consumer Center	General Affairs Section Municipal Administration Section Community Activities Section Employment & Labor Policy Section Consumer Center
Human Rights Office	Diversity Promotion Office
Planning and Coordination Section Human Rights Education & Consultation Center	Human Rights Planning Section Gender Equality Section Human Rights Education & Consultation Center

policies. Diversity management has been an important research area in management studies since the 1970s, and the Osaka City approach to human rights for gender and sexual minorities must be considered in this light (Shingae 2021).

The new Diversity Promotion Office within the Osaka City Citizens Bureau was established in October 2013. Three sections were set up within that office: the Human Rights Planning Section, the Gender Equality Section, and the Human Rights Education and Consultation Center. Prior to the establishment of the Diversity Promotion Office, the Osaka City Citizens' Affairs Bureau had two divisions, the Citizens' Affairs Department and the Human Rights Office, with the latter in charge of human rights policies. The Human Rights Office was renamed the Diversity Promotion Office in 2013, and the Human Rights Planning Section, in charge of human rights policies, was placed within that office. In other words, diversity is a higher-level concept, and the Human Rights Planning Section is subordinate to it (see Table 10.1).

This change of signage was no mere change of nomenclature. It means that the logic of diversity management has penetrated human rights policies. The key point of diversity management lies in the utilization of diverse human resources. If human rights policies heretofore have been implemented to protect the human rights of individuals with various political, economic, cultural, and social backgrounds, and to educate people to eliminate discrimination, then diversity policies must also protect those human rights while utilizing the individuality of minorities for the invigoration of society. At a meeting of the Osaka City Council for Gender Equality in October 2013, a city official explained the organizational reform of the Citizens' Affairs Bureau in terms of diversity as follows:

> To respect people's differences in values and lifestyles, not only in terms of gender, nationality, age, physical condition, and external appearance, and for all to give full play to their individuality and live in a way true to themselves, *are vital* not only from a human rights perspective *but also from the perspective of maintaining and enhancing the vitality of the city; and the challenge is to understand that diversity and to capitalize upon it.*[3]

Using *katakana* – the Japanese script commonly used to transliterate foreign words – to spell out "diversity" (*daibāshiti*) as an abbreviation for the English expression "diversity and inclusion," Osaka City states that it aims for "acceptance of diversity" and "inclusion of diversity."[4] The Same-sex Partnership Oath System initiated by the municipality was one of the measures initiated under this conceptualization of diversity.

This diversity policy is positioned within Osaka City's "Municipal Reform Plan." The "Municipal Reform Plan 2.0" for fiscal years 2016 through 2019 aimed to promote "reforms that create new values." The plan clearly stated that while "efficient and effective administrative management through the thorough elimination of waste" would be carried out by such means as reducing expenditure and securing revenue,

---

3   From minutes of the 25th Osaka City Council for Gender Equality meeting, October 21, 2013 (emphasis added).

4   https://www.city.osaka.lg.jp/shimin/cmsfiles/contents/0000348/348740/3siryou1.pdf.

reducing the number of employees, and reviewing external organizations, "reforms to improve quality by thoroughly utilizing ICT [Information and Communications Technology] and drawing out the abilities of employees to the maximum extent" would be promoted.[5] In other words, the city had to make the best use of its limited budget and personnel in the face of tight finances. The diversity policy was to be rolled out based on the logic that the active participation of a diverse workforce was required to generate innovation throughout Osaka City, and that proactively utilizing this diversity would foster economic growth.

The city's diversity policy appears to have been further strengthened in recent years, with its human rights policy being reinforced by its labor policy. In April 2020, the Citizens' Affairs Bureau was again reorganized, and a new "Promotion of Women's Participation and Advancement in the Workplace Section" was established within the Diversity Promotion Office. The new structure was designed to further promote the utilization of diverse human resources as part of the workforce.

"Pinkwashing" in Osaka City

At first glance, the change of signage from "human rights" to "diversity" may appear to have been a harmless move. However, what was happening behind the scenes was a clear retreat from human rights policies.

First, after a visit in April 2012 by Osaka Mayor Tōru Hashimoto and Osaka Prefecture Governor Ichirō Matsui – another member of the Osaka Restoration Association – the prefectural and municipal governments decided to stop subsidizing Liberty Osaka, the Osaka Museum of Human Rights. They argued that the museum's exhibits on comfort women and feminism were one-sided and biased, and that "we asked the museum to be a place where children can think about their future, but the exhibits are not compliant" (*Sankei shinbun* 2015). For many years, the facility had also been used as a training facility for elementary and junior high school students and city employees and had served as a base for the city's

---

5   Osaka City "Municipal Reform Plan 2.0: Reforms to Create New Value," August 2016.

human rights awareness activities. In November 2013, the city demanded a fee for the use of the city-owned land where the facility is located, and, in a further step, in July 2015 Mayor Hashimoto unilaterally filed a lawsuit against the museum.[6] However, on June 19, 2020, the city and the museum reached a settlement at the Osaka District Court whereby the land would be cleared by June 2021 and the museum would be exempted from paying the approximately 190 million yen in rent owing since 2015. The museum would be closed temporarily on May 28, 2020, and reopened in a different location, and operated independently by donations and membership fees.

Similar municipal interventions in human rights-related facilities occurred at the Osaka International Peace Center (Peace Osaka), which announced in April 2013 that it would reopen in 2014 with revised exhibits, minus its previous exhibit on Japanese military aggression during WWII. After the reopening, Mayor Hashimoto continued to express his disapproval of the "Nanjing Massacre" exhibit and demanded that its content be changed to focus on damage caused by air raids on Osaka. Citizens and academic societies sent letters of protest to the governor and mayor in response to these alterations to the exhibit. In particular, the citizens' group "Liaison Group to Think about Peace Osaka's Crisis" (Peace Osaka *no kiki o kangaeru renraku kai*) filed a lawsuit against the prefectural and city governments and the center's management body, demanding the disclosure of official documents showing how and why the center changed its exhibits. In May 2019, the Osaka District Court ruled that withholding of that information was illegal and rejected the prefectural and city governments' appeal to the Supreme Court (*Asahi shinbun* 2019).

The breakdown of the sister city relationship between San Francisco and Osaka occurred in a similar context: in February 2017, the then Osaka Mayor Hirofumi Yoshimura sent an open letter to the mayor of

---

6   The land on which this museum stood had originally been donated by *Buraku* community members for the purpose of building an educational facility for eliminating discrimination against *Buraku* (*Kaihō shinbun* 2018).

Photo 10.1: Statue of comfort
women near Chinatown,
in San Francisco
(photo by author, February 27, 2019)

San Francisco to protest its erection of a memorial to comfort women (BBC 2018). The Mayor of Osaka's concerns were that individuals differ in their interpretations of history, and that the inscription made one-sided claims based on uncertain historical evidence. The reply from the mayor of San Francisco was that the City Council had unanimously approved the installation of the comfort women's memorial which had been donated by a citizens' group. In response, the Mayor of Osaka demanded that the statue be withdrawn from city ownership and informed the City of San Francisco that if it did not comply, it would dissolve their sister city relationship. The dissolution came to pass in October 2018.

Each of these incidents appears to have undermined the human rights policies that the City of Osaka and its citizens had been working on for decades. In fact, the discriminated-against *Buraku* communities involved in the establishment of the Osaka City Human Rights Museum, the war victims who engaged in peace activities, and the citizens of San Francisco who fostered interaction with Osaka for sixty years have all been directly and negatively affected by these incidents. What is unique about them is that they were all top-down decisions made by the prefectural governor and mayor. The Osaka Museum of Human Rights was closed in 2020, although the department in charge of this museum was the Diversity

Promotion Office, which operates the Same-sex Partnership Oath System. Thus, dual moves were simultaneously underway: on the one hand, the exclusion of human rights issues relating to war and wartime sexual violence; and on the other hand, the inclusion of new foci such as LGBT rights.

The Osaka City government's stance on human rights could probably be characterized as "pinkwashing," which refers to the practice of powerful actors appearing to defend human rights for some sexual minorities while at the same time covering up human rights violations against other minorities (Ritchie 2015). This has been discussed by US political scientist Lisa Duggan as part of her discussion of "new homonormativity" (Duggan 2002). The development of friendly policies toward sexual minorities by Israel and Tokyo's Shibuya City, while behind the scenes repeatedly violating human rights vis-à-vis Palestinians and excluding homeless people from public spaces, qualify as examples of such pinkwashing (Shimizu 2017). Compared to Shibuya City, Osaka City's pinkwashing exudes a more nationalistic flavor, while at the same time discriminating against elderly people who have long been involved in human rights activities. Osaka City has officially adopted a position of addressing various human rights issues that arise in the city, but in practice not everyone is recognized as an individual with dignity; rather, the diversity of minorities is utilized by the city's economic strategy, and minorities are included in the framework of "good citizens" to that limited extent. The human rights that have been fought for and won by those who have worked for years for the social integration of *Buraku* and for proper recognition of war damages are treated coldly, while new diversity issues such as multiculturalism and LGBT are emphasized.

The Same-sex Partnership Oath System in Osaka City

When the Same-sex Partnership Oath System in Osaka City is discussed in the above context, a new perspective emerges, namely, the symbolic meaning of same-sex partnership. How can same-sex partners be included as "good citizens?"

Osaka City launched its Same-sex Partnership Oath System on July 9, 2018, based on the "Osaka City Guideline for Certification of Oath of Partnership." The key point is that the system was implemented in the form of a "guideline" (*yōkō*) rather than an "ordinance" (*jōrei*). Ordinances require the approval of the City Council to be enacted, and once enacted, they have external force and binding effect, while guidelines are internal rules created autonomously by the administration, and do not require City Council approval. The first municipality to enact this system in the form of an ordinance was Tokyo's Shibuya City.[7]

Accordingly, when an ordinance is enacted, its approval or disapproval is determined by the council's power structure. When such human rights issues are decided by a majority vote of the council, minorities may be disadvantaged.

---

7   In Shibuya City's case, in 2015 there was no ordinance, action plan or suchlike that would form the basis for systematizing a same-sex partnership system: prior to the enactment of the "Shibuya City Gender Equality and Diversity Promotion Ordinance" on March 31, 2015, "LGBT" was not even mentioned in the gender equality plan. Neither was there any ordinance to serve as the basis for its establishment (Kamikawa 2016: 232). In the process of creating an ordinance on gender equality, Shibuya City chose to include the same-sex partnership system in the ordinance. However, after the ordinance was passed in March 2015, the way former Mayor Kuwabara and current Mayor Hasebe had conducted themselves in this matter caused lingering resentment in the City Assembly. Some Assembly members who voted in favor of the ordinance's passage criticized the hurried manner of the discussion. For example, they were rebuked in statements by Kenpō Suzuki (DPP) at the March 2015 General Affairs and Community Affairs Committee meeting, Mari Satō (LDP) at the regular Assembly session the same month, and Takumi Tanaka, a member of the groups *Shibuya o egao ni suru kai* (Make Shibuya smile) and *Nihon o genki ni suru kai* (Invigorate Japan), at the May 2016 regular session. In particular, the enactment of the ordinance triggered a change in the name of the Women's Center Iris, which had played a central role in gender equality and women's civic activities in Shibuya City, to the Shibuya Gender Equality Diversity Center. The draft ordinance was submitted without hearing from the 139 registered women's action groups in the city according to Mari Satō (LDP) at the March 2015 regular session and by Kenpō Suzuki (DPP) at the General Affairs and Community Affairs Committee meeting the same month. In an interview, a Shibuya City official (September 22, 2017) mentioned that similar criticism had been made by citizens.

In contrast, a guideline is characterized as an internal administrative manual or regulation with no legally binding force. Currently, several local governments across Japan have launched systems similar to Osaka City's Same-sex Partnership Oath System, but only Tokyo's Shibuya City has passed an ordinance; all other local governments have adopted guidelines, which can be implemented at the discretion of the head of the municipality. Setagaya City in Tokyo was the first to enact a same-sex partnership system in this form.[8] Some may argue that issues which should not be decided by a majority vote, such as human rights measures, are better addressed in the form of a guideline, to the extent allowed by the Constitution. The greatest vulnerability of this approach is that although it progresses without going through a municipal council, it is not legally binding.

The "Osaka City Guideline for Certification of Partnership Oath" is, as the title suggests, a document showing that a couple has "sworn an oath" to the mayor that they are in a partnership, and the city government has then "certified" their relationship. Article 2 of the guideline defines "gender and sexual minority" and "partnership relationship" as follows:

Article 2.1: The term "sexual minorities" as used in this guideline shall mean persons whose sexual orientation is not necessarily heterosexual or whose gender identity differs from that of their sex [assigned] at birth.

Article 2.2: The term "partnership relationship" as used in this guideline shall mean a relationship between two persons, one or both of whom are

---

8   When the same-sex partnership system was being discussed in Setagaya City, the mayor was affiliated with the Social Democratic Party, but half of the assembly was made up of an "anti-mayoral" faction, including the LDP and the New Komeito party. Although the mayor had the authority to propose the ordinance, there was a chance that it would be rejected by the assembly. Furthermore, if the ordinance had been rejected by the assembly, there would be widespread outrage if the mayor then introduced it as a guideline. Hence, Aya Kamikawa, an Assembly member who was involved in the design of the system, was determined to introduce it as a guideline rather than an ordinance from the beginning (interview with Kamikawa, December 10, 2018).

sexual minorities, who have committed to cooperate with each other in their daily lives, making each other their life partner.[9]

According to this definition, for example, heterosexuals in a de facto marriage relationship cannot use this system; it is a system specifically for gender and sexual minorities.[10] The gist of the same-sex partnership oath system is that gender and sexual minority partners "swear" to the mayor that they will cooperate with each other in their daily lives and the mayor "certifies" that oath. In other words, they undergo an equivalent process to a heterosexual couple submitting a marriage license to have their relationship recognized. This is in accordance with the principle of inclusion of gender and sexual minority couples in society on par with heterosexual couples.[11]

So, what are the specific benefits of the city issuing this certification? Table 10.2 compares the three forms of partnership, namely, legal marriage, de facto marriage, and the same-sex partnership oath certification (referred to in the table as SSPC). It shows that a same-sex partnership certificate does not convey the same benefits as legal marriage. Designation of the beneficiary for life insurance and the right to visit a hospitalized partner and consent to medical treatment on their behalf are handled differently by different insurance companies and hospitals. In addition, the right to claim a share of property and the right to inherit are not recognized without notarization, and a same-sex partnership certificate alone has no legal effect. Even when children are raised by same-sex partners, a parent who is not related to the child or children by blood has no legal rights vis-à-vis the children, and plenary adoptions are not permitted. However, legal scholars argue that this certificate may be treated in the future as equivalent to legal protection as a de facto

---

9   https://www.city.osaka.lg.jp/shimin/page/0000439064.html

10 In Chiba City, by contrast, the system permits heterosexual couples in de facto marriages to also use it.

11 Note, however, that this system continues to exclude gender and sexual minorities identifying as asexual, polygamous or other than LGBT.

Table 10.2: Differences among legal marriage, de facto marriage and same-sex partnership certification

	Legal marriage	De facto marriage	SSPC
Spousal deduction for income/residents' tax	✓	✕	✕
Eligibility for survivor's pension	✓	✓	✕
Obligation of cohabitation/cooperation/assistance*	✓	✓	Notarized document**
Shared custody of children	✓	✕	✕
Plenary adoption	✓	✕	✕
Right to claim a share of property	✓	✓	Notarized document**
Right to inherit	✓	✕	Notarized document**
Designation as life insurance beneficiary†	✓	✓/✕	✓/✕
Application for public housing	✓	✓	✓
Right to visit when partner hospitalized/consent to partner's medical treatment	✓	✓	✓

*   Article 752 of the Japanese Civil Code stipulates: (Duty to Live Together, Cooperate, and Be of Assistance to Each Other) A husband and wife must live together, cooperate with each other, and act so as to be of assistance to each other.

** Because the Japanese Civil Code does not recognize same-sex couples and its provisions on marriage do not apply to them, many same-sex couples draft a notarial deed to declare their relationship to be the equivalent of a legal marriage, which typically includes a commitment to comply with the Civil Codes provisions for legal marriage, such as the obligation to cohabitate, the right to property, and the right to inherit.

†   Some Japanese insurance companies recognize same-sex partners as beneficiaries, but conditions vary.

relationship without a marriage, and that it is incorrect to say that it has no legal effect (Nakagawa 2016: 221–222).

Therefore, at present, the same-sex partnership certificate does not have legal substance, but is "symbolic," giving the impression that same-sex couples are equal to opposite-sex couples. If one wants to enjoy legal and financial benefits in a partnership, a notarized document is sufficient without a same-sex partnership certificate. What is important in the certificate is that the relationship is sworn before and approved by a mayor. Despite the individuals in question being gender and sexual minorities, the mayor's recognition of their lifelong partnership is at the same time recognition of "good citizens," despite the system affirming that their partnership is not in fact equal to legal marriages between heterosexuals. For example, couples receive their oath certification at the Human Rights and Education Consultation Center in Osaka City's Nishi Ward. According to a city survey of those who have gone through the procedure and sworn the oath, some reported that the location gave them a "sense of alienation, and had the image of being hidden away." The city's expressed intention in choosing that location was to ensure privacy, and to connect applicants to available consultation services, but beneath those intentions were deep-seated concerns that conducting these ceremonies in a more prominent location would cause trouble, given the many different views on the matter.[12]

Establishing the Same-sex Partnership Oath System in Osaka City

Councilors and mayors

From here on, we will focus on how the Same-sex Partnership Oath System was established in Osaka City. To foreshadow the conclusion, the implementation of the system in Osaka City was decided in a top-down manner, mainly between Osaka Restoration Association councilor Itō and Mayor Yoshimura. The following is an examination of the process.

Questions were first raised at the Osaka City Council about LGBT issues that would lead to the enactment of the Same-sex Partnership Oath System at a regular meeting of the Standing Committee in March 2017. Councilor Tomoko Yamamoto from the New Komeito Party and former Osaka Restoration Association Councilor Makoto Umezono[13] asked about efforts being made vis-à-vis LGBT and other gender and sexual minorities in Osaka City.

---

12 Interview with an Osaka City Hall employee, September 6, 2018.

13 Osaka City Councilor Umezono originally represented the Osaka Restoration Association but left that group in October 2016.

Councilor Yamamoto was first to raise the question. She said that her interest in LGBT issues was triggered when she had traveled to Brazil before becoming a council member, where she had encountered an LGBT parade. She had also worked as a care worker before joining the council, and suspected that gender and sexual minorities would face a variety of problems in their old age. After becoming a councilor, she reportedly heard directly from gender and sexual minorities when meeting with members of NPOs active in Osaka City, and by participating in LGBT events. Based on these experiences, Yamamoto took the opportunity to ask questions at the city council.

Before Councilor Umezono became a councilor, he had worked for a well-known foreign apparel brand, where he met gender and sexual minorities. After becoming a councilor, he attended an LGBT lecture in Osaka City, where he was exposed to the complex issues faced by LGBT people, such as coming out. Becoming more interested in the issue, he began to study it, and then to ask questions at city council meetings. However, Councilors Yamamoto and Umezono did not mention a partnership system at the March 2017 meeting.

It was at the council's regular session in March 2018 that concrete steps were first taken towards enacting a same-sex partnership oath system. This time, Councilor Yoshika Itō, a member of the Osaka Restoration Association, asked about the system at the council's regular session. Prior to joining the city council, she had worked as a model overseas alongside many gender and sexual minorities. As she was also single when first becoming a councilor, she experienced sexual harassment by fellow councilors who asked her such things as whether she was going to marry, and why she did not have children despite the declining birthrate. She was thus sympathetic to the situation of gender and sexual minorities, as well as being aware of the male chauvinism that is deeply rooted in political culture, and its impact on people's ability to freely choose their life-style. With this background, Itō was strongly committed to realizing a same-sex partnership oath system.

During a briefing with Mayor Yoshimura, when Councilor Itō said she wanted to question the council about this partnership system, the mayor reportedly stated that while he did not tolerate discrimination against LGBT people, it would be impossible to implement a same-sex partnership system in Osaka City. When Councilor Itō first contacted the Citizens' Affairs Bureau, the answer was similar. Some councilors from the Osaka Restoration Association also opposed the idea. In the end, however, Councilor Itō persuaded the mayor and the Citizens' Affairs Bureau to move forward with passing the same-sex partnership oath system.

Gender and sexual minorities with systemic needs

One thing Councilors Yamamoto, Umezono, and Itō had in common was that they had all had close contact with gender and sexual minority members in the past; and, based on the efforts of other local governments, they believed that similar efforts were needed in Osaka City. However, while Komeito Councilor Yamamoto had met directly with gender and sexual minorities residing in Osaka City, Osaka Restoration Association Councilor Itō and former Osaka Restoration Association Councilor Umezono had not heard directly from any Osaka City residents about their needs. For example, Councilor Umezono stated in the City Council's Question Time that he had not dared to contact any who were active in the city. He said that this was because he was afraid that if he listened to too many different opinions, his way of thinking might become blurred in various ways, and he might become biased in a certain direction if he became involved with gender and sexual minorities whose ideology or thinking differed from his own. Councilor Itō, in turn, said that she heard from a sexual minority in her local constituency, but that person had already moved away from Osaka; however, she had heard various opinions via social media about the need for such a system.

In response to Councilor Itō's question at the council session in March 2018, the mayor announced that he would like to create a same-sex partnership system in Osaka City. The Osaka City Diversity Promotion Office was thus instructed to begin preparations for the specific operation of the system. However, the idea of establishing a same-sex partnership system in Osaka City was a complete surprise to individuals and organizations supporting gender and sexual minorities, who quickly began to prepare a written submission requesting that the city government make the system easy to use for those involved. A draft of the request was prepared by volunteers from several NPOs, the Osaka Bar Association, and academics, who then solicited for support through their networks. The request was submitted to Osaka City Hall on April 12, 2018.

To the best of my knowledge, this written submission was never made public, but we understand the basic demands to be (1) an easy-to-use and effective system developed through consultation with the parties concerned, as well as support groups, lawyers, academic researchers and other experts; (2) that the partnership registration system should be available without limiting legal gender combinations, just like in Sapporo and Fukuoka Cities;[14] (3) that a certificate be issued to couples who register their partnership; and (4) that couples who register their partnership be eligible for family administrative services provided by the City of Osaka, and that the city thoroughly review the scope of "family" across its administrative services to ensure that same-sex couples can enjoy the same benefits as family members even if they do not register their partnerships. Furthermore, the petitioners asked (5) that the city seek to ensure that citizens and businesses respect partnership registrations; and that the city should be able to condemn, or even penalize, discriminatory treatment.

My examination of the same-sex partnership oath system in Osaka City clearly indicates that the system's designers took the above concerns into account. Nevertheless, as the system was initially discussed by Councilor Itō and Mayor Yoshimura and debated at the City Council before any consultation with the gender and sexual minorities involved, this was very much a "top-down" approach. Although the opinions of

---

14 Sapporo City initiated its partnership system on June 1, 2018, and Fukuoka City on April 1, 2018. The expression "without limiting legal gender combinations" refers to the fact that in those cities "couples in which one or both parties are gender and sexual minorities may use the system without limiting combinations of legal gender combinations."

some gender and sexual minorities were reflected in the submission and subsequently in the system design, the system was arguably established without sufficient input from the people most affected.

Conclusion

In this chapter, we have examined the process leading to the creation of the Same-sex Partnership Oath System in Osaka City in relation to the city's human rights and diversity policies, and have clarified the actors involved in its creation. We concluded that this system in Osaka City was established by the mayor as a top-down measure. The mayor, representing the Osaka Restoration Association, adopted a new corporate management approach in his administration, with a view to Osaka City's growth strategy. While on the one hand he eliminated conventional human rights policies, on the other he adopted gender and sexual minorities as a new policy target from the perspective of diversity management. Diversity management, which has been incorporated into Osaka City's regional revitalization efforts, seeks to develop measures that protect the human rights of diverse minorities, such as women, foreigners, and LGBT people, as well as utilizing their human resources.

What is particularly striking throughout this analysis is the change in the administration's attitude toward human rights issues. Human rights measures that had been in place since WWII, such as the *Buraku* Liberation Movement and the peace movement, were forced to scrap or change their projects due to the mayor's nationalistic beliefs, while the topic of gender and sexual minorities emerged rapidly as a new human rights issue. In the 2010s, some human rights policies that had been cultivated over the years were eliminated through the mayor's top-down approach as his emphasis shifted towards diversity management in terms of urban revitalization and growth strategies. In other words, the conventional measures that recognized basic human rights and individual dignity were reinterpreted to focus on marshalling diverse human resources toward revitalizing the economy. Similarly, the human rights agenda that focused on individual dignity and equality has become a mere shell, while meek gender and sexual minorities who do not vocally claim their rights or criticize seem to be privileged as "good citizens."[15]

So, how should we regard the relationship between human rights and diversity? Are human rights and diversity opposites, or can they work together? Unlike traditional human rights measures, new diversity policies represent gender and sexual minorities in connection with urban corporate business and marketing. This representation seems to be stripped of the politics of advocating for, winning and fighting for human rights and entitlements.[16] Only those gender and sexual minorities who fit the logic of the marketplace are included in society as "good citizens." But the representation of such gender and sexual minorities is also political.

In either case, human rights policies have reached a major turning point. Are human rights becoming outdated and old-fashioned? Will gender and sexual minorities be positioned as second-class citizens despite surface appearances of acceptance? Will diversity policies truly protect the human rights of minorities? We will need to monitor these issues closely in the future.

---

15 Gender and sexual minorities may have a greater affinity with economic stimulus than other segments of the population that are prioritized in human rights measures, such as foreigners, women, and the *Buraku* communities. For example, the marketization of gender and sexual minorities, including "pink tourism," makes it easier to link human rights advocacy and neoliberalism. Gender and sexual minority issues also have a high affinity with nationalism in a globalized society (Puar 2007), and further examination of why gender and sexual minorities have become an important human rights issue in recent years is warranted.

16 Gon Matsunaka, for one, who was highly instrumental in establishing the same-sex partnership system in Shibuya City, said:

When I hear the words 'same-sex marriage' or 'same-sex partnership,' I get a strong image of a 'rights-oriented approach.' Of course, it is important, but I myself have always thought in relation to the activities [of the group called] "Good Aging Yells (GAY)," as well, that I wanted to take a different approach from 'seeking a system,' wanting not to do anything political. (cited in Esumuraruda and Kira 2015: 39)

PART III

Identity Dynamics and Everyday Politics

11

"Kathoey" and *"Kee"* (Gay) are Equally Acceptable: Cisgender Men Who Desire Men and the *"Kathoey"* Category in Urban Laos

Yūsuke Ōmura[1]

Introduction

This chapter is a study of the categories *"kathoey"* (ກະເທີຍ) and *"kee"* (gay) (ເກ)[2] used in Laos, based on anthropological fieldwork conducted by the author in Vientiane, its capital.

From among the categories relating to gender and sexual minorities[3] in Laos, this chapter will focus on situations in which cisgender men living in urban Laos who desire men[4] use the word *"kathoey"* as a self-identifying category; or, conversely, distance themselves by using it as a term to denote persons different than themselves; and it will scrutinize and analyze the micro-politics of self-awareness and self-expression at work in this process.

The analysis in this paper was initiated by a word that appeared nonchalantly in a conversation with a research collaborator: on March 13,

1 This study was made possible by Konosuke Matsushita International Scholarship (from 2019 to 2021) and Grant-in-Aid for JSPS Fellows (Grant Number 23KJ0317) (in 2023).

2 The term "kee" (ເກ) discussed in this chapter is a Lao word derived from the English word "gay." In Romanized transcription, it is spelt "kee," but is pronounced [ge:].

3 The term "gender and sexual minorities" in this paper is used to refer to minorities in sexual orientation and gender identity (SOGI minorities).

4 The term "cisgender men who desire men" is used to refer to persons who have a male gender identity and are also sexually and emotionally attracted to men, regardless of their self-identification as homosexual, bisexual, or heterosexual.

2022, I was in Japan on a video call with Jan,[5] a friend and collaborator living in Vientiane. Jan was having a beer with his friend, Tho outside the front of the tenement house where Jan lived. Both Jan and Tho are cisgender men who desire men and describe themselves as "*kee*" (gay). During the conversation, Jan and Tho had different opinions about the word "*kathoey*." Tho stated that a *kathoey* was a person with long hair and feminine appearance, while Jan, in contrast, said that for him, "'*kathoey*' or '*kee*,' either way is fine," thus affirming his use of the word "*kathoey*" as a self-identifier, despite his masculine gender expression. This case will be described in detail below.

This chapter is an attempt to analyze the relationship between individuals and their categories of self-identification, including how latent understandings of categories influence individual behaviors. To understand the disagreement between Jan and Tho, and the implications of Jan's expression, "either way is fine," the first section of the chapter discusses previous research on categories in Thai discourse, which has a close linguistic relationship with Lao and is widely accepted and consumed (albeit to varying degrees) by the Lao people. I will review discussions of the Thai system of "*phet*," which encompasses matters relating to gender and sexuality, especially the positioning of and changes in the categories "*kathoey*" and "gay." In the second section I will provide an overview of the usage of the words "*kathoey*" and "*kee*"[6] in Lao, based on previous studies and the author's research, noting differences from the Thai situation and influences from Thai discourses.

The third section outlines findings from anthropological fieldwork conducted in Vientiane from February 2019 to May 2021, in August–September 2021, and in August 2023. First, I will describe in detail the scene in which Jan made the statement mentioned above, examining the

---

5   Personal names of people appearing in this chapter in accounts from the author's survey are pseudonyms.

6   In this chapter, the word "gay" as cited in prior studies related to Thailand and Laos is spelt according to its usage in those studies. In accounts based on the author's own research, the Romanized Lao spelling of "ເກ" as "*kee*" is used to emphasize that the English word "gay" has been accepted into the Lao vocabulary.

difference of opinion between the two friends. Further, I will introduce other situations in which Jan used the word *"kathoey"* as a self-designating category, and present relevant parts of my interviews with him; and analyze these with reference to his background, his current living situation, and the broad discourse on gender and sexuality in contemporary Laos. Finally, the chapter will address the possible implications of a study such as this, which focuses on individual practices of categorization.

"Kathoey" and "gay" in the *phet* system: A review of prior studies on Thailand

The term *kathoey* is understood to refer mainly to transgender women in contemporary Thai and Lao languages, but it is necessary to understand the broader categorization of gender and sexuality in Laos to tease out the nuances of the word and its relationship with cisgender men who desire men. Given the abundance of previous studies on Thailand and the linguistic proximity between Lao and Thai, as well as the active movement of people between the two countries (to be discussed in the next section), here I will introduce some previous studies on Thailand and then review the usage of the categories *kathoey* and gay in Thailand.

Rosalind Morris describes the conceptualization of gender and sexuality in contemporary Thailand as "a trinity of three sexes" and "a system of four sexualities" (Morris 1994: 17). The former is a framework based on the three gender categories: male, female, and *kathoey*, which predates modern times and persists despite significant historical transformations, while the "system of four sexualities" is a newer framework originating in the modern West, consisting of four sexual orientations based on a combination of gender binaries and homosexual/ heterosexual oppositions. By comparison, Peter Jackson points out that Morris's model is based on Western-centric assumptions distinguishing "gender" from "sexuality."[7] Instead, Jackson describes a system of

---

7   Here, I followed Jackson (2000) in employing the terms "gender" and "sexuality," but more strictly speaking, what Jackson calls "gender" refers to "gender identity"

"eroticized gender," called "*phet*" (เพศ) in Thailand, where a number of categories including male, female, *kathoey*, gay, and *tom* (a Thai category for lesbian women with masculine gender expression) have appeared and disappeared over time (Jackson 2000: 409–411).

Inspired by Arjun Appadurai's concept of "scapes," Dredge Byung'chu Käng conceptualizes a Thai genderscape spread across multiple nodes or clusters with a certain degree of stability (Käng 2014: 423–424). Käng points to five categories – "*tom* : woman : *kathoey* : gay : man" (Käng 2014: 410) – as nodes that form the core of the contemporary Thai genderscape. While Jackson (2000) outlined a system in which numerous categories of *phet* proliferate, diverge, and disappear from one era to the next, Käng presents an image in which the categories of *phet* cluster around these five core nodes (Käng 2014: 424). Importantly, Käng observes that perceptions of a genderscape vary from actor to actor (just as perceptions of space varies from person to person) (Käng 2014: 424); hence, a genderscape is a conceptualization of "how gender categories are grounded but also fluid in everyday life" (Käng 2012: 476).

Let us now look at previous studies of the relationship between cisgender men who desire men in Thailand and the categories *kathoey* and gay (within the system of the *phet* or genderscape). Peter Jackson points out that the word gay first appeared in Bangkok newspapers in 1965, and argues that this was a sign that the word *kathoey* was beginning to change (Jackson, 1999a: 388–389). *Kathoey* had previously broadly encompassed cisgender men who desired men, or had sex with men, regardless of gender expression, but the term gay came to be used to differentiate those among them who were masculine in their gender expression and were "high class" (Jackson 1999a: 395–396). This trend has since transcended regions and classes, and in the 1990s there was a strong tendency for some cisgender men among those who desire men and expressed a masculine gender identity to identify as gay, differentiating themselves from *kathoey* (Jackson 1999a: 395–396; Jackson and Allyn 1995: 268–269).

---

or "gender category," and "sexuality" refers to "sexual orientation."

Note, however, that the trend to identify as gay and not *kathoey* was not all-encompassing, and that while some men might want to sharply distinguish the two identities, there remains considerable fluidity between them. Jackson and Allyn (1995) posited a continuum between the three categories: man,[8] gay and *kathoey*, and indicated that individuals might be positioned between these categories, or move among them. In terms of Käng's (2014) genderscape, we might think of these as three proximate nodes, though, rather than a continuum.

In the early 2010s Käng reported that, at least in Bangkok, the term *kathoey* was used only in reference to transgender women, but it continued to be used differently in other parts of the country (Käng 2012: 477). Käng observed that although many gay men disliked being called *kathoey*, it was common for gay men to refer to others as *kathoey* when joking with other gay men (Käng 2012: 477); and the term *"kathoey-noi"* was used to refer to something "just a little transgendered" (Käng 2012: 477–478). Furthermore, the word gay is ambiguous, with some interpretations emphasizing its masculinity, some perceiving it as feminine, while others think it refers to something like "versatility" in one's sexual preferences (Käng 2012: 478).

In other words, over the past few decades the term gay has been increasingly associated with cisgender men who desire men and differentiated from the category *kathoey*, which has become much more closely associated with transgender women.[9] In the process, though, *kathoey* and gay are increasingly perceived as distinct nodes; and it is important to recognize that different actors have different perceptions of the distance and differences between the two categories. In short, the

---

8 Here, "men" mainly refers to cisgender, heterosexual men.

9 This account discusses *kathoey* mainly from the perspective of cisgender homosexual men's relationship with them, but conceptions of *kathoey* from the perspective of transgender women would likely be different. Winter (2006), for example, reports the results of a survey conducted in Bangkok, Thailand in 2001–2002, in which 46.9% of the 195 respondents chose "woman," 12.3% *"kathoey,"* and 36.1% *"phu ying praphet song"* (meaning "second type of woman") in answer to a question about what category the respondent used to describe themself (Winter 2006: 21).

meanings and positioning of the two categories remain fluid, ambiguous and are still being negotiated.

Kathoey and *Kee* in Laos: An overview

The studies in Thai outlined above provide a point of reference for considering the connotations and relationships between the categories *kathoey* (กะเทย) and *kee* (เก) in Laos. Laos and Thailand border each other across the Mekong River, and have a long history of prolific interchange of people and goods as well as linguistic proximity (in particular, the Isan language spoken in northeastern Thailand is very close to Lao). Moreover, many people in Laos watch Thai television broadcasts, and more recently, it has become common to watch Thai dramas and other content on YouTube and Tiktok. Thus, many Laos people are exposed to Thai-language content from an early age, and with the spread of the internet and social media, access to information in Thai has become dramatically easier in recent years. In this context, understanding the relationship with Thai discourse is crucial when examining language use in Laos, and this holds true for gender and sexual categories.[10]

The perception that gender identity and sexual identity can be considered under a single system (or set) of *phet*, as suggested by Jackson and Käng's discussion on Thailand, probably holds true for Laos, as well.[11] The Lao term for "gender and sexual minorities" is a clear indication of this. Currently, the expression *"khon lak lai thang*

---

10   The term used in Thai to refer to a transgender woman, *"phu ying praphet song"* or *"sao praphet song,"* ("second type of woman") (see Note 9), is also used in Lao, albeit with a slight difference in pronunciation: *"phu nying paphet song"* or *"sao paphet song."* In addition, the terms used in Laos among cisgender men who desire men in reference to the roles taken in sexual activity are *"luk"* and *"hap,"* meaning "inserter (top)" and "insertee (bottom)," respectively. While the latter term, *"hap"* (ຮັບ) expresses "receiving" or "accepting" in Lao, the former, *"luk"* does not have any other meaning in Lao. This suggests that the Thai word *"ruk"* (รุก), meaning "push" or "offend," has been phonetically borrowed into Lao.

11   The word *"phet"* is written "เพศ," in Thai script, and "ເພດ" in Lao. I am not implying that people in Laos make no distinction between gender identity and sexual identity. What is at issue is the conceptual grouping in Thai and Lao.

phet" (ຄົນຫລາຽກາຫລາຽທາງເພດ) is often used in official documents and events involving international organizations, international NGOs, and national organizations (such as the National University of Laos and the Lao Women's Union). Literally translated, it means "people of various *phet*," but it is used to refer to gender and sexual minorities.[12] Moreover, the slang term *"phet thi sam"* (ເພດທີສາມ)" (meaning "third *phet*") is often used both by gender and sexual minorities, and other people in general.[13] If we turn our attention to the word *"phet,"* whether as "various *phet*" or "third *phet*," we will see that the concept *phet* includes both gender identity and sexual identity.

The categories *kathoey* and *kee* are positioned within this *phet* framework, as they are in Thailand (Thai language) as we saw above. As in Thai, the imported foreign word "gay" has been embraced by certain groups of cisgender men who desire men to self-identify as other than *kathoey*, a vernacular word and concept. There are very few studies of the use of *kathoey* and *kee* in Laos, but according to Chris Lyttleton (2008), who conducted a survey in 2006–2007, before 2000, the category of choice for self-identification by men who desired men was *kathoey*, regardless of whether they expressed a masculine or feminine gender identity. Since the 2000s, however, especially in urban areas, the English-derived gay has begun to be used to distinguish themselves from men who express a feminine gender identity, or *kathoey* (Lyttleton 2008: 1, 8).

Furthermore, based on data from 2010–2011, Chanthavilay and Sychareun (2014: 362) note that the word gay is becoming vernacular,

---

12 However, English-language concepts such as lesbian, transgender, LGBT and LGBTQ are often used by staff from SOGI minority groups during events and are frequently employed in web-based media articles. In such contexts, the expression "people with diverse genders and sexualities" is rather more ambiguous than LGBT, which specifies the members of a category, and "gender and sexual minorities," which specifies being in a "minority," so it is a moderate expression commonly used in public events and activities.

13 However, there are also some SOGI minority members who dislike this terminology, which considers "men" and "women" as being cisgender and heterosexual, and puts the rest into a "third" category. Implicit in this term is the recognition that SOGI minorities are viewed (or named by the minorities themselves) as being different from cisgender, heterosexual men and women.

but is not used much outside the capital. For example, they introduce a 25-year-old man from outside the capital who explains that he used to know only the word *kathoey*, but when he was in high school, he encountered the word gay and was confused at first, but later came to identify as gay (Chanthavilay and Sychareun 2014: 378–379).

By the time of my fieldwork in 2019, the use of *kee* as a category had become more widespread, with several *kee* groups having been formed on Facebook, giving the impression that at least in urban areas, it had become popular among men who desire men in Laos.[14] However, I could find no data that establishes the scope or scale of its diffusion. As discussed above, previous research found that the word *kee* was primarily used in urban areas, and it is likely to remain very different between urban and rural areas today. However, it has become easier in recent years for people to access media from neighboring Thailand through social networking services and online video, and for those who identify as *kee* to communicate with others without regional restrictions, which may have the effect of reducing regional differences in the diffusion of the *kee* category. Nevertheless, despite information and images being widely distributed through the media in neighboring Thailand, and expressions such as LGBT and gay becoming more commonly used in online media, it can be assumed that the term *kee* is generally only common among a small number of people in urban areas.

The word *kathoey*, though, is not as limited, being widely recognized by people of all gender and sexual identities as a vernacular Lao word. What follows is a summary of how *kathoey* is used in contemporary Lao based on my research. First, the main usage of "*kathoey*" is to refer to transgender women and male-to-female cross-dressers, both as a self-description by such individuals, and as an other-description.[15]

---

14 It is unclear precisely when and how the English-derived category gay became popular in Laos, but it seems likely that it was introduced via Thailand.

15 Chanthavilay and Sychareun observe a distinction within "*kathoey*" between "long-haired" and "short-haired" *kathoey*, the former always behaving and dressing as women, while the latter behave in what is considered to be a "feminine" manner, but dress in a "masculine" manner (Chanthavilay & Sychareun 2014: 368–369).

In Thailand, as mentioned, as more cisgender men who desire men embrace the word gay as distinct from *kathoey*, the latter has been more clearly differentiated and now primarily refers to transgender women. A similar trend can be seen in Laos. However, as per the example at the beginning of this chapter, there are still cisgender men who desire men who understand the word *kathoey* as referring to a category that includes them, even though they have a male gender identity.

Notably, when employed by cisgender heterosexuals, *kathoey* is occasionally still used as a blanket term to refer indiscriminately to transgender women, male-to-female cross-dressers, and cisgender men who desire men. In such cases, the term is sometimes used with a teasing or contemptuous nuance, but it is not uncommon for people to recognize the word *kathoey* in non-pejorative ways.[16] These are the circumstances in which Jan, introduced at the beginning of this chapter, calls himself *kee*, but says that *kathoey* is also acceptable. Now the question arises: Is the distinction between the two categories *kee* and *kathoey* not clear to Jan, or does he clearly distinguish between the two words, yet ventures to identify with both? In the next section, I will elaborate on the relationship between cisgender men who desire men in contemporary Laos and the two categories of *kee* and *kathoey*.

---

16 This is similar to the relationship between *bakla* and gay in the Philippines, as discussed by Kusaka in this volume (Ch. 13). While people who have embraced the concept of gay based on a male homosexual orientation emphasize its difference from the vernacular concept of *bakla* – "a man with a woman's heart" – for the majority, the two concepts are significantly overlapping categories, as are *kee* and *kathoey* in Laos. However, the structure of conflict and class distinction that Kusaka describes, in which middle-class gay men and transgender women emphasize "good conduct" and being "good citizens" to distinguish themselves from poor *bakla* is not as prevalent in Laos.

Kathoey or *kee* (gay)? A case study in Vientiane about categories

A conversation between Jan and Tho

The conversation between Jan and Tho mentioned at the beginning of this chapter had a particular background. A few days earlier, Tho had posted an episode on Facebook describing how, upon sharing a photo of himself with a man who had approached him on social media, he was coldly told that he looked "*kee*-ish" and "*ok sao*" (feminine). Jan and Tho seemed to be talking about this when Jan made a video call to me, and while looking at Tho, who was angry, Jan jokingly said to me, "Tho is *kathoey*-like, isn't he?" When I expressed my confusion at Jan's comment, Tho explained that a *kathoey* is a person with long hair and a feminine figure.

In response to his calling Tho "*kathoey*-like," I asked Jan: "What about yourself?" Jan replied, "If other people say I'm '*kee*,' then I am *kee*, and if they call me '*kathoey*,' I am *kathoey*, and I don't care, as long as it's fun."

Jan and Tho are both cisgender men who express their gender identity as men, desire men, and use the word *kee* to refer to themselves. However, it is obvious that they have different views about the word *kathoey*, what it means, and how it relates to them. Tho defines *kathoey* in terms of feminine gender expression, and then clearly differentiates it from himself. Jan, too, seems to characterize *kathoey* in terms of femininity, using "*kathoey*-like" to tease Tho, who is disgruntled at being called effeminate. However, Jan recognizes *kathoey* as a term that refers to himself. In this respect, whether Jan thinks that *kathoey* is not reducible to femininity, or that it expresses feminine elements in his gender identity, he clearly sees it as a valid referent to him.

In terms of the previous studies outlined above, it appears that Tho conforms to the trend of cisgender men who desire men choosing to identify as *kee* rather than *kathoey*. This suggests that Tho perceives *kathoey* to be a referent to transgender women or male-to-female cross-dressers, and as distinct from the word *kee*. In contrast, Jan's identification with both terms suggests that he understands the term *kathoey* as a broader category that encompasses both transgender women and men who desire men.

Furthermore, the man who called Tho effeminate also used the term *"kee*-ish," which suggests that he associated the word *kee* with femininity. This appears to be quite a different conception of *kee* than Tho's. Whereas some men, including Tho, have adopted the word *kee* and rejected the word *kathoey* to express their masculine identities, many heterosexual men, such as the one who offended Tho, do not recognize this distinction, and see *kee* as largely equivalent to *kathoey*, referring to a person who is somehow feminine and different from them. Thus, this casual conversation reveals a complex interplay of different ways of interpreting the words *kathoey* and *kee*.

Kathoey in Jan's daily life

What I found particularly interesting was Jan's statement that both terms were acceptable to him. Does this statement perhaps indicate that Jan does not distinguish between the two categories? It is hard to imagine, though, that Jan is not at least aware that there are people who (in their own view, notwithstanding) make a clear distinction between them. Jan had worked in Bangkok, Thailand for about ten years, starting from the age of eighteen, and would often talk about the nightlife there. Jan must have had a close association with people who identified themselves as being gay, or simply male, distinguishing themselves from *kathoey*.

Why, then, does Jan say it does not matter which term defines him? To understand this, I will describe the relationship between *kee* and *kathoey* in other situations in Jan's daily life. By closely examining the context of his use of the two words, we will find that Jan attached a unique importance to the word *kathoey*.

First, Jan uses the term *kee* to refer to himself, especially when he talks about his background, as in: "My relatives on my father's side did not like that I was *kee*," or when expressing his opinion, such as: "I know most *kee*s in the Lao capital, but I do not like them because they are gossips compared to *kee*s in Thailand."

At the same time, Jan also understands the word *kathoey* as a referent to a category that describes him, but not because of his gender identity or feminine expression. Although Jan routinely applies lipstick and beauty cream when going to bars or nightclubs, he says: "I don't want to dress like a woman," and: "I have been told I look like a ladyboy, but I'm not," clearly seeing himself as different than women and cross-dressers.

Yet, Jan frequently uses the word *kathoey* as an important means of self-expression or self-description in everyday life. For example, when making the rounds of markets and stores as a wholesaler of imported seafood and seasonings, Jan would often joke with his customers: "I'll throw in a *kathoey* with it." Even during shopping trips for everyday necessities, Jan would typically engage in light-hearted conversation with market vendors, saying, for example: "Pick out some good mangoes for the *kathoey*!" or provoking laughter with a lewd joke to a familiar vendor: "Do you have any cock (*khoi*)?" One time, Jan explained: "It's fun wherever I go. Everyone says it's fun when the *kathoey* is around." Whenever he saw small children at family or neighborhood gatherings, he would address them delightedly: "Do you want to come with the *kathoey*? I have lots of snacks," or "Are you going to be a *kathoey*, too?" Many relatives and acquaintances called Jan a *kathoey* when they referred to him.

Having witnessed this on numerous occasions, one day I asked Jan again, "Are you a *kathoey*?" to which he replied:

> I'm not really a *kathoey*. But people [around the community] generally wouldn't be expected to know the [categorical] distinction, and everyone says it's fun to be with the *kathoey*, and so that's fine. (Field notes, December 5, 2022)

When I later asked: "By '*kathoey*,' do you mean someone who looks like a woman?" Jan explained as follows:

> We call those people *"sao paphet song"* [lit.: "women of the second type"]. A *"kathoey"* is a *"hap,"* and a *"kee"* is a *"luk."*[17] (Field notes, December 5, 2022)

This explanation is peculiar. First, while routinely describing himself as a *kathoey*, Jan said: "I'm not really a *kathoey"* when directly asked. Moreover, Jan explains that *kathoey* refers to the person who is penetrated in the sexual act, while *kee* refers to the penetrator.

Indeed, a study of transgender women in Thailand (Winter 2006) found that the term "woman" or "second type of woman" was preferred over *kathoey*, so Jan's view might be a reflection of this trend of category usage among transgender women in contemporary Thailand and Laos. However, I had never encountered an understanding of the *kathoey* category as referring to typing in sexual acts. As mentioned above, Jan's understanding of *kathoey* and *kee* appears to be much broader than Tho's, but the difference can be seen as not just a choice of words, but as expressing an individual's perception of the two categories, linked with other concepts such as *"sao paphet song."* This shows that Jan clearly differentiates between *kathoey* and *kee*, but uses them both as categories of self-identification.

Another question arises here. Why does Jan perform as a *kathoey* in so many situations while clearly declaring that he is "not really a *kathoey"*? To answer this question, we must shift our focus from how individuals perceive the semantic content of the categories, to what is being done by using those categories, and what kind of emotions and atmosphere are being fostered by them, so let us next look at the word "fun" (*muan*) in Jan's declaration that *"kathoey* or *kee*, either way is fine. I don't care, as long as it's fun."

17　For detailed information about the Lao words "hap" and "luk," see Note 10.

Being "fun" (*muan*) and *kathoey*

Jan used the word "fun" in numerous situations. For example, at the end of 2021, when I was in Japan speaking to Jan on a video call, he said:

> I don't have a job right now, but they [good friends in the neighborhood] say it's fun to hang out with the *kathoey*, and they buy me beer and food. So, I can eat even if I don't have a job. (Field notes, November 24, 2021)

Jan had worked in the tourism industry for many years but lost his job in 2020 due to the COVID-19 pandemic, and as of 2021, he had been unable to find a stable job because the Lao government continued to restrict tourists entry to the country. He was sustained by financial support from friends and others, and during that time, Jan visited his neighbors and acquaintances almost daily to chat, play cards, and join them for meals and parties.

I previously described Jan's behavior in the marketplace, where he joked around and elicited laughter. In the same way, Jan brought laughter to his circle of neighbors by firing off jokes and generally clowning around. The neighbors, and Jan himself, seemed to enjoy laughter-filled chats as well as discussing problems and disputes in their lives.

During my fieldwork, I observed the neighbors calling Jan a *kathoey* (he was rarely called "Jan"),[18] and he often referred to himself as a *kathoey* ("Here comes the *kathoey*!"). At first glance, this might suggest that Jan is not recognized by his personal name or attributes, but is instead understood as a manifestation of the *kathoey* category or set. From this perspective, Jan's eliciting laughter conforms to a stereotype of a *kathoey* playing a comedy relief role in Lao and Thai entertainment.[19] Hence, while Jan does not see himself as a *kathoey*, he performs to the stereotypes

---

18 A wedding invitation sent to Jan was addressed simply to "*Thoey*" (an abbreviation of "*kathoey*").

19 Jan enjoyed watching comedy shows on television (mostly programs from Thailand) and videos on social media featuring *kathoey* characters. Sakagawa (Ch. 2) in this volume discusses visual media works featuring *kathoey*.

for the sake of survival in his community. Kusaka (Chapter 13 in this volume) discusses *bakla* in the Philippines who identify as "men with a woman's heart" and recount their "grief" that their relationships never last and they are excluded from their extended families. Kusaka explains how *bakla* try to "heal" and earn respect with good social skills and humor, and by establishing pseudo-familial relationships with their peers and adopted children. Jan differs from *bakla* in that he has a male gender identity and male gender expression, but by performing the *kathoey* role and making the people around him laugh, he has similarly earned respect and secured his place in the intimate sphere.

Indeed, the Lao word *"muan"* which Jan had used as a baseline ("it's fine, as long as it's *muan*") has a much broader meaning than being funny, as in provoking laughter: the expression *"wao muan"* (*"wao"* meaning "to speak"), for example, means: to speak softly in a harmless and inoffensive manner so as not to spoil the mood; to speak so as to align with the intentions of the other person; or to speak in a polite manner. In this respect, Jan's *"muan"* behaving as a *kathoey* is not limited to his personal sense of fun, but more generally means behaving so as not to spoil the mood, or conforming to the role of a *kathoey* in accordance with the other person's expectations. Moreover, such behavior is associated with maintaining ties with relatives and acquaintances, facilitating communication in the workplace, bringing personal pleasure and surviving life's difficulties.

Thus, to some extent, Jan performing a *kathoey* in accordance with the stereotyped expectations of those around him might be seen as a survival strategy to cope with life's difficulties. But the "fun and comfortable feeling" he gets from walking around the marketplace making people laugh, or when immersed in card games and conversations with neighbors are highly valued in themselves by Jan, and need no other purpose or strategy. Notably, we can only appreciate the irreducible self-sufficiency of this "fun" when we let go of the instrumentalist interpretation that performing to stereotypes is simply a survival strategy.

While Jan proactively uses the word *kathoey* in everyday situations, when quizzed by the author, he displayed multiple points of view, saying, for example, that he was "*kathoey* or *kee*, either way is fine," or that he was "not really a *kathoey*." While on the one hand, a view like Tho's clearly differentiates the word *kathoey* (and what it signifies) from himself, on the other hand, Jan playfully engages with the collective image of the term *kathoey* while alternately approaching and retreating from the category, and "doing *kathoey*"[20] through his own unique interpretation of it. This attitude is not limited to "performing" in accordance with the stereotypes of his surroundings, and he untiringly evades questions (such as those the author asked repeatedly) like "*Are* you *kathoey*"? or "What does the '*kathoey*' category *mean*?" Without clearly defining whether he "*is*" *kathoey*, Jan certainly "*lives*" a *kathoey* life without "venturing to pretend to be *kathoey*."

Returning to Käng's (2014) concept of a genderscape, the *phet* that encompasses gender and sexual categories in Thailand and Laos can be seen on the one hand as a constellation of multiple categories that change over time, while on the other hand it contains the movements of people who interpret, cite, and embody the constellation in their own practices in various ways. Within it, there are ways of life that incorporate "doing X," which cannot be reduced to the category of "being X" (whether *kathoey* or *kee*, as in Jan's case).

Conclusion

As mentioned at the outset, instead of presenting an overall picture of the usage of gender and sexual categories in Laos, this chapter takes one scene encountered during my fieldwork in Vientiane as its starting point, and the discussion proceeded with a narrow focus on the relationship between men who desire men, and the two categories, *kathoey* and *kee*.

I first reviewed the Thai word "*phet*," which has close proximity to Lao, and referred to prior studies of the categories *kathoey* and *gay* within the *phet* system, which encompasses both gender and sexual

---

20 This word, "doing," does not ask whether someone "*is* a *kathoey* or not," but instead expresses the idea of 'living *kathoey*."

identity. I then explained that shifting conceptions of these categories in Thai are likely to have spilled over into Laos, and examined the usage of the categories *kee* and *kathoey* in Lao, based on published research and my own fieldwork. In Laos, the category *kee* (gay), began to be accepted from around the early 2000s as a category of self-designation by urban men who desire men; and as this concept spread, some cisgender men embraced it to differentiate themselves from the *kathoey*, a vernacular term that historically included both transgender women and cisgender men who desire men. However, recognition of the category *kee* is not so widespread among the heterosexual and cisgender majority of the population, with most continuing to understand the word *kathoey* in its traditionally broader terms.

The constellation of categories is always somewhat ambiguous, with ample room for interpretation and change as we saw in the case study of particular categories being interpreted, expressed, and "done" in daily practices. Jan's indifference to being called either *kathoey* or *kee* suggests that in his interpretation, the two words are not mutually exclusive categories between which one must choose. Through life experience, Jan found a way of living with the category *kathoey* without clearly defining whether he identifies himself *as* it.

Thus, we can see that under certain circumstances, the category becomes a nexus between the self and the world around it, evoking emotions and driving practices, underpinned by personal history. Although there is a discernible tendency among cisgender men who desire men in urban Laos to choose *kee* and reject *kathoey*, within the system of *phet*, the latter continues to evoke diverse interpretations and practices among cisgender men who desire men as men.

12 | Gender and Sexual Minorities and the LGBT Rights Movement in Contemporary Myanmar

Takahiro Kojima

Introduction

This chapter analyses the development of the LGBT rights movement and the transformation of the lives of gender and sexual minorities in Myanmar after the 1988 democracy movement from the perspective of the country's rapidly shifting political and economic situation during this period. It is based on intermittent surveys conducted from 2015 to 2023 by qualitative interviews with LGBT-related organizations, gender and sexual minorities and non-LGBT Buddhists in the Yangon and Mandalay regions and Shan State, as well as referencing pamphlets, magazines and websites published by various LGBT-related organizations. The language used for these qualitative interviews was Burmese.

Following the military coup d'état that had suppressed the 1988 democracy movement, the new military junta in Myanmar abandoned socialism and introduced a capitalist economy. Although democratic elections were held in 1990, the junta ignored the results and the generals continued to govern until a military-led transition to civilian rule in 2011 established the military-backed Thein Sein government. The National League for Democracy (NLD) headed by Aung San Suu Kyi won the 2015 general election, resulting in a civilian government in 2016. Although the long-standing repressive political system was changing and Myanmar had begun to attract foreign investment, the situation remained unstable, and the military seized power again in yet another coup d'état in 2021.

In this volatile political situation, the lives of gender and sexual minorities have also undergone transformation. The Burmese nomenclature referring to gender and sexual minorities in Myanmar is complex, and has changed over time, reflecting changing attitudes to diversity. A brief introduction is given below.[1]

In Burmese, close synonyms *meinmasha* and *achauk* are loosely understood as "transgendered/effeminate homosexual men" (Ho 2009: 287). *Achauk* (dry one) is also routinely used, albeit somewhat derogatorily.[2] The neutral term *mami* (from the English mummy) has come into use as both a self-description and a title since the early 2000s. By contrast, transgendered/masculine homosexual women are called *yaukhkasha*.

It is difficult to translate the words into English because while English distinguishes between words that express sexual orientation and gender identity, *meinmasha/achauk* and *yaukhkasha* contains nuances of both. In Burmese, sexual orientation is often explained on the assumption of heterosexuality, with *meinmasha*, whose physical sex at birth are male but female in mind (*seik*), preferring men as romantic partners, and *yaukhkasha*,[3] whose physical sex at birth are female but male in mind, preferring women. The English loanword "gay" has come into use since the 1980s to describe a male whose sexual orientation is towards males, while "lesbian" is used to describe a female whose sexual orientation is female.[4] Recently, the word *leintu chit thu* ("the person who loves the same sex/gender") is also used to mean homosexuals, but it is a rather literary

---

1   In this chapter, "Myanmar" refers to the name of the country, and "Burmese" to the language of Bama. The military regime changed the English name of the country from "Burma" to "Myanmar" in 1989, however, some people who opposed the military rule deliberately continued to use "Burma" in the English names of the country. In those cases, we will respect the original name. Romanized forms in parentheses are, in principle, Burmese, but words with a P: are Pali.

2   *Bawpya* (flat balls), is also used derogatorily.

3   Although some consider this term to be derogatory, others use it for self-identification. *Bawkwe* (broken balls), however, is always derogatory.

4   Informants recalled that the term "gay" became widely used in Myanmar after the American actor Rock Hudson "came out" after contracting AIDS in 1985.

expression. People whose sexual orientation is towards both genders are called *hnat hpet chun* (meaning "good at both" or "ambidextrous").

The term "LGBT" has also come into use in Myanmar in recent years, mainly by human-rights groups. LGBT rights advocacy did not exist in Myanmar during the military regime, mainly because there was no freedom of association. However, since the transition to civilian rule in 2011, LGBT rights groups have gradually increased their activities, and the NLD government has indicated a desire to protect the human rights of gender and sexual minorities. For example, in the Youth Policy (*Lungeyeiya Muwada*) published by the NLD Government in 2017, "youth with different sexual orientations and gender identities" is cited as a subject requiring special attention (Pyidaungzu Thanmada Myanma Naingngandaw 2017: 10). The publication explains that "youth with different sexual orientations and gender identities" refers specifically to LGBT, that is, homosexual, bisexual, transgender and intersex persons.

Article 33(n) of the Youth Policy discusses prohibiting gender discrimination and granting equal rights to those with different sexual orientations and gender identities (Pyidaungzu Thanmada Myanma Naingngandaw 2017: 26). Although Article 33(n) does not specify the types of discrimination that have been experienced by gender and sexual minorities, a publication by Colors Rainbow, the largest LGBT human rights organization in Myanmar, presents examples of oppressive language and behavior by family, friends, employers, and teachers (Colors Rainbow 2013: 32–36). We will discuss Colors Rainbow in more detail below.

Previous studies have noted that discrimination against gender and sexual minorities in Myanmar has been based in Buddhist values (Chua and Gilbert 2015, for example).[5] Theravada Buddhists, who constitute the vast majority of Myanmar's population (87.9% according to 2014 statistics), believe that men's *hpon* (glory or power resulting from deeds

---

5   Of course, discrimination against gender and sexual minorities is not exclusive to Buddhists but is also common among Muslims and Christians (Chua and Gilbert 2015: 14).

in a previous life) is greater than women's. Parents therefore want their sons to grow up to be manly,[6] and strongly oppose intentional behaviors that diminish their power, such as the *meinmasha*. Myanmar's Buddhists often explain that gender and sexual minorities have become *meinmasha* in this life because in their past lives they violated the third of the five precepts to be observed by lay Buddhists: (1) abstain from killing; (2) abstain from stealing; (3) abstain from sexual misconduct; (4) abstain from lying; (5) abstain from intoxication. As we will see, these beliefs are not directly grounded in the Pali Tipiṭaka but are instead variations of interpretations based on the doctrine of cause and effect. My informants described that when boys behave like girls, their fathers may resort to violence, force them to enlist in the army or police to bring out their masculinity, or pressure them to be ordained as a Buddhist monk.

It should be noted that confirmation of male sex is a precondition to being ordained, but it is possible for *meinmasha* to be ordained unless they are hermaphrodite, missing male genitalia, or have undergone breast augmentation. Sexual activity after ordination is prohibited by precept.

Several informants testified that discrimination has intensified since the 1990s; as the number of HIV/AIDS cases increased, so did the oppression of gay men.[7]

Let us look now at how Myanmar's gender and sexual minorities have responded to social marginalization, beginning with anthropological or ethnographic studies. Iikuni (2010), for example, focuses on the growing tendency for *meinmasha* to become *nat kadaw* (mediums), a role traditionally performed by women. Iikuni explains that women have increasingly been inclined towards Buddhist practice, which in turn reduced the number of potential candidates for *nat kadaw*, while at the same time the role is consistent with the interests of *meinmasha*. Keeler (2016), however, posits that *meinmasha* in Mandalay have transitioned

---

6   Chua and Gilbert (2015: 14) explain that male same-sex sexual activity is abhorred because of the belief that being a receptive partner reduces male *hpon*.

7   The National AIDS Program (2014: 8–9) indicates that the number of HIV cases in Myanmar increased rapidly in the 1990s and peaked in the early 2000s.

from *nat kadaw* to beauticians, makeup artists and similar livelihoods, and attributes this to the forces of modernization. Gilbert (2022) describes how the spirit networks and the practices of trans "kinship" play crucial roles in the everyday lives of spirit mediums. In the same edited volume, Brac de la Perrière (2022) depicts a medium's dilemma between LGBT rights advocacy and the spirit world.

Previous studies of gender and sexual minority rights advocacy in Myanmar include a monograph on the development of LGBT human rights activism and the experiences of the activists (Chua 2018); a study of the activities of Colors Rainbow (Sanders 2015a); a report on changes in the legal situation of LGBT people after the transition to civilian rule (Chua and Gilbert 2015); and a report on the current situation of discrimination and human rights violations against gender and sexual minorities (Colors Rainbow 2013).

While these studies have shed light on the situation of gender and sexual minorities in Myanmar, anthropological research has tended to focus on the relationship between gender/sexual minorities and spirit worship, while ignoring the diverse views of the Buddhist mainstream. At the same time, studies of rights-advocacy groups have been based mainly on interviews with participants, and there has been scant research into the reactions towards such activities by gender and sexual minorities who were not directly involved in them. Furthermore, LGBT rights advocacy in Myanmar suffered a significant setback following the 2021 coup d'état and the effects on the lives of gender and sexual minorities are as yet unknown.

This chapter, therefore, first focuses on the period from 2011 to 2021, when a limited democratic regime governed the country, and examines: 1) how Buddhist doctrines were perceived by Buddhists who support development of the LGBT rights advocacy groups across Myanmar or oppose their activities; and 2) how the activities of LGBT rights advocacy were recognized by gender and sexual minorities who were not directly involved in the movement. Then, turning to the situation since the 2021 coup d'état, the study 3) clarifies the situations of both gender/sexual minorities and the LGBT rights advocacy groups in terms of the general social transformation in Myanmar.

The political system and LGBT rights organizations in Myanmar

The military regime (1988–2011)

During the 1988–2011 military regime in Myanmar, forming associations required permission from the government, and violations were punished in accordance with Law 6/88, a measure enacted against the 1988 pro-democracy movement (Chua and Gilbert 2015: 7–8). Human rights NGOs were not allowed to organize within Myanmar, so they based themselves in Chiang Mai in neighboring Thailand, which had become a refuge for students who had engaged in the pro-democracy movement. One of the driving forces behind these activities was Aung Myo Min, who had participated in the 1988 pro-democracy movement as a student. After engaging in armed resistance to government repression as a member of the All Burma Students' Democratic Front (ABSDF), he received a scholarship to study in the Human Rights Advocates Program at Columbia University in the US and earned a master's degree in 1995. In 2000, with funding from the US government, he established the Human Rights Education Institute of Burma (HREIB) in Chiang Mai. Chiang Mai was home to many human rights organizations and was also a place where international support for them was thriving. Aung Myo Min's activities can be seen as part of this trend, but during the military regime, it was impossible to operate within Myanmar.

The Thein Sein regime (2011–2015)

After Thein Sein became president in 2011, with the transition to civilian rule there were marked changes in this situation. Thein Sein's government released political prisoners and encouraged exiles to return home. It also began to collaborate with the NLD, led by Aung San Suu Kyi.

The Thein Sein era also saw significant changes to the human rights situation in Myanmar, perhaps most notably by recognizing the legitimacy of human rights groups. A significant development in the LGBT rights movement in Myanmar was the establishment of the Myanmar National Human Rights Commission in 2011, made up of fifteen members, including former ambassadors, education officials and civil servants, some of whom interacted with members of Colors Rainbow and Equality Myanmar, to be discussed below (Sanders 2015a: 27).

The 2014 Registration of Associations Law (*Athin Ahpwe mya Hmatpontin chin Hsainya Upadei*) regulated the registration of local and international NGOs.[8] Following these changes in the political situation, numerous foreign-based human rights organizations began to set-up in Myanmar. HREIB moved from Chiang Mai to Myanmar in 2012 and was renamed Equality Myanmar; in 2013, Aung Myo Min returned from Chiang Mai and assumed the position Executive Director of Equality Myanmar, setting up offices in Yangon and Mandalay with 34 staff. Many other political exiles also returned to Myanmar and organized gender/sexual minority rights advocacy groups.

The socialist censorship regime in place since 1962 was abolished in 2013, lifting the ban on magazines and web-sites published by gender and sexual minority rights organizations, as discussed below. Additionally, lectures on human rights that had not been permitted during the military regime were allowed. Furthermore, as the media situation was greatly improved, television dramas were aired to raise awareness about discrimination against gender/sexual minorities and awareness-raising programs on LGBT rights were broadcast on FM radio.

In summary, the situation of gender and sexual minorities improved significantly during the Thein Sein regime.

---

8   However, none of the local NGOs or CBOs on LGBT rights were registered at that time. Some researchers have cited the annual registration fee of 100,000 kyats as the reason for this (e.g., Chua and Gilbert 2015: 8), but it is conceivable that they did not register because it was not required.

The NLD regime (2016–2021)

The NLD won the general election in 2015, resulting in a change of government in 2016. The new civilian government announced the Youth Policy in 2017, which included a clause prohibiting discrimination against gender and sexual minorities (Pyidaunzu Thamada Myanmar Naingngandaw 2017).

Myanmar's leading LGBT rights organizations, Colors Rainbow and Kings N Queens (to be discussed below), were yet to be registered at the period of my fieldwork in March 2019, but a local NGO, Lashio Tomboy and Lesbian Group, was authorized in 2018 by Lashio District. To be clear, none of these groups had been specifically restricted by the Thein Sein government, and the NLD basically continued its predecessor's policies on LGBT human rights organizations.

In fact, concrete moves around improving the rights of gender and sexual minorities were somewhat limited under the NLD government, as can be seen in the reply of NLD aide Win Htein, when asked if the government would take any steps towards LGBT rights: "I'm not interested. Burma is not like the West. Gender issues are not important" (Carroll 2016).

In reality, compared to Thein Sein's government, which had been proactive on human rights in order to rid itself of the negative image of the military regime, the NLD government did little to protect the rights of LGBT people despite officially adopting a pro-human rights stance, as it was preoccupied with various issues that arose after it took office, including economic problems, the Rohingya issue and reconciliation with ethnic minorities.

LGBT rights organizations and their activities in Myanmar

This section examines the prominent LGBT rights organizations that were active nationwide in Myanmar prior to the 2021 coup d'état. One of the main goals of LGBT rights organizations was the repeal of Section 377 of the Criminal Code, the so-called "sodomy law," which prohibits sexual acts that go "against the order of nature," a successor to the Criminal Code of 1861 introduced during British colonial rule (1824–1948). It prohibits homosexual intercourse, with violations punishable by up to ten years' imprisonment or a fine. Similar provisions were enacted in many British colonies in Asia, including Pakistan, India, Bangladesh, Malaysia, Singapore, Brunei, as well as settler societies such as New Zealand and Australia. Although Myanmar has amended numerous laws since its new constitution was enacted in 2008, Article 377 of the Penal Code remains unchanged to date.

However, as sexual acts are generally not performed in public, their occurrence is difficult to prove, so Section 377 of the Penal Code is generally only applied in cases where (a) the act or attempt is performed in public; (b) there is no consent (rape, for example), or (c) the police are undercover (Sanders 2015a: 18). According to Mr. Z, a lawyer in his 60s who I interviewed in 2015, to the best of his knowledge, the last arrest under Section 377 of the Criminal Code was in 1991, as AIDS was breaking out in Myanmar. According to Mr. Z, police at the time used that law to conduct sting operations against homosexuals, but it is unheard of for homosexuals to be arrested under Section 377 of the Criminal Code simply for living their daily lives.

In practice, the police powers most commonly used to arrest gender and sexual minorities are Section 30(c), 30(d) of the Rangoon Police Act of 1899, and Section 35(c), 35(d) of the Police Act of 1945. These Acts, primarily targeting thieves, state that "any person found between sunset and sunrise having his face covered or otherwise disguised, who is unable to give a satisfactory account of himself; any person found within the precincts of any dwelling-house or other building whatsoever, or in any back-drainage space, or on board any vessel, without being able satisfactorily to account for his presence therein" is punishable by imprisonment for a term of up to three months. On this basis, transgender people can be questioned by police simply for walking or standing on a public street at night and detained for offering insufficient explanation (Chua and Gilbert 2015: 18). In a prominent case in 2013, twelve gay men and transgender people were detained by police officers near the moat of the Royal Palace, a well-know "gay beat."[9] Over several hours, the detainees were verbally insulted, as well as being physically and sexually assaulted by ten officers at the Mandalay Regional Police Headquarters. Before their release, they were made to sign a statement that they would never again visit the south-eastern area of the moat dressed as women (Colors Rainbow 2013: 50).

After this incident, the LGBT Rights Network filed a complaint with the Myanmar National Human Rights Commission and demanded a response from the Ministry of Home Affairs (Sanders 2015a: 24).

Aiming to improve this situation, many LGBT rights organizations were active across Myanmar before the 2021 coup. Below I will describe how they came to be established.

Colors Rainbow

Colors Rainbow was a local NGO that inherited the legacy of the LGBT rights advocacy body, Committee for Lesbigay Rights in Burma, which was part of the previously mentioned HREIB established in Chiang Mai, Thailand, in 2007. It was the first, as well as the largest, LGBT rights advocacy organization in Myanmar, having relocated from Chiang Mai to Yangon in 2013 and, at the time of my fieldwork in 2016, had permanent staff in Yangon and Dawei. Its objectives were to achieve respect for human equality, guarantee LGBT human rights and eliminate discrimination against LGBT in Myanmar.

After moving to Yangon in 2013, Hla Myat Tun was appointed Deputy Director. He had graduated from university in Myanmar in 2004 and worked for the UN Population Fund there until 2008, when he received a scholarship from the international NGO Freedom House. With this scholarship, he studied for a master's degree at the University of the Philippines until 2010. From 2010 to 2011, he interned at M-Plus (in Chiang Mai), an HIV/AIDS organization run by gay men, before joining Colors Rainbow in 2012.

---

9   An LGBT rights advocate claimed that the police conduct such crackdowns to "boost their arrest quota" or to solicit bribes.

Colors Rainbow's activities include: 1) raising awareness through lectures on LGBT rights; 2) publishing *Colors Rainbow*, a magazine about LGBT rights, and distributing it to partner organizations nationwide (launched in Chiang Mai in 2009, with a circulation of about 1500 copies every two to three months); 3) strengthening its solidarity with other groups through organizing commemorative events such as IDAHOBIT (International Day against Homophobia, Biphobia and Transphobia, May 17) and TDoR (Transgender Day of Remembrance, November 20); 4) networking with relevant domestic and international organizations by, for example, organizing the domestic Myanmar LGBT Rights Network (formed in 2012) and holding quarterly meetings on LGBT rights with assembled representatives of related organizations from 30 districts across the country, as well as participating in the ASEAN SOGIE Caucus;[10] 5) disseminating LGBT-related information from Myanmar and other countries of the world via its website,[11] in addition to lobbying members of the Myanmar parliament to repeal laws that oppress LGBT people.

Kings N Queens

One of the largest of the LGBT organizations affiliated under the Colors Rainbow umbrella was the Yangon-based Kings N Queens, with around 90 members nationwide. Its founder, Myat No Phyu, was a cisgender woman. After attending a human rights course run by Equality Myanmar in Chiang Mai in 2009, she decided that a similar course should be organized in Myanmar, and founded Kings N Queens in 2010 with a dedicated staff of nine. However, as Myanmar was still under military rule and human rights activities were prohibited, she positioned the group's activities as HIV/AIDS-related. At the time of writing, like Colors Rainbow, it is not officially recognized by the government, but until the coup in 2021, the government did not hinder its activities.

Kings N Queens' activities focused on awareness-raising at the local level, such as organizing workshops on human rights and

10 https://aseansogiecaucus.org/about
11 https://www.colorsrainbow.org

gender, discussing legal matters, and holding events. It also screened documentary film and staged performances on IDAHOBIT and TDoR days. For example, one of its officers held a ceremony in a hotel in Yangon in 2014 to celebrate the tenth anniversary of a gay couple which was widely publicized and described in local newspaper reports as a "wedding ceremony." This event will be discussed later.

CAN-Myanmar

CAN stands for Civil Authorize Negotiate Organization, founded in Mandalay in 2011. Its founder, Saw Zin Maung Soe, was a former monk who was ordained as a novice at a young age. He received a scholarship to study clinical psychology at the International Institute of Social Studies in the Netherlands, and then attended the International Theravāda Buddhist Missionary University of Mandalay, where he received a Bachelor of Arts. He also passed the Myanmar government-sponsored doctrinal examinations at an advanced level. During his time as a monk, he hid the fact that he was gay, as the introduction of stimuli such as sexual desire into a *sangha* (monastic communities of monks) is avoided in Theravada Buddhism. However, after attending HREIB's LGBT human rights course in Chiang Mai in 2011, he decided to return to secular life and founded CAN-Myanmar to work in the rights advocacy movement.

CAN-Myanmar held public dialogues for Parents, Friends of Lesbians and Gays (PFLAG) twice a month, with the aim of providing social and psychological support on LGBT issues. It provided advice to gender and sexual minorities who had been wrongfully arrested and referred them to lawyers. It also published *The Corner (of 26 & 66 Street) Magazine* monthly, providing information for gender and sexual minorities. The magazine's name refers to the gay beat and the 2013 mass arrests mentioned above. Furthermore, the magazine published articles in the media advocating for legislation to ban discrimination against gender and sexual minorities because, while seeking the repeal of the so-called sodomy law, CAN-Myanmar recognized that in some countries, such as

India, the situation had deteriorated after the repeal of Article 377, with rapes increasing.

Other organizations

Other organizations include the Bright Pride Myanmar Lesbian Organization, which supports lesbians and trans men, and &PROUD, which has held an LGBT photo and video contest since 2014. According to &PROUD's website,[12] the group ran LGBT filmmaking workshops since 2014 in collaboration with Colors Rainbow and other organizations. YG is another NGO affiliated with Colors Rainbow, which held large gay and lesbian parties on the last Saturday of every month from 2013. These parties were frequently attended by foreigners.

Furthermore, the Human Rights Human Dignity International Film Festival was held in 2013, awarding its top prize to *This Kind of Love*, a film about Aung Myo Min's work, and the Miss Red Ribbon Beauty Contests were held for trans women in 2009, 2012 and 2014 to raise funds for HIV-infected and AIDS patients in the Yangon District.

Reactions to LGBT rights advocacy campaigns

Buddhist criticism

Activities by human rights organizations have sought to raise awareness of human rights in the broader society. However, they have provoked backlash from conservative Buddhists: in 2013, when photos of a "wedding ceremony" in Mon State for a gay man and his trans bride circulated on the internet, the couple was accused of violating traditional values and were threatened by the local community and authorities. In 2014, when about 100 guests attended a celebration of the tenth anniversary of a gay couple involved in the Kings N Queens, the local newspapers described it as a wedding ceremony and speculated that they would be punished for violating Article 377, but they were not. However, these actions invited a backlash (Human Rights in Asean 2014).

---

12 https://web.archive.org/web/20210223005956/https://www.andproud.net/about/

Commenting on this situation, Mr. Z stated:

It has only been since 2013 that gay rights have come to be spoken
about in this way. Of course, gay men existed before. But it was the
influence of the West that led to the holding of "weddings" and parties.
Democratization brings an influx of both the good and the bad. During
the military regime, they feared crackdowns and could not take this
kind of action, but with democratization they are no longer afraid.
However, it was Britain in its colonial years that introduced Section 377
of the Penal Code to Myanmar in the first place. The British made a law
prohibiting homosexuality, imposed it on the countries they colonized,
and now they are breaking it themselves and imposing it once more.
(Interview March 18, 2015)

Mr. Z, a committed Buddhist, showed the author a book written by the
rector of International Theravāda Buddhist Missionary University, the
Venerable Nandamālābiwuntha. His interpretation can be summarized as
follows (Nandamālābiwuntha 2011: 38–43):

In the third of the five precepts to be observed by a lay person, the
definition of "sexual misconduct" (P: *Kāmesumicchācāra*), literally
means "wrong or evil conduct with regard to sensual things." Some
Western countries, such as the Netherlands, have legalized homosexuality, which is included in "wrong conduct," but it is written in
the *Dīgha Nikāya* [Collection of Long Discourses on scriptures], the
Pāthika-vagga [the third section of the former], and the *Cakkavatti-
sutta* [Wheel-turning Monarch Sutra], which form part of the *Tipiṭaka*
[collections of primary Pali texts], that when man's life span was 500
years, his children's life span shrank to 200 to 250 years due to his
acts of abnormal lust (P: *adhamma-rāga*), excessive greed (P: *visama-
lobha*) and misguided action (P: *micchā-dhamma*). According to the
Atthakatha [commentaries on the Pali Buddhist canon], "abnormal
lust" means "lust for inappropriate objects such as one's mother, aunt,
or uncle's wife," "excessive greed" means "dark vexations that occur

in non-time and in non-place" and "misguided action" means "male covetousness towards men and female covetousness towards women." The Buddha taught more than 2,500 years ago that the world would be defiled if homosexuality increased; the emergence of incurable diseases such as HIV/AIDS was therefore due to the prevalence of "misguided actions."[13]

However, when I asked Ven. K, then head of the State Sangha Maha Nayaka Committee, the highest administrative body in the *sangha* in Myanmar, to confirm his interpretation of "sexual misconduct" as part of the Five Precepts that lay Buddhists should observe daily, he replied: "Same-sex sexual relations do not violate the precept of sexual misconduct. In the first place, it is an issue unrelated to Buddhism."

Furthermore, *The Teachings of the Buddha* (Higher Level), published by the Myanmar government's Department of the Promotion and Propagation of the Sasana (2018: 19), describes sexual misconduct (P: *Kāmesumicchācāra*) as "a man has sex with any woman who is under the guardianship of someone," which is the common interpretation in Myanmar. This is the general understanding of "sexual misconduct" in Myanmar, and the interpretation of Ven. Nandamālābiwuntha, who relates the content of the precept of sexual misconduct to the descriptions about "misguided actions" from the *Atthakatha* on the Wheel-turning Monarch Sutra, is a departure from the prevailing view in Myanmar. Of course, in Myanmar, "even though priority will be given to the original text in a choice between it and the *Atthakatha*, the standard for interpretation was always sought in the latter, and the tale of causes and conditions is valued not as a kind of interpretation by Buddhaghosa or other commentators, but rather as a more detailed explanation of what the Buddha himself revealed" (Harada 1991: 173), and is therefore the traditional interpretation of the Wheel-turning Sutra. Generally, however,

---

13 Translation of Pali words in the main text are based on notes and references on the Myanmar *Buddhasasana Samiti* Sixth Buddhist Council edition, in Katayama, trans. (2005: 153).

the interpretation of the precept against sexual misconduct is not linked
with the description about "misguided actions" in the *Atthakatha*. As can
be seen from the opening of the Ven. Nandamālābiwuntha's account,
in which he expresses his concern over the legalization of same-sex
marriage in the Netherlands, a backlash against the influx in recent years
of Western values such as the defense of LGBT rights lurks behind
such insistences.

Counterarguments from gender and sexual minorities

In response to the Buddhists' criticisms, Ms. T (a trans woman) from
Colors Rainbow offers the following refutation. The precept against
"sexual misconduct" prohibits adultery (sexual relations with a man or
woman who is married to someone else) or irresponsible sexual relations
(premarital sex) with a man or woman who is dependent on their parents.
Same-sex couples cannot be legally married in Myanmar at this stage, but
if both parties take responsibility, they do not violate the precept against
"sexual misconduct." Nor does Buddhist doctrine stipulate that LGBTs
are despicable. On the contrary, those who attack LGBT people are in
violation of the doctrine for two reasons: 1) they should have compassion
(*metta*) for all living beings, but they lack such feelings; and 2) contrary
to the teaching that their activities by body, mouth and mind should be
purified, they say bad things of others.

Ms. A from the previously mentioned Bright Pride Myanmar Lesbian
Organization also notes that people who are attached to a religion,
whether Buddhist, Christian or Muslim, often oppose LGBT people and
lifestyles. In the case of Buddhism, the main text of the *Tipiṭaka* (the
teachings directly attributed to the Buddha) only mentions "abnormal
lust" (P: *adhamma-rāga*), "excessive greed" (P: *visama-lobha*) and
"misguided actions" (*micchā-dhamma*): Buddhaghosa, who interpreted
this as including same-sex sexual relations, was only a latter-day monk.
Indeed, it is "verbal karma" to say something that is beneficial neither
to oneself nor to others. It is impossible to know whether a gender and
sexual minority has committed the sin of sexual misconduct in a past life,
and even if they have done so, they cannot redress it. The only thing that

matters is doing good deeds in this life. As such, LGBT rights advocates have presented a counter-narrative that interprets the Buddha himself as not having preached a doctrine that discriminates against gender and sexual minorities.

Reactions of gender and sexual minorities not directly involved in rights advocacy

Those gender and sexual minorities who participate in the LGBT rights advocacy groups mainly spring from the university-educated elite or urban middle class, while activists who make a living as makeup artists, hairdressers or spirit mediums – favorite targets of anthropological research – were rarely encountered in this survey. How, then, do such individuals perceive the work of rights organizations? The author interviewed many members of gender and sexual minorities, but for reasons of space, only the case of Ms. M (a trans woman) is outlined below.

Ms. M had been aware of her *mami* identity since childhood and attended high school wearing *longyi* (a cloth worn around the waist) in a feminine way and *tanathka* (a natural cosmetic that also works as a sunscreen) on her cheeks. Her teachers and friends said nothing about it, but as an only son, she was scolded, especially by her father, who expected her to grow up like a man.

After finishing high school, she worked in the family business for a while, but her interest in beauty led her to become a makeup artist when she was about seventeen years old. She did not have a specific mentor, but sought out those who had the skills, observed their methods, and stole the techniques she liked. At the time of our interview, she had been working as a makeup artist for twenty years. In the 2000s, her client-base grew and she averaged five to six jobs per month, earning 50,000 kyat per job,[14] or an average of 250,000 to 300,000 kyat monthly.[15] Her father

---

14 Some highly skilled practitioners charge 100,000 kyat per assignment.

15 In 2017, when this interview was conducted, 1 kyat was worth approximately 0.0007 US Dollars. The median monthly starting salary for high school graduates was estimated at about 200,000 kyats (USD 146) in 2018 (MyJobs Myanmar 2018: 28).

came to realize that she earned a lot of money from her makeup work, and had not scolded her in the past decade.

She also worked for an LGBT rights and HIV/AIDS-related NGO called The Health from 2014 to 2016, but left because she could no longer continue full-time due to an overlap with her makeup work. When she had a makeup job, she woke up at 4 am and started work, but finished at 8 am. She was asked to work at weddings, Buddhist offering ceremonies, monk ordination ceremonies, graduation ceremonies (for women only), etc.

Mami makeup artists have a reputation as being better than women artists because of their aesthetic sense. As a result, *mami* came to enjoy a higher reputation and began to be treated more equally. *Mami* used to be laughed at because their only occupation was to dance and sell digestive medicines made from citrus fruit (*shauk-thi*), and their income was low, but now they earn more than company employees and thus have more dignity (*theikhka*). However, this dignity is due to their economic power rather than the result of LGBT rights organizations: she had never heard of Colors Rainbow. However, it is obvious that since democratization, awareness of LGBT rights has improved, which has in turn improved their situation. During the military regime, Ms. M was wrongfully arrested by the police near the moat of the Mandalay Royal Palace. During interrogation she was asked to pay a bribe. She paid and was released. Compared to these situations, the NLD government which respects human rights was expected to better protect *mami* rights. In recent years, for example, university teachers have stopped trying to dictate what *mami* should wear, due to growing awareness of their rights.

According to my interviews, many respondents were of the opinion that the increase in trans women's mediumship had occurred since the military era in the 1990s, when the nation transitioned from socialism to a capitalist economy.[16] Iikuni (2010) suggests that the main reason

---

16 Ho (2009: 274) claims that "Since the 1980s, an increasing number of *nat kadaws* are transgendered gay men," but according to the older respondents I interviewed, the growing number of trans women who are *nat kadaws* began in the 1990s.

for this uptake was that demand for mediums' services rose alongside increased suffering during the transition from socialism to capitalism. Income for mediums varies greatly from person to person, but if they garner enough clients, their income can be considerable.

As for makeup artists, Ms. M explained that it was only since the 2000s that trans women had gained a reputation and increased in number. According to Keeler (2016), it was after the 1988 democratic movement that trans women in Mandalay moved from *nat kadaw* to livelihoods such as hairdressers and makeup artists. The subsequent transition from socialism to a capitalist economy was a significant factor in improving life and raising the dignity of trans women.

Thus, gender and sexual minorities who earn their living as *nat kadaw*, hairdressers, makeup artists and other professionals are often not directly involved in the LGBT rights advocacy groups driven mainly by the university-educated and urban middle class, but the number of people who know about the latter's activities is gradually increasing, and at the time of my fieldwork prior to the 2021 coup d'état, the majority had a favorable opinion of it.

Gender and sexual minorities and the rights movement after the coup

In 2021, when LGBT rights advocacy groups were becoming increasingly active, the military staged another coup d'état. According to LGBT rights advocates, the post-coup environment for gender and sexual minorities was worse than before the 2011 military regime. Colors Rainbow moved its activities out of the country because it became impossible to operate there. The human rights organization Equality Myanmar also ceased activities in Myanmar, but its founder, Aung Myo Min, was appointed Human Rights Minister in the National Unity Government (NUG) established by pro-democracy forces opposed to the military regime. The previously discussed *Youth Policy* were suspended, and all events related to LGBT rights advocacy were cancelled. About the only programs to continue were online awareness-raising courses.

Many transgender people participated in the anti-coup demonstrations that immediately followed the coup, and many activists were detained by the military. Sections 505(a) and (b) of the Penal Code for "Statements conducing to public mischief" and Article 50(j) of the Counter Terrorism Law for aiding and abetting murder were often applied to those who were detained. For example, Sue Sha Shin Thant, a trans woman who had been involved in a campaign for a Law on Prevention of Violence against Women before the coup and was a national representative in the Mandalay District Youth Committee, was detained for playing a leading role in the anti-dictatorship movement in Mandalay. She was charged under Sections 505(a) and (b) of the Penal Code and Article 50(j) of the Counter Terrorism Law, and sentenced to a total of 25 years' imprisonment (RFA Burmese 2022). In addition, the original draft of the Law on the Prevention of Violence against Women had aimed to include trans women, but work on it was suspended after the key members of the drafting team were detained or fled the country. In this situation, gender and sexual minorities found themselves in constant fear of arrest.

Furthermore, the COVID-19 pandemic, which caused numerous deaths in Myanmar in 2020–21, exacerbated the situation: according to LGBT rights advocacy groups, the Taung Byon festival, which attracts *nat kadaw* from all over the country, was cancelled due to COVID-19, and the economic situation deteriorated, so that their income from offerings dried up. Many *nat kadaw* were fortune-tellers, but it became difficult for them to operate because of the risk of being arrested under Article 505 of the Criminal Code if they said anything contrary to the interests of the government. Particularly in the Sagaing region, where fighting between the national army and the People's Defense Force (PDF) continues, many *nat kadaw* and other gender/sexual minorities who earned their livelihoods as hairdressers, makeup artists, and the like lost their jobs and housing. Nevertheless, rights advocacy groups continued to work under the radar, supplying aid money to gender and sexual minorities and providing technical training to enable them to open food stalls.

Thus, Myanmar's gender and sexual minorities were worse off than ever after the post-2020 COVID-19 pandemic, the 2021 coup d'état and the subsequent civil war. However, mutual aid activities among gender and sexual minorities, led by LGBT rights activists, continued covertly, providing a safety net for gender and sexual minorities.

Conclusion

Finally, let us summarize this chapter. A major influence on gender and sexual minority human rights advocacy in Myanmar was former students who sought asylum in Chiang Mai, Thailand. Following the 1988 pro-democracy movement, they began advocating for the human rights of gender and sexual minorities. When freedom of association was granted in Myanmar in concert with the transition to civilian rule in 2011, the influx of pro-democracy activists and international NGOs from abroad encouraged the formation of local LGBT rights advocacy groups. Their activities were facilitated by funding from the West and deregulation by the Myanmar government, such as lifting the ban on politically sensitive websites and abolishing the system of censorship. They established networks with local and international rights organizations, running programs to promote awareness and calling for changes to discriminatory laws.

Such activities by LGBT rights organizations provided an opportunity to raise awareness of the human rights not only of gender and sexual minorities, but also of the people who interact with them. On the one hand, the activities of those involved in LGBT rights organizations provoked a backlash from conservative Buddhists who claimed that they do not align with traditional values, with some Buddhists arguing that acts such as same-sex sexual relations are contrary to doctrine, based on accounts in commentaries on Pali Buddhist canon. On the other hand, members of gender and sexual minorities who are also Buddhists have attempted to refute these claims by presenting alternative interpretations, arguing that such views were later interpretations and do not represent the Buddha's own teachings. In a sense, this is a hegemonic struggle over who is a "good citizen" in the context of the influx of various values associated with democratization and the concomitant upheavals in the established order. In other words, it can be understood as a struggle between forces that sought to define "good citizens" narrowly from a conservative Buddhist perspective, and elite-oriented forces that sought to define it more broadly, using concepts originating from the West, such as human rights.

In these circumstances of wavering traditional values, over the four years between 2015 and 2019 when I conducted the bulk of my research, I witnessed a transformation as the term LGBT rapidly spread in Myanmar and the activities of rights advocacy groups became more widely known. However, many of those directly involved in rights-advocacy groups hail from the relatively well-educated urban middle class, which is a very small proportion of gender and sexual minorities in Myanmar. Most gender and sexual minorities built their lives as spirit mediums, hairdressers, makeup artists, and so on. Although many of them experience discrimination and hardship, it is noteworthy that a considerable number have been recognized for their abilities in their communities and have been able to support themselves, sometimes comfortably. The transition to a capitalist economy, especially after the democratic movement of 1988, probably played a role in enabling them to build a dignified life as a gender and sexual minority. Although never actively participating in LGBT rights advocacy movement, many had positive opinions of those activities.

However, the COVID-19 pandemic that began in 2020, the 2021 coup d'état and the subsequent civil war all brought significant changes, and gender/sexual minorities in Myanmar, at the time of writing, face unprecedented difficulties. Mutual assistance activities to support gender and sexual minorities will be a focus of my future research.

13 Public Rights, Everyday Dignity, and Intimate Sorrow: LGBT and *Bakla* in the Philippines

Wataru Kusaka

Introduction

The Philippines has no laws that directly persecute gender and sexual minorities, but nor are there any national laws that support them. Attempting to remedy this situation, a number of LGBT organizations have taken advantage of the liberal democratic system and relatively free civil society to pursue legal rights.

The results, however, have not always been satisfactory. At the local level, starting with Quezon City in 2003, six out of 81 provinces and 21 out of 1643 cities and municipalities had enacted anti-discrimination ordinances as of 2019 (United Nations Phillipines 2019). At the national level, however, an anti-discrimination bill first introduced in 2000 has yet to pass Congress. In electoral politics, Ang Ladlad, the first "LGBT political party" in Southeast Asia, was founded in 2003 and campaigned for election. However, its candidates never won a seat, and the party has not fielded a candidate since 2019. In the 2016 elections, a trans woman, Geraldine Roman, was elected to the House of Representatives, but she was from a local political dynasty whose parents had both served in the same position, and she was not dependent on support from the LGBT movement.

Why has it been so difficult for the LGBT movement to make progress in acquiring legal rights, despite its lively activities in the Philippines? Three main factors have been identified: first, opposition from the Catholic Church and conservative religious groups stoked moral panics in the 2000s and blocked the passage of legislation in the 2010s, claiming that their faith would be violated by laws protecting LGBT rights (Cornelio and Dagle 2019). However, the political influence of religious forces is not absolute, as evidenced by the passing in 2012 of Reproductive Health Law that included the promotion of sex education and family planning, in defiance of opposition from the Catholic Church (Miyawaki, Chapter 5 in this volume).

Second, the majority that prides itself on "tolerance" effectively offers only "conditional acceptance" to gender and sexual minorities. For example, "*bakla*," loosely characterized as male-to-female vernacular transgender individuals, are accepted by the majority only when fulfilling prevailing expectations such as performing household chores while supporting the family financially, entertaining others in an amusing manner, and contributing to local or school events (Tan 2001; Presto 2020). Thus, they court a backlash when they demand rights, breaking such stereotypes. However, the majority's thinking seems to be gradually changing. According to a 2019 survey, for example, as many as 73% of Filipino respondents indicated that homosexuality should be accepted; and this tendency was strongest among the younger demographics (Poushter and Kent 2020).

Third, the LGBT movement has been divided. While the left calls for measures to tackle poverty and inequality, liberals focus on the identity and legal rights of gender and sexual minorities (Thoreson 2012: 540–541; Evangelista 2020). Within the movement, as well, gay men and trans women tend to take the initiative more often than lesbians and trans men (Soriano 2014: 8).[1] Even among gender and sexual minorities, there are homophobes, biphobes, and transphobes, and there has been confrontation between activists holding different positions (Evangelista 2018). Despite these tensions, though, the LGBT movement, through deliberations based on affective ties, has developed broad consensus and cooperation over advocacy for anti-discrimination laws, and holding

---

1   Gay men and *bakla* are more concerned with laws prohibiting public indecency, police entrapment and professional discrimination, whereas lesbians and tomboys are more concerned with civil law and recognition of family relationships (Thoreson 2012: 541).

pride parades to reject any sense of "shame" imposed under heterosexual norms (Evangelista 2018; 2024). The Ladlad Party, too, has collaborated with diverse groups to work toward the equality of diverse identities.

As examined, these three obstructive factors against the LGBT movement are not necessarily absolute, leaving considerable room for them. In this chapter, we will focus on another disincentive: the discrepancy arising between those who participate in the LGBT movement and those who do not, based on social divisions such as social class, generation, and region.

The LGBT movement has been led by the urban middle class, who define themselves by modern Western concepts such as "gay" and "transgender." While making full use of their fluency in English to work with the international LGBT movement, they have sought legal rights such as the prohibition of discrimination in official institutions including schools, employment, and public services, as well as same-sex marriage. Meanwhile, many poor, elderly, and rural residents who understand themselves in terms of vernacular identities such as *bakla* have been more reluctant or indifferent to participate in the LGBT movement (Garcia 1996: xvi; Tan 2001). Rather, they have sought everyday dignity through success in niche occupations and economic contributions to their families and communities while resisting ridicule and ostracism.

There are interactions and commonalities between these two groups beyond the division. As the acquisition of legal rights has stalled, the LGBT movement has become more attuned to the needs of the poor (Thoreson 2012). In addition, the poor and middle class alike seek to achieve everyday dignity through economic success. Moreover, the two groups' hopes overlap. It is common for young rural *bakla* to speak of hopes such as: "I wish we were equal," even if they do not fully recognize the need for legal rights (Presto 2020).

However, although LGBT activists often emphasize the importance of educating and raising awareness of marginalized gender and sexual minorities, such efforts are not always sufficient to motivate the latter to join the LGBT movement for legal rights. This is because, I argue, there is a risk that the LGBT movement's appeal to being recognized as "good citizens" deepens its divergence from those who prioritize everyday dignity and the healing of intimate sorrow, further marginalizing those who do not fit the mold of "good citizens." This discussion is based on participant observation and interviews I conducted intermittently from 2017 to 2020 with four gay men, three trans women, and five *bakla* in Cebu City and Tagbilaran City, where open urban and conservative rural cultures intersect. In Cebuano and Boholano, the local languages of the places, vernacular trans women are referred to as *bayot*, and there is much regional and linguistic diversity in nomenclature, but for simplicity, this chapter uses the Tagalog word *bakla* as a general term for trans women in the Philippines.

Two identities and politics

Bakla stereotypes

In pre-colonial society, "*asog*" who transitioned from male to female gender were common. The role of the "*babaylan*," the shaman/healer in the vernacular belief system, was primarily assumed by women and *asog*, who were respected in the community. However, the role of the *babaylan* was abolished when Spanish colonial rule introduced male chauvinism (*machismo*) along with Catholicism. The status of the *asog* fell, and they came to be called "*bakla*," which refers to "effeminacy/delusion/indecision" in Tagalog (Brewer 2001; Quintos 2012; Garcia 2013; Ildefonso 2022).

Today, *bakla* are generally understood as "men with a woman's heart" or "women trapped in a man's body," and those who embrace this identity are often older, rural, and/or poor (Tan 2001). From a modern Western perspective, *bakla* combine a gender transition to women with a sexual orientation toward men in an undifferentiated way. Some *bakla* actively express their femininity, while others maintain a masculine outward appearance.

Many studies have noted the difficulties faced by *bakla*. For example, the older *bakla* are more likely to have experienced violence from their fathers seeking to "correct" their gender expression under the belief that they can be cured by beating. At the same time, because *bakla* generally do not marry or have children of their own, their families expect more from them than from their cisgender, heterosexual brothers and sisters in terms of domestic labor, parental and nursing care, and financial support for their nephews and nieces. However, even though *bakla* work hard to seek acceptance from their families, they do not always receive support and care from those to whom they have devoted themselves, which frequently leads to loneliness and anxiety as they age (Guevara 2016; Ceperiano et. al. 2016).

Often, *bakla* receive the personal care that they need in close, intimate relationships with fellow *bakla* (Guevara 2016: 148). Intimate relationships also help *bakla* enter occupational niches, such as hairdressers or beauticians, as successful and elder *bakla* hire younger fellows in their beauty parlors and look after them. However, low income in such occupations and their obligations to support their families have trapped many of them in poverty. Thus, many of them feel a sense of sorrow that they cannot become as beautiful as they wish, being unable to purchase enough cosmetics and clothing (Thoreson 2011).

In romantic relationships, following the gender norm that "women are supposed to love men," many *bakla* desire a "real man" with whom to live. However, "real men" often financially and sexually exploit those *bakla* (Ceperiano et. al. 2016; Johnson 1997; 1998). The men seek to enhance their own masculinity and gain economic benefit by manipulating risky sexual relationships with *bakla* (Johnson 1998: 700–701).[2] Moreover, these relationships are ephemeral, since the men eventually marry women and start families. Hence, the *bakla* find that no matter how much she devotes herself to a "real man," she will never win "true love." Since the "real man" who has a relationship with a *bakla* does not perceive himself or his partner as "homosexual," neither do the

---

2   Tan (2001: 121) describes men who have relationships with *bakla* as victims of the Philippines' madonna/whore culture in which they are unable to have sexual relations with girlfriends, but also have no money to pay for services from female sex workers.

two enter into a stable same-sex relationship (Cannell 1999: 214–15).[3] However, *bakla* are well aware that in other countries, relationships between *bakla* and "real men" based on emotional connections become possible. Therefore, *bakla* imagine and yearn for an "America" where "real love" could perhaps be realized, where they would be treated as a "real woman" by a "real man" (Johnson 1997; 1998).

The Flores de Mayo (May Flower Festival) devoted to the Virgin Mary and "Miss Contests" in various fiestas are opportunities for *bakla* to reverse the dominant hierarchical order, overcoming the sense that they are not "real women" and do not possess the beauty of the upper class. *Bakla* seek to be showered with admiration by dressing in glitzy costumes on stage and on the boulevards, embodying the ideals of beauty and affluence that "America" exemplifies. The pleasure of imitating upper-class culture and disrupting the hierarchical order from below is simultaneously accompanied by the pain that imitation can never be full emulation (Tolentino 2007), Indeed, if a *bakla* fails at a beauty contest, she runs the risk of being accused of being a vulgar imitator (Cannell 1999: 222–26).

Thus, while the *bakla* have been forced to conform to the stereotypes of serving their families, occupying occupational niches, entertaining people, or being outlets for men's sexual desires, they have also disrupted the symbolic hierarchical order on fleeting, extraordinary occasions.[4] Meanwhile, many *bakla* who dislike these stereotypes have suppressed their femininity, trying to maintain masculine appearances and behaviors in accordance with dominant norms (Tan 2001: 123).

Although my research on vernacular identities is limited to *bakla*, there are also people called "*tomboy*," who are characterized by gender transition to males. They are constructed as "males trapped in a female

---

3 *Bakla* having sexual relations with each other is described as a "clashing of two cymbals" (*pompyangan*) or "lesbianism," and is abhorred by *bakla* themselves (Tan 1995: 92).

4 *Bakla* slang expressions called "Sward speak," disrupt the symbolic categories and hierarchical order in the language and negotiate the dominant culture (Tolentino 2007: 176–179).

body" and often work in occupations associated with men, such as security guards or bus conductors (Tan 2001: 122). *Tomboys* seek approval from their own and their female partners' families by contributing economically as masculine breadwinners. Their relationships with partners emphasize care and respect, unlike the ephemeral relationships of the *bakla* (Ceperiano et. al. 2016: 20–27).

The othering of *bakla* by gay men and trans women

The term "gay" was introduced in Manila in the 1960s by elite individuals with Western experience. The gay scene was characterized by wealth and beauty, and in the 1970s some gays were favored by First Lady Imelda Marcos (Tan 2001). In the 1980s, the urban middle class with no overseas experience began to absorb Western gay culture through the media; and in the 1990s, gay magazines proliferated. A series of gay organizations were formed: some claimed their rights as a part of the student movement, and others developed countermeasures to address the HIV/AIDS crisis (Tan 2001).

Bakla is a performative gender expression while gay is defined by sexual orientation. Neil Garcia (1996; 2013) argues that the change in the idea of the *bakla* has facilitated the acceptance of the gay concept. Originally, *bakla* were thought to be sexually orientated toward men due to having a female *loob* (literally, inside) inhabiting a male *labas* (literally, outside). However, the spread of the gay concept reversed the causal relationship among many people. Namely, those who have accepted the concept of gay came to think that they gender-shifted to women because of having *loob* with a sexual orientation toward men. The mainstream Philippine population, however, continues to conflate *bakla* and gay as alternative concepts. Therefore, gay men who did not gender-transition to women were categorized as "*silahis*:" *bakla* who conceal their femininity (Garcia 1996: 97–98).

For middle-class gay men, calling each other *bakla* can be an expression of familiarity among peers, but to be called so by heterosexuals is insulting. They are uncomfortable being identified with entertainers, *parlorista* (hairdressers), or the *bakla* caricatured by the media (cf. Sakagawa,

Chapter 2 in this volume). Therefore, to differentiate themselves from *bakla*, they typically try to maintain masculine appearances and enter professional careers such as teaching, the civil service, and so on.

Some gay men, emphasizing their own "decency," accuse *bakla* with having a propensity towards irresponsibility, excessive drinking, drug abuse, steal and cross-dressing (Guevara 2016: 140).[5] A kind of elitism dogged the HIV/AIDS prevention movement, with middle-class gay men who trumpeted their own decency under the idea that HIV/AIDS was someone else's problem, saying that they would do poor *bakla* the favor of enlightening them (Tan 1995: 96; 2001: 137). A statement from the 1996 Pride Parade protested: "As gay men, we are portrayed as limp-wristed weaklings who crumble in the face of danger. We are also shown as sex-starved effeminate sissies who exploit minors" (Tan 2001: 132). A gay student organization required as a condition of membership "no girlie attire" or long hair and even "strictly adhere to a social norm of being straight" (ibid: 127). Such statements show that middle-class gay men's efforts to de-pathologize and mainstream homosexuality paradox-ically endorsed the male-centered norms that good gays are masculine (Tan 2001).

In romantic relationships, middle-class gay men also attempt to develop lifelong relationships to differentiate themselves from *bakla* who usually flirt with ephemeral, money-mediated relationships (Canoy 2015). However, such efforts are often thwarted by physical desires. Moreover, the more they are haunted by the ghosts of heterosexual norms in trying to establish "normal" relationships, the more they risk falling into the gap between the "gay world" and the "straight world," and being marginalized by both (Canoy 2015).

As for middle-class people who actively gender-transition to women, they have adopted the Western-derived identity as "trans women" to emphasize they have intentionally chosen their gender and to differentiate

---

5 Conversely, *bakla* also tease "yuppie gays" for being closeted cowards, saying, for example: "Whom (*sic*) is he trying to fool? You can smell his uterus" (Tan 2001: 127).

themselves from the *bakla*. In my research, many trans women were interested in gender affirmation surgery in Thailand and elsewhere, but most *bakla* did not seek such surgery, despite taking female hormones.

As we saw above, traditionally, *bakla* have had limited employment opportunities. Since the 2000s, however, many trans women with English fluency have found employment in the business process outsourcing (BPO) industry, typically in call centers of US companies emphasizing "diversity," earning higher salaries and gaining social recognition (David 2015; 2016). Although the state and BPO companies hail the call center agents as *"bagong bayani"* (new heroes) who contribute to economic development and nation-building, they do not enjoy unconditional recognition and emancipation. While being allowed to dress as women in the workplace, they are asked to tone down their dress and gender expression. They are also required to perform unpaid emotional labor in stereotypical ways, such as relieving their colleagues' work stress by making them laugh at their jokes. Some attempt to establish a level of intimacy with customers by using a romantic-sounding voice to increase sales. As such, trans women who work at call centers can enjoy "freedom" only within the dominant neoliberal framework (David 2015; 2016).

Certainly, through higher education, new identities, and higher-income employment, middle-class gay men and trans women have been able to free themselves to some extent from the stereotypes imposed on *bakla*. However, their freedom remains conditional, and their differentiation from *bakla* hampers the building of broader solidarity.

The "good citizens" LGBT movement

Challenges and issues for the LGBT movement

The LGBT movement in the Philippines was spawned in the aftermath of the 1986 democratization and the 1992 Communist Party split, raising diverse identities, ideologies, and demands. In the early 1990s, issues related to gender and sexuality were considered secondary within the leftist movement, but feminists helped the nascent LGBT movement to articulate and sharpen their issues (Evangelista 2018; 2020; 2024).

The Progressive Organization of Gays in the Philippines (Progay) and Kapederasyon LGBT Sectoral Organization were organized from the leftist camp. UP Babaylan, formed as a student organization at the University of the Philippines Diliman, aligned with the Akbayan party, which emphasized policy advocacy and social democracy. The Lesbian Collective (TLC) was founded as a voice for lesbians, and the Reach Out Foundation (ROF) formed as an HIV/AIDS policy advocacy body. The Metropolitan Community Church (MCC), which seeks to include gender and sexual minorities, also began activities in the Philippines.

According to John Andrew Evangelista (2018: 59–61), LGBT organizations in the Philippines have attempted to identify and address gender and sexual minorities' rights through four different frames. The "class frame" seeks to destroy the feudal, patriarchal system and establish socialism; the "legal frame" seeks to overthrow the conservative system of collusion between the state and the church and enact anti-discrimination laws; the "consciousness frame" seeks to change people's prejudices through education on gender and sexuality; and the "intersectional frame" seeks to address multilayered marginalization.

There are tensions and conflicts between organizations that espouse these different frames. However, in the late 1990s and early 2000s, contending groups created deliberative fora based on affective ties and agonism in which opponents recognize each other as worthy adversaries, which led to a broad consensus that they share the common causes of holding annual pride parades and promoting advocacy for anti-discrimination laws. However, the pursuit of legalized same-sex marriage was not included in a shared agenda because of disagreements within the movement (Evangelista 2018; 2020; 2024).

The first pride parade in the Philippines, led by Progay and the MCC in 1994, reportedly developed out of protest action about soaring oil prices and other problems. However, urged to return to the left's basic mobilization, Progay did not hold a pride event the following year. From 1996 to 1998, ROF, with financial support from national and international donors, took the reins in holding a pride parade with a more festive atmosphere which was attended by a diverse range of organizations. After ROF's funding declined, Task Force Pride began to lead the pride event from 1999. Its diverse mix of combative, festive, and queer elements culminated in 15,000 attendees in 2018 (Evangelista 2018; 2020).

Party-list elections for 20% of members of the House of Representatives from marginalized social groups provided the LGBT movement with a favorable political opportunity structure. Akbayan won a seat in the 1998 election, which vitalized the LGBT movement's policy advocacy activities. The Lesbian and Gay Legislative Advocacy Network (LAGABLAB) was formed to persistently lobby conservative forces to enact anti-discrimination legislation. Anti-discrimination bills, which aim to prohibit discrimination in workplaces, schools, health care, housing, social services, and the like has been introduced in Congress by various members since 1995. While the bills passed the Lower House in 2004 and 2018, they were rejected by the Upper House and had yet to be enacted as of 2024.

To promote policy advocacy, Ang Ladlad, the first LGBT political party founded in 2003, also sought to participate in the party-list election.[6] However, the Commission on Elections rejected the party's application to participate in the 2006 elections on the grounds that it did not have enough regional chapters (Coloma 2013: 492), and refused its application in 2009 on the grounds that it endangered youth by "advocating immoral doctrines," citing the Bible and the Quran, respectively (Coloma 2013: 495). In response to the latter decision, the party and others launched the "LGBTs are not immoral" and "I'm moral" (imMORAL) campaigns (Coloma 2013: 501) and took the case to court. The Supreme Court ruled that the Commission on Elections' decision based on religion was unconstitutional, opening the way for the party to participate in future elections. However, the party did not win any seats in the 2010 and 2013 elections; and in 2019, its founder, a famous public intellectual named

---

6   Originally named the *Lunduyan* (Center) Party to resituate LGBT people from the periphery to the center, it was renamed the Ladlad Party, from the Filipino word *magladlad*, meaning "to unfurl the cape that used to cover your body like a shield" (Coloma 2013: 483–484).

Danton Remoto, ran for Quezon City Council as an independent but was unsuccessful.

The LGBT movement has also worked hard to change prejudices in society by crafting counter-discourses. For example, it has challenged the dominant discourse that "LGBT people are already accepted by society" by arguing that they are only accepted on the condition that they do not claim rights, and that they conform to existing stereotypes. To counter the religious view that "LGBTs are immoral," its activists have pointed out, through their work to reconcile faith and sexuality, how such a biased view has fostered discrimination, oppression, human rights violations, and hate crimes (Thoreson 2012; Coloma 2013: 499–500; Soriano 2014).[7]

Furthermore, the middle class, which plays a central role in LGBT activism, has attempted to recruit new members from depressed communities into the movement. In the process, middle class activists have tried to explain the concepts of sexual orientation and gender identity, situate various vernacular identities within the Western conceptual map, and teach the poorer members their "correct" identities.

While these endeavors have not always been successful, middle-class activists, while recognizing their limitations, strategically use "LGBT" as a symbol for a movement seeking rights and recognition (Thoreson 2012: 545–49).

The Cebu City LGBT movement

The LGBT movement in Cebu City is led by millennials who have embraced a Western identity. Many graduated from college with the support of overseas parents or relatives and work in global service industries such as fashion, tourism, and call centers, which have grown since the mid-2000s. Their relatively high salaries have helped them enjoy dignity and social recognition in their families and communities.

---

7   Between 1996 and 2013, 156 SOGI (sexual orientation and gender identity) minority people were reportedly murdered due to discrimination (Philippine LGBT Hate Crimes Watch 2012).

Their English fluency and internet access have allowed them to have more liberal romantic relationships with foreigners.

One of the key figures in the movement was a trans woman known by the nickname Magda (Interviewed September 27, 2017 and March 20, 2018). She was bullied as a child with such calls as: "Crucify the *Bakla*!," but came out when she was in high school and had breast-augmentation surgery when she was in college. She paid for her university tuition with remittances from her father, who was working in Saudi Arabia, but when he was unable to renew his contract, she was forced to take a two-year leave of absence. During that time, she met a Korean man who had come to Cebu to study English. She explained: "At first, he seemed to think I was a woman, and when I told him I was gay, he rejected me, but when I told him I was a trans woman, he accepted me." Later, a Spanish lover she met online helped her with tuition fees to finish university.

However, San Carlos University, a Catholic school, had a strict dress code, forcing her to remove her earrings and bra, and cut her long hair, and she was preached to by conservative faculty who invoked God. In response, in 2006, she and her fellow students petitioned for free dress and hairstyles. In the process, she says, she found herself transformed, despite having once cared only about beauty and partying. After graduating from the university, she founded the transgender organization Coalition for Liberation of Reassigned Sex (COLORS) in 2010, and a coalition called Cebu United Rainbow LGBT Sector in 2011. She successfully lobbied the city council to enact Cebu Anti-Discrimination Ordinance in 2012. In 2016, she was appointed chair of the anti-discrimination committee, and took the initiative to craft the Implementing Rules and Regulations of the ordinance in 2018. While the law established penalties such as suspension of the licenses of entities that violated the ordinance, its primary purpose was to forge a broad consensus to prevent discrimination against any and all people, including people with disabilities and women.

As of 2017, public services for gender and sexual minorities in Cebu City included: LGBT Help Desks, which holds activities such as job fairs with invited foreign companies, including call centers that actively employ gender and sexual minorities, and SOGIE (sexual orientation, gender identity and gender expression) awareness activities; and the Gender and Development Office, responsible for organizing the LGBT community in each *barangay* (the smallest local political and administrative unit) as well as bringing government programs to the furthest reaches of society, including the elderly, the disabled, children, fathers providing child care,[8] and single parents.

In September 2017, I accompanied Magda and others on a tour of the city's *barangays* to explain the Department of Social Welfare and Development's Sustainable Livelihood Project, which provided small-scale three-year loans to LGBT local communities. She stressed the importance of creating a viable business plan, taking pride in their business, being decent and socially responsible, and promoting the high quality of LGBT communities. However, while there was enthusiastic participation of LGBT organizations in some *barangay*, this was not the case in poorer areas.

A trans woman working at the LGBT Help Desk lamented:

> LGBTs, also, should think about what they can contribute to the community and the government as citizens. But it is very difficult to get LGBT people to attend meetings in poor areas. Many of them work at night or enjoy nightlife and don't get up in the early morning. They are so focused on their immediate enjoyment and work that it is hard to get them to commit to activities. It's like teaching fish to climb trees. (Interview, March 20, 2018)

A staff member at the Gender and Development Office also expressed similar concerns:

> LGBT people seldom participate even when we offer them programs. When one NGO offered HIV/AIDS prevention seminars and testing,

---

8   In the programs, fathers providing child care are called ERPAT. Originally, the term was a *bakla* slang of "father," reverse-engineered from the Latin *pater*, meaning "father," but reconfigured as the acronym of Empowerment Reaffirmation of Paternal Abilities and Trainings in the formal programs.

the only people there were the doctors. Some don't want to participate in pride parades. No matter how much we try to help them, they have no intention of helping themselves. (Interview, March 23, 2018)

Thus, in addition to rights, diversity, and dignity, LGBT activists emphasize terms such as decency, entrepreneurship, social responsibility, good governance, and participation. This is not surprising, considering that marginalized minorities are often forced to demonstrate that they are also "good citizens" when demanding public recognition and rights. The dilemma, however, is that not all gender and sexual minorities can be or want to be the "good citizens" thus described.

Bakla work, dignity and sorrow

Itinerant merchants and entertainers

The ways to resist marginalization for gender and sexual minorities are not limited to LGBT movements. One practice for *bakla* is to seek dignity through success in their niche professions. I conducted participant observation with an itinerant merchants' group of the Zizmore company for three days in September 2017. The company employs many *bakla*, *silahis* and others as door-to-door salespeople for massage oils and other products because they excel at sales talk. They live an itinerant life, touring the regional cities of the Central Visayas region to sell their products. Payment is on a commission basis, so the more they sell, the more they earn. The best salespeople reportedly earn as much as 1,000 pesos per day, which is good compared to the legal minimum wage in Cebu City of about 400 pesos per day as of 2017. Nevertheless, at the time of my visit, the salespeople had chosen cheap accommodation in a depressed community during their life on the move. The salespeople and their female managers sharing their life on the road had formed a family-like relationship.

When I accompanied their sales activities, they visited government offices and schools without appointments, approaching puzzled-looking officials and teachers willy-nilly and beginning to massage them, and making obscene jokes, such as: "Your uric acid level looks high. You shouldn't eat eggplant with eggs on it," provoking gales of laughter. Capitalizing on the amicable atmosphere, the salespeople then read clients' palms, listening to their health concerns, and grooming their eyebrows, while selling their products. On one occasion, when we entered a kindergarten, a difficult-looking female teacher coldly told the salespeople to leave because she had no money. But when Jessica, a top salesperson, joked and gently began massaging her, the teacher's expression softened and she offered to cooperate in Jessica's sales efforts, saying: "I haven't been able to raise my shoulders for a long time, but neither my husband nor my children ever give me a massage. You are the only one. You should come back next time when the parents assemble. I'll tell the other teachers, too."

In this way, the salespeople establish a brief intimacy with even skeptical and curious strangers, and offer healing and care. Thus, to some extent, such practices involve emotional labor – the "commodification of emotion" – but they seemed to reduce the stress of the labor through a patterned approach to their clients.

After marrying a childhood sweetheart and having two children, Jessica, from a poor farming family in Mindanao, began living as a *bakla*, albeit retaining a masculine appearance. Now one of the biggest earners at Zizmore, Jessica says, "It's exhausting to constantly entertain customers, but it's lovely to give a massage to old people because they enjoy it so much." Jessica dreams of saving enough to open her own store in her hometown. Jessica also says: "I'm a hard worker, different than many *bakla* who don't value life and are riddled with vices."

The salespeople are kind and caring, but there are flickers of sadness in their intimacy. Elsa is from a slum in Manila, and jokes that she is a "transformer," attractive because she is "exotic and macho" (Interviewed September 24, 2017 and February 24, 2019). Having taken hormones and being feminine in appearance, Elsa explained that she had started to realize she was a *bakla* when she was about six years old because she "danced well and played with girls all the time." Almost daily, her father would beat her with a bamboo cane, or put her into a bag and hang her from the ceiling; at age seven she was raped by a relative; and at age fifteen she ran away from home because she was afraid of her father and wanted to see another world. She started calling herself Elsa, working as a "call gay" taking rich middle-aged men as clients, participating in Miss Gay contests, and dancing and performing fire-breathing shows at village festivals.

At 23, Elsa started living with a fourteen-year-old boy. But while she was performing at a bar to earn money to celebrate the boy's sixteenth birthday, he was seeing a woman. Shocked by this, Elsa left Manila, taking a ferry alone to Negros Island. She boasts, "I can live anywhere, just with my own body," thanks to her good social skills and talent for entertaining. On Negros, she stayed at the home of some *bakla* she met on the ferry and lived with them while performing shows, but left because she disliked that they were on methamphetamines. While sleeping rough in a cemetery, she met a twelve-year-old boy. Under the pretense of dating his older brother, Elsa moved in with the boy's family, who made their living making tombstones. Eventually, Elsa began a relationship not only with the younger boy, but also with his older brother and uncle, and they kept begging her for money. When she won 10,000 pesos at a show, she gave them money because, as Elsa says: "A *bakla* who doesn't hand over money is worthless." On the boy's birthday, Elsa presented him with a guitar, which pleased him. When Elsa joined Zizmore and was selling in Cebu, however, the now sixteen-year-old boy found a girlfriend. Shocked by this, Elsa returned to the slum in Manila, where she now works in a gay bar and enjoys spending time with her nieces and nephews.

Elsa laments: "It's hard to love men. My love interests were getting younger and younger. But no matter how much love and money you devote to dating youngsters, when they grow up, they eventually fall in love with women." Jessica worries about her, saying: "Elsa is very sweet, but she gets too caught up in her lover, so she loses sight of everything else. I advise her to think more about herself, but she just won't change."

Perhaps the realization of legal rights by the LGBT movement will not save Elsa from sorrow. Also, many activists detest *bakla* like her as "criminal pedophiles," saying that they tarnish the image of LGBTs and hinder their quest for rights. However, Elsa's role is to provide sexual services, and although she may have seduced, she has never coerced. Nor has she broken the law, since the age of sexual consent in the Philippines is twelve, regardless of whether it involves the same or the opposite sex.

An elderly hairdresser

Jojo, who runs a beauty parlor in a town on the island of Bohol, is also very sad (Interview, May 2, 2018). Born to a poor fishing family in northern Mindanao, she left home at age fifteen for Manila, where she worked as a live-in domestic helper in the homes of rich people and sex workers who were sharing accommodation. At nineteen, Jojo was invited by an older *bakla* named Sosing, whom she met in a park, to return to her home island of Bohol. Since Jojo had no boat fare, she offered the captain and others massages and sexual services in return for her passage on the boat.

In Bohol, Jojo worked in a beauty salon with Sosing, who was a talented hairdresser, but three years later Sosing died of illness. While lying beside Sosing's body, Jojo prayed: "At least leave your talent with me," upon which she heard Sosing's voice saying: "Very well. You have a good heart," and so Jojo acquired hairdressing skills. To return the favor, she supported Sosing's family financially for a long time. After Sosing's demise, Jojo worked for about nine years at a beauty parlor run by another *bakla* named Yayot, but Yayot also became ill. Even while employees and customers had been leaving, Jojo continued to work there all along, which lead to Yayot giving Jojo the beauty parlor. Feeling indebted, Jojo took better care of Yayot than her own family did until Yayot's death.

When Jojo became independent and opened her own beauty salon, women who had their makeup done at Jojo's salon won the Miss Bohol contest five years in a row, making the salon very popular. Business was thriving. As of my research in 2017, Jojo had retired as a hairdresser and employed seven *bakla*. She stressed that her financial success helped her regain dignity in her family. Jojo's eldest brother, who joined the private army of a local politician involved in drug trafficking, did not allow Jojo to return home, saying that it was shameful to have a *bakla* in the family. However, Jojo subsidized her brother's sons' tuition to become seafarers, and when her brother developed cancer, Jojo paid for his treatment. Then, shortly before the brother died, he rubbed Jojo's knee with his fingertips, which Jojo took to mean he was saying sorry.

Nevertheless, despite her financial success and sense of dignity, Jojo still carried a deep sadness in her heart. She says, "I helped many men become sailors or electricians by paying their tuition, but none of them ever returned to me. They took advantage of me, but I took advantage of their bodies too, so it was mutual." She explains that young men approach *bakla,* saying: "What do you lose if you sleep with a *bakla*? Just juice, right? Let's have some fun," but when they have a family, they will leave *bakla.* Jojo laments that the only time love between *bakla* and a man lasts long is when there is money or other purposes. "*Bakla* don't know real love. We're good at entertaining people, but there's a hole deep down inside, where drugs and sex can easily enter." Jojo confessed that she was once addicted to methamphetamines and arrested, which she was encouraged to take by brokers who sent young Filipino women to nightclubs in Japan, and by *bakla* film crews.

> For a long time, I wished for a short life. What is the point of this life if I can never know true love? I wonder why God made me a *bakla*. I just wanted to be a woman directly. *Bakla* are the most pitiful people in the world. We have had hard lives, so God will surely save us first.

Jojo learned when she was nearly sixty years old that this deep sadness could be assuaged by love and care for others. A mother and two young girls were begging in her neighborhood, all three having intellectual disabilities. One of the children became ill, and when Jojo took her to hospital, she was diagnosed as malnourished. The grandmother who had cared for the children had died, so Jojo adopted the two girls. At first, she felt she *had* to take care of them, but now she says that spending time with the children is her greatest happiness and purpose in life. However, if Jojo had not had the financial resources to support the children, it would have been difficult for her to assuage her sadness through love and care.

Jojo has no interest in the LGBT movement for legal rights, saying that the term LGBT, also, "will soon be obsolete, and is meaningless," and that "*bakla* is a much cuter and more beautiful word." As for legal rights, she says: "Same-sex marriage is impossible, of course. If such a law were to be enacted, it would only cause more confusion. A *bakla* is a man with a woman's heart, and she will only fall in love with real men. A *bakla*'s love is fleeting, after all." As for prohibiting discrimination, she emphasizes the importance of love and care over the law, saying, "Even the word '*bakla*' will not hurt anyone if it is spoken slowly and with love and care."

Conclusion

The various practices of gender and sexual minorities who resist marginalization discussed in this chapter can be typified as follows (see Table 13.1). First, the middle-class-led LGBT movement primarily seeks legal rights in the public sphere (the realm of open debate with unspecified others over the desired social order). Second, both the poor and middle class seek everyday dignity through economic success in niche or professional occupations in the market and contributions to their families and communities. Third, in the intimate sphere (the sphere bound together by care for the lives of specific others), *bakla* seek to heal their deep sadness at not being able to establish stable relationships with "real men." These practices are not mutually exclusive, and people can engage simultaneously in more than one practice.

From this, we can identify two difficulties the young middle-class-led LGBT movement will have when trying to span the social rifts of class and generation. First, the more the LGBT movement emphasizes the acquisition of legal rights, the deeper the discrepancy with *bakla*, who prioritize everyday dignity and the healing of grief. LGBT activists seem to value legal rights because they have experienced discrimination and exclusion within formal institutions such as schools and workplaces,

Table 13.1: Sexual minority practices

Objectives	Legal rights	Everyday dignity	Assuaging of grief
Means	Policy advocacy by the LGBT movement	Personal economic success	Rebuilding of care relationships
Agents	Middle-class activists	Diverse gender and sexual minorities	Poor/elderly *bakla*
Location	Public sphere	Marketplace	Intimate sphere
Challenges	Indifference of the poor; exclusion by "good citizens"	Necessity for contribution to family and neighbors; exclusion by "good citizens"	Necessity for economic capacity to care for others

in addition to international influences. However, many among the poor and elderly have had less opportunity to face institutional discrimination without opportunities to have higher education and employment in corporate enterprises. Moreover, they do not believe that legal rights will provide dignity or soothe their sorrows. Second, the more the LGBT movement emphasizes being "good citizens," the more it morally marginalizes *bakla* who make their livings through sex work, love young boys in pursuit of "true love," or use illicit drugs to drown sadness.

How, then, can the LGBT movement seek broader solidarity across these divisions? Aware of this chapter's failure to survey people who identify as lesbian, tomboy, bisexual and others, I will conclude with a tentative thought experiment. First, one possibility would be to create a nexus of diverse individuals by emphasizing economic activities that support everyday dignity. Nancy Fraser (1997: 11–40) argues that even though gays and lesbians can be economically successful, they will remain culturally marginalized, which is not necessarily true in the Philippines. Gender and sexual minorities in the country, regardless of differences in class or identity, have achieved everyday dignity by economically succeeding in their respective occupations and contributing to their families and communities. The LGBT movement may therefore be able to transcend divisions by supporting the livelihoods of poor gender and sexual minorities in partnership with the government, as in the Livelihood Assistance Project.

However, approaches that support the livelihoods of the poor cannot transform the marginalizing structure of "conditional acceptance" if taking place only within the dominant culture. For example, support for economic activities alone preserves a situation in which gender and sexual minorities who cannot contribute to their families and communities continue to be subjected to unjust treatment. For a more radical change, it is essential to dismantle the belief that people who deviate from the heterosexual norm must meet the majority's expectations in order to be accepted and respected. Another problem is that making support for economic activities conditional on being a "good citizen" and living "decently" will further marginalize the poor who deviate from that norm, such as sex workers. To avoid these problems, it will be necessary to critique the situation in which the majority requires the minority seeking rights to prove its worthiness by meeting certain moral and normative standards. In other words, if the majority cannot explain why only they can enjoy privileges, then the minority can legitimately complain of the unfairness that only they have shouldered the burden of proof for deserving those rights.[9]

Another possibility for solidarity would be for the LGBT movement to approach intimate sorrow of more marginalized people. For example, the *bakla* were saddened by their inability to attain "true love" with a "real man" as a "real woman," and by tragic relationships with men who exploit them. This sadness seemed to stem from their internalization of the rigid gender norms assigned to "real women" and "real men" and their belief that a "*bakla* with a woman's heart will seek a real man." In contrast, urban middle-class youth who embrace Western-derived identities such as gays and trans women seem to be less burdened by this sadness and enjoy more opportunities to develop more stable romantic relationships with Filipino or foreign partners. Therefore, by conveying "correct" identities to the *bakla*, LGBT movements may offer them an opportunity to disembed themselves from the vernacular culture causing this sadness. However, for many *bakla*, such cultural disembedding

---

9   This argument follows multiculturalism according to Will Kymlicka (2002).

and identity transitioning would not be easy. Moreover, such intervention could reinforce the pecking order of "progressive gays and trans/ignorant *bakla*."

Rather, a more effective approach would be for the LGBT movement to support the practices of gender and sexual minorities who seek to build "new families," based on diverse care relationships. Many *bakla* have attempted to heal their own grief by reconstructing their intimate sphere, by establishing various family-like relationships based on care with their peers or by adopting children. Yet, such "new families" that *bakla* built have tended to be formed mainly by those with the economic power to care for others, suggesting that those without economic power would have difficulty comforting their sorrow through new care relations. Therefore, developing programs to financially support more diverse intimate relationships, rather than exclusively focusing on a narrow, formal marital status such as same-sex marriage, may provide opportunities for new solidarity and improvement of welfare among diverse gender and sexual minorities. For instance, promoting advocacy for livelihood support, social security, cash transfer, and basic income for "new families" may be effective, but they should be provided on an individual basis, not on a household basis, so that the "new families" do not reproduce the domination and subordination of patriarchy.

14 | Gender and Sexual Minorities in Cambodia: External Influences and Internally Generated Movements

Naomi Hatsukano

Introduction

Cambodia, like its neighbor Thailand, is relatively tolerant toward gender and sexual minorities, and has not adopted a religious position that actively excludes sexual minorities.[1] Moreover, former King Norodom Sihanouk declared in 2004 that gay men and lesbians should be respected and that as a "liberal democracy", Cambodia must allow "marriage between man and man... or between woman and woman." This is often mentioned in reports and articles on sexual minorities in Cambodia (UNDP, USAID 2014; Hunt and Pann 2017; Vachon 2004).

Because of this ostensible tolerance, discrimination has not been seen as a major issue, nor has there been a sensationalized movement demanding the rights of gender and sexual minorities. In Cambodia, gender and sexual minorities have not always been conspicuous, and there is no evidence of a flourishing gay culture such as the one in the entertainment quarters of Bangkok or Pattaya in Thailand. Instead, there has been only minor development of gathering places in downtown Phnom Penh, the capital, and Siem Reap, a world-class tourist city.

Under these circumstances, it is not uncommon for people who are generally tolerant of gender and sexual minorities and support eliminating discrimination in principle to be intolerant of members of their own

---

1   Most of Cambodia's population adheres to Theravada Buddhism, while a Muslim Cham population accounts for 1–2% (National Institute of Statistics 2021). Freedom of religion is ensured by Article 43 of the Constitution of the Kingdom of Cambodia.

family. For example, In 2007, when the adopted daughter of the then Prime Minister Hun Sen came out publicly as a lesbian, he disowned her, but he also made positive statements about eliminating discrimination against sexual minorities at the same time (Vong 2007).

Cambodia has received foreign aid support and assistance from around the world since 1991, when the Paris Peace Accords were signed. Amid the influx of support, people, and culture from outside, HIV/AIDS became a major social issue, which fostered solidarity among gay men which in turn fueled movements seeking rights for gender and sexual minorities. This chapter will provide an outline of the environment in which gender and sexual minorities find themselves in Cambodia, and then discuss how that environment has been affected by "outside" influences. It will then explore recent trends in the gender and sexual minority movement and same-sex marriage.

The environment for gender and sexual minorities in Cambodia

In the Cambodian language, the word *khteuy*, similar to the Thai word *kathoey*, is the most commonly used term to describe genders other than male (*pros*) and female (*srei*). Headley's 1977 *Cambodian-English Dictionary* defines it as "hermaphrodite." Sakamoto's 1988 *Dictionary of the Cambodian Language* (Cambodian-Japanese) concurs. A more recent edition of Sakamoto's dictionary (Sakamoto 2006) provides a second meaning: "a man who is womanish; a man dressed as a woman."

There are several other Cambodian expressions that refer to sexual minorities. According to Catalla et al., "*sak veng*" (long hairs) and "*srei sros*" (pretty girls) are used to refer to men who dress and act like women, while "*sak klay*" (short hairs) is sometimes used to refer to women who dress and act like men. English origin expressions such as "WLW", "LB", "LG" and "LT" are used among young lesbians. Furthermore, expressions such as "*SIM pi*," likening bisexuality to a smartphone that can accommodate two SIM cards, demonstrate how novel expressions are flexibly adopted. A more descriptive and formal expression used on occasion is *"phet ti bey"* (third gender) (UNDP, USAID 2014; Catalla et al. 2003; Hoefinger et al. 2017). However, when people other than gender and sexual minorities use these expressions, there is often a connotation of ridicule.

Historically, in Cambodia, being a gender and sexual minority and engaging in homosexual acts was not a criminal offense, nor were there any religious prohibitions. Surveys and studies in the 1950s and 1970s documented cases of same-sex couples living together and homosexual acts (Hoefinger and Srun 2017; Tan 2008; Ebihara 1974). However, during the Democratic Kampuchea period (the Pol Pot regime, 1975–1979), when millions were persecuted, sexual minorities were sometimes subject to violence and torture, forced into heterosexual marriages, and otherwise abused.[2] After the Pol Pot regime, the Marriage and Family Law enacted in 1989 under the Kampuchea People's Revolutionary Party's government explicitly prohibited marriage of "a person whose sex is the same sex as the other," along with that of "a person whose penis is impotent; a person who has leprous, tuberculosis, cancer or venereal diseases which are not completely cured; a person who is insane, and a person who has mental defect; [and] a person who was bound by prior marriage which is not yet dissolved" (Article 6). It is unclear how strictly the law was applied during the social turmoil that continued until the Paris Peace Accords in 1991, but the fact that despite its historical tolerance of sexual minorities, Cambodia had a period of official exclusion, helps to explain the discrimination that has continued since then.

In December 2016, a doctored image originating in Thailand was posted on Facebook, ridiculing King Norodom Sihamoni of Cambodia for being gay. The Cambodian government protested that insulting the King was an insult to the country itself (Hutt 2017).[3] The fact that such a

---

2 In August 2016, the Extraordinary Chambers in the Courts of Cambodia, prosecuting alleged crimes committed between April 17, 1975 and January 6, 1979, heard testimony about harm to sexual minorities. https://www.eccc.gov.kh/en/witness-expert-civil-party/sou-sotheavy. Accessed December 3, 2023.

3 King Sihamoni is unmarried, but has never made any specific statement about his sexual orientation. Cambodia did not have a lèse-majesté law at the time, but in February 2018, a new crime of lèse-majesté was established in the Criminal Code.

message originated in Thailand, where disrespect to the King is a serious offense, indicates the sensitive relationship between the people of the two countries, while demonstrating that in Cambodia, whatever the laws and official position, sexual orientation can be the basis for an insult.

According to a survey on family violence among sixty-one lesbian, bisexual, and transgender people, 81% (twenty-five people) of LBT people under the age of thirty-five had experienced emotional violence; six people reported being pressured to have a heterosexual marriage and to end their same-sex marriage; and 35% (eleven people) of LBT people under the age of thirty-five in this survey had considered suicide because of family members' rejection of their sexual orientation (RoCK 2019). There have also been reported cases where gender and sexual minority couples have been punished under the Anti-Trafficking Law for rejecting their parents' attempts to force them into a heterosexual marriage and running away from home (Hoefinger et al. 2017). Another study from 2014–2015 established that many LGBT children are likely to face bullying at school, which negatively effects educational and economic opportunities (CCHR 2015).

"Traditional" values and things from "outside"

When asked about the general image of gender and sexual minorities in Cambodia in the late 2010s, respondents who had not interacted with gender and sexual minority activists or their supporters often replied: "Urban life has changed people. Gender and sexual minorities do not exist in rural areas," or "It is the influence of Western culture." Furthermore, many people attributed the presence of gender and sexual minorities to eating contaminated food from Thailand.[4] Those who

---

There was also a theory that a Cambodian national in Thailand was responsible for the incident, but the matter was never resolved and eventually fell off the radar.

4   Responses from private school teachers and officials in Stung Treng Province (all of whom had graduated from universities in Phnom Penh or had overseas experience) when asked about their perceptions of sexual minorities (Author's fieldnotes January 2018).

believed this hypothesis are not necessarily unintelligent: I heard it expressed by people with university education or higher, who claimed to have read articles which reported that this had been scientifically proven. Whether it is a matter of food or cultural influences, many people have viewed gender and sexual minorities negatively. More common is the belief that such "bad things" did not originate domestically, but came from "outside," that is, from Thailand or Western countries, and are not Cambodian traditions.

Of course, this does not mean that gender and sexual minorities have not historically existed in Cambodia. The image of "none being in rural areas" unmistakably derives from the fact that gender and sexual minorities are more apparent in urban areas, but this is only because the difficulties of living in rural areas have driven them underground. *Zhenla fengtu ji* (The customs of Cambodia) (Zhou 1989), composed by a 13th century monk who traveled throughout Indochina, includes a passage describing Cambodia as follows: "There are many catamites in this country who stroll around the markets every day in groups of ten or more, always trying to attract the attention of Chinese men, and receive generous gifts in return. It is quite detestable."[5] Similarly, the *Chbab Srey* (Women's code of conduct), allegedly composed by elite men and monks in the 19th century, declares that a bad wife who behaves inappropriately towards her husband would become a *khteuy* in the next life.[6] All of this indicates that historically, gender and sexual minorities have lived in Cambodia, and they have been discriminated against to some extent.

Why, then, are foreign influences blamed for gender and sexual minorities? Why are they are not accepted by society or recognized as having historically been present in Cambodia? There appear to have been two major turning points in two stages, namely, the period before and after independence; and the period of recovery from the civil war. In the French colonial era, there was a movement to clarify the distinction

---

5   Originally written in Chinese. This passage is based on a Japanese translation by Wada Hisanori.

6   On the content of the *Chbab Srey,* see Jacobsen (2008).

between men and women, because the common people of both sexes wore similar clothes and hairstyles, and the distinction was not rigid in the 19th century (Edwards 2007). When Cambodia was building a new independent nation in 1953, after ninety years of French rule, it had to consult pre-colonial literature to explore its national identity and counter the imperialism of other countries. Under the circumstances, a text such as *Chbab Srey*, a guide for the daughters of good families which was not widely followed by ordinary people, was considered to be representative of traditional sexual roles. At the same time, any action or relationship outside of the heteronormative, androcentric family system was increasingly seen as unethical and un-Cambodian (Jacobsen 2008; Hoefinger and Sron 2017). A system based on binary rather than ambiguous genders was also deemed to be more conducive to governing the state (Brún 2019).

Furthermore, after the Paris Peace Accords, Cambodia was rapidly internationalized with the United Nations Peace Keeping Operations (PKO) personnel deployed throughout the country in the 1990s. As the economy moved towards recovery, there was a huge influx of foreigners and a great increase in the mobility of the domestic populace, all of which coincided with the spread of HIV/AIDS. As the HIV/AIDS program focused on those deemed most at risk, such as sex workers and male homosexuals, they were stigmatized. The then Prime Minister Hun Sen and his wife Bun Rany Hun Sen, concerned about the impact of globalization, information technology and the influx of foreign cultures on young people, expressed their fear that people would engage in unethical behavior and lose sight of family values, in the context of prevention of HIV/AIDS.[7] These fears were not necessarily directed at gender and sexual minorities, but they reinforce the idea that the things which were negatively impacting the people had come from "outside" (Hoefinger and Srun 2017; Sandy 2013).

---

7   Hoefinger and Srun noted that gender nonconforming people and sex/entertainment workers were often framed as immoral and "un-Cambodian" by the government, referring to the then Prime Minister Hun Sen's speech in 2010 and his wife Bun Rany's speech in 2009 (Hoefinger and Srun 2017).

We have already established that gender and sexual minorities and homosexual behavior had a long history in Cambodia, but ever since the HIV/AIDS epidemic, there has been a tendency for anyone who deviates from the heteronormative, androcentric family system to be regarded as coming from outside and threatening the Cambodian tradition, which has given rise to covert discrimination, teasing and bullying.

Rise of the gender and sexual minority rights movement

Domestic NGOs often filled gaps in government capacity with the influx of aid from the international community and served as domestic partners for international donors within Cambodia. NGOs played an important role in the emergence of the gender and the sexual minority movement in Cambodia, but there were also some grassroots movements that arose independently of international donors. More recently, there has been activism within the arts world and a growing number of commercial initiatives. Generally, the range of people who understand the movement is expanding with the broadening scope of its activities.

The initial movement began in the mid to late 1990s. At the time, HIV/AIDS was a major global challenge, and Cambodia was particularly hard hit: by the end of the 1990s, more than one in forty adults (1.25%) of reproductive age had the virus (Beyrer 2017). The international community invested significant funds in Cambodia for measures to combat the disease. Most of the funding was provided by the US President's Emergency Plan for AIDS Relief (PEPFAR)[8] and the Global Fund to Fight AIDS, Tuberculosis and Malaria (Global Fund), conducting activities such as distributing condoms and disseminating information about prevention. In the late 1990s and early 2000s, male homosexuals were targets of focused efforts as one of the most vulnerable groups, and NGO activities sought to empower gender and sexual minorities to deal

---

8 PEPFAR, established in 2003, was a five-year US plan to address the international HIV/AIDS problem. The initiative was developed with the goal of eliminating HIV and malaria in Cambodia by 2025.

with their own health issues. Through the combined efforts of foreign donors, domestic government agencies and gender and sexual minority-led NGOs, the HIV prevalence rate in the Cambodian population aged 15–49 decreased to 0.6% by 2013.

From the 2000s, activities were expanded beyond technical issues such as combatting HIV/AIDS, and were taking on a new challenge, namely, defending the human rights of gender and sexual minorities. Initial support for these activities came from domestic NGOs that had long worked on health issues. In 1999, Sou Sotheavy, a founder of Cambodia's gender and sexual minority rights advocacy movement, launched the Cambodian Network for Men Women Development (CMWD),[9] which aimed to support gender and sexual minorities in addition to preventing HIV/AIDS. In 2006, Bandanh Chaktomok (BC) was established as a gay men's and transgender network (Hoefinger et al. 2017).

The first pride parade was held in Phnom Penh in 2003, and since 2009 a film festival (screening films related to gender and sexual minorities from around the world as well as those from Cambodia),[10] elaborate *tuk-tuk* races,[11] and other events have been held in one coherent week in Phnom Penh and Siem Reap, drawing crowds of more than 400, according to the organizers (Hoefinger et al. 2017). The event was reported in English-language newspapers in Cambodia, and photos and videos of it were shared broadly on social media.

Rainbow Community Kampuchea (RoCK) started in 2009 and was registered as an NGO in 2014 as a network to more effectively develop plans and strategies for engaging the government in the pursuit of human rights for gender and sexual minorities. In 2012, a grassroots group led

---

9   Mr. Sotheavy was internationally recognized in 2014 when he was given the David Kato Vision & Voice Award for outstanding leadership in support of sexual minorities (Chhay and Woodside 2014).

10 When I attended the festival in May 2018, there were only small audiences during the screening of foreign sexual minority films, but about 50–80 Cambodians and foreigners attended the screening of a documentary short film about Cambodian gender and sexual minorities.

11 A *tuk-tuk* is a motorized tricycle. A *rumok,* a motorcycle with a cargo bed attached to the back, is often also referred to as a *tuk-tuk,* and also joins this event.

by young activists called CamASEAN Youth's Future began working to combat various forms of discrimination, including that against LGBT.[12] These new groups encouraged the use of social media to promote their activities (Hoefinger et al. 2017). NGOs have engaged in the work of various groups since the 2010s, including groups that led the fight against HIV/AIDS (mainly male homosexuals and transgender people); groups primarily focused on women's rights; groups dealing with a wide range of human rights issues; and groups focused specifically on issues related to gender and sexual minorities. As well as their efforts to protect the rights of gender and sexual minorities, NGOs continued to expand their cooperation with organizations representing the socially alienated and marginalized, such as sex workers and drug users.

NGOs that formed to fight HIV/AIDS in the 1990s began pursuing the rights of gender and sexual minorities relatively early. Around 2010, the Cambodian Center for Human Rights (CCHR), originally created to advocate for civil and political rights, began working with the Swedish Association for Sexuality Education (RFSU) to address challenges faced by the gender and sexual minority community. In 2014, the United Nations and USAID, in cooperation with various domestic NGOs, published the Cambodian segment of a report on the status of gender and sexual minority rights in Asian countries, entitled: "Being LGBT in ASIA: Cambodia Country Report" (UNDP, USAID 2014).

According to Brún (2019), who worked with human rights organizations and activists in Cambodia, most domestic NGOs in Cambodia have been embedded in a hierarchical structure in which projects are funded by international donors. Since the 1990s, NGOs have proven effective in fields of endeavor that ought to be handled by the government. Brún points out that the movement for gender and sexual minority rights has taken an exceptional direction among NGO-led movements in Cambodia. Unlike "hot" human rights issues in that country, such as land grabbing and freedom of speech, which have

---

12 This was a result of the ASEAN Grassroots People's Conference which coincided with Cambodia's one-year ASEAN Presidency in 2012 (Hoefinger et al. 2017).

attracted the attention of many and have sometimes become political and resulted in arrests, the gender and sexual minority rights movement started off relatively quietly. Although international donors began to show some interest in this field from around 2010, there was still very little until 2017 when the dissolution of opposition party and the arrest of opposition politicians prompted some donors to shift their support to "less sensitive human rights issues," and jumped on the opportunities to focus on gender and sexual minority rights. It is difficult to ascertain the donors' true motivation, as local Cambodian agencies were becoming more attuned to sexual minority rights at the same time that international interest in the issue increased significantly. Regardless, political interest in gender and sexual minorities in Cambodia certainly started from a low base, and understanding gradually spread among the population from the mid to late 2010s.

Leaders of the movement that began in the 2000s to pursue the rights of gender and sexual minorities engaged in dialogue with local government officials (at the village and commune level) to promote better understanding of the movement's aims, while simultaneously holding pride events that attract little attention. They have also initiated radio broadcasts to bring solitary sexual minority individuals out of isolation; released documentary films on video streaming sites; and promoted solidarity with local gender and sexual minorities through social media.[13] More recently, they have begun to organize workshops at the central government level and to hold dialogue with the Ministry of the Interior to promote understanding of gender and sexual minorities.[14] Behind this experience there appears to lie a sense of pride in the fact that they have not been strongly influenced by donor funding or intentions, but have instead taken the initiative in developing their own activities. The increased use of social media has underpinned their ability to decentralize

---

13 Based on interviews with relevant NGOs in June 2017 and October 2018.

14 RoCK organized National Dialogues on Law and Policy promoting LGBTIQ Rights. https://rockcambodia.org/what-we-do/advocacy-and-communication/ Accessed 30 September 2024.

activities focused on gender and sexual minorities. Furthermore, NGOs formed to combat HIV/AIDS, for example, have explained that "we are involved in human rights activities insofar as they are related to our original endeavors, which we continue to conduct."[15] In other words, they expanded their scope by drawing on and contributing to the expertise of their networks, while maintaining their own axis of activity.

There have also been moves to engage gender and sexual minorities in artistic and cultural activities. In 2017, Prumsodun Ok, a second-generation refugee who grew up in the US, founded Prumsodun Ok & NATYARASA, a classical dance troupe (*Robam Boran*) composed of gay performers.[16] The troupe has provided a training ground for bearers and inheritors of Cambodian culture, and has provided opportunities for gay dancers in Cambodia (Hagai 2021).

In addition, a film directed by Sok Visal in 2016, *Poppy Goes to Hollywood Redux*, featured at the Busan International Film Festival and the Osaka Asian Film Festival. At the time of its release, the Ministry of Culture and the Arts reportedly (Meta and Kijewsji 2017) had (undisclosed) film guidelines that deemed films with homosexual themes to be "adult films," revealing the government's intolerance of sexual minorities. However, *Hello, Neighbor*, directed by Un Bunthouern (2022), premiered at a large cinema in Phnom Penh in 2022 (*Khmer Times* 2022). Recently, streaming services have been offering LGBT-friendly dramas online. There have also been popular songs about same-sex love, such as *Chong srolanh monus pros doch knea vinh* (I want to love the same-sex man (instead of a woman) in 2021), *Chong srolanh monus srei doch knea vinh* (I want to love the same-sex woman (instead of a man) in 2021), *Srei beh daung pros* (Woman with a man's heart in 2015), and so on. These indicate that local understanding of sexual minorities is growing.

Commercially, the number of overtly "gay bars" in cities is also growing. Meanwhile, social media promotes numerous examples of

---

15 Based on interviews with relevant NGOs in June 2017 and October 2018.

16 For more information on Prumsodun Ok & NATYARASA, see: https://www. prumsodun.com/. Accessed December 3, 2023.

transgender celebrities achieving great success in business or becoming well-known for their charity work, heightening the public's recognition of gender and sexual minorities in the 2020s.

As interest from international and local actors has grown, some activists have begun to worry that the influx of funds and more diverse groups of people will make it more difficult to be effective. Another fear is that the government might resort to pinkwashing (Brún 2019).

Although public activism has succeeded in heightening awareness and understanding of gender and sexual minority issues among the general population, in the 2020s, there are still no legal provisions against discrimination or for same-sex marriage, and discriminatory sentiment among the public has certainly not disappeared. The government of Cambodia received the UN Independent Expert on protection against violence and discrimination based on sexual orientation and gender identity, Victor Madrigal-Borloz's visit and survey in January 2023. He found that the situation in Cambodia is positive. At the same time, he raised three recommendations: a) establishing a basic knowledge base that documents the current state of persons of diverse sexual orientation and gender identity, through the human rights-based approach; b) formulating policies and protocols for key institutions with a role in promoting the social inclusion of LGBT persons; c) adopting legislation against discrimination based on sexual orientation and gender identity and legalizing same sex marriage (Madrigal-Borloz 2023). In June 2023, responding to the growing numbers of people infected with HIV/AIDS, then-Prime Minister Hun Sen spoke against legalizing same-sex marriage, while insisting there would be no discrimination against the LGBT+ community (Nimol 2013). Prime Minister Hun Manet, who took office in August 2023, also supports the relatively tolerant attitude towards LGBT community. On June 20, 2024, the Cambodian Human Rights Committee (CHRC) announced that the Cambodian government supported France for the Joint Statement on the Universal Decriminalization of Homosexuality to be issued at the 56th session of the UN Human Rights Council in Geneva, Switzerland.[17]

---

17 CHRC press release, dated June 20, 2024, https://www.facebook.com/share/p/12DbDgWdLiL/

In October 2023, in response to Nop Dane's performance on the popular television show, *Cambodia's Got Talent*, judge and comedian Neay Krem said: "If five to six million of Cambodia's seventeen million people were gay, we would be short of manpower," for which he was widely condemned on social media, under the hashtag #RespectBongDane. The CHRC has promised to establish a working group on the case (*Khmer Times* 2023).

Although the situation for gender and sexual minorities in Cambodia is not progressing in a linear fashion, the movement seeking rights for gender and sexual minorities in Cambodia is entering a new era as it includes more local people.

Toward the realization of rights: The same-sex marriage debate

While there are various demands within the movement for protecting the human rights of gender and sexual minorities, in this section, the legal situation surrounding same-sex marriage, and activities aimed at its legalization will be discussed. Personal information such as births, deaths and marriages was destroyed during the Pol Pot era, and during the turmoil that followed in the 1980s, drafting a Marriage and Family Law was a low priority. When it finally passed, in 1989, it explicitly prohibited same-sex marriage, as mentioned above.

In the Constitution enacted in 1993, Article 45 stipulates that "Marriage shall be conducted according to law, based on the principle of mutual consent between one husband and one wife." The 2007 Civil Code, repeals the 1989 Marriage and Family Law article prohibiting same-sex marriage.[18] The Civil Code also stipulates that the minimum age for marriage is eighteen for both males and females (Article 948).[19] The

---

18 The Marriage and Family Law has not been repealed, but some provisions have been partially superseded by new provisions in the Civil Code.

19 Article 1023(2) of the Civil Code also prohibits "simple adoption" if the adoption is to be "abused" for the purpose of "heterosexual or homosexual marriage" to an adoptee by an adopter or any other "unjust purpose."

current Cambodian legal system does not prohibit same-sex marriages, but this does not mean they are approved, either.

Some proponents of same-sex marriage point out that the Constitution does not mention the gender of the husband (*pdei*) or wife (*propun*) and argue that same-sex marriage is therefore allowed (UNDP, USAID 2014), but this view has not been widely accepted. Furthermore, the Law on Civil Status, Civil Status Statistics and Identification, which was enacted in 2023, mentions that "one man" (*boros mneak*) and "one woman" (*srey mneak*) can register their marriage (Section7), therefore same-sex marriage is clearly not recognized under the current legal system.

Many foreign legal experts were involved in drafting the 2007 Civil Code. Former King Sihanouk's 2004 statement in favor of same-sex marriage was made in the midst of the drafting process.[20] The experts felt that rather than it being explicitly stipulated in the Civil Code, this was a matter best left to the Constitution, which takes precedence over the Civil Code; and that before the government passed any amendments to more explicitly permit same-sex marriage, it should first engage in thorough community discussions, with the citizenry taking the lead.[21] Under these circumstances, it is hard to interpret the current Constitution and Civil Code as permissive of same-sex marriage.

Although same-sex marriage is not legally recognized, proponents of the rights of sexual minorities sometimes claim: "There are a certain number of same-sex marriages in Cambodia every year " (Kunthear and Drennan 2013) and social networking sites are rife with photos of Cambodian same-sex couples getting married and cohabitating. So how have they achieved "marriage"? There are two types of "marriage" in Cambodia: traditional marriage and legal marriage.[22] A traditional

---

20 Drafting of the Cambodian Civil Code began in 1999 with support by the Japan International Cooperation Agency (JICA), and many Japanese experts were involved.

21 Based on an interview with an expert who participated in the Legal System Development Support Project (January 2018).

22 Many Cambodians, especially in the countryside, attached more value to the traditional Buddhist marriage ceremony instead of legal registration (Keur 2014; Kuong 2016).

marriage involves inviting guests to the "wife's" home, holding a marriage ceremony, and feasting on food. Such a ceremony confers approval for the marriage from parents, relatives, and the community, and is of great importance in Cambodian culture. However, permission from the local authorities is necessary to hold any kind of wedding ceremony, and obtaining such permission remains a major barrier to same-sex weddings. People who are afraid of discrimination in the local community only hold small parties under the guise of birthday or house warming parties, which do not require permission from the local authorities. As efforts to promote understanding of gender and sexual minorities among local governments are beginning to bear fruit, traditional weddings were becoming more common in the early 2020s.

Out of the practical necessity to continue living together and a desire for official recognition, gender and sexual minority couples sometimes register their relationship in a "family record book" (*siupau kruosar*), a booklet that lists the composition of the household, names, and relationships, and allows same-sex couples to register as "brother" or "sister," or even as "husband and wife," even if they are not related (UNDP, USAID 2014).[23] This makes the fact of their cohabitation somewhat acceptable in the local community. For example, UN Independent Expert Victor Madrigal-Borloz's end of mission statement in January 2023 cites a transgender couple in their seventies who hold a family record book of their registration as sisters (Madrigal-Borloz 2023), although not really siblings. One might infer that this is, or was, an acceptable method because the family record book used to be a relatively loosely administered institution.[24] However, like the traditional marriage, this does not change the couple's legal status. In future, if same-sex marriage is still not legalized and only the administrative structure is strictly regulated and streamlined, while the gender framework retains its

---

23 There seems to be more cases of sisters or brothers than husbands and wives.

24 In 2020, the Ministry of Interior guideline for registering or updating information in the family book requires official documents such as marriage certificate, birth certificate and so on. Therefore, if the local officials strictly follow the guidelines, it is difficult for the same sex couples to register as brothers/sisters.

traditional "male-female" configuration, such modest "certification" may be no longer feasible.

One way for same-sex couples to enjoy rights similar to heterosexual couples under the current legal system is through a formal contract, which is called a Declaration of Family Relationship. This is a practical method promoted by RoCK advocating for same-sex marriage; the parties agree on a contract as an alternative to a legal marriage to protect the property and assets of same sex couples, their biological and adopted children, and family as an interim strategy. Obtaining official recognition of a contract requires lengthy procedures, including filing the contract with the local government office, which is a significant barrier for the average couple. Still, it is an important route for those seeking something close to a legal marriage.

Although Cambodia's Constitution has been amended relatively frequently, since 1993 the main concerns of constitutional reform have been governance issues, such as how many National Assembly votes are needed to approve the Cabinet, or the structure of the electoral commission. Matters concerning marriage and family have not been on the agenda.

Realizing the rights of gender and sexual minorities has never been an election promise of the political parties, nor has it ever been the focus of policy discussions. Even among opposition parties, there has been almost no positive action on the issue. In sum, domestically, it appears to be a topic of political indifference.

In the absence of a legal system that allows same-sex marriage, members of gender and sexual minorities have appealed to local governments, village chiefs, and others for permission to hold weddings, or have pursued their rights through everyday activities that exploit the operational ambiguity of the family record book system. Moreover, those who have the capacity are pursuing legal rights through official mechanisms such as property contracts. These are the strategies of those hoping for same-sex marriage in Cambodia, following all avenues within the existing system to achieve rights and spiritual fulfillment.

The 2019 Universal Periodic Review (UPR) of the UN Human Rights Council recommended same-sex marriage be legally recognized through an amendment to Article 45 of the Constitution, and the government has formally accepted the recommendation.[25] Civil society, in cooperation with the Cambodian government, local authorities, and LGBTQ+ activists, launched the I Accept campaign in December 2021 to push for development of legislation for same-sex marriage. While there appears to be increasing tolerance for traditional marriage and cohabitation of same-sex couples, the legal system is slow to put it in place. In the 2024 UPR, the government of Cambodia explained that even though the same-sex marriage is not recognized by law, the government "has paid attention to strengthening the enforcement of laws and regulations in the fight against all forms of discrimination, as well as LGBT discrimination, and expanding individual, family, community and social education for greater recognition of LGBT rights" (Government of Cambodia 2024).

Conclusion

Although there ought not to be a religious or legal basis for banning gender and sexual minorities in Cambodia, they have been treated as outsiders in the process of nation-building, bullied and teased in schools, and often marginalized by their families as not being good daughters or sons. In HIV/AIDS prevention measures, sexual minorities were "targeted" for support, which triggered increased activism in pursuit of their human rights. This joint effort among NGOs engaged in health, medical, gender, and human rights movements with which gender and sexual minorities were involved, initially received little attention from international donors and domestic political movements. In that sense it remained outside of the hierarchical relationships between other domestic NGOs and international donors that have been prevalent since the 1990s.

---

25 Recommendations on the human rights of sexual minorities in the UPR include amending Article 45 of the Constitution to allow equality for sexual minorities in legal marriage, enacting a law to prohibit gender discrimination, and legislating recognition for transgender persons. However, these would not be mandatory.

Some who have sought same-sex marriages have attempted to obtain verification of their marital status by holding traditional weddings or registering their names in family registers, although these practices have no legal validity or basis. There have been no concrete moves toward legalizing same-sex marriage yet. In recent years, the human rights of gender and sexual minorities have garnered great international attention, and a more diverse range of people have become involved. Gender and sexual minorities in Cambodia have communicated more through social media, and their slow and steady type of activism has resulted in some changes in the environment. As a result, understanding of gender and sexual minorities has steadily grown and deepened in the 2020s. However, it remains necessary to continue building dialogue among people to ensure this understanding is guaranteed in concrete form, such as legally.

Acknowledgements

The author wishes to thank Dr. Lim Lyhong and other friends for valuable comments on an earlier version of this paper.

15 | Rainbows over the Church: The Indonesian Christian Church and Gender and Sexual Minorities

Yumi Kitamura and Khanis Suvianita

Introduction

"LGBT can be cured if we cast out the evil spirits." In April 2019, we were in Manado, the capital of North Sulawesi, Indonesia, listening to a woman evangelist of the Minahasa Evangelical Christian Church (Gereja Masehi Injili di Minahasa: GMIM) purported to be an exorcist with the power to cast out evil spirits. Indonesia is known for having the largest Islamic population in the world, but of its thirty-eight provinces, North Sulawesi, Maluku, East Nusa Tenggara, and the Papuan provinces are majority Christian. The Minahasa Evangelical Christian Church is the largest in North Sulawesi and in sheer numbers is one of the largest congregations in Indonesia. The evangelist was the model of sincerity, and she was praying that even if only for a moment before drawing their last breath, gender and sexual minorities would return to the image of men and women as depicted in the Bible, and that as many as possible would be led to heaven. While she acknowledged that some members of gender and sexual minorities would never change through prayer alone, she told us that such persons had become habituated to being LGBT due to early childhood trauma.

The idea that LGBT people can be cured or, with help, "rehabilitated," and should be actively rehabilitated, is frequently heard in contemporary Indonesia, regardless of religion. It is also generally believed that belonging to a sexual or transgender minority stems from early childhood trauma. "LGBT" is a relatively new term in Indonesia. Rehabilitation is deemed necessary because homosexuality or disobedience to one's natural gender is contrary to religious norms and threatens the "proper" shape of the family.

This understanding of gender and sexual minorities, and this configuration of religious norms, are not unique to Indonesia, but can also be found, for example, in the same-sex marriage debate in the United States. Opposition to same-sex marriage on the basis that it runs contrary to Christian religious and family norms has always had significant support in both countries. In Indonesia, however, although Islam is the majority religion, there are six other recognized religions or broad denominations, including Protestantism, Catholicism, Hinduism, Buddhism, and Confucianism, and there is a unique religious foundation upon which differences and similarities among faiths create subtle tensions at times.

Since January 2016, however, religious discourses critical of gender and sexual minorities have become much more pronounced and the issue has become a political battleground. It began when the Higher Education Minister Muhammad Nasir released a statement banning LGBT students from university campuses. Numerous politicians and professionals read the statement as an invitation to use "anti-LGBT" discourses and policies as political bargaining chips. Gender and sexual minorities and the activism related to them became targets of verbal and non-verbal violence, especially from politicians pandering to religious voters. Gradually anti-LGBT policies spread to local government levels.

While in the 2014 presidential election, gender and sexual minorities, including transgender women's groups across the country, publicly supported Joko Widodo, their overt public activity provoked a strong backlash. In some respects, this was exploited by those opposed to a Widodo regime, but this was not the primary motivation of religious figures who publicly opposed gender and sexual minorities.

This chapter focuses on the fact that of all the national bodies from the six recognized religions, only the Protestant PGI (Persekutuan Gereja-gereja di Indonesia: PGI) openly embraced gender and sexual minorities. We will explain why the PGI adopted such a position and examine the extent of its influence. Specifically, the aim of this chapter is to draw a multilayered picture of the theological understanding of gender and sexual minorities in the Indonesian Christian community, the involvement of local parties, and their respective positions, based on findings in Jakarta and North Sulawesi, where 70% of the population is Christian.

The Minahasa Evangelical Christian Church (GMIM) is very strong in Manado and its surroundings, where this research was conducted, and many of the individuals appearing in this chapter are connected with it. GMIM boasts an especially large membership even among the various Protestant churches in Indonesia. It is a Calvinist-leaning congregation and is formally opposed to LGBT positions. However, the congregation includes many who take a liberal feminist stance in defense of gender and sexual minorities, as well as activists who, as Christians, choose to walk with gender and sexual minorities even while sharing the mainline of the Minahasa Evangelical Christian Church's views.

In this chapter, the term "gender and sexual minorities" will be used as much as possible, but in cases where the term "LGBT" was used by local speakers, the latter expression will be used.

The positioning of gender and sexual minorities in Indonesian society

In Indonesia, sexual and gender diversity was historically accepted as a matter of course, but the Christian ethic introduced by Dutch colonization from the 17th century and the influence of the Islamic revival movement in the 20th century led to the repudiation of sexual and gender diversity (Okamoto 2021). After independence, Suharto's authoritarian regime promoted a patriarchal view of the family, which lasted for more than 30 years until 1998, and heterosexual marriage became the national norm (Boellstorff 2005; Suryakusuma 2011).

Among the first groups formed by gender and sexual minorities and their supporters was Himpunan Wadam Djakarta (Hiwad: Jakarta Association of Transgender Women), which was established at the suggestion of Jakarta Governor Ali Sadikin (1966–1977) to provide support for trans women in economic distress (Okamoto 2021).[1] Following the establishment of many more organizations, including Lambda Indonesia by gay activists in 1982,[2] and Persatuan Lesbian Indonesia (Perselin) in 1986, the first Indonesian Lesbian and Gay Congress (KLGI I) was held in 1993 (UNDP, USAID 2014). In the 1990s, the spread of HIV/ AIDS impelled these organizations to expand the scope of their activities (Okamoto 2021).

Activities by gender and sexual minority groups were intended to promote recognition and mutual assistance, and were not the sort that would attract outside interest. However, following Indonesia's democratization in 1998, there were moves to reject gender and sexual minorities' demands for human rights as a threat to the state (Boellstorff 2005; Okamoto 2021). From this *Era Reformasi*, LGBT became a focus of attention and a target for religious groups. These hostilities toward gender and sexual minorities have become more overt since 2016, with the endorsement of religious figures and gender and sexual minorities gradually came to be governed under local by-laws that were based on Islamic law.

Religious rejection and cultural acceptance

The position of gender and sexual minorities is inseparable from the role of religion in Indonesian society. Although Indonesia is ostensibly a secular country, "monotheistic faith" is explicitly embedded in its national policy, and religion has a central role in social life. Personal identification cards specify religious affiliation, and in 2017, the Supreme Court determined that the (estimated) 600 different indigenous beliefs (*kepercayaan*) could be recognized on the cards, but having no faith is not

---

1   Ali Sadikin coined the term *wadam* (from *wanita Adam*) (female Adam) to replace the derogatory words previously used to indicate transwomen, namely *bencong* (effeminate man) or *banci* (referring generally to gender and sexual difference). However, Islamic groups objected to this use of the prophet Adam's name, so it was amended to *waria* (from *wanita pria*) (female man) in 1978 (UNDP, USAID 2014).

2   In 1987 Lambda Indonesia changed its name to GAYa NUSANTARA.

acceptable. Suharto's authoritarian regime was strongly anti-communist, which contributed to its vehement opposition to a non-religious public life.[3] In conversations, many religious people express a belief that the number of atheists will increase in coming generations, but for now, atheists and those who are not aligned with a particular religion face difficulties if they are open about their beliefs.

This can be seen in the foreword to a special 2020 issue on atheism in *Inside Indonesia*, an online journal on contemporary Indonesia, which observes that atheist organizations are subject to dissolution in accordance with Article 59 of Government Regulation in Lieu of Law Number 2 of 2017 concerning Community Organizations (Lembaran Negara Republik Indonesia 2017).[4] The various articles in the special journal issue explore the dilemmas and difficulties facing young people who cannot reveal to their family and friends that they are atheists, and the life stories of those in the doubly difficult position of being both atheist and gay (Farhan and van Klinken 2020).

Another issue of *Inside Indonesia* contains an article discussing gender and sexual minority members with deep religious beliefs. Their suffering, whether atheists or religious devotees, could be largely attributed to the great importance of religion in Indonesian society. Atheist members of gender and sexual minorities feel rejected by society, while deeply religious ones feel rejected by both society and God and tend to be tormented by guilt.

---

3 Suharto suppressed a coup d'etat supposedly mounted by the Indonesia Communist Party late on September 30, 1965 (in the early hours of October 1) in a series of massacres known as the 9/30 Incident. He assumed the presidency in March 1968 after years of purging the country of anyone allegedly associated with the Communist Party. To "prove" that one was not a member of the Communist Party, it was necessary to demonstrate religious devotion.

4 Article 59 clearly states that mass organizations that accept, develop, and disseminate teachings and ideas that are contrary to the national motto, the *Pancasila*, are prohibited. The explanatory text clearly states "atheism, communism/ Marxism-Leninism, or other ideas aimed at replacing/changing the *Pancasila* and the 1945 Constitution," thus indicating the government's understanding that atheism contravenes national policy.

Nearly 90% of the Indonesian population is Muslim, and while there are some liberal religious leaders in Islam, they are a small minority.[5] The vast majority consider it their duty to "correct" gender and sexual minorities and lead them to become good Muslims by forcing LGBT people to "return to" their *fitrah* (being straight). In 2014, the Majelis Ulama Indonesia (MUI) Council issued a *fatwa* (Islamic legal ruling) on homosexuality in general. This *fatwa* states that the government is obligated to provide "rehabilitation" to the parties in question and, at the same time, through strict and robust enforcement of the law, to ensure that deviance in sexual orientation does not become more widespread (Atriana 2016).[6]

In Christianity, too, gender and sexual minorities, and especially homosexual acts, have been condemned based on the Old Testament verses Leviticus 18:22 and 20:13, and Genesis 19:4–16; and many Christian churches in Indonesia have censured homosexuals. Of these Old Testament texts, the first prohibits sexual intercourse between two men, and the second tells the story of the inhabitants of the cities of Sodom and Gomorrah, who are destroyed for committing a grave sin, but it is not necessarily clear from the biblical text whether the sin is homosexuality. Nevertheless, it has been widely referenced as the theological basis for Christianity's prohibition of homosexuality, as exemplified by the legal term referring to homosexuality, namely "sodomy."

---

5   For example, in Jogjakarta, Pondok Pesantren Al-Fatah, a weekly Islamic school that grew out of a prayer group of transgender women (*waria* as per Note 1), was launched with the cooperation of several religious leaders in the wake of the 2006 Central Java earthquake. As the venues and clothing for prayer differ between men and women in Islam, the hurdles for transgender believers to participate in religious practices are high. Hence, such Islamic schools have become safe places where attendees can practice their religion with peace of mind. On liberal Islamic legal interpretations relating to sexuality, see Husein Muhammad, Siti Musdah Mulia, and Marzuki Wahid (2011).

6   It is worth mentioning an earlier *fatwa*, issued in 1997, which allows reassignment surgery for *khunsa* (intersex) but forbids it for transgender women who are not intersex, declaring the latter should be rehabilitated to "return to" their *kotrat* (nature) through government intervention.

At the same time, one often sees and hears that gender and sexual minorities have a long history of being culturally included in Indonesia. For example, Dédé Oetomo, a gay human rights activist and founder of Gaya Nusantara, a non-profit organization that promotes sexual and gender diversity, has often proclaimed that Indonesian society was historically inclusive of transgender and homosexual people (Oetomo 2001).

Like other Southeast Asian countries, there are regions in Indonesia, too, where women and transgender women have historically played important roles in religious rituals (Andaya 2006: 70–103). These historical facts are referenced by activists such as Oetomo to explain why Indonesian society should be accepting of gender and sexual minorities, independently of Western discourses on sexual and gender minority rights. In other words, they invoke Indonesian traditions to counter the false claims that homosexuality is of Western origin, which often appears in anti-LGBT discourse in Indonesia.

However, gender and sexual minorities do not necessarily position themselves in traditional culture: each is different, with some, especially gay men, identifying themselves in modern terms (Boellstorff 2004). Moreover, discourses that promote inclusion based on tradition and history have been insufficiently powerful counters to religious opposition, which is imbued with a more public hue. When sexual and gender minorities seek religious salvation, religious and theological inclusion, rather than inclusion based on tradition and local historical circumstances, is essential.

Pastoral statement of the Communion of Churches in Indonesia

Trends concerning gender and sexual minorities since 2016

However, as these initial moves towards religious and theological inclusion of gender and sexual minorities began to spread, they were met with a strong backlash that combined religious opposition and a growing discomfort about gender and sexual minorities, which came to a head in January 2016 as mentioned above. Specifically, on January 24, 2016, Higher Education Minister Muhammad Nasir released a statement banning LGBT students from entering campuses as well as the activities of student groups in support of gender and sexual minorities at all Indonesian universities, triggering an outpouring of statements by ministers, politicians, local governments, professionals, and religious leaders that "LGBT behavior" should not be tolerated.

These statements shared a conviction that identifying as a sexual or gender minority is not a matter of intrinsic personality or dignity but is rather an individual choice to engage in particular acts, and that choice is modifiable. The anti-LGBT discourse was reinforced by the endorsement of religious leaders of most faiths. In February 2016, representatives of the respective non-Islamic national religious organizations gathered with the Indonesian Council of Ulama, issuing a statement banning "LGBT behavior" and activism.[7] Since then, loud condemnations of LGBT acts as being "against religious norms" and "threatening religions" have been amplified, such that during the 2018 Central Sulawesi earthquake, for example, the claim that this was a "divine punishment for LGBT people" spread online (Listiorini 2020). Since 2016, several cities, subregions, and provinces, gradually introduced local by-laws (*peraturan daerah*) to control people's bodies and behaviors.

Against the anti-LGBT backlash since 2016, the only nationally recognized religious organization to respond differently was the Communion of Churches in Indonesia (Persekutuan Gereja-gereja di Indonesia: PGI), which includes 89 of the country's Protestant churches as members. The PGI did not endorse the Indonesian Council of Ulama condemnation, and on May 17, released a pastoral statement saying that discrimination against LGBT people should be eliminated in the church and LGBT rights should be respected as human rights. However, views on gender and sexual minorities within the PGI are diverse and highly contested, and many members rejected the sentiments of this pastoral statement. Moreover, the PGI has no power to punish members who do

---

7   Reported in numerous online newspapers. See, for example, Atriana 2016.

not comply with the decisions in the letter. As such, the letter is merely an appeal to members to recognize gender and sexual minorities as God's creations and human beings whose basic rights should be respected.

Summary and background of the pastoral letter from the Communion of Churches in Indonesia

The Pastoral Letter from the Communion of Churches in Indonesia (PGI) Concerning the LGBT Community has four sections: "Introduction," "Starting Point," "Recommendations," and "Conclusion." The "Introduction" states the theological position that it is God's will that humanity, God's creatures, be diverse in race, ethnicity, gender, sexual orientation, and religion, and that we should respect each other. The "Starting Point" section then states that gender and sexual minorities are by no means a product of modern culture, and then cites the biblical misinterpretations that the Christian church has used as the basis for its rejection of them, including the relevant section of Genesis. The "Recommendations" section encourages churches to accept gender and sexual minorities as they are. However, it states that same-sex marriage is not yet acceptable, and further discussion is needed.

According to one of the three authors of the pastoral letter, Albertus Patty, a pastor of the Church of Christ Indonesia (GKI), the three members of the Assembly of Daily Workers (Majelis Pekerja Harian) who manage PGI and had originally taken progressive positions on the issue of gender and sexual minorities in the church were assigned to compose the draft, which they completed in a few days. According to Albertus, the draft was approved by the Assembly of Daily Workers virtually unchanged.

The impetus for the pastoral letter was apparently the request from the Indonesian Council of Ulama (MUI) for PGI to join its anti-LGBT statement. As the national organizations of five other religions had already committed to do so, PGI felt it necessary to clearly express its dissenting position.

As mentioned, PGI has 89 member churches throughout Indonesia, and we cannot assume that they all agree with the pastoral letter. However, it is important to note that publication of the letter has provided theological grounding for many pastors and gender minority Christians. In North Sulawesi, as will be discussed, the Minahasa Evangelical Christian Church staunchly opposed the pastoral letter, but theologians and activists highly appreciated the fact that PGI, a national organization, had issued it.

The theological background of the PGI pastoral letter

Although Christians are a minority in Indonesia, they are by no means insignificant, given that Protestants and Catholics comprise 7% and 3% of the total population, respectively, with a total of approximately 23 million believers. Nevertheless, Islam is the overwhelming majority, and anti-LGBT discourse by Islamic organizations, as mentioned earlier, has permeated widely throughout society. In such circumstances, several efforts since the 2000s have underpinned PGI's ability to demonstrate a progressive theological perspective.

First, the Jakarta Theological Seminary (STFT) has been one of the most prominent theological training schools in the country. Stephen Suleeman, a faculty member at the school (retired 2018) and a pastor of the Church of Christ in Indonesia (GKI), had studied in the United States on two occasions in the 1990s and 2000s. During his first visit, he was impressed by the work that local churches were doing to reach out to gay communities.[8]

A new generation of pastors in Protestant churches across Indonesia has studied the foundation and practices of queer theology under Suleeman at STFT (see below). According to Suleeman, his students at the seminary had always included gender and sexual minorities, but prior to his experiences in the United States he did not know how to embrace their identities. After his second visit to the United States, he began organizing international symposia on gender and sexual minori-

---

8   Following our first interview with Suleeman on March 23, 2016, we had oppor-
    tunities to meet and talk with him each year at various venues. This chapter
    incorporates information from our frequent conversations with Suleeman as well
    as a 2019 interview.

ties as well as seminars on queer theology with his students in 2009 (Suleeman 2019).

Suleeman has also worked outside the seminary in collaboration with sexual and gender minority organizations and the Network of Women Theologians in Indonesia (Persekutuan Perempuan Berpendidikan Teologi: PERUATI) and in 2012, he began sending students to work with sexual and gender minority organizations. We attended one workshop organized by Suleeman and PERUATI aimed to assist religious leaders in their practice, using real-life case studies of gender and sexual minority people's experiences in churches.[9] PERUATI has been a leading teacher of accepting gender and sexual minorities from the perspective of feminist theology. The network was established in 1995 in Tomohon, North Sulawesi, by the PGI Women's Affairs Office and the Association of Theological Schools in Indonesia (Perhimpunan Sekolah-Sekolah Teologi di Indonesia: PERSETIA). PERUATI began working toward the inclusion of gender and sexual minorities in the church in 2013, revising its constitution in 2015 to state its support for them (Perempuan Berpendidikan Teologi di Indonesia 2015).

According to Ruth Ketsia Wangkai, a seminary professor from Minahasa Christian Evangelical Church who served two terms as president of PERUATI from 2011 to 2019, the network began to commit to gender and sexual minorities from 2013 (Interview, August 31, 2017). Wangkai's theological turning point came when she attended lectures on critical feminist theology conducted intermittently over a period of three years between 2002 and 2005 under the auspices of PERUATI with invited guests Lieve Troch, a Catholic feminist theologian based in the Netherlands, and Chung Hyun-kyung, a Korean Presbyterian Church theologian residing in the US (Troch 2002). Troch has taught feminist theology in Brazil, Sri Lanka, Latin America, and Asia since the 1980s (Troch 2002). Wangkai said that from their lectures, she learned that feminist theology is not just abstract knowledge, but the concrete practice

---

9   The authors were given the opportunity to participate in workshops held in Cirebon in February 2008 through the kind auspices of the organizers and others.

of being inclusive of others. In the 2010s, when issues surrounding gender and sexual minorities surfaced in Indonesia, PERUATI, under Wangkai's leadership, began advocating and practicing their inclusion.

While some national church bodies have moved in a similar direction, there are still few local churches open to gender and sexual minorities, and even fewer that are open advocates of inclusion. One notably outspoken advocate is the Grace Community Church (Gereja Komunitas: GKA), one of Jakarta's Reformed Baptist Churches. GKA is run by a group of about twenty young university and high school students under the leadership of Pastor Suar Budaya Rahadian and his wife. Although it does not specialize in activities for gender and sexual minorities, support for those minorities lies at the core of its activities, along with the victims of the 9/30 Incident (see Note 3) and the Papuan Independence Movement.

Certainly, when these activities began within Protestant churches in the 2000s they were quite limited. Since 2016, however, against a mounting anti-LGBT backlash, their efforts, including PGI's pastoral statement on LGBT, have provided the groundwork for Protestant churches to take a different approach than others.

These developments in Indonesia are of course influenced by global trends in the more progressive Protestant churches. In the post-democratization period, while gender and sexual minorities were becoming increasingly active in politics and suffering the backlash, domestic theologians such as Suleeman and Wangkai, in the process of solving their own problems by referring to theology and practice in the West, accepted and shared these ideas through education and group activities.

From feminist theology to queer theology

Let us turn now to the origins of queer theology. Since the 1960s, many new religious practices and theological developments can be understood as responses to movements, theories and social changes in the West in relation to gender and sexuality, such as the feminist movement, the gay and lesbian movement, and queer theory.

In the 1960s, feminist theology began to be discussed under the influence of the American feminist movement, and spread throughout the world in the 1970s, including Latin America, Asia, and Africa (Fulkerson and Briggs 2012: 1). As early as 1968, gay pastor and activist Troy Perry founded the Metropolitan Community Church in Los Angeles specifically to minister to gender and sexual minorities. In 1969, James Lewis Stoll was ordained in Unitarian Universalism as the first openly gay minister in a major North American denomination.

In the 1970s, gay theology began to form in the wake of the Stonewall Riots of 1969, a reaction to police raids on the Stonewall Inn, a hangout for homosexuals in New York City (Stuart 1999: 371–373). Then lesbian theology was formulated by lesbians who felt marginalized by gay and feminist theology (Stuart 1999: 373). Although based on different foundations, with gay theology influenced by liberation theology, and lesbian theology developing under the influence of feminist theology, they shared core values and beliefs, focused on the "liberation" of homosexuals who had, individually and collectively, been subject to oppression for their homosexuality (Stuart 1999; Kudō 2018: 27–30). The Aids epidemic in the 1980s fueled a strong backlash against sexual minorities, but also provided a catalyst for them to come together as "queers" (Stuart 2015: 20).

In the 1990s, queer theology emerged as a response to the queer theory formulated by scholars such as Judith Butler (Stuart 1999; Asaka 2018: 56). According to Asaka, queer theology has a variety of objects and methodologies, but they share a "focus on the experiences of queerly positioned people, reveal the constructed nature of Christian heterosexual norms, and find within Christianity itself the beginnings of a move beyond such fixed norms" (Asaka 2018: 63). To augment the third point, the resurrection of Christ, for example, can be seen as queer in the sense that it challenges biological conventions about life and death (Cheng 2011), or in the sense that it challenges dualistic norms that are not limited to worldly gender, in that God is an entity that transcends gender.

This theological positioning of gender and sexual minorities in Christianity has changed even in the West as a response to their positioning in secular society. At the extremes, on the one hand, there is a conservative Christian theology and practice that sees homosexuality and cross-dressing as evil, while on the other hand, a position that proactively accepts gender and sexual minorities based on the belief that being queer is a blessing that enriches the church. When polarized like that, it seems necessary to choose between the two, but many lay and religious people have sought a compromise between them, both in Asia and the West.

Sexual and gender minorities in the Christian province of North Sulawesi

Christianity in North Sulawesi

The questions of how Christian churches accept gender and sexual minorities, and how Christians in general, including LGBT people, come to terms with issues of sexuality and faith, are interrelated, but not the same. We will examine these issues from several perspectives through the case of North Sulawesi Province, where Christians are the majority, accounting for about 70% of the population, with Protestants making up about 62% and Catholics about 6%. The main ethnic group is Minahasa (Badan Pusat Statistik Provinsi Sulawesi Utara 2020).

Christian missionary work in what is now Eastern Indonesia, including Sulawesi, began in the early 16th century. Influenced by the European Reformation, both Catholics and Protestants started proselytizing outside Europe: in 1511, having been granted missionary protectorship from the Pope, Portugal began proselytizing in Ternate and Ambon (Kimura 2004: 135–137). The Jesuit Francis Xavier, well known for his missionary work in Japan, had also been a missionary in the Maluku Islands for several years in the 1500s (Kimura 2004: 137–139). When Portuguese influence weakened in the region and Dutch hegemony began, Catholic missionary work was banned. The ban was not lifted for nearly 200 years (Makkelo 2010: 81–83).

From the early 17th century, Protestant Calvinists proselytized under the Dutch East India Company (Makkelo 2010: 81–83). Under Dutch colonial rule in the 1830s, the Dutch Missionary Society (Nederlandsch Zendeling Genootschap: NZG) sent two missions to begin work in the

Minahasan areas of Tondano and Tomohon (Henley 1996: 52–56). As a result, more than 90% of the Minahasa people were Protestant according to the 1930 census (Makkelo 2010: 86). In 1934, the Minahasa Christian Evangelical Church (GMIM) was established.

Before colonization, women had high social status in Minahasa society and had played a central role in religious rituals (Schouten 1998: 33–35). With the arrival of Christianity, women's status declined. However, missionaries saw women playing a major role in teaching and maintaining Christian morals in the home and promoted the education of girls from the late 19th century. As a result, the Minahasa community at the time had the highest percentage of girls in primary education in the Dutch East Indies at 43.5% (Schouten 1998: 118–121).

Today, nearly 70% of pastors in the Minahasa Christian Evangelical Church are women. Although there is a twist in that few women hold important positions in the church's decision-making council, the church has produced many women who have been active in Indonesian Christian circles, including Ruth Ketsia Wangkai, mentioned earlier. The relatively low status of women historically in GMIM is seen as an important factor in its more active acceptance and practice of feminist theology.

The Minahasa Christian Evangelical Church (GMIM) and sexual and gender minorities

The Minahasa Christian Evangelical Church is a member of PGI, but takes a very different position toward gender and sexual minorities. Specifically, its 2013 Code of Ethics forbids gender and sexual minorities from becoming teachers, and its 2017 election regulations for church officers state that those who are guilty of "gambling, drunkenness, cohabitation, adultery, LGBT, and divorce" cannot be candidates for deacon or elder (Gereja Masehi Injili di Minahasa 2013: 4, Gereja Masehi Injili di Minahasa 2017: 11). When we asked Church Board Chair Hein Arina about this, his response was that as a Calvinist church it needed to uphold the Christian conservative tradition; and that he had been concerned about the issue of homosexuality in the seminary for many years (Interview, April 6, 2019).

Sexual and gender minority and the Church in North Sulawesi Province

What are gender and sexual minorities experiences and how do they and their supporters respond to the anti-LGBT stance of the majority Minahasa Christian Evangelical Church?

LGBT organizations

Several sexual and gender minority organizations are active in Manado, the capital of North Sulawesi. Many of these grew from HIV/AIDS related and other health support activities. We focus here on GWL Kawanua (Gaya Warna Lentera Kawanua), which has been active since 2007, and Salut (Sanubari Sulawesi Utara), active since 2012. The former focuses on HIV issues, while the latter aims to educate people about human rights and SOGIE-SC (Sexual Orientation, Gender Identity and Expression – Sex Characteristic). There are various other groups that have branched from these two, including Satu Hati Sulawesi Utara, an HIV-related organization of young transgender women and gay men, and Forum Berdikari Tomohon, a community consisting mainly of lesbians and gay men, based in Tomohon (Fieldnotes, September 3, 2017).

Both GWL and Salut were founded by gay men who had dropped out of seminary (of different denominations) because they could not publicly declare their sexuality and become ministers of religion, but neither abandoned his Christian faith; rather, they seem to have come to terms with it through their own interpretations of queer theology. In addition, both have engaged in outreach to seminary students and clergy, attending lectures at one of the two seminaries of the Minahasa Christian Evangelical Church in Tomohon, and participating as witnesses in seminars by Wangkai and others. In their interviews with the authors, both also discussed PGI's pastoral letter (Fieldnotes, August 31 and September 3, 2017).

Transgender women's thoughts on the church

Coincidentally, the fact that the founders of the two major gender and sexual minority groups had been seminary students might be indicative of how pervasive Christianity is in North Sulawesi. But what about the many other individuals who did not receive a theological education? Among the lesbians interviewed by the authors, many went to church on Sundays and found clergy with whom they could talk about their sexuality, although not always in their own church, and there was a greater problem of discrimination in both the workplace and the church for those who presented as "butch" rather than "femme."

In contrast, in a group discussion with six transgender women (September 1, 2017) from rural areas – one of whom was Muslim – they described the dilemmas they face when they want to attend church services. Their gender expression is not always accepted by the church leaders but they want to express themselves as female, to be "authentic." Many had experienced not being accepted in the church and expressed fear that the experience might be repeated. They therefore felt unable to go to church despite their very strong religious beliefs. They informed us:

> I want to go to church, but I have long hair and shaved eyebrows, so it's hard for me to attend.

> When I go to church, I am of two minds: that I should go as a male, my birth gender; or that I want to go dressed up as far as possible as a woman, which reflects my true self.

> I still go to church, but I go dressed as a man because of my parents' respectability.

> I was created by God as a male, but I became trans on my own volition. I am sinning (because it is not God's will).

> I have been to a church where the sermon suddenly changed as soon as I entered, and the content was offensive to transgender people, so it's hard for me to go.

> I am a Muslim, but I attend a Christian women's prayer group that comes to my apartment. I am pressured to go back to being a man, but I still want to hear about religion.

Of these, the statement "I was created by God as a male, but I became trans on my own volition. I am sinning (because it is not God's will)," seemed to be what everyone in the group was feeling, as several asked: "It's still a sin, right?"

These statements reveal how religious teachings and practices that were internalized during childhood socialization permeate their belief systems and understandings of their gender identity and sexuality. Self-blaming and self-punishment seems to be common to their respective life journeys, especially in difficult conditions. They appear to have accepted conventional doctrines on binary gender and heteronormativity as the truth. They did not appear to be familiar with progressive theology or religious teaching on gender and sexual minorities. Unfortunately, several reported experiences with conservative churches that actively welcomed them but then slowly tried to "rehabilitate" them.

People who pray for the rehabilitation of gender and sexual minorities

This group of transgender women's desires are partially, if not entirely, fulfilled by a Christian woman who comes to their apartment every weekend, whom they referred to as Lydia (not her real name). Lydia belongs to the Minahasa Christian Evangelical Church, but finds it meaningful to practice her Christianity outside of the church. For more than a decade, she has been running a school for the children of poverty-stricken garbage collectors (Interview with Lydia, April 6, 2019).

Lydia first became involved with transgender women in 2010. She and the children at the school she managed watched the soccer World Cup on television and did not return home until 3:00 in the morning. On the way home, she saw three women on the side of the road and offered them a lift in her car. When they got in, she realized that they were transgender women. At that moment, she says, she suddenly had an image of God showing her what she should do: "You have been asking me for a long time to clear a path for you, so this is your path." She went to visit where they and others were prostituting themselves and realized that they were struggling with their sinfulness. So she established a prayer group for transgender women, and while teaching them the ways of God she has been holding a camp once a year, inviting her friends in the clergy to attend, trying to build bridges towards greater understanding of and compassion for transgender women.

Lydia holds the extremely orthodox view that if a person is born male, they should live as a male, because God never makes mistakes. At her prayer meetings, too, all participants are called by their original male names. Lydia's ultimate goal is for these transgender women to return to the path she believes God determined for them, of living as men. In her involvement with transgender women, she has gone above and beyond what should be the bounds of her concern, treating them as friends and even inviting them to her own wedding. Despite claiming to wonder occasionally whether what she is doing has any meaning, she gleefully told us she was happy to take charge of their makeup and dresses for her wedding and had once made an appearance in male clothing to please them. From the way she looked, it was easy to imagine that her instant acceptance of transgender women as they are would have struck a chord with them.

From the perspective of representatives of sexual and gender minority groups, Lydia's attitude of accepting their sexuality, an important part of their identity, while also trying to "rehabilitate" would seem outrageous. However, for transgender women who hold conservative religious views, people with conservative Christian views, such as Lydia and the exorcist mentioned at the beginning of this chapter, can be helpful as sincere Christians who take them seriously.

Of course, both the exorcist and Lydia have gradually changed their views on gender and sexual minorities and Christianity as they have become more involved with said minorities. The day may never come when they become evangelists of queer theology, but we suggest it would be just as important for them to deepen their personal Christian practice, neither black nor white, as it would be to pursue cutting-edge theological theories.

Conclusion

This chapter has examined the issue of gender and sexual minorities and faith, using as a key the pastoral letter of the PGI, the only one of six nationally recognized religious organizations to have articulated a position advocating for acceptance of gender and sexual minorities since the backlash against them in Indonesia began in 2016. First, we reviewed how the theologies on sexual and gender minorities that developed in the West, and especially in North America, spread to Indonesia after 1960 started through feminist theology. We then discussed how information on theology and religious practice relating to gender and sexual minorities has been shared since 2000 by seminary faculty and women theologians who have studied feminist theology, and how they have tackled the interpretation of texts on sexual minorities and gender issues.

Furthermore, through the case of North Sulawesi, we showed how an ally with conservative Christian views can be of great help to gender and sexual minority individuals with traditional religious views. PGI's pastoral letter hints at new developments for the Christian church in Indonesia, but not many religious and lay people can immediately accept or adopt it, and it will probably take time to percolate. Nevertheless, it appears to have created an opening for those within the Christian church in Indonesia to find a space between liberal positions such as queer theology, and conservative positions that reject gender and sexual minorities based on biblical interpretations, or perhaps to go somewhere else entirely.

Conclusion

The Sexual is Political: "LGBT" Questions the Market, the State, Religion, Human Rights, and Survival

Kaoru Aoyama

The new meaning of "LGBT" and sexual politics

LGBT has long been an acronym for lesbian, gay, bisexual, and transgender. More recently, I has been added for intersex, A for asexual, and Q for questioning/queer to include diverse minority groups. But no matter how many letters are added, something is missing. We are seeking to first legitimately name those who are stigmatized and discriminated against because they have a sexual orientation, gender identity, gender expression, or sexual characteristics (SOGIESC)[1] that have been deemed non-normative and marginal in contemporary society.

This book attempts to explore this gap between the name and the named in the socio-political context of Asian societies. This chapter summarizes the book as a whole, shedding light on the new meanings that the short form LGBT has come to have, especially in Asia, and critically examines these meanings.

Initially, LGBT was a term expressing solidarity in the pursuit of minority rights. The movements demanding human rights for gays, transgenders, and lesbians, which began in the US Civil Rights Movement and the contemporaneous "political seasons" in Europe, respectively, evolved into a call for solidarity among L, G, B, and T, for the poor, and

---

1 The Yogyakarta Principles, which appealed to the international community to protect human rights, were updated in 2017, and international human rights law now recognizes human rights violations related to "gender expression" and "sexual characteristics." SOGIESC, an acronym for each of these gender phases, is a concept that sees sexual rights as equally relevant to all people, rather than a minority issue.

for all other minorities, in the wake of the Stonewall Rebellion in 1969 and the so-called AIDS Panic in the late 1980s. Gradually, the designation, which positions the parties as a collective, spread around the world (Edsall 2003; Hubbard 2012). Junko Mitsuhashi, a gender and cultural historian and transgender activist, blogged at the first International Conference of Asian Queer Studies held in Bangkok in 2005 that the term was already being used by activists in the West and Asia (Mitsuhashi 2015).

However, "LGBT" has at some point come to highlight fragmentation rather than solidarity, and some minorities appear to have become more equal than others. Some minorities have become more normalized and have achieved more political and/or economic power than others. Most notably, middleclass gay men of society's dominant ethnic group have achieved more recognition and have more opportunities to exercise their rights than lesbians, bisexuals, transgenders, or working-class and ethnic minority counterparts. There is today growing awareness of inequality that divides gender and sexual minorities.

Reflecting the unequal divisions, the meaning of LGBT has changed substantially over time. This is also indicative of broader changes in Asian societies, including Japan. The changes are in state, religious, and market power that affect human rights, self-formation, daily lives, and the very survival of gender and sexual minorities through their workplaces, churches and mosques, schools, communities, and NGOs, as well as with their families, relatives, friends, and associates. The meaning of LGBT has changed as some minorities have negotiated in good terms with the status quo and climbed the social ladder while others have gone down in response to modernization and post-colonial conditions as well as globalization and the neoliberalization of the political economy in the 21st century. Particularly in Asia, however, the contemporary meaning of the term also reflects "compressed modernity"[2] in which contradictory

---

2   According to social theorist Chang Kyun Sup (2010), contemporary Asia reflects a state of civilization in which economic, political, and cultural changes occurred in a compressed form, both in time and space, compared to European modernization, and in which conflicting historical and social elements coexist, resulting in a complex and fluid social system.

historical and social elements coexist, though with intra-regional differences: the original meaning of LGBT solidarity and new meaning of "LGBT" diverge within their struggle.

In the Asian context, it is clear that sexual desire, gender identity, and sexual expression are at once personal and private, as well as political and public. Radical feminism (Millett 2000; Hanisch 2006) began from the realization of the power relations that Kate Millett called "sexual politics," by which male domination over women has long been constructed as "natural" matters of the "private sphere" and thus irrelevant to the politics of the public sphere. Sexual politics has always been sustained through fostering the belief, in both men and women, that "private" matters are insignificant compared to public matters. In turn, not many individuals, until feminists changed the game, had a ground to discuss this in public as a political problem. With respect to these ideas, this chapter will attempt to elucidate the ways in which LGBT (as a symbol of solidarity among gender and sexual minorities against the status quo) and newer "LGBT" (as a symbol of negotiation with and utilization by the status quo thus of division among gender and sexual minorities) appear, are used, and are avoided in each of the societies discussed in the chapters of this book. In the process, this chapter will also draw out trends in sexual politics in contemporary Asia that are not limited to the male domination of women.

Market leader

In Japan, the market has had a great impact on spreading the term "LGBT." For example, in 2007, Nikkei Business (February 26) published an article titled "The Huge 'LGBT' Market," beginning a years-long trend of analyzing this new market in business magazines. A high-profile 2012 Dentsu survey (its first) led to a boom of "LGBT market" as a lever to pull out of the recession. The Dentsu survey is an Internet monitor survey and does not reflect overall trends in Japan (Hagiwara 2009; Ishida 2019). Nevertheless, according to Dentsu's consecutive surveys (2015; 2019; 2021), the penetration rate of the term "LGBT" (the total of those who "know" and those who "somewhat know" that it is a generic term for gender and sexual minorities) rose from 37.6% in 2015 to 69.8% in 2020 (termed the "LGBTQ+" survey from that year), a dramatic increase. To invoke the considerable size and growth potential of the "LGBT-affiliated market," Dentsu – Japan's 5th largest ad agency – introduced the catchy expression "rainbow consumption" (Dentsu 2015).

Led by the market, "LGBT" is used in distinctive ways in other areas. For example, newspaper articles and news headlines such as "LGBT Women, Shining" and "LGBT man sues university for suicide" appear to treat the term simply as a synonym for "gender and sexual minority" (LGBT Law Coalition 2019; NHK 2015). By definition, it is impossible for a single individual to be L, G, B, *and* T at the same time. Nevertheless, the mass media used it with impunity, producing and reproducing a peculiar meaning of "LGBT."[3]

"LGBT" is used as a substitute for "gender and sexual minority," but not as a symbol of solidarity and the human rights movement. The journalist responsible for the headline, "LGBT Women, Shining," explained, "I used 'LGBT women' because 'lesbian' or 'homosexual' would be too direct" (LGBT Law Coalition 2019: 6). In this case, the term was a euphemism to avoid using "lesbian" or "gay," which are stigmatized and associated with discrimination due to their sexualities. This euphemism, reminiscent of avoiding sexual politics in public, also avoids the need to ask why the majority is, as the journalist felt, uncomfortable with using these names or acknowledging their existence. Furthermore, lumping L, G, B, and T together without asking what they are masks the disparities among them, and thus without evoking criticism of norms or the complexity and harshness of reality, euphemisms can represent what is easy for the majority to take in, "positive," "upbeat," and, in turn, "looking good." The media and the market define these representations in contemporary Japanese society. Thus, we also cannot overlook the minority people themselves and their movements that welcome or utilize euphemisms (see Shingae, Chapter 10). Psychological counselor Sayoko

---

3   Due in part to the news media's self-reflections, such expressions appear less frequently by the late 2010s (*Mainichi Shimbun* 2018).

Nobuta said to Koyuki Azuma, an actress who publicized a "wedding" in 2015 between two women, "The fact that [their dresses] were 'beautiful' was really good from a media strategy point of view," and observed that "compared to gay people, lesbians are darker or more poignant." The contrast between the two images was symbolic (Azuma and Nobuta 2015).

Thus – to cover up the "dark lesbians" – "LGBT" has come to be a euphemism that supports the status quo by avoiding mention of discrimination by gender norms and stigma against so-called deviants.[4] This new meaning is quite contrary to the solidarity of the people the rights movement originally aimed to represent by the term.

Use of "LGBT" by state and religious powers

However, there is a positive aspect to the new "LGBT" use. It conveys the hope that remaining quiet about the minority's rights and not challenging the status quo might evade oppression and eventually bring about changes that lead to different opportunities, depending on who uses the term. These hopes are expressed in some cases by the gender and sexual minorities themselves, in others by their opponents, and in still others by state and religious authorities who wish to control and regulate them. This is true not only of the market-spun concept in Japan, but also in other Asian societies.

A straightforward example of this use of "LGBT" by state and religious authorities can be found in Malaysia, which changed government in 2018 for the first time since independence. As discussed by Tsukasa Iga (Chapter 3), the "New Malaysia" of the Pakatan Harapan (Alliance of Hope) government was the focus of much national and international attention for its commitment to "create an inclusive, moderate and

---

4   Nobuta rightly argues that LGBT suffering and discrimination against them are rooted in the patriarchal and gendered division of labor in heterosexual families. However, while being aware of her own majority, Nobuta has the "LGBT" take on the role of subverting it (Azuma and Nobuta 2015: 44–45). As with the media's use of the term, this is too uncritical of the current state of discrimination against gender and sexual minorities.

globally respected Malaysia." This policy appeared to break from the Mahathir line of the 1980s and 1990s, which oppressed gender and sexual minorities as violating "Asian values" and other theories, marking them as deviant and Western-influenced decadents. What has emerged in Malaysia, however, is a discourse that is both pro-LGBT and anti-discrimination, and a "sexuality politics" emanating from the same government that tolerates the existence of "LGBTs" as long as they do not publicly demand human rights and keep their activities private. Moreover, this "sexuality politics" is accompanied by the pathologization of homosexuality and cross-dressing, and the intervention of state and religious power to forcibly uphold the norm, sometimes through conversion treatment (Iga, Chapter 3). Hence, Malaysia presents itself as "LGBT" inclusive to maintain the appearance of tolerating "diversity" at home and abroad, while reducing the difficulties faced by gender and sexual minorities to personal troubles to appease conservatives. It also plays sexual politics in which the "private lives" of the sexually deviant (and its normative counterpart) are in fact public matters to be managed and controlled by the state. In this respect, the "New Malaysia" upholds those so-called "Asian values."

The state's use of "LGBT" is also clearly visible in Myanmar, where LGBT human rights advocacy became possible during the transition from military dictatorship to civilian rule. According to Takahiro Kojima (Chapter 12), this new freedom to advocate may have been permitted by the government of the time to signal "its stance on human rights protection and assert the legitimacy of the regime" to other countries. More interestingly, however, the National Democratic Party (NLD) government, which came to power in 2016, proclaimed support for LGBT human rights, but did not put forward any specific measures to advance such rights. Kojima cites senior NLD officials who claimed that gender was only a secondary issue for the new government, which faced a multitude of challenges, and that same-sex marriage and other issues were "not traditional Myanmar customs and should not be voiced in public." He notes that treating homosexual expression as a negative import from the West is in accord with the views of conservative

Theravada Buddhists (Kojima, Chapter 12). Here, too, "LGBT" works as a doubly-useful discursive device, both outwardly to rub shoulders with the West and inwardly to distance Myanmar authorities from the West. This device simultaneously tells us that sexuality is a political issue, and that politicians desperately seek to keep sexuality outside of politics, as a "private" and therefore non-priority issue.

Use of "love" by the party movement

By contrast, gender and sexual minorities and their supporters in the administrative control of state and religious power, to avoid conflicts with social norms while implicitly seeking change, sometimes appear to adopt a form of strategic individualism to challenge the discourse in which sexual issues are "private." Instead of questioning the politics of sexuality, they foreshadow "love."

Nara Oda's (Chapter 7) analysis of the same-sex marriage movement in Vietnamese society illustrates this point. Although the international news media in recent years have described Vietnam as a "gay-friendly country," the internal situation is complex: the Vietnamese "LGBT" movement and its supporters have become more active and diverse since around 2008. An explicit assertion of the human rights of gender and sexual minorities risks being seen as an implicit criticism of the one-party system, which could lead to suppression. Therefore, instead of rights, they advanced the slogan "love is fair," to advocate for social and government acceptance. To avoid criticism from the international community for suppressing civic political activities and to avoid a conservative backlash, the national government has, since around 2012–13, tacitly accepted same-sex "weddings," pride parades, and drag queen art exhibitions, but not legal rights or questioning the gender dichotomy, revealing a double standard. According to Oda, there is an understanding on both sides that the "LGBT issue is not considered a political issue," which is itself a form of suppression. As a result, the strategy of "love" did little to move the Vietnamese government towards the minorities' rights.

Similarly, in Singapore, where freedom of assembly and association is heavily restricted, the "love" strategy is at work. According to Keiko Tsuji Tamura (Chapter 9), in Singapore, an emerging but influential Christian group seems to have succeeded in pressuring the government to make new rules stipulating that "providers of sex education inform students that homosexual acts [are] illegal". The gender and sexual minority communities responded by creating Pink Dot, "a new step forward in the minorities' rights advocacy movement." Pink Dot "proposed that many people gather freely under the banner of 'Freedom to Love' instead of protest rallies," and held large-scale events to attract public attention. Again, Christian and Muslim groups reacted negatively, and the government, while signaling to the international community that "gender and sexual orientation [equality] is protected by the Constitution," tightened restrictions on the participation of foreign companies and foreigners in "controversial events such as on the LGBT issue." Since then, however, Pink Dot has continued to attract no fewer than 20,000 participants.

We may recall #LoveWins, which became a global slogan for the same-sex marriage movement before and after the 2015 US Supreme Court decision that declared state laws that prohibited same-sex marriage were unconstitutional. It was also used before and after Taiwan's 2019 vote on a bill legalizing same-sex marriage. Notably, at the time, US President Barack Obama and Taiwan President Tsai Ing-wen also used it as a show of governing power. Obama, who had previously taken advantage of #LoveWins to speak out, touted the guarantee of "marriage equality" as a "victory for all Americans who are born free" in his presidential address following the Supreme Court decision (June 26, 2015). On the day the same-sex marriage bill was passed in Taiwan, Tsai tweeted in English, "Love has won, we have taken a big step toward true equality and made Taiwan a better country" (May 17, 2019). This is a form of the highest state authority standing on the side of the minority and displaying its power to lead a country divided by sexuality politics with "love" and its ability to promote freedom and equality. For Taiwan, it may also have been a policy aimed to communicate its difference from China to the international community (Fukunaga, Chapter 6).

However, regimes that have legislation that guarantees the right to same-sex marriage have treated "love" quite differently from those that keep LGBT rights "private" and "non-political." The "love" that the former made into a political symbol was used to emphasize the "non-political" nature of "love" by gender and sexual minorities in countries with the latter type of regime. Here we see examples of minorities attempting to gain social recognition and rights by allying themselves with the powerful, or the state, much as Pierre Bourdieu theorized (2018). Yet, the cisgender cum heterosexual norm does not decline in national and societal politics especially where the one-party long-term government has more control over what are rights and wrongs. In Singapore, Tsuji Tamura notes, the colonial de-facto anti-homosexual law was repealed in 2023 to go along with the international trend and, at the same time, the government amended the Constitution to specify that "marriage shall be between a man and a woman" (Chapter 9).

Homonormative "LGBT"

After all, only some gender and sexual minorities directly benefit from "love," legal and social recognition, and rights guaranteed in same-sex couple relationships and same-sex marriage, which is incompatible with the original concept of LGBT solidarity. Those whose needs are not met by the state or guarantees of "love" and couple-hood remain marginalized precisely because they are minorities. For example, recognition and rights to inheritance, support, and benefits for both spouses, often a central demand of the same-sex marriage movement, marginalizes those who have no spouse to take care of each other or inheritance to pass on. Moreover, instead of equalizing the haves and have-nots, it puts the responsibility and cost of care onto the family – the main function of the "private sphere" – centered on the spousal relationship. In this sense, the "non-political" and "private" "love" that both state power and the gender and sexual minorities advocates exploit is akin to the heterosexual family norm (Aoyama 2021). It is also compatible with neoliberalism, which exempts the state from its public responsibilities regarding equality of distribution and socialization of care, while allowing "human resources" who can contribute to the economy to rise without regard to their sexuality. In other words, this kind of "love" is precisely in line with what Lisa Duggan has named the "new homo-normativity" (Duggan 2003).

Duggan's point was that the LGBT movement, which was aware not only of minorities within the LGBT population, but also of the poor, ethnic minorities, single mothers, and various other vulnerable groups in society, and which aimed at equality of distribution through institutional reform rather than inclusion in the current system, was being transformed by a homonormativity (Duggan 2003). Neoliberalism, so to speak, is evident in the establishment of the "same-sex partnership" system in Osaka City, which Akitomo Shingae examines in Chapter 10. A remarkable change is taking place. Diversity management, based on the utilization of diverse human resources, has been introduced and human rights policies have been rolled back. Most notably, the anti-*Buraku* discrimination movement, the peace movement, and the women's movement took hits. However, while excluding these movements and parties, the "double movement" included "LGBT" and recognition of same-sex partnerships through a sort of pinkwashing (Shingae, Chapter 10). What was worse in a roundabout way was that this same-sex partnership system was not initiated by gender and sexual minority people, had no legal effect, and was basically only a symbolic system in which the mayor could recognize "good citizens." In other words, what was given to "LGBT" here is a miniscule "right" convenient to a "miniscule government" that is minimized even for those it was meant to benefit.

In contrast, the Filipino *bakla* discussed by Wataru Kusaka (Chapter 13) are a clear example of the have-nots marginalized by homonormativity. *Bakla* transcend gender binaries (see below) and have been recognized in Philippine society since long before the introduction of the English word "transgender." However, *bakla* simultaneously love "real men" and live with "sadness" because "men are supposed to love women" and they therefore cannot find "real love." It is easy to criticize *bakla* for being trapped by heteronormativity, but this "sadness" also highlights their distance from the "LGBT" movement. One *bakla*, whom Kusaka interviewed, "shows no interest in the LGBT movement for legal rights," and said that "the term LGBT 'won't last long and is meaningless'." This can be read as resistance to the new homonormativity[5] of middle-class intellectual gays and transgenders, who emphasize decency, entrepreneurship and participation, and advocate "good citizenship." Kusaka calls the situation of the *bakla* – who enjoy economic freedom as long as they work in occupations that conform to stereotypes, and who support both their families and the men who will eventually leave them – "inclusive marginalization." The *bakla* resist neoliberal homonormativity by creating a "new family" united in care while not seeking official recognition and rights. At the same time, they are also included in the society that marginalizes them as long as they contribute to the economy and do not seek equality of distribution.

Gender pluralism in Asia

Arguably, the *bakla*s' experience of "inclusive marginalization" is a relatively higher status than many other marginalized gender and sexual minorities in Southeast Asia, and is perhaps attributable to the long-term visibility of transgender women at large. This book discusses many cases of transgender people becoming the center or forerunners of international rights movements (Iga, Chapter 3, Okamoto, Chapter 4); benefiting from neoliberalism (which is more tolerant than religious fundamentalism and sexual essentialism) and gaining economic power (Kusaka, Chapter 13); moving into the role of spiritual guides in response to new competition

---

5 The "new homonormativity," which represents one feature of the gay and lesbian movement in the United States in the 2000s, has been described as a "third way" that opposes both conservative homophobia and the radical queer movement. It assumes that American values such as freedom and rights depend on a free-market economy and small government, that gay and lesbian people do not threaten morality and order, and they do not support fundamental social change (Dugan 2003: 48–50). This reflects a "theory of practice" that is often employed by minority groups and individuals in societies dominated by a neoliberal political economy, even if they are not homosexual parties and even if they are not in the United States.

and insecurity (Kojima, Chapter 12); achieving social recognition and economic security through their artistic expression (Oda, Chapter 7; Sakagawa, Chapter 2); and becoming the focus of an international tourism development that attracts Orientalism and nationalism (Hinata, Chapter 8).

One shortcoming of this book, however, is that other minorities such as lesbians, transgender men, and bisexuals, to name but a few, are infrequently mentioned and are not the focus of any of the studies reported herein. The research presented here concentrated on cases of gay men and transgender women, which reflects social biases in previous research, their prominence in social movements, and that the educated middle-class is generally more responsive to interviews and other forms of communication. One manifestation of this bias in this book is that only female authors (Kitamura, Oda, Hatsukano, and Tsuji Tamura) go beyond objective descriptions to consider the lived experiences of lesbians. Naoya Sakagawa's examination of moving images on gender and sexual minorities in Southeast Asian countries similarly found that lesbians, transgender men, and bisexuals are less prominent in visual media (Chapter 2) and are less visible in the public sphere than gays and transgender women. In this sense, the research community bears responsibility for the invisibility of minorities within minorities.[6]

How, then, might we explain the relative visibility of transgender women, which includes marginalized non-elites, in contrast to the middle-class intellectual gays who are driving the new homonormativity? This may be related to the so-called vernacular "gender transgressors" and

---

6 In some cases, lesbians, transgender men, and bisexual women are quite visible and accepted in everyday life, as for example with *Tom* (local slang adapted from "tomboy", also interpreted as butch lesbian or transgender men) and *Dee* (local slang from "lady", also interpreted as femme lesbian or bisexual woman) in Thailand. Megan Sinnott (2004) explains their existence and visibility with a logic similar to that of "sexual pluralism" (see below). However, it is precisely because of sexual pluralism that gender and sexual minorities do not identify with or conform to these categories, making them invisible or confusing to observers attempting to grasp them by the contemporary gender/sexuality dichotomy.

their social recognition (Imamura, Chapter 1), which have a history that cannot be explained by a foreign concept of "transgender."

Southeast Asia scholars have demonstrated that gender/sexuality dualism is a Western bias that misrepresents the phenomena in question by dichotomizing men and women, hetero-homo, and trans and cis (Jackson 1997; Johnson 1997; Blackwood and Wieringa eds. 1999; Sinnott 2004; Blackwood 2005; Peletz 2009). According to Michael Peletz, by the 17th and 18th centuries, the expansion of European influence, the concentration of wealth and political power, and the legitimization of patriarchy and authoritarian religions had degraded the status of previous cosmologies, the "transsexuals" (as they were called by the Europeans later) who embodied these cosmologies, and women in general. Colonialism imposed heterosexist, patriarchal, and discriminatory gender/sexuality regimes that signified, criminalized, and pathologized transsexuality and subordinated women. In some areas, female mediums were labeled as witches (Peletz 2009).[7]

In contrast, Peletz examined the history of "transgenderism" – the term I would argue as synonymous with "gender transgressing" in this book – in multiple communities and nations in the Southeast Asian region from the early modern period to the present. With over 500 years of history across a vast and diverse region, Peletz emphasizes commonalities rather than differences between communities and nations. The study of "transgenders" is a very important part of Peletz's work that resulted in his theory of "gender pluralism" in Southeast Asia. Until the early modern period, people with both male and female characteristics (perhaps including both transgenders and intersex people in the Western notion) held positions close to royal authority as "mediums" who embodied a cosmological vision. Their status was not exceptional, but common to gender pluralism. Gender pluralism is based on three

---

7   Peletz's account has been criticized for its reliance on European records, which is unavoidable for historical researchers in a multi-regional area with few written records. Nevertheless, critics argue that the decline of the pluralistic cosmology began before the 17th century and the loss of women's status was much earlier (e.g., Blackwood 2005).

norms: 1) social identity as determined by dress, occupation, and ritual roles; 2) the legitimacy of sexual relations between people of different social identities; and 3) an understanding that the physical (anatomical) characteristics of the parties in a sexual relationship is irrelevant. Gender pluralism is therefore quite different from the modern sex/gender/ sexuality binaries that seek to distinguish between physical sex, social sex, gender identity, and the sex of the object of desire, as well as the combination of these identities. In addition, the status of women in the production of life was relatively high at the time of gender pluralism, according to Peletz (2009).

The gender pluralism found in Southeast Asia can also be seen in historical East Asian sex/gender/sexuality systems. For example, according to Junko Mitsuhashi (2022), in premodern Japan, people were not categorized by dichotomized gender or physical characteristics. They were categorized instead mainly by their appearance, which depended on the combination of sex, age, class, occupation, etc. For example, a male-dressing prostitute and a young man dressed similarly to young women (*wakashu*) were both considered to be in the same category vis-à-vis "adult man." Also, the sexual orientation was neither a fixed nor an important attribute, and there was no oppositional classification of homosexuals and heterosexuals.

As a cultural historian, Mitsuhashi (2022) also traces the histories of sex/gender/sexuality in China, the Korean peninsula and India, and finds "gender transgressors" in all these cultures. She calls this the "universality of gender transgressing." Their social roles cum occupations were also similar to those in Southeast Asia, as they were reported to have been intermediaries between gods and humans, and providers of arts and entertainment, food and drink, and sexual services. Across premodern Asia, these important roles were based on the power of crossing and transgressing categories, endowing them with a distinct holiness.

These historical Asian sex/gender/sexuality concepts have been transformed but not erased by centralization, colonization, modernization, and industrialization. In Chapter 1 of this book, Imamura outlines changes flowing from intra- and inter-regional and Western influences. He reveals that while gender and sexual minorities have been constructed and marginalized, they have also continuously existed as forms of resistance or compromise.

Imamura (Chapter 1) discusses how English terminology has been adopted to express diverse sex/gender/sexuality in Asian languages. Focusing on the Japanese case, he points out that the vernacular did not have terms to clearly distinguish "sex,", "gender," and "sexuality," the terrain of the burgeoning field of gender studies since around 1990. Japanese academia entered these fields and adopted their English terminology without translation, namely, by writing them in *katakana* phonograms to represent the original sounds and meanings. In the lives of people in the regions of Chinese linguistic influence, however, before and after 1990, "sex/gender/sexuality" was represented by one word/character 性 or its equivalent used to refer to a vague mixture of "sex," "gender" and "sexuality" in accordance with everyday sense.

Yūsuke Ōmura reveals that in Lao society, strongly influenced by Thai, the field of gender and sexuality, or "genderscape," has been understood under the single term *"phet"* (Ōmura, Chapter 11). *Phet* originates from the Chinese word for sex/gender/sexuality. Drawing on Peter Jackson and others, Ōmura explains the complexity of the Laotian genderscape through the vernacular (originally Thai) category *kathoey*, which historically had broadly referred to men who have sex with men regardless of gender expression, but is increasingly being distinguished from the more contemporary Western influenced "gay." More specifically, urban and middle-class men who express a masculine gender and a same-sex sexuality are identifying as "gay" as distinct from "transgender women" – or *kathoey* – which in this context connotes "non-masculine." But this change in meaning is neither absolute, ubiquitous, nor irreversible. The term *kathoey* in contemporary urban Laos is used differently in different contexts, depending on "what is being done by using those categories, and what kind of emotions and atmosphere are being fostered by them." Here we see a pluralistic conception of gender and a clear example of what West and Zimmerman called "doing gender" (1987).

The discrimination and marginalization/visibility or "inclusive marginalization" of transgender women discussed in this book always highlights the harmful effects of dichotomous thinking. Peletz's examination of diverse local context to identify regional commonalities may be useful for translating sex/gender/sexuality systems and practices from the region to the global context. Blackwood and Johnson (2012) and Sinnott (2010) have proposed using "Asian queer" as a concept and entity for questioning norms, transgressions, and revealing the challenges of multiple sex/gender/sexuality regimes. This proposal sounds particularly valid after editing this book and, from a gender/sexuality studies perspective, Asian queer is not only about Asia; we should be able to connect this to global queer theory and movements.

Gender and sexual minorities as interaction

Studies of sex/gender/sexuality in Asia, including those presented in this book, reveal the pitfalls of nostalgically representing the "vernacular gender" structure of pre-modern societies as complementary to men and women, and blaming modernization cum colonialism alone for the crimes of ostracizing women and gender transgressors.[8] Regardless of how it is represented, there is no such thing as a purely localized vernacular gender in an already globalized society. For example, as discussed in various chapters of this book, the young middle-class, college educated cohort with overseas experience and familiarity with Internet media viewed the transformations influenced by foreign trends positively and demanded new conceptions of "LGBT." These demands sometimes triggered strong backlashes from the state and religious authorities which resulted in further marginalization of gender and sexual minorities, even in states seeking recognition from the international community for their progress in respecting human rights (Iga, Chapter 3; Okamoto, Chapter 4; Oda, Chapter 7; Tsuji Tamura, Chapter 9; Ōmura, Chapter 11; Kojima,

---

8   The term "vernacular gender" and the ideas attached to it by Ivan Illich (1982) were sharply criticized by feminists in the 1980s. See Yokoyama (2007) for a discussion of the controversy and its aftermath.

Chapter 12; Kusaka, Chapter 13; Kitamura and Suvianita, Chapter 15). Nevertheless, these power relations introduced concepts of the rights of sexual and gender minorities which are compatible with globalization and the neo-liberal political economy. The current "LGBT" movement has arisen to pursue such rights. In this sense, the current movement, that is led by the above cohort, often ostracizing other minorities, is also seeking certain kinds of rights in a different way from the original intention of LGBT solidarity movement of the 1980s. At the same time, the current sex/gender/sexuality systems in Asia are being transformed by the new "LGBT" concept that has been asserted by the college educated, Internet and foreign influenced young middleclass (often gay men).

Conceptions of "lesbian," "gay," "bisexual," or "transgender," and possibly who is a gender or sexual minority, have been formed and reformed repeatedly through interactions between Western cultures and local societies across Asia throughout the history of colonization and decolonization, the Cold War and proxy wars, and into the globalized and neoliberal present.

In Chapter 8, Shinsuke Hinata vividly describes how even the Orientalist gaze that mediates interaction between the East and the West has only come to the present through the utilization of the gazer. At the center of this is Pattaya, which substantively informs the international image of Thailand, a country known for its hetero-male sex clubs, drag shows and contests, gay towns, and sexual diversity. Pattaya was a minor beach resort before the Vietnam War and its transformation into a recreation area for the US military, eventually became a kind of safe haven for gay Westerners.[9] Tourism development typically involved a combination of Western and Thai investors. In the 1980s, a period of rapid economic growth in Thailand, the Western-Thai business "culture" became normalized. Thai investors successfully interwove development

---

9　At the time, sodomy laws were just beginning to be repealed in northwestern Europe and North America, while Australia and New Zealand did not repeal them until the 1980s and 90s, whereas Thailand had repealed them in 1954 (Carroll and Itaborahy 2015; Mitsunari 2015), which no doubt enhanced its appeal as a safe haven.

and nationalism, as Hinata demonstrates, quoting the founder of the Tiffany Show – a famous drag show that remains a highlight of Pattaya tourism today – who was proud of the employment opportunities provided to *kathoey* (see above) dancers and extolled their role in "introducing the Thai nation to the world" (Hinata, Chapter 8). However, lesbians, transgender men and cis women rarely appear in this history. This seems to indicate that Pattaya became a sanctuary for "bonds between men"[10] to be enjoyed safe from the homophobia in the West.

Naomi Hatsukano discusses how the daily lives of gender and sexual minorities in Cambodia have been affected by "outside influences." In 1991, after the civil war ended, there was a sudden influx of foreign aid workers, which coincided with the HIV/AIDS epidemic and the corresponding emergence of a gay men's movement related to sexual health and rights. A gender and sexual minority rights movement and commercialization rapidly developed. At the same time, however, there is a continuing tendency for those who do not conform to the family system to be regarded as outsiders of the Khmer "tradition," says Hatsukano, "which has given rise to covert discrimination, teasing and bullying." Although *khteuy* (synonymous with *kathoey* in Thailand and Laos) and same-sex relationships have been observed since the Middle Ages (supporting Peletz's theory of indigeneity), as a modern nation in search of its identity following its independence from France, Cambodia adopted sexual dualism, heterosexism, and male-centered norms as its "tradition" (Hatsukano, Chapter 14).

Attributing non-normative sexuality to decadent Western influences has become common in both Southeast and East Asia, a reaction to colonization and subordination.[11] Anthony Reed referred to this

---

10 Eve K. Sedgwick's (1985) concept of the homosocial bond between men that has constructed modern Western society. It calls for homophobia, the suppression of sexual relations between men to maintain the patriarchy through the "exchange of women" (marriage), but paradoxically, it proves the fascination of sexual relations that must be suppressed.

11 In the relationship between Western colonialism and colonial Asia, Japan's position as the dominant colonial power is of course different from other Asian nations.

phenomenon as "neo-traditionalism," a nationalism that opposes the West and therefore cannot escape being defined in relation to Western standards (cf. Kusaka et al., Introduction to this volume). But the West is not the only opponent. According to Hatsukano, Sakagawa, Kojima and Ōmura, Thailand's influence in the phenomena, discourses, and representations of gender and sexual minorities in Southeast Asian societies has been no less significant than that of the West. For example, Hatsukano notes that some Cambodians claim that they have become gender or sexual minorities "because they ate contaminated food from Thailand" (Hatsukano, Chapter 14), indicating Thailand's cultural influence in the region, and the belief that the influence of a powerful and familiar outside/other can be experienced as a flesh and blood threat that could transform the self from within. This has hardened Cambodia's neo-traditionalism in terms of "LGBT" within Asia as well as vis-à-vis the West.

Religion in the politics of sexuality

Several chapters in this book focus on the importance of religion as a factor in Asian societies. Among them, Islam and Christianity in the region tends to be highly heterosexist, patriarchal, and intolerant of non-normative sexuality. In contrast, in Thailand, where Theravada Buddhism is the predominant religion, occupying an important position in the monarchy and national politics, sexual diversity is widely accepted. Similarly, in Cambodia, Theravada Buddhism, the state religion which claims more than 90% of the population as followers, is generally considered to be "relatively tolerant of gender and sexual minorities" (Hatsukano, Chapter 14). In Myanmar, where Theravada Buddhism is also the prevalent religion, constituting almost 90% of the population, some conservatives have declared that a commentary on the Buddhist canon warns against "male covetousness toward men and female covetousness toward women," but the head of the Sangha counters that

---

Thailand also occupies a unique politico-historical position in relation to Western colonialism, but that is beyond the scope of this chapter.

homosexuality "does not violate the precept of sexual misconduct, it is an issue unrelated to Buddhism" (Kojima, Chapter 12). However, although state and religious powers in Thailand and Cambodia appear to have decided against legal intervention in same-sex relationships and gender transgression, "discursive sanctions" (Jackson 1997) that stigmatize and dishonor are also prevalent. And while Myanmar appears to be generally tolerant of gender and sexual minorities, the sodomy laws introduced by British colonialism remain in effect, as they are in Malaysia (Singapore repealed its sodomy law in 2023). It is somewhat ironic that Myanmar's conservative Buddhists' efforts to intervene against gender and sexual minorities invoke this legacy of colonialism. As Kojima learned from activists in Myanmar (Chapter 12), gender and sexual minorities are oppressed when the sexuality politics of a society reflect and apply religious interpretations and doctrines.

Similarly, the Foucauldian explanation that religion constructs sexuality to form heterosexist patriarchal families to assert its own political power in the management and control of individuals can be applied to Masaaki Okamoto's (Chapter 4) discussion of the Indonesian Islamist regime and Satoshi Miyawaki's (Chapter 5) discussion of the Philippine Catholic Church.

As mentioned, the term LGBT began to be used and the respective parties began to seek solidarity with each other in Asian countries even as a new, more fragmentary meaning of "LGBT" in this chapter began to emerge in the information, support and media representations from abroad. This manifestation of "compressed modernity" is clearly visible in Indonesia, as Okamoto observed.

The LGBT solidarity movement that arose in the wake of Indonesia's democratization in 1998 triggered a backlash. First, the main council of Islamic leaders declared that same-sex orientation and behavior is a deviant aberration to be cured, and in the wake of the US Supreme Court's 2015 decision on marriage equality, major Indonesian universities began to control speech about LGBT and repress gender and sexual minorities for violating religious doctrine. The backlash expanded to anti-American nationalism, opposing gender and sexual minority rights as symbols of liberalism; the Indonesian Minister of Defense declared that LGBTs were enemies of the state and tools of a proxy war seeking to dominate Indonesia. Indonesia stands out among Asian countries for its thorough pathologization of deviations from heterosexual norms even as the global consensus was depathologizing sexual diversity. There was a revival of Islamic psychiatry and psychology, based on Islamic values, which entailed a move by the Society of Clinical Psychology and the Society of Psychiatry to promote the term "normal lifestyle" to ensure that LGBT was neither promoted nor recognized even as a target for prevention or treatment. More recently, the international community's criticism of the pathologization of homosexual orientation and "gender identity disorder" has added fuel to the fire (Okamoto, Chapter 4). It is notable that although the American Psychiatric Association and WHO reversed their 19th century positions (in 1990 and in 2010 respectively) on the pathologization of non-normative sexual orientation, behavior, and gender expression, this has not been recognized in Indonesia. Superseded psychiatric cannons are being used by neo-traditionalists for much the same purpose as some conservatives in some former British colonies are reverting to outdated sodomy laws.

According to Satoshi Miyawaki (Chapter 5), the Catholic Church in the Philippines likewise avoids the use of the term LGBT to avoid legitimizing it. The Church's focus is almost entirely on homosexual activities; and, unlike the Malaysian Coalition of Hope (see Iga, Chapter 3), for example, it has no need to appease the international community. The Catholic Church has been a major force in the fight against same-sex marriage in the Philippines. It condemns the pursuit of same-sex rights as an "imperialist plot" and an "invasion of foreign thought" that overlaps with abortion and birth control. The Church grounds its opposition to homosexuality and contraception in both nationalism and international Catholicism. It maintains that a "Christian husband and wife united by the sacraments of the Church" are "always in a sexual relationship open to the possibility of childbearing" and that the family borne and nurtured by this "healthy" couple is considered "the foundation of the Church."

This principle is also reflected in the Philippine Constitution, which gives substance to ecclesiastical nationalism.

The spaces in daily life to circumvent authoritative power

However, as it appears to be increasingly fundamentalist, support for the Catholic Church in the Philippines is declining among both the public and Congress. The heterosexist patriarchal family has been shaken, affected by the long-standing emigrant labor policy and the even longer-standing practice of extended families providing care (Miyawaki, Chapter 5). In the daily lives of ordinary people, there is much scope in Philippine society for the marginalized like *bakla* to create a "new family based on care" as an alternative to the heteronormative family. Creating such alternative families can be seen as a violation of prevailing norms that offers both dignity and hope (Kusaka, Chapter 13).

Okamoto (Chapter 4) describes the suffocating atmosphere in Indonesia, where religious opposition to LGBT people and practices have prevailed in academia, psychiatry, and psychotherapy as well as politics, steadily narrowing the spaces in which minorities can breathe. However, Kitamura and Suvianita (Chapter 15) demonstrate that such spaces can still be found in Indonesia. In their case study of Christian transgender women, the space is not characterized by disapproval of or resistance to religious fundamentalism; even though they feel pressured to conform to the status quo, a space has been made for them to "seek salvation" in their local religious community.

Indonesia is not constitutionally an Islamic state although the constitution states the country is based on the belief in a single supreme god. It recognizes individual freedom of religion. Among the recognized religious organizations, the Protestant Indonesian Church Solidarity Community "accepts gender and sexual minorities as they are." There are currents, albeit minor, of radical liberalism in the Christian faith in Indonesia, including queer theology, which challenges dualisms such as life and death, men and women. Kitamura and Suvianita's case study, however, is not about conflicting ideals or principles between Islam and Christianity or between fundamentalism and liberalism. They instead focus on the "neither black nor white" daily lives of those seeking religious salvation in a society where faith is an important part of an individual's identity. They found that transgender women with little primary or secondary education who had moved to Manado (the province capital) from rural villages sought solace in a space like the conservative church they had attended as children, but without being discriminated against by the congregation. They were helped to create such a space by a conservative "sister" who had changed her attitude toward gender and sexual minorities through her association with them and found "it meaningful to practice her Christianity outside the church" (Kitamura and Suvianita, Chapter 15). Spaces in everyday life where people operate away from the direct action of authoritative power may be able to shift the politics of sexuality from a politics of domination to more interactive and creative relationships, even if only in small ways.

One may measure the treatment of gender and sexual minorities in the various societies discussed in this book on a spectrum of how strong the forces of state, religion and the market, whether through family, legal systems and norms, or through money, manage and control the everyday lives of ordinary people. At the weaker end of the spectrum is the Philippines, and at the stronger end is Indonesia. Vietnam and Cambodia, where same-sex couples hold "weddings," register as families that are recognized in daily life, although not in family law or the Constitution (Oda, Chapter 7; Hatsukano, Chapter 14), are close to the Philippines, while in Myanmar, the democratic government, albeit abstractly, recognizes the human rights of gender and sexual minorities and more-or-less tolerates the human rights movement and foreign NGOs, and where the trickle-down of capitalism has created new opportunities for sexual minorities. The "New Malaysia," by contrast, claims to be inclusive of diversity but is not inclusive of gender and sexual minorities; while in Japan, human rights claims against the current legal system have been eliminated and only homonormative gender and sexual minorities are recognized; and in Singapore, the cultural movement for minorities' rights is restrained by the government's strict administrative control, which approaches Indonesia in its suppression of gender and sexual minorities. Thailand, however, or at least Pattaya – a city that offers sanctuary from homophobia and represents the international image of Thailand – lies somewhere beyond the Philippines' end of the spectrum. Similarly, as will be discussed below, Taiwan occupies a special place in Asian sexuality politics and cannot be located on that spectrum, as it has both decisive state control and great acceptance of gender and sexual minorities; the rights, recognition, and thus freedom of gender and sexual minorities are publicly promoted through the strong administrative control power of an LGBT-friendly government.

The spectrum of how much the state, religion, and market control and manage everyday life, and how much they diverge from the everyday, overlaps with Sakagawa's typology of visual representations of these societies (with the exceptions of Cambodia and Japan) in Chapter 2. The public acceptance of images of gender and sexual minorities (i.e., not excluded from public space by censorship or prohibition) is high in Taiwan, Thailand, the Philippines, and Vietnam (and was for a brief period in Indonesia). Prohibitions are gradually being lifted in Myanmar, and there are new developments in Malaysia and Laos. While Singapore maintains its international reputation by holding a queer film festival, Indonesia is "reverting" to a society in which gender and sexual minorities are concealed, and their imagery is absent. In societies where gender and sexual minority images are highly acceptable, it is increasingly common for the minorities in focus to be at the center of both the images and their makers. Positive representations of gender and sexual minorities are increasingly common, and are shifting from images of deviance and exclusion to more "realistic" portrayals and "friendly neighbor images."

Visual expression, however, does not directly improve the patriarchal family structure, the legal system, social norms, or the human rights situation. Moreover, if it does not somehow satisfy the market's demands, it has little public effect. But when they can find a market, the transwomen's comedies Sakagawa cites that have achieved massive popularity in the Philippines and Thailand, portraying accepting and inclusive social norms without overtly challenging the status quo, can have significant impact on advancing the LGBT cause. Moving images convey enormous amounts of information, combining linguistic with audiovisual information, providing great opportunity to represent lives and peoples that are not "black and white," or generalized, but result from micro-level creative relationships, as described by Kitamura and Suvianita (Chapter 15). For example, Sakagawa sees the emergence of lesbian and transwomen directors in Southeast Asia creating a space for a minority within a minority that has been re-marginalized within the "LGBT" movement defined by the success of middleclass gay men.

The "terminal vocabulary" of Asian sexuality

Some of the central themes that recur throughout this book were reviewed by Masao Imamura in Chapter 1. For Asian gender and sexual minorities, there are three key points: whether there is a "terminal vocabulary" to describe themselves in everyday language; whether the history of gender and sexual minorities is their own; and whether sexual diversity is really diverse.

For gender and sexual minorities in Asia in the contemporary period, the term LGBT was originally meant to be a "final vocabulary" defined as "a set of words used to justify one's actions, beliefs, and life" (Rorty 2000 cited in Imamura, Chapter 1) that "describes admiration for friends and contempt for enemies, long-term plans, the most deep-seated self-doubts, the most noble hopes." The adoption and development of the term was influenced by the following intertwined factors: the term's English origins; the post-colonial conditions in Asia; the global neoliberalism that adopted it to exploit diversity; and the emergence of a homonormative movement that sought inclusion in the ranks of "good citizens." At the same time, the respective states ranged from indifference to hostility towards minority rights. Some governments expressed their ideological opposition to the West while condemning the "LGBT" movement, even while economically trying to take advantage of global neoliberalism. This can be seen in Shingae's (Chapter 10) includes Japan's Osaka government, which is opposed to the Western ideology of gender equality, but does not admit it. The fundamentalist religious powers that oppose them have taken the position of rejecting both "LGBT" and LGBTs.

In contrast, Taiwan, "the most LGBT-friendly society in Asia," is unique. According to Genya Fukunaga, Taiwan, the first country in Asia to legalize same-sex marriage (in 2019) and to abolish the prerequisite of gender reassignment surgery to legally change gender (in 2023), has promoted human rights for gender and sexual minorities through party politics. As seen in the President's #LoveWins tweet, the government and the activists involved in the "equal marriage" movement both use "LGBT" in terms of a mainstreaming discourse of homonationalism that promotes national superiority and tolerance to the international community. Importantly, this discourse is oriented toward "gender equality," meaning not only equality between "men" and "women" but also equality between lesbians, transgender people, and others with non-typical sexual orientations and gender identities. Moreover, in Taiwan, these gender politics are an extension of the historical solidarity between the feminist movement and gender/sexual minorities' movement (Fukunaga, Chapter 6). These developments each distinguish Taiwan from the other Asian countries examined in this book. Fukunaga attributes this to Taiwan's marginalization in the international community and its corresponding need to differentiate itself from China. It is a meaningful irony that Taiwan, which was expelled from the United Nations and has no official diplomatic relations with many nations, demonstrates its moral superiority by embodying the human rights and gender equality principles of the United Nations as well as the West, exercising the most powerful national strategy of sexuality politics.

At the same time, according to Imamura (Chapter 1):

> In Japan, the Anglo-American norm is hegemonic today. It is easy to find a Japanese book about the history of the gay movement in the US or the history of homosexuality in Europe, but it is extremely difficult to find such a book on Japan… Japanese history and … literature … are rarely discussed by scholars of gender and sexuality, who keep themselves busy by introducing the latest Euro-American norms. While they raise awareness about heteronormativity, they hardly ever question Euro-American normativity.

English standardization of the concept of diversity has become wide-spread. This is a reality for which policymakers who rely on UN discussions and activists and researchers who rely on Western-language discourse and literature bear responsibility.

In contrast, Taiwan has a vernacular term for "gay and lesbian" that is not derived from English but rather from the Chinese word "*dongzhi*" 同志, the Chinese communist word for "comrade," as if to outdo both the UN and Communist China. In Japan, Imamura sees "low brow" culture such as the BL genre reconstructing "sexual diversity" by redefining masculinity,[12] and many chapters in this book have revealed similar openings or possibilities in their respective societies, in terms of politics, history, and the daily lives of ordinary people. The historical and vernacular diversity evidenced in this volume suggests that we should pursue the possibilities of "Asian queer" studies. Perhaps in the nexus between area studies and gender/sexuality studies we can find a final vocabulary of our own (Nakamura 2003).

---

12 A fiction genre originated in Japanese manga aimed for the sexual gratification of a female audience. Typically, what the audience enjoys is an explicit sexual relationship between two young male protagonists. It is considered to be a queer expression/consumption because it confuses homo-hetero binary sexual attractions as well as the gender power dynamics of the male gaze and objectified female. BL has spread into moving images and to other Asian countries such as Thailand.

Bibliography

Aberigo, Guiseppe, 2007(2005). *Dai-ni Vatikan kōkaigi: sono konnichi-teki imi* (The Second Ecumenical Council of the Vatican: Its contemporary meaning). Trans. by Takeshi Odaka, Shiho Ōmori, and Takuji Kuwata. Tokyo: Kyōbunkan.

Achmad Syalaby, 2016. 'LGBT Direkomendasikan Masuk dalam ODMK. (LGBT recommended to be categorized as person with mental health problems).' *Republika.co.id.* 12 February. republika.co.id/berita/nasional/umum/16/02/12/o2fnvx394-lgbt-direkomendasikan-masuk-dalam-odmk

Adam, Aulia, 2019. 'Salah Kaprah Ruqyah "Menyembuhkan" LGBT yang Nirfaedah (Mistaken Ruqyah "healing" LGBT is useless).' *Tirto.or.id.* 4 September. tirto.id/salah-kaprah-ruqyah-menyembuhkan-lgbt-yang-nirfaedah-ehtE. Accessed 21 November 2024.

Adam, Barry D., Jan Willem Duyvendak and Andre Krouwel, 1999. *The Global Emergence of Gay and Lesbian Politics: National Imprints of a Worldwide Movement.* Philadelphia: Temple University Press.

Aedi Asri Abdullah, 2017. 'Organiser defends "Gay Iftar" breaking of fast event.' *Free Malaysia Today*, 15 June. https://www.freemalaysiatoday.com/category/nation/2017/06/15/sponsor-defends-gay-iftar-breaking-of-fast-event/. Accessed 31 August 2019.

AFP, 2018. 'Activists call for movement on transgender rights law in Vietnam.' *VnExpress*, 18 November. https://e.vnexpress.net/news/world/southeast-asia/activists-call-for-movement-on-transgender-rights-law-in-vietnam-3837611.html. Accessed 1 October 2024.

Agence France-Presse, 2015. 'Vietnam law change introduces transgender right.' *The Guardian*, 24 November, https://www.theguardian.com/world/2015/nov/24/vietnam-law-change-introduces-transgender-rights. Accessed 1 October 2024.

Agus Lukman, 2016. 'Diprotes Asosiasi Psikiater Amerika Soal LGBT, Ini Tanggapan PDSKJI.' (Response of the Indonesian Association of Psychiatric Specialists to the American Psychiatric Association on LGBT). *KBR.* 17 March. kbr.id/nasional/03-2016/diprotes_asosiasi_psikiater_amerika_soal_lgbt_ini_tanggapan_pdskji/79483.html

Alave, Kristine L., 2012. 'Catholic bishop goes after Ateneo professors for heresy.' *Philippine Daily Inquirer*, 21 August. http://newsinfo.inquirer.net/254188/catholic-church-wants-pro-rh-bill-ateneo-professors-sacked#ixzz4B4PPSieF

Alexander, Jacqui M., 1994. 'Not Just (Any) Body Can be a Citizen: The Politics of Law, Sexuality and Postcoloniality in Trinidad Tobago and the Bahamas.' *Feminist Review*, 48: 5–23.

Alfred Dama, 2019. 'Ustadz Abdul Somad UAS Ditanya tentang LGBT, Begini Penjelasan Sahabat Ustadz Yusuf Mandur (Ustadz Abdul Somad UAS asked about LGBT: Here's Ustadz Yusuf Mansur's close friend's explanation).' *Pos-Kupang. com,* 28 August. https://kupang.tribunnews.com/2019/08/28/ustadz-abdul-somad-uas-ditanya-tentang-lgbt-begini-penjelasan-sahabat-ustadzyusuf-mansur

Alhadjri, Alyaa, 2023. 'Lawyer slams "illegal" Swatch raids, ban order made three months after.' *Malaysiakini,* 10 August. https://malaysiakini.com/news/675224. Accessed 15 August 2023.

Altman, Dennis, 2004. 'Sexuality and Globalization.' *Sexuality Research and Social Policy,* 1(1): 63–68.

Altman, Dennis, 2008. 'AIDS and the Globalization of Sexualities.' *Social Identities,* 14(2): 145–160.

American Psychiatric Association, 2016. *Letter to Indonesia Psychiatrists Association,* 8 March. https://psychiatryonline.org/doi/full/10.1176/appi.pn.2016.4a10. Accessed 21 November 2024.

Andaya, Barbara Watson, 2006. *The Flaming Womb: Repositioning Women in Early Modern Southeast Asia.* Honolulu: University of Hawaii Press.

Andaya, Leonard Y., 2000. 'The Bissu: Study of a Third Gender in Indonesia.' In Barbara Watson Andaya, ed., *Other Pasts: Women, Gender and History in Early Modern Southeast Asia.* Honolulu: Center for Southeast Asian Studies, University of Hawaii, pp. 27–46.

Anderson, Benedict, 1983 / 2006. *Imagined Communities: Reflections on the Origins and Spread of Nationalism.* London: Verso.

Anderson, Benedict, 1990. 'Professional Dreams: Reflections on Two Javanese Classics.' In Benedict Anderson ed., *Language and Power: Exploring Political Cultures in Indonesia.* Ithaca: Cornell University Press. pp. 271–298.

Anon, 1990. 'Queer Read This.' http://www.qrd.org/qrd/misc/text/queers.read.this. Accessed 22 October 2024.

Anten, Todd, 2006. 'Self-disparaging trademarks and social change: Factoring the reappropriation of slurs into Section 2 (a) of the Lanham Act.' *Colum. L. Rev.,* 106: 388.

Aoyama, Kaoru, 2016. '"Ai koso subete": Dōseikon/partnership seido to "yoki shimin" no kakudai ('All you need is love': Same-sex marriage/partnership and expansion of the 'good citizen').' *Jendā Shigaku* (Gender history), 12: 19–36.

Aoyama, Kaoru, 2021. 'Sore hodo atarashikunai "atarashii kazoku": Dōseikon no hoshusei, kakushinsei (Not-so-new 'new families': The conservativeness and progressiveness of same-sex marriage).' In Emiko Ochiai, ed., *Dō suru Nihon no kazoku seisaku* (Japan's family policy: What are they going to do about it?). Kyoto: Minerva Shobō, pp. 258–272.

Apilado, Digna B., 2009. 'The issue of HIV/AIDS in the Philippines: The Roman Catholic Church and the Philippine government.' In Julius Bautista and Francis Khek Gee Lim, eds., *Christianity and the State in Asia*. London and New York: Routledge, pp. 131–154.

Arun Sampunthawiwat, ed., 2017. *The Legendary Life of a True Scout.* Bangkok: Amarin Printing.

Asahi shinbun, 2019. 'Osaka-fu to shi no haiso kakutei (Osaka Prefecture and Osaka City lose lawsuit).' 28 May.

Asaka, Tomoki, 2018. 'Kuia shingaku no teigi o meguru shomondai (Issues in defining queer theology).' *Fukuin to Sekai* (The Gospel and the World), 73(7): 12–17.

Atriana, Rina, 2016. 'Majelis-majelis Agama: Kami Menolak Propaganda, Promosi dan Dukungan ke LGBT! (+Religious Councils: We reject LGBT propaganda, promotion and support).' *detikNews*, 18 February.

Au, Alex, 2009. 'Soft Exterior, Hard Core, Policies towards Gays.' In Bridget Welsh, James Chin, Arun Mahizhnan and Tan Tarn How, eds., *Impressions of the Goh Chok Tong Years in Singapore*. Singapore: NUS Press, pp. 399–408.

Au, Alex, 2011. 'Speaking of Bangkok: Thailand in the History of Gay Singapore.' In Peter A. Jackson, ed., *Queer Bangkok: 21ˢᵗ Century Markets, Media and Rights*. Hong Kong: Hong Kong University Press, pp. 181–192.

Augustin, Andreas, 2007. 'Kurt Wachtveitl: 40 years with The Oriental.' *The Most Famous Hotels in the World*. https://famoushotels.org/news/kurt-wachtveitl-40-years-with-the-oriental. Accessed 21 November 2024.

Aulia Adam, 2019. 'Salah Kaprah Ruqyah "Menyembuhkan" LGBT yang Nirfaedah (Misguided Islamic healing practices: 'Curing' LGBT with no benefit).' *Tirto.or.id.* 4 September. tirto.id/salah-kaprah-ruqyah-menyembuhkan-lgbt-yang-nirfaedah-ehtE

Ayoub, Phillip M., 2016. *When States Come Out: Europe's Sexual Minorities and Politics of Visibility*. Chicago: Chicago University Press.

Azuma, Koyuki and Sayoko Nobuta, 2015. 'Tōron: Watashitachi ga tsukuru "kazoku" no katachi (Debate: The form of the 'family' we create).' *Gendai shisō* (Review of contemporary thought), 43(16): 30–45.

Badan Pusat Statistik Provinsi Sulawesi Utara, 2020. 'Jumlah Penduduk Menurut Kabupaten/Kota dan Agama di Provinsi Sulawesi Utara (Jiwa), 2015–2018 (Population by regency/city and religion in North Sulawesi Province (Jiwa), 2015–2018).' https://sulut.bps.go.id/indicator/108/617/1/jumlah-penduduk-menurut-kabupaten-kota-dan-agama-di-provinsi-sulawesi-utara.html. Accessed 28 October 2020.

Bangkok Post, 2007. 'The Royal Varuna: 50 years young.' https://www.pressreader.com/thailand/bangkok-post/20070701/282595963499919

Banning-Lover, Rachel and Joe Sandler Clarke, 2016. 'Six countries make progress on LGBT rights.' *The Guardian*, 10 February. https://www.theguardian.com/global-development-professionals-network/2016/feb/10/lgbt-rights-six-countries-progress. Accessed 5 December 2024.

Bao, Hongwei, 2018. *Queer Comrades: Gay identity and Tongzhi activism in postsocialist China*. Copenhagen: Nordic Institute of Asian Studies Press.

Baudinette, Thomas, 2023. *Boys love media in Thailand: Celebrity, fans, and transnational Asian queer popular culture*. London: Bloomsbury.

Bayoran, Gilbert, 2013. 'Diocese defies Comelec on Team Patay poster.' *Rappler*, 26 February. http://www.rappler.com/nation/politics/elections-2013/22631-diocese-defies-comelec-on-team-patay-poster

BBC Indonesia (bbc.com), 2018. 'Marak Perda Anti-LGBT "demi moral publik," bagaimana nalar hukumnya? (Mushrooming anti-LGBT regulations for public morality: What is the legal reasoning?).' 12 November. https://www.bbc.com/indonesia/indonesia-46170154

BBC, 2018. 'Osaka cuts San Francisco ties over "comfort women" statue.' 4 October. https://www.bbc.com/news/world-us-canada-45747803

Beyrer, Chris, 2017. *War in the Blood: Sex, Politics and AIDS in Southeast Asia*. London: Zed Books.

Bih, Herng-Dar, 2000a. 'Zouru qitu de nanxing qigai yangcheng guocheng (The process of cultivating misguided masculinity).' *Liangxing pingdeng jiaoyu jikan* (Both-sexes equal education quarterly), 12: 44–46.

Bih, Herng-Dar, 2000b. 'Zuotan jilu (Symposium records).' *Liangxing pingdeng jiaoyu jikan* (Both-sexes equal education quarterly), 12: 59–90.

Bih, Herng-Dar, 2000c. 'Cong liangxing pingdeng dao xingbie pingdeng (From equity for both sexes to gender equity).' *Xingbie pingdeng jiaoyu jikan* (Gender equity education quarterly), 13: 123–132.

Bih, Herng-Dar, 2004. 'Xingbie pingdeng jiaoyu fa tongguo le yihou (After the passing of the Gender Equity Education Act).' *Xingbie pingdeng jiaoyu jikan* (Gender equity education quarterly), 28: 4–5.

Bin Abdul Aziz, Johannis, Gillian Koh, Mathew Mathews and Min-Wei Tan, 2016. *SG50 and Beyond: Protecting the Public Space in the New Era of Singaporean Pluralism*. IPS Working Paper No. 25. Singapore: Institute of Policy Studies.

Blackwood, Evelyn and Mark Johnson, 2012. 'Queer Asian Subjects: Transgressive Sexualities and Heteronormative Meanings.' *Asian Studies Review*, 36(4): 441–451.

Blackwood, Evelyn and Saskia Wieringa, eds., 1999. *Female desires: Same-sex relations and transgender practices across cultures*. New York: Columbia University Press.

Blackwood, Evelyn, 2005. 'Gender transgression in colonial and postcolonial Indonesia.' *The Journal of Asian Studies*, 64: 849–807.

Blackwood, Evelyn, 2010. *Falling into the Lesbi World: Desire and Difference in Indonesia.* Honolulu: University of Hawaii Press.

Bloomberg News, 2015. 'Vietnam takes gay-rights lead in SE Asia.' *Bangkok Post*, 8 January. https://www.bangkokpost.com/world/455253/vietnam-takes-gay-rights-lead-in-se-asia. Accessed 5 December 2024.

Boellstorff, Tom, 2004. 'The emergence of political homophobia in Indonesia: Masculinity and national belonging.' *Ethnos*, 69(4): 465–486.

Boellstorff, Tom, 2005. *The Gay Archipelago: Sexuality and Nation in Indonesia.* Princeton: Princeton University Press.

Boellstorff, Tom, 2007. *A Coincidence of Desires: Anthropology, Queer Studies, Indonesia.* Durham: Duke University Press.

Bolasco, Mario, 1994. *Points of Departure: Essays on Christianity, Power, and Social Change.* Manila: St. Scholastica's College.

Bosia, Michael J. and Meredith L. Weiss, 2013. 'Political Homophobia in Comparative Perspective.' In Meredith L. Weiss and Michael J. Bosia, eds., *Global Homophobia: States, Movements, and the Politics of Oppression.* Urbana: University of Illinois Press, pp. 1–29.

Bosia, Michael J., Sandra M. McEvoy and Momin Rahman, eds., 2020. *The Oxford Handbook of Global LGBT and Sexual Diversity Politics.* Oxford: Oxford University Press.

Boswell, John, 1980. *Christianity, Social Tolerance, and Homosexuality.* Chicago: Chicago University Press.

Bourdieu, Pierre, 2018. *Jissen kankaku 1,* shinsōban (Practical Senses 1, New Edition). Trans. by Hitoshi Imamura and Michitaka Minato. Tokyo: Misuzu Shobo. (1980. *Le Sens pratique*, Maison Des Sciences De L'Homme.)

Brac de la Perrière, Bénédicte and Peter A. Jackson, eds., 2022. *Spirit Possession in Buddhist Southeast Asia: Worlds Ever More Enchanted.* Copenhagen: Nordic Institute of Asian Studies Press.

Brac de la Perrière, Bénédicte, 2022. 'Hpyo's Choice: Activism or Mediumship? A Gay Person's Dilemma in Contemporary Myanmar.' In Peter A. Jackson and Benjamin Baumann, eds., *Deities and Divas: Queer Ritual Specialists in Myanmar, Thailand and Beyond.* Copenhagen: Nordic Institute of Asian Studies Press, pp. 192–221.

Brandzel, Amy, 2005. 'Queering Citizenship? Same Sex Marriage and the State.' *GLQ: A Journal of Gay and Lesbian Studies*, 11(2): 171–204.

Brewer, Carolyn, 2001. *Holy Confrontation: Religion, Gender, and Sexuality in the Philippines, 1521–1685.* Manila: St. Scholastica's College.

Brown, Gavin, Kath Browne, Rebecca Elmhirst and Simon Hutta, 2010. 'Sexualities in/of the Global South.' *Geography Compass*, 4(10): 1567–1579.

Brún, Pat de, 2019. *Queering Kampuchea: LGBT rights discourse and post colonial queer subject-formation in Cambodian queer politics.* LLM Thesis. Human Rights, Conflict and Justice at SOAS, University of London.

Bui, Thi Hong Minh, 2015. Kon-in Kazoku Hou (Marriage and family law). https://www.jica.go.jp/project/vietnam/021/legal/ku57pq00001j1wzj-att/legal_44_20150109.pdf. Accessed 5 December 2024.

Burchall, Michael J., 2008. *Boyztown 1982–2008: My Life, and the History of Cockpit Bar, Le Bistro Restaurant and the Story of Boyztown, Pattaya, Thailand.* Chonburi: Self-published by 87 Print Co Ltd.

Butler, Judith, 1990. *Gender Trouble: Feminism and the Subversion of Identity.* New York and London: Routledge.

Canaday, Margot, 2009. *The Straight State: Sexuality and Citizenship in Twentieth-Century America.* Princeton: Princeton University Press.

Cannell, Fenella, 1999. *Power and Intimacy in the Christian Philippines.* Cambridge: Cambridge University Press.

Canoy, Nico Arevalo, 2015. '"Intimacy is Not Free of Charge:" An intersectional analysis of cultural and classed discourses of intimacy among gay and transgender identities.' *Sexualities*, 18(8): 921–940.

Carroll, Aengus and Lucas Paoli Itaborahy, 2015. *State-sponsored Homophobia: A World Survey of Laws: Criminalisation, Protection and Recognition of Same-sex Love*, 10th ed. International Lesbian Gay Bisexual Trans and Intersex Association. https://ilga.org/downloads/ILGA_State_Sponsored_Homophobia_2015.pdf. Accessed 21 November 2024.

Carroll, Joshua, 2016. 'LGBT Burmese Missed the Revolution.' *Daily Beast*, 22 August. https://www.thedailybeast.com/lgbt-burmese-missed-the-revolution. Accessed 14 November 2020.

Carvajal, Orlando P., ed., 2014. *A Conversation about Life: Points of View on Reproductive Health.* Quezon City: Claretian Publications.

Catalla, Teodoro Ambrosio P., Sovanara Kha and Gerard van Mourik, 2003. *Out of the Shadows: Male to Male Sexual Behavior in Cambodia.* Phnom Penh: International HIV/AIDS Alliance & KHANA.

CBCP (Catholic Bishops' Conference of the Philippines), 1997. Catechism for Filipino Catholics. https://cbcponline.net. Accessed 21 November 2024.

CBCP Pastoral 1968. On the Encyclical Letter "Humanae Vitae"

CBCP Pastoral 1969. On Public Policy regarding Population Growth Control

CBCP Pastoral 1973a. On the Population Problem and Family Life

CBCP Pastoral 1973b. Moral Norms for Catholic Hospitals and Catholics in Health Services

CBCP Pastoral 1976a. On the Doctrine of the Church on Christian Marriage

CBCP Pastoral 1976b. On Christian Marriage and Family Life

CBCP Pastoral 1990a. Love is Life

CBCP Pastoral 1990b. Guiding Principles on Population Control

CBCP Pastoral 1990c. Church/Government Dialogue on Family Planning

CBCP Pastoral 1993. Save the Family and Live

CBCP Pastoral 1994. On the Cairo International Conference on Population and Development

CBCP Pastoral 1999. On Pornography

CBCP Pastoral 2000a. On the Defense of Life and Family

CBCP Pastoral 2000b. "That They May Have Life, and Have It Abundantly"

CBCP Pastoral 2001. Saving and Strengthening the Filipino Family

CBCP Pastoral 2002. The Christian Family: Good News for the Third Millennium

CBCP Pastoral 2003. We Must Reject House Bill 4110

CBCP Pastoral 2005. On the National Celebration of Family Week on September 19 – 25, 2005

CBCP Pastoral 2006. Shepherding and Prophesying in Hope

CBCP Pastoral 2008. Standing Up for the Gospel of Life

CBCP Pastoral 2009. Reiterating CBCP Position on Family

CBCP Pastoral 2010a. On the Government's Revitalized Promotion of Condoms

CBCP Pastoral 2010b. Securing our Moral Heritage

CBCP Pastoral 2011a. Choosing Life, Rejecting the RH Bill

CBCP Pastoral 2011b. Proclaim Life … In Season and Out of Season

CBCP Pastoral 2013a. Contraception is Corruption!

CBCP Pastoral 2013b. On Certain Social Issues of Today

CBCP Pastoral 2014. On Stewardship of Health

CBCP Pastoral 2015a. Moral Guidance on the Anti-Discrimination Bill

CBCP Pastoral 2015b. On the US Supreme Court Ruling on Same Sex Marriage

CBCP Pastoral 2015c. The Dignity and Vocation of Homosexual Persons - Response to the Acceptance of Homosexual Lifestyle and the Legalization of Homosexual Unions

CBCP Pastoral 2015d. Understanding Pope Francis' Gesture Rightly

CCHR, 2010. *Coming out in the Kingdom: LGBT People in Cambodia*. Phnom Penh: Cambodian Center for Human Rights. http://cchrcambodia.org/public/en/publications/general-reports/8. Accessed 21 November 2024.

CCHR, 2015. *LGBT Bullying in Cambodia's Schools*. Phnom Penh: Cambodian Center for Human Rights. https://cchrcambodia.org/index_old.php?url=media/media.php&p=report_detail.php&reid=110&id=5

CCHR, 2017. *Cambodia's Rainbow Families: Marriage, Adoption and Gender Recognition Rights in the Kingdom*. Phnom Penh: Cambodian Center for Human Rights. https://cchrcambodia.org/storage/posts/1672/2017-11-23-reports-eng-cambodia-s-rainbow-families.pdf. Accessed 21 November 2024.

Ceperiano, Arjohn, Emmanuel Santos Jr., Daniella Celine Alonzo and Mira Alexis Ofreneo, 2016. '"Girl, Bi, Bakla, Tomboy:" The intersectionality of sexuality, gender, and class in urban poor context.' *Philippine Journal of Psychology*, 49(2): 5–34.

Chakrabarty, Dipesh. 2000. *Provincializing Europe: Postcolonial Thought and Historical Difference*. Princeton: Princeton University Press.

Chan, Kenneth, 2015. *Yonfan's Bugis Street* (妖街皇后). Hong Kong: Hong Kong University Press.

Chang, Kyung-Sup, 2010. *South Korea under Compressed Modernity: Familial Political Economy in Transition*. London and New York: Routledge.

Chanthavilay, Phetsavanh and Vanphanom Sychareun, 2014. 'Mobile Phones' Effects on Gender and Sexuality among MSM and TGs in Lao PDR.' In Pimpawun Boonmongkon and Timo Tapani Ojanen,eds., *Mobile Sexualities: Transformations of Gender and Sexuality in Southeast Asia*. Bangkok: Southeast Asian Consortium on Gender, Sexuality, and Health, pp. 357–402.

Châu Mỹ, 2022. 'Sài Gòn quán: Độc đáo "Lẩu pê đê" (Saigon restaurant: Unique 'Gay hotpot').' *Dân Việt*, 13 August. https://danviet.vn/sai-gon-quan-doc-dao-lau-pe-de-20220813013648887.htm. Accessed 5 December 2024.

Chauncey, George, 2019. *Gay New York: Gender, Urban Culture, and the Making of the Gay Male World, 1890–1940*. New York: Basic Books.

CHECO/CORONA Harvest Division, Directorate of Operations Analysis, HQ PACAF, 1973. 'Project CHECO Report: Base Defense in Thailand.' (Formerly confidential document declassified in 1999). https://apps.dtic.mil/sti/pdfs/ADA586193.pdf. Accessed 21 November 2024.

Chen, Hwei-Syin, 2001. 'Jiaoyu bu 'liangxing pingdeng jiaoyu fa cao'an' de lifa guocheng yu neirong (The legislative process and content of the Ministry of Education's 'Draft Act on Gender Equity Education').' In Taiwan Ministry of Education, ed., *Liangxing pingdeng jiaoyu fa cao'an' yanni jihua qimo baogao* (Final report of the 'Draft Act on Both-Sexes Equal Education'), pp. 14–21.

Chen, Hwei-Syin, 2006. 'Yeh Yung-Chih anyu xingbie de guanxi: yige falüren de guandian (The relationship between the case of Yeh Yung-Chih and gender: A jurist's view).' In Taiwan xingbie pingdeng jiaoyu xiehui (Taiwan Gender Equity Education Association), ed., *Yongbao meigui shaonian* (Embracing the rose boy). Taipei: Fembooks, pp. 60–69.

Chen, Kuan-Hsing. 2010. *Asia as Method: Towards Deimperialization*. Durham: Duke University Press.

Cheng, Patrick S., 2011. *Radical Love: An Introduction to Queer Theology*. New York: Church Publishing.

Chhay, Channyda and Amelia Woodside, 2014. 'LGBT rights campaigner awarded.' *The Phnom Penh Post*, 21 February. https://www.phnompenhpost.com/7days/lgbt-rights-campaigner-awarded. Accessed 3 December 2023.

Chong, Jean, 2017. 'LGBTQ activism in Singapore.' In Jiyoung Song, ed., *A History of Human Rights Society in Singapore 1965–2015*. New York: Routledge, pp. 150–168.

Chong, Terence, 2011. 'Introduction.' In Terence Chong, ed., *The AWARE Saga: Civil Society and Public Morality in Singapore*. Singapore: NUS Press, pp. 1–13.

Chonwilai, Sulaiporn, 2012. 'Kathoey: Male-to-Female Transgender or Transsexuals.' In Pimpawun Boonmongkon and Peter A. Jackson, eds., *Thai Sex Talk: The Language of Sex and Sexuality in Thailand*. Trans. by Timo Ojansen. Chiang Mai: Mekong Press, pp. 109–117.

Choong, Jerry, 2018. 'After caning backlash, PAS Youth warns against domestic, global LGBT forces.' *Malay Mail Online*, 16 September. https://www.malaymail.com/news/malaysia/2018/09/16/after-caning-backlash-pas-youth-warns-against-domestic-global-lgbt-forces/1673154. Accessed 31 August 2019.

Chow, Jonathan Tseung-Hao, 2011. *Religion, Politics and Sex: Contesting Catholic Teaching and Transnational Reproductive Health Norms in the Contemporary Philippines.* PhD Thesis. University of California, Berkley.

Chu, Mei Mei, 2018. 'Syed Saddiq's "call me bro" backfires after Numan Afifi's resignation.' *The Star Online*, 10 July. https://www.thestar.com.my/news/nation/2018/07/10/syed-saddiqs-call-me-bro-backfires-after-numan-afifis-resignation#BlCI5E89U8SALQgD.99. Accessed 31 August 2019.

Chua, Lynette J. and David Gilbert, 2015. 'Sexual Orientation and Gender Identity Minorities in Transition: LGBT rights and activism in Myanmar.' *Human Rights Quarterly*, 37: 1–28.

Chua, Lynette J., 2014. *Mobilizing Gay Singapore: Rights and Resistance in an Authoritarian State*. Singapore: NUS Press.

Chua, Lynette J., 2018. *The Politics of Love in Myanmar: LGBT Mobilization and Human Rights as a Way of Life*. Stanford: Stanford University Press.

Cochran, Susan D., Jack Drescher, Eszter Kismödi, Alain Giami, Claudia García-Moreno, Elham Atalla, Adele Marais, Elisabeth Meloni Vieira and Geoffrey M Reed, 2014. 'Proposed Declassification of Disease Categories Related to Sexual Orientation in the International Statistical Classification of Diseases and Related Health Problems (ICD-11).' *Bulletin of World Health Organization*, 92: 672–679. https://pubmed.ncbi.nlm.nih.gov/25378758/ Accessed 21 November 2024.

Collins, Patricia Hill and Sirma Bilge, 2020. *Intersectionality* (2nd Edition). London: Polity Press.

Coloma, Roland Sintos, 2013. 'Ladlad and Parrhesiastic Pedagogy: Unfurling LGBT Politics and Education in the Global South.' *Curriculum Inquiry*, 43(4): 483–511.

Colors Rainbow, 2013. 'Facing 377: Discrimination and Human Rights Abuses against Transgender, Gay and Bisexual Men in Myanmar.' https://equalitymyanmar.org/book/wp-content/uploads/2015/02/AnnualReport-rainbow.pdf. Accessed 21 November 2024.

Comptroller General of the United States, 1977. 'Withdrawal of U.S. Forces from Thailand: Ways to Improve Future Withdrawal Operations.' (Unclassified Version of GAO's Secret report LCD-77-402, dated June 3, 1977). https://www.gao.gov/assets/130/120410.pdf. Accessed 21 November 2024.

Cornelio, Jayeel, and Robbin Charles M. Dagle, 2019. 'Weaponising Religious Freedom: Same-Sex marriage and Gender Equality in the Philippines.' *Religion and Human Rights*, 14: 65–94.

Cornelio, Jayeel, and Robbin Charles M. Dagle, 2024. 'Who am I? Who can I Love? And Why Me? Queer Christians and the Spirituality of Struggle.' *Critical Research on Religion*. https://doi.org/10.1177/20503032241277494. Accessed 21 November 2024.

Corrales, Nestor, 2018. 'Duterte favors same-sex civil union, not same-sex marriage.' *Philippine Daily Inquirer*, 2 July. https://newsinfo.inquirer.net/1006205/duterte-favors-same-sex-civil-union-not-same-sex-marriage. Accessed 21 November 2024.

Courage Philippines http://couragephilippines.blogspot.jp/ Accessed 21 November 2024.

Crenshaw, Kimberlé, 1989. 'Demarginalizing the Intersection of Race and Sex: A Black feminist critique of antidiscrimination doctrine, feminist theory and antiracist politics.' *University of Chicago Legal Forum*, 1: 139–167.

Đào, Duy Anh, ed., 1936. *Pháp-Việt Từ Điển* (French-Vietnamese Dictionary). Hue: Quan-hai Tung-thu.

Đào, Duy Anh, ed., 1950. *Pháp-Việt Từ Điển* (French-Vietnamese Dictionary). Paris: Minh Tân.

Đào, Duy Anh, ed., 1957. *Hán Việt Từ Điển* (Chinese-Vietnamese Dictionary). Saigon: Trường Thi Xuất bản.

David, Emmanuel, 2015. 'Purple-Collar Labor: Transgender workers and queer value at global call centers in the Philippines.' *Gender and Society*, 29(2): 169–194.

David, Emmanuel, 2016. 'Outsourced Heroes and Queer Incorporations: Labor brokerage and the politics of inclusion in the Philippines call center industry.' *GLQ: A Journal of Lesbian and Gay Studies*, 22(3): 381–408.

Davy, Zowie, 2015. 'The DSM-5 and the Politics of Diagnosing Transpeople.' *Archives of Sexual Behavior*, 44: 1165–1176. DOI: 10.1007/s10508-015-0573-6. Accessed 21 November 2024.

D'Emilio, John, 1983. 'Capitalism and Gay Identity.' In Ann Snitow Christine Stansell and Sharan Thompson, eds., *Powers of Desire: The Politics of Sexuality.* New York: Monthly Review Press, pp. 100–113.

Dentsu, 2015. 'Dentsu Diversity Labo LGBT Chosa (Dentsu Diversity Lab LGBT Survey) 2015,' 23 April. https://www.dentsu.co.jp/news/release/2015/0423-004032.html. Accessed 3 March 2024.

Dentsu, 2019. 'Dentsu Diversity Labo LGBT Chosa (Dentsu Diversity Lab LGBT Survey) 2018,' 10 January. https://www.dentsu.co.jp/news/release/2019/0110-009728.html. Accessed 3 March 2024.

Dentsu, 2021. 'Dentsu Diversity Labo LGBT Chosa (Dentsu Conducts LGBTQ+ Survey) 2020,' 8 April. https://www.dentsu.co.jp/news/release/2021/0408-010364.html. Accessed 3 March 2024.

Department for the Promotion and Propagation of Sāsanā, 2018. *The Teachings of the Buddha (Higher Level) Volume II.* Yangon: Ministry of Religious Affairs & Culture.

Department of Statistics, Singapore, 2010. 'Key Indicators of the Resident Households.' *Singapore Census of Population 2010.*

Dewi, Suzy Yusna, 2016. 'LGBT vs. PHN-Stigma (Stigma of LGBT vs. normal relationship behavior).' *kompasiana*, 22 February. kompasiana.com/drsuzyyusna/56ca840597937334153430fb/lgbt-vs-phn-stigma.

Drescher, Jack, 2015. 'Out of DSM: Depathologizing Homosexuality.' *Behavioral Sciences*, 5(4): 565–575. DOI: 10.3390/bs5040565. Accessed 21 November 2024.

Duggan, Lisa, 2002. 'The new homonormativity: The sexual politics of neoliberalism.' In Russ Castronovo and Dana D. Nelson eds., *Materializing Democracy: Toward a Revitalized Cultural Politics.* Durham: Duke University Press, pp. 175–194.

Duggan, Lisa, 2003. *The Twilight of Equality? Neoliberalism, Cultural Politics, and the Attack on Democracy.* Boston: Beacon Press.

Dunlap, David W., 2017. 'How The Times Gave "Gay" Its Own Voice (Again).' *The New York Times*, 19 June. https://www.nytimes.com/2017/06/19/us/gay-pride-lgbtq-new-york-times.html. Accessed 22 October 2024.

Dương Ngoc, 2016. '"Một nửa của các đại sứ (*): Đại sứ Mỹ và mối tình đặc biệt ("Half" of the ambassadors (*): The US Ambassador and his special love).' *Người,' Lao động*, 19 May. https://nld.com.vn/thoi-su-trong-nuoc/mot-nua-cua-cac-dai-su-dai-su-my-va-moi-tinh-dac-biet-20160519221126824.htm. Accessed 5 December 2024.

Ebihara, May M., 1974. 'Khmer village women in Cambodia.' In Carolyn Matthiasson ed., *Many Sisters: Cross-Cultural Perspective.* New York: Free Press, pp. 305–47.

Edsall, Nicholas C., 2003. *Toward Stonewall: Homosexuality and Society in the Modern Western World.* Charlottesville: University of Virginia Press.

Edwards, Penny, 2007. *Cambodge: The Cultivation of a Nation, 1860–1945*. Honolulu: University of Hawai'i Press.

Ellison, Ralph, 1970. 'What America would be like without Blacks.' https://teachin-gamericanhistory.org/library/document/what-america-would-be-like-without-blacks/. Accessed 22 October 2024.

Empower Foundation, ed., 2015. *This is Us: EMPOWER Foundation Museum of Sex Works in Thai Society*. Nonthaburi: Empower University Press.

Encarnacion, Omar, 2014. 'Gay Rights: Why Democracy Matters.' *Journal of Democracy*, 25(3): 90–104.

Endō, Satoshi, 2012. 'Nenpyō (Timeline).' In Akio Imai and Misaki Iwai, eds., *Gendai Betonamu wo shirutameno 60 shō* (60 chapters for understanding modern Vietnam), 2nd edition. Tokyo: Akashi Shoten, pp.375–391.

Esumuraruda and Kira, 2015. *Dōsei pātonāshippu shōmei, hajimarimashita: Shibuya-ku, Setagaya-ku no seiritsu monogatari to tetsuzuki no hōhō* (The beginning of same-sex partnership certificates: Stories and methods of their establishment in Shibuya City and Setagaya City). Tokyo: Potto Shuppan.

Evan, Vania, 2020. 'Tren Ruqyah LGBTQ: Tak Efektif tapi Justru Tambah Pop-uler di Indonesia (LGBTQ Ruqyah Trend: Ineffective but increasingly pop-ular in Indonesia).' *Vice.com.*, 14 February. www.vice.com/id/article/n7j3y7/tren-ruqyah-lgbtq-tak-efektif-tapi-justru-tambah-populer-di-indonesia. Accessed 21 November 2024.

Evangelista, John Andrew G., 2018. 'Beyond Partying: Characterizing the LGBTQ movement in the Philippines.' *Philippine Social Science Review*, 70(2): 46–74.

Evangelista, John Andrew G., 2020. 'Mess Up the Empire: Deploying and disrupting homonationalism.' *Sexualities*, 25(4): 347–364.

Evangelista, John Andrew G., 2024. '"You've Got Me Feeling Emotions": Affective norms of deliberation in the Philippine lgbtqia+ rights movement.' *Philippine Political Science Journal*, 45: 117–145.

Evans, David T., 1993. *Sexual Citizenship: The Material Construction of Sexualities*. London and New York: Routledge.

Fairclough, Gordon, 2004. 'Gay Asia: Tolerance pays.' *Far Eastern Economic Review*, 167(43): 52–63.

Farhan, Farwiza and Gerry van Klinken, 2020. 'Atheism in Indonesia.' *Inside Indonesia 140*. https://www.insideindonesia.org/atheism-in-indonesia. Accessed 21 November 2024.

Finke, Roger and Amy Adamczyk, 2008. 'Cross-national Moral Beliefs: The influence of national religious context.' *Sociological Quarterly*, 49(4): 617–52.

Fjelstad, Karen and Nguyen Thi Hien, 2012. *Spirits without Borders: Vietnamese Spirit Mediums in a Transnational Age*. London and New York: Palgrave Macmillan.

Florida, Richard, 2002. *The Rise of the Creative Class: And How It's Transforming Work, Leisure, Community and Everyday Life*. New York. Basic Books.

Fraser, Nancy, 1997. *Justice Interruptus: Critical Reflections on the "Postsocialist" Condition*. New York: Routledge.

Fuhrmann, Arnika, 2016. *Ghostly Desires: Queer Sexuality and Vernacular Buddhism in Contemporary Thai Cinema*. Durham and London: Duke University Press.

Fukunaga, Genya, 2017a. 'Seiteki mainoriti no seido e no hōsetsu o meguru poritikusu: Taiwan no jendā byōdō kyōiku hō o jirei ni (The politics of inclusion of sexual minorities in the system: Gender equity education law in Taiwan as a case study).' *Nihon Taiwan gakkai hō* (Journal of the Japan Association for Taiwan studies), 19: 29–49.

Fukunaga, Genya, 2017b. 'Taiwan ni okeru feminizumuteki sei kaihō undō no tenkai: josei undō no shuryūka to, itsudatsuteki sekushuariti shutai no rentai (The development of the feminist sexual liberation movement in Taiwan: Mainstreaming the women's movement and solidarity of subjects of deviant sexuality).' In Kaku Sechiyama, ed., *Jendā to sekushuariti de miru higashi ajia* (East Asia from the perspective of gender and sexuality). Tokkyo: Keisō Shobō, pp. 92–135.

Fukunaga, Genya, 2017c. '"LGBT furendorī-na Taiwan" no tanjō (The birth of 'LGBT-friendly Taiwan').' In Kaku Sechiyama, ed., *Jendā to sekushuariti de miru Higashi Ajia* (East Asia from the perspective of gender and sexuality). Tokyo: Keisō Shobō, pp. 187–225.

Fukunaga, Genya, 2022a. 'Reisen taisei to gunjika sareta masukyuriniti: Taiwan to Kankoku no chōheisei o jirei ni (Cold War regimes and militarised masculinity: Taiwan and Korea's conscription system as a case study).' In Masako Kohama and Akiko Itabashi, eds., *Higashi ajia no kazoku to sekushuariti* (Family and sexuality in East Asia). Kyoto: Kyoto University Press, pp. 21–54.

Fukunaga, Genya, 2022b. '"Kika, haikon" kara "kon'in byōdō" e: Taiwan ni okeru dōseikon no hōseika to "yoki shimin" no seiji (From 'destruction of the family/abolition of marriage' to 'marriage equality:' The legalization of same-sex marriage and the politics of 'good citizenship' in Taiwan).' *Sociologos*, 45: 39–58.

Fukunaga, Genya, 2022c. 'Feminisuto to hoshu no kimyō-na "rentai": Kankoku no toransu haijo gensetsu o chūshin ni (The strange 'solidarity' between feminists and conservatives: With a focus on Korean discourses of transgender exclusion).' *Jendā shigaku* (Gender history), 18: 75–85.

Fukunaga, Genya, 2024. 'Queer Politics and Solidarity: Post-Cold War Homonationalism in East Asia.' In Kazuyoshi Kawasaka and Stefan Würrer ed., *Beyond Diversity: Queer Politics, Activism and Representation in Contemporary Japan*. Dusseldorf: Dusseldorf University Press, pp. 99–115.

Fukunaga, Genya, 2025. *Sei/sei o meguru tōsō: Taiwan to Kankoku ni okeru seiteki mainoriti no undo to seiji* (The Struggle over Sexuality/Gender: Queer movements and politics in Taiwan and Korea), Tokyo: Akashi Shoten.

Fukuoka, Madoka, 2012. '"Joseisei" to "danseisei" o kangaeru: Indoneshia no popyurā karuchā ni okeru jendā to sekushuariti (Thinking about 'femininity' and 'masculinity': Gender and sexuality in Indonesian popular culture).' *Ōsaka daigaku daigakuin ningen kagaku kenkyū kiyō* (Bulletin of the Graduate School of Human Sciences, Osaka University), 38: 79–103.

Fukuoka, Madoka, 2016. 'Eiga ni okeru jendā, sekushuariti no hyōshō o kangaeru: Indoneshia no 2000-nen ikō no sakuhin o jirei toshite (Considering the representation of gender and sexuality in films: A case study of Indonesian films since 2000).' *Ōsaka daigaku daigakuin ningen kagaku kenkyū kiyō* (Bulletin of the Graduate School of Human Sciences, Osaka University), 42: 19–42.

Fukutomi, Wataru, 2017. *Tai gendai bungaku shiron: Bungakushi, tekisuto, dokuritsu-kei shoten o tōshite miru 21-seiki no Tai bungaku* (An essay on contemporary Thai literature: Thai literature in the 21st century seen through literary history, textbooks, and independent bookstores). Tokyo: Fuji Xerox Co. Kobayashi Foundation.

Fulkerson, Mary McClintock and Sheila Briggs eds., 2013. *The Oxford Handbook of Feminist Theology*. Oxford: Oxford University Press.

Fushimi, Noriaki, ed., 2002. *"Okama" wa sabetsuka* (Is "Okama" a Slur?). Tokyo: Potto Shuppan.

Garcia, Neil C., 1996. *Philippine Gay Culture: Binabae to Bakla, Silahis to MSM*. Quezon City: University of the Philippine Press.

Garcia, Neil C., 2013. 'Nativism or Universalism: Situating LGBT Discourses in the Philippines.' *Kritika Kultura,* 20: 48–68.

Gereja Masehi Injili di Minahasa, 2013. *Kode Etik Pendeta* (Code of Ethics for Pastors). Tomohon: Sinode GMIM.

Gereja Masehi Injili di Minahasa, 2017. *Petunjuk Pelaksanaan Pemilihan di Semua Aras Tahun 2017/2018* (Guidelines for Conducting Elections at All Levels Year 2017/2018). Tomohon: Sinode GMIM.

Gilbert, David F., 2022. 'Spirits in Trans Kinship Networks: An Ethnographic Exploration of Ritual and Recognition in Queer Myanmar.' In Peter A. Jackson and Benjamin Baumann, eds., *Deities and Divas: Queer Ritual Specialists in Myanmar, Thailand and Beyond*. Copenhagen: Nordic Institute of Asian Studies Press, pp. 169–191.

Gilbert, David, 2013. 'Categorizing Gender in Queer Yangon.' *Sojourn*, 28(2): 241–271.

Glanzberg, Al, 1993. 'Hotel opportunities in Thailand.' *The Cornell Hotel and Restaurant Administration Quarterly*, 34(3): 56–59.

Goh, Joseph N., 2019. 'Practical Guidelines for SOGIESC theologising in Southeast Asia: Foregrounding gender nonconformity, sexual diversity and non-dyadic embodiment.' In Stephen Suleeman and Amadeo D. Udampoh, eds., *Siapakah Sesamaku? Pergumulan Teologi Dengan Isu-Isu Keadilan Gender* (Who are my fellows? Theological struggle with the issues of gender justice). Jakarta: Sekolah Tinggi Filsafat Teologi, pp. 185–210.

Goh, Yan Han, 2022. '8 highlights from NDR 2022: Masks optional in most indoor settings, Section 377A to be repealed.' *The Straits Times*, 21 August. https://www. straitstimes.com/singapore/politics/8-highlights-from-ndr-2022-masks- optional-in-most-indoor-settings-section-377a-to-be-repealed. Accessed 24 November 2024.

Government of Cambodia, 2024. 'National report submitted pursuant to Human Rights Council resolutions 5/1 and 16/21: Cambodia.' https://undocs.org/en/A/HRC/WG.6/46/KHM/1. Accessed 17 January 2025.

Guevara, Celline Charmaigne Angeles, 2016. 'Life Satisfaction among Older Filipino Sexual Minorities and their Experiences of Support.' *Philippine Journal of Psychology*, 49(2): 135–155.

Guo, Lifu, 2020. 'Owaru eizu, kenkō-na Chūgoku: Chūgoku AIDS Walk o jirei ni. Chūgoku ni okeru gei eizu undō o saikō suru (End AIDS for a healthy China: Reconsidering the Gay AIDS movement in China with the China AIDS Walk as a case study),' *Joseigaku* (Journal of Women's Studies Association of Japan), 28: 12–33.

Hadi Awang, 2018. 'Isu sebat di Terengganu.' Facebook Page by Dato' Seri Tuan Guru Haji Abdul Hadi Awang, 9 September. https://www.facebook.com/abdulhadiawang/videos/257021745147355/. Accessed 31 August 2019.

Hafidz Muftisany, 2016. 'Gerakan Indonesia Beradab Bangun Kembali Bangunan Adab Masyarakat (Civilized Indonesia Movement rebuilds the Civilized Society's foundation).' *Republika.co.id.*, 18 March. www.republika.co.id/berita/koran/dialog-jumat/16/03/18/o47v4613-gerakan-indonesia-beradab-bangun-kembali-bangunan-adab-masyarakat.

Hagai, Saori, 2021. 'Kanbojia koten buyō robamu boran no keishō ni okeru Kumēru kei diasupora no eikyō (The influence of the Khmer diaspora in the transmission of Khmer classical dance, *robam boran*).' *Ritsumeikan daigaku jinbun kagaku kenkyūjo kiyō* (Journal of Human Sciences Research Centre, Ritsumeikan University), 125: 315–341.

Hagiwara, Makiko, 2009. 'Internet monitor chousa ha dono youni katayotte irunoka: Juurai-gata chousa shuhou ni daitai suru chousa shuhou no mosaku (How biased are Internet monitor surveys: The search for alternative survey methods).' *Works Review*, 4(1): 1–12.

Hanisch, Carol, 2006. 'The Personal Is Political' (Originally published: 1969), https://webhome.cs.uvic. ca/~mserra/AttachedFiles/PersonalPolitical.pdf. Accessed 3 March 2024.

Hanoi Pride, 2018. *Vietnam Queer History Month: The Portrait of History* (English Version) [Brochure].

Harada, Masami, 1991. 'Attakatā ga monogataru bukkyō sekai: Danmapada o chūshin ni (The Buddhist world as told by the Atthakatha: Focusing on the Dhammapada scripture).' In Yoneo Ishii, ed., *Kōza bukkyō no juyō to hen'yō 2: Tōnan Ajia hen* (Lectures on the reception and transformation of Buddhism 2: Southeast Asia). Tokyo: Kōsei shuppansha, pp. 163–196.

Harborne, Ben, 2017. 'Pattaya: Where it all began!' https://lovepattayathailand.com/pattaya-history/. Accessed 21 November 2024.

Harrison, Rachel and Peter A. Jackson, eds., 2010. *The Ambiguous Allure of the West: Traces of the Colonial in Thailand*. Hong Kong and Ithaca, NY: Hong Kong University Press and Cornell University Southeast Asia Program Publications.

Harrison, Rachel V. 2000. 'The Disruption of Female Desire and the Thai Literary Tradition of Eroticism, Religion and Aesthetics.' *Tenggara*, 41: 88–125.

Hart, Donn and Harriet Hart, 1990. 'Visayan Swardspeak: The language of a gay community in the Philippines.' *Crossroads: An Interdisciplinary Journal of Southeast Asian Studies*, 5(2): 27–49.

Hasanul Rizqa, 2016. 'PDSKJI: Homoseksual Masuk Kategori Masalah Kejiwaan (The Indonesian Association of Psychiatric Specialists: Homosexuality is categorized as a mental health problem).' *Republika.co.id.*, 20 February. republika. co.id/berita/nasional/umum/16/02/20/o2ul0i394-pdskji-homoseksual-masuk-kategori-masalah-kejiwaan.

Hayami, Yōko, ed., 2019. *Tōnan ajia ni okeru kea no senzairyoku: sei no tsunagari no jissen* (Potentialities of care in Southeast Asia: Practices of relatedness in life). Kyoto: Kyoto University Press.

Headley, Robert K. Jr., Kylin Chhor, Lam Kheng Lim, Lim Hak Kheang and Chen Chun, 1977. *Cambodian- English Dictionary*. Washington, D.C.: The Catholic University of America Press.

Heiman, Elliot M. and Cao Van Lê, 1975. 'Transsexualism in Vietnam.' *Archives of Sexual Behavior*, 4(1): 89–95.

Hekma, Gert, 2015. 'Sexual Citizenship.' In Claude J. Summers ed., *GLBTQ: An Encyclopedia of Gay, Lesbian, Bisexual, Transgender, & Queer Culture*. Chicago: Glbtq, inc.

Henley, David, 1996. *Nationalism and Regionalism in a Colonial Context: Minahasa in the Dutch East Indies*. Leiden: KITLV Press.

Hiramatsu, Hideki, 2017. 'Tai no nanshoku to LGBT (Male homosexuality and LGBT in Thailand).' In Tomoyuki Someya and Chiaki Hatanaka, eds., *Nanshoku o egaku Saikaku no BL komikaraizu to Ajia no 'sei'* (The BL comicalization of Saikaku's portrayal of male homosexuality and Asian 'sexuality'). Tokyo: Benseisha, pp. 167–177.

Hiramori, Daiki and Saori Kamano, 2020. 'Asking about Sexual Orientation and Gender Identity in Japan: Case report on the Osaka City Residents' Survey and related preparatory studies.' *Annual Meeting of the Population Association of America*, April 2020.

Hirata, Toshiaki, 2016. 'Seiyō seishin igaku ni okeru dōseiai no atsukai no hensen (Changes in the handling of homosexuality in Western psychiatry).' *Seishinka chiryōgaku* (Japanese journal of psychiatric treatment), 31(8): 985–990.

Ho, Josephine Chuen-Juei, 2017. *Xingbie zhili* (Gender governance). Taoyuan: National Central University Center for Study of Sexualities.

Ho, Josephine Chuen-Juei, Ding Nai-Fei (Fifi), and Ning Yin-Bin, 2005. *Xing zhengzhi rumen: Taiwan xing yun yanjiang ji* (Introduction to sexual politics: Collected lectures on the Taiwan sexuality movement). Taoyuan: National Central University Center for Study of Sexualities.

Ho, Tamara C., 2009. 'Transgender, Transgression, and Translation: A Cartography of Nat Kadaws Notes on Gender and Sexuality within the Spirit Cult of Burma.' *Discourse,* 31(3): 273–317.

Hoefinger, Heidi and Srorn Srun, 2017. '"At-Risk" or "Socially Deviant"? Conflicting narratives and grassroots organizing of sex/entertainment workers and LGBT communities in Cambodia.' *Social Sciences, Special Issue: Sex Workers' Rights: Looking toward the Future*, 6: 93. DOI:10.3390/socsci6030093. Accessed 21 November 2024.

Hoefinger, Heidi, Pisey Ly, and Srorn Srun, 2017. 'Sex Politics and Moral Panics.' In Katherine Brickell and Simon Springer, eds., *The Handbook of Contemporary Cambodia.* New York: Routledge, pp. 315–325.

Holy See, 1965. Documents of the Second Vatican Council. https://www.vatican.va/archive/hist_councils/ii_vatican_council/index.htm. Accessed 21 November 2024.

Holy See, 1993. Catechism of the Catholic Church https://www.vatican.va/archive/ENG0015/_INDEX.HTM

Horie, Yuri, 2015. *Rezubian aidentitīzu* (Lesbian identities). Kyoto: Rakuhoku shuppan.

Huang, Ke-Hsien, 2017. '"Culture Wars" in a Globalized East: How Taiwanese Conservative Christianity turned public during the same-sex marriage controversy and a secularist backlash.' *Review of Religion and Chinese Society*, 4(1): 108–136.

Hubbard, Jim, 2012. *United in Anger: A History of ACT UP* (DVD). United in Anger, Inc. https://www.unitedinanger.com. Accessed 21 November 2024.

Human Rights in Asean, 2014. 'Couple Lives in Fear after Myanmar's First Public Same-Sex Wedding,' 1 April. https://humanrightsinasean.info/news/couple-lives-in-fear-after-myanmars-first-public-same-sex-wedding/. Accessed 14 November 2020.

Human Rights Watch, 2014. 'I'm Scared to Be a Woman: Human Rights Abuse Against Transgender People in Malaysia.' *Human Rights Watch.* https://www.hrw.org/sites/default/files/reports/malaysia0914_ForUpload.pdf. Accessed 31 August 2019.

Human Rights Watch, 2015. 'Việt Nam: Bước đi Tích cực về Quyền của Người Chuyển giới (Vietnam: Positive steps for transgender rights: Vietnam's National Assembly passes new law on gender reassignment),' 30 November. https://www.hrw.org/vi/news/2015/11/30/283937. Accessed 5 December 2024.

Human Rights Watch, 2016a. *Letter to the Minister of Health, Republic of Indonesia*, 11 April.

Human Rights Watch, 2016b. 'Singapore bans foreign funding of gay pride rally,' 21 October. http:/www.ndtv.com/world-news/Singapore-bans-foreign-funding-of-gay-pride-rally-1477386. Accessed 24 August 2016.

Human Rights Watch, 2018. *Sacred in Public and Now No Privacy: Human Rights and Public Health Impacts of Indonesia's Anti-LGBT Moral Panic.* Washington DC: Human Rights Watch.

Hun, Sen, 2010. 'Keynote address at the 99th Anniversary of International Women's Day.' Phnom Penh: Royal University of Phnom Penh. http://en.cnv.org.kh/keynote-address-at-the-99th-anniversary-of-international-womens-day/. Accessed 21 November 2024.

Hung, Hui-Lin, 2007. *Xingbie pingdeng jiaoyu fa xingcheng zhi lunshu fenxi* (The Formation of the Gender Equity Education Act: A Discourse Analysis). Thesis. Department of Education, National Taiwan Normal University.

Hunt, Luke and Molyny Pann, 2017. 'Cambodia's Gays: Out of the Shadows? A closer look at the state of LGBTs in the country amid the recent Pride Week.' May 26. *The Diplomat.* https://thediplomat.com/2017/05/cambodias-gays-out-of-the-shadows/. Accessed 17 January 2025.

Hutt, David, 2017. 'The Real Danger of Cambodia's "Gay King" Episode: A recent incident could have broader implications for democracy and human rights in the country.' https://thediplomat.com/2017/01/the-real-danger-of-cambodias-gay-king-episode/. Accessed 21 November 2024.

Iga, Tsukasa, 2017. 'Gendai Marēshia ni okeru "sekushuariti poritikkusu" no tanjō: 1980 nendai ikō no kokka to LGBT undō (The birth of 'sexuality politics' in contemporary Malaysia: The state and the LGBT Movement since the 1980s).' *Ajia/Afurika chiiki kenkyū* (Asian and African Area Studies), 17(1): 73–102.

Iikuni, Yukako, 2010. 'Seiteki shōsūsha toshite no sei/sei no saikōchiku: gendai Myanmā seirei shinkō ni okeru reibai no hen'yō (Reconstructing life/sexuality as a sexual minority: the transformation of mediums in contemporary Myanmar spirit worship).' *Hyūman raitsu* (Human Rights), 271: 50–56.

Ikatan Psikologi Klinis (IPK-HIMPSI), 2016. *Pernyataan Sikap Ikatan Psiklogi Klinis (IPK-HIMPSI) mengenai "Lesbian, Gay, Bisexual, and Transgender (LGBG),'* 16 February. https://www.facebook.com/permalink.php?story_fbid=117442355591 0570&id=291070504245884&_rdr

Ildefonso, Tracy Mae, 2022. 'From Asog to Bakla: Genealogical analysis of the Philippine history to diagnose the roots of homophobia.' *Humanities Bulletin*, 5(2): 213–238.

Illich, Ivan D., 1982. *Gender.* New York: Pantheon Books.

Ilyasova, K. Alex, 2006. 'Dykes on Bikes and the Regulation of Vulgarity.' *International Journal of Motorcycle Studies*, 2(3). https://web.archive.org/web/20180424010931/http://ijms.nova.edu/November2006/IJMS_Artcl.Ilyasova.html. Accessed 21 November 2024.

Imanuel Nicolas Manafe, 2016. 'Majelis Agama-agama Indonesia Tolak Legalisasi LGBT (Religious councils in Indonesia reject the legalisation of LGBT).' *Tribunnews.com.*, 18 February. www.tribunnews.com/nasional/2016/02/18/majelis-agama-agama-indonesia-tolak-legalisasi-lgbt

Immigration and Refugee Board of Canada, 2010. https://www.refworld.org/docid/4b7cee8e37.html. Accessed 5 December 2024.

Inglehart, Ronald and Pippa Norris, 2003. *Rising Tide: Gender Equality and Cultural Change Around the World*. Cambridge: Cambridge University Press.

Institute of Policy Studies (IPS), 2013. *Our Singapore Conversation Survey.* Singapore: Institute of Policy Studies.

Inton, Michael Nuñez, 2017. *The* bakla *and the silver screen: Queer cinema in the Philippines*. PhD Thesis. Lingnan University.

Irawan Sapto Adhi, 2016. 'Fenomena LGBT: Begini Cara Para Dokter Sosialisasikan Perilaku Hubungan Normal (LGBT Phenomenon: How doctors promote normal relationship behaviors).' *Solopos.com.*, 14 March. www.solopos.com/fenomena-lgbt-begini-cara-para-dokter-sosialisasikan-perilaku-hubungan-normal-700460.

Ishida, Hitoshi, 2019. *Hajimete manabu LGBT: Kiso kara torendo made* (The first study of LGBT: From basics to trends). Tokyo: Natsumesha.

Itō, Makoto, 2000. 'Charabai, bissu, benchon: minami suraweshi ni okeru toransujendā (Calabai, bissu, bencong: Transgenders in South Sulawesi).' *Jinbun gakuhō* (The journal of social sciences and humanities), 309: 82–109.

Itō, Makoto, 2003. 'Onna no kokoro o motsu "karera": Indoneshia no charabai (The 'men' with women's hearts: The *calabai* of Indonesia).' In Makio Matsuzono, ed., *Kurashi no bunka jinruigaku 4: Sei no bunmyaku* (The cultural anthropology of living 4: The context of sex). Tokyo: Yuzankaku, pp. 226–249.

Iwama, Akiko, Reiko Yamato and Yasuko Tama, 2015. *Toi kara hajimeru kazoku shakaigaku: Tayōka suru kazoku no hōsetsu ni mukete* (Family sociology that [we] start from questions: Towards inclusion of the diversifying family). Tokyo: Yūhikaku.

Jackson, Peter A. and Eric Allyn, 1995. 'The Emergence of Thai Gay Identity.' In Peter A. Jackson, ed., *Dear Uncle Go: Male Homosexuality in Thailand*. Bangkok: Bua Lunag Books, pp. 226–281.

Jackson, Peter A. and Benjamin Baumann, eds., 2022. *Deities and Divas: Queer Ritual Specialists in Myanmar, Thailand and Beyond*. Copenhagen: Nordic Institute of Asian Studies Press.

Jackson, Peter A., 1995. 'Thai Buddhist Accounts of Homosexuality and AIDS.' *The Australian Journal of Anthropology (TAJA)*, 6 (3): 140–153.

Jackson, Peter A., 1997. 'Thai Research on Male Homosexuality and Transgenderism and the Cultural Limits of Foucaultian Analysis.' *Journal of the History of Sexuality*, 8(1): 52–85.

Jackson, Peter A., 1998. 'Male Homosexuality and Transgenderism in the Thai Buddhist Tradition.' In Winston Leyland, ed., *Queer Dharma: Voices of Gay Buddhists*. San Francisco: Gay Sunshine Press, pp. 55–89.

Jackson, Peter A., 1999a. 'Tolerant But Unaccepting: The Myth of a Thai "Gay Paradise."' In Peter A. Jackson and Nerida Cook eds., *Genders and Sexualities in Modern Thailand*. Chiang Mai: Silkworm Books, pp. 226–242.

Jackson, Peter A., 1999b. 'An American Death in Bangkok: The Murder of Darrell Berrigan and the Hybrid Origins of Gay Identity in 1960s Thailand.' *GLQ: A Journal of Lesbian and Gay Studies*, 5 (3): 361–411.

Jackson, Peter A., 2000. 'An Explosion of Thai Identities: Global Queering and Re-imagining Queer Theory.' *Culture, Health & Sexuality*, 2(4): 405–424.

Jackson, Peter A., 2001. 'Pre-Gay, Post-Queer: Thai Perspectives on Proliferating Gender/Sex Diversity in Asia.' In G. Sullivan and Peter A. Jackson eds., *Gay and Lesbian Asia: Culture, Identity, Community*. New York: Harrington Park Press.

Jackson, Peter A., 2003. 'Performative Genders, Perverse Desires: A Bio-History of Thailand's Same-sex and Transgender Cultures.' *Intersections: Gender, History & Culture in the Asian Context*, 9. http://intersections.anu.edu.au/issue9/jackson.html. Accessed 21 November 2024.

Jackson, Peter A., 2004. 'Gay Adaptation, Tom-Dee Resistance, and Kathoey Indifference: Thailand's gender/sex minorities and the episodic allure of queer English.' In William L. Leap and Tom Boellstorff eds., *Speaking in Queer Tongues: Globalization and Gay Languages*. Urbana: University of Illinois Press, pp. 202–230.

Jackson, Peter A., 2007. 'Autonomy and Subordination in Thai History: The Case for Semicolonial Analysis.' *Inter-Asia Cultural Studies*, 8(3): 329–348.

Jackson, Peter A., 2009a. 'Capitalism and Global Queering: National Markets, Parallels Among Sexual Cultures, and Multiple Queer Modernities.' *GLQ: A Journal of Lesbian and Gay Studies*, 15(3): 357–395.

Jackson, Peter A., 2009b. 'Global Queering and Global Queer Theory: Thai (Trans) Genders and (Homo)Sexualities in World History.' *Autrepart: Revue de Sciences Social du Sud*, March, 49: 15–30.

Jackson, Peter A., 2011a. 'Queer Bangkok After the Millennium: Beyond 20th Century Paradigms.' In Peter A. Jackson ed., *Queer Bangkok: 21st Century Markets, Media and Right*. Hong Kong: Hong Kong University Press, pp. 1–14.

Jackson, Peter A., 2011b. 'Bangkok's Early 21st Century Queer Boom.' In Peter A. Jackson ed., *Queer Bangkok: 21st Century Markets, Media and Rights*. Hong Kong: Hong Kong University Press, pp. 17–40.

Jackson, Peter A., 2011c. 'Capitalism, LGBT Activism, and Queer Autonomy in Thailand.' In Peter A. Jackson ed., *Queer Bangkok: 21st Century Markets, Media, and Rights*. Hong Kong: Hong Kong University Press, pp. 195–204.

Jacobsen, Trudy, 2008. *Lost Goddesses: The denial of female power in Cambodian history*. Copenhagen: Nordic Institute of Asian Studies Press.

Jacobsen, Trudy, 2017. 'Misogyny, Malice, and Male Privilege in Cambodia: The Cbpab Srei' [c.1800]. https://www.academia.edu/15042099/Misogyny_Malice_and_Male_Privilege_in_Cambodia_The_Cbpab_Srei_c_1800_.

James, Jamie, 2016. 'Boys in Love.' *The New Yorker*, 8 January. https://www.newyorker.com/culture/culture-desk/boys-in-love. Accessed 22 October 2024.

Japan International Cooperation Agency, 1976. *Tai koku pataya chiku kiban seibi keikaku jizen chōsa* (Preliminary survey [for] Pattaya district, Thailand infrastructure development plan). http://open_jicareport.jica.go.jp/pdf/10502706.pdf. Accessed 21 November 2024.

Japan International Cooperation Agency, 1977. *Tai koku pataya chiku kiban seibi keikaku chōsa hōkokusho* (Survey report [on] Pattaya district, Thailand infrastructure development plan). http://open_jicareport.jica.go.jp/759/759/759_122_10502748.html. Accessed 21 November 2024.

Japan International Cooperation Agency, 2008. *Civil Code of Cambodia*. https://www.jica.go.jp/Resource/project/english/cambodia/0701047/materials/c8h0vm000000zsb2-att/01_02e_1.pdf. Accessed 23 July 2024.

Johnson, Mark, 1997. *Beauty and Power: Transgendering and Cultural Transformation in the Southern Philippines*. Oxford and New York: Berg.

Johnson, Mark, 1998. 'Global Desiring and Translocal Loves: Transgendering and Same-Sex Sexualities in the Southern Philippines.' *American Ethnologist*, 25(4): 695–711.

Jonathan, ed., n.d. *Tam Roi Tamnan Mueang Phatthaya kap Parin'ya Chawalitthamrong: Phu Phalikfuen Phaendin Mueang Phatthaya*. Bangkok: Amarin Printing.

Jones, Cleve, 2016. *When We Rise: My life in the movement*. New York: Hachette Books.

Jowett, Adam, 2016. 'Editorial: LGBTQ Psychology in a Globalised World: Taking a Stand against Homophobia, Transphobia and Biphobia Internationally.' *Psychology of Sexualities Review*, 7(1): 2–9.

Kaihō shinbun, 2018. 'Shōnenba o mukaeta Ribati Osaka no saiban tōsō to jishu unei o shien shiyō (Let's support Liberty Osaka's court battle and independent management at a critical moment).' 9 July.

Kamikawa, Aya, 2016. 'Jichitai ni okeru dōsei pātonāshippu seido no dōnyū: Setagaya-ku ni okeru dōsei pātonāshippu seido no torikumi ni tsuite (Introduction of the same-sex partnership system in local governments: Initiatives for the same-sex partnership system in Setagaya City).' In Masayuki Tanamura and Shigenori Nakagawa eds., *Dōsei pātonāshippu seido: Sekai no dōkō, Nihon no jichitai ni okeru dōnyū no jissai to tenbō* (The same-sex partnership system: World trends and the realities of and outlook for introduction in Japanese local government). Tokyo: Nihon kajo shuppan, pp. 180–209.

Käng, Dredge Byung'chu, 2012. 'Kathoey "In Trend": Emergent Genderscapes, National Anxieties and the Re-Signification of Male-Bodied Effeminacy in Thailand.' *Asian Studies Review*, 36(4): 475–494.

Käng, Dredge Byung'chu, 2014. 'Conceptualizing Thai Genderscapes: Transformation and Continuity in the Thai Sex/Gender System.' In Pranee Liamputtong ed., *Contemporary Socio-Cultural and Political Perspectives in Thailand*. Dordrecht: Springer, pp. 409–429.

Kasinathan, Shathana. 2023. 'PM Anwar says Home Ministry seizure on rainbow swatches "excessive," but defends Malaysia's anti-LGBT stance.' *Malay Mail Online*, 23 September. https://www.malaymail.com/news/malaysia/2023/09/23/pm-anwar-says-home-ministry-seizure-on-rainbow-swatches-excessive-but-defends-malaysias-anti-lgbt-stance/92465. Accessed 24 September 2023.

Katayama, Ichirō, trans., 2005. *Chōbu (Dīganikāya) Pātika hen I* (The collection of long discourses (*Dīgha* Nikāya): *Pāthika* I). Tokyo: Daizō shuppan.

Kawasaka, Kazuyoshi, 2015. '"Jinken" ka "tokken" ka "onkei" ka?: Nihon ni okeru LGBT no kenri ('Human rights?' 'Privileges?' Or 'benefits?': LGBT rights in Japan).' *Gendai shisō* (Review of contemporary thought), 43(16): 86–95.

Kazama, Takashi and Kazuya Kawaguchi, 2010. *Dōseiai to iseiai* (Homosexuality and heterosexuality). Tokyo: Iwanami Shoten.

Keeler, Ward, 2016. 'Shifting Transversals: Trans Women Move from Spirit Mediumship to Beauty Work in Mandalay.' *Ethnos: Journal of Anthropology*, 81(5): 792–820.

Kennedy, Randall, 2002. *Nigger: The Strange Career of a Troublesome Word*. New York: Pantheon.

Kerkvliet, Benedict, 1990. *Everyday Politics in the Philippines: Class and Status Relations in a Central Luzon Village*. Berkeley: University of California Press.

Keur, Dorine Van Der, 2014. 'Legal and Gender Issues of Marriage and Divorce in Cambodia.' *The Cambodia Law and Policy Journal*. 3. https://www.cambodialpj.org/article/legal-and-gender-issues-of-marriage-and-divorce-in-cambodia/ Accessed 21 November 2024.

Khmer Times, 2022. 'Cambodian LGBT film "Hello Neighbor" receives rapturous response at premiere.' 24 August. https://www.khmertimeskh.com/501138086/cambodian-lgbt-film-hello-neighbor-receives-rapturous-response-at-premiere/. Accessed 3 December 2023.

Khmer Times, 2023. 'Minister confirms investigation into "discriminatory" remarks by Cambodia Got Talent judge against LGBT+ competitor LGBT+ community in Cambodia.' 31 October. https://www.khmertimeskh.com/501384501/minister-confirms-investigation-into-discriminatory-remarks-by-cambodia-got-talent-judge-against-lgbt-competitor-lgbt-community-in-cambodia/. Accessed 3 December 2023.

Khng, Russell Heng Hiang, 2001. 'Tiptoe Out of the Closet: The Before and After of the Increasingly Visible Gay Community in Singapore.' *Journal of Homosexuality*, 40(3/4): 82–83.

Khor, Diana, Denise Tse-Shang Tang and Saori Kamano, 2020. 'Global Norms, State Regulations, and Local Activism: Marriage Equality and Same-Sex Partnership, Sexual Orientation, and Gender Identity Rights in Japan and Hong Kong.' In Michael J. Bosia, Sandra M. McEvoy and Momin Rahman eds., *The Oxford Handbook of Global LGBT and Sexual Diversity Politics*. Oxford: Oxford University Press.

Kim Anh, 2018. 'LGBT community in Vietnam's path to recognition.' *Vietnam plus*, 14 May. https://en.vietnamplus.vn/lgbt-community-in-vietnams-path-to-recognition/131049.vnp. Accessed 5 December 2024.

Kim, Nami, 2016. *The Gendered Politics of the Korean Protestant Right*. Cham, Switzerland: Palgrave Macmillan.

Kim Thanh, 2013. 'Sửa đổi Luật Hôn nhân và gia đình: Hạ độ tuổi kết hôn (Amending the Marriage and Family Law: Lowering the age of marriage).' *Hà Nội Mới*, 7 November. https://hanoimoi.com.vn/tin-tuc/Chinh-tri/637740/-sua-doi-luat-hon-nhan-va-gia-dinh-ha-do-tuoi-ket-hon-352076.html. Accessed 5 December 2024.

Kimura, Kōichi, 2004. *Indoneshia kyōkai no senkyō to shingaku* (The mission and theology of the Indonesian church). Tokyo: Shinkyō Shuppansha.

Kohama, Masako, 2023. 'Jendā no shiten kara mita rekishi (Higashi Ajia) (History from the perspective of gender (Southeast Asia)).' In Jendā jiten henshu iinkai (Editorial committee of dictionary of gender) ed., *Jendā jiten* (Dictionary of gender). Tokyo: Maruzen Shuppan, pp. 26–27.

Komori, Yoichi, 2003. *Kenkyuu suru imi* (The meaning of research). Tokyo: Tokyo Tosho.

Kudō, Marie, 2018. '"Shingaku towa kuia na mono"? Erizabesu Schuāto no "kuia shingaku" rikai no hihanteki kōsatsu ('Theology is a Queer Thing'? A Critical Study of Elizabeth Stuart's 'Queer Theology').' *Nihon no shingaku* (Japanese Theology), 57: 26–48.

Kugle, Scott Siraj al-Haqq, 2014. *Living Out Islam: Voices of Gay, Lesbian, and Transgender Muslims*. New York and London: New York University Press.

Kumamoto, Risa, 2020. *Hisabetsu buraku josei no shutaisei keisei ni kansuru kenkyū* (Study on the subjectivity formation of women from discriminated-against *buraku*). Osaka: Kaihō Shuppansha (Liberation Press).

Kunthear, Mom and Justice Drennan, 2013. 'Laws can't stop lovers marrying.' *The Phnom Penh Post*, 20 May. https:// www.phnompenhpost.com/national/laws-can%E2%80%99t-stop-lovers-marrying. Accessed 3 December 2023.

Kuong, Teilee, 2016. 'Development of Legal Norms on Marriage and Divorce in Cambodia: The Civil Code Between Foreign Inputs and Local Growth (I).' *Nagoya University Asian Law Bulletin*, 1: 69–81.

Kwankaew, Udomboonyanuparp, 2003. *Kamnoet lae Kankhayaitua khong Mueang Phatthaya* (The origin and expansion of Pattaya). M.A. Thesis. Chulalongkorn University.

Kymlicka, Will, 2002. *Contemporary Political Philosophy: An Introduction* 2nd edition. Oxford: Oxford University Press.

Lan Anh, 2013. Bộ Y tế ủng hộ kết hôn đồng tính (The Ministry of Health supports same-sex marriage). *Tuổi trẻ*, 15 April. https://tuoitre.vn/bo-y-te-ung-ho-ket-hon-dong-tinh-543174.htm. Accessed 5 December 2024.

Lawi Weng, 2012. 'Rohingya Refuse to Register as "Bengali".' *The Irrawaddy*, 13 November. https://www.irrawaddy.com/news/burma/rohingya-refuse-to-register-as-bengali.html. Accessed 22 October 2024).

Leap, William, and Tom Boellstorff, eds., 2004. *Speaking in Queer Tongues: Gay Language and Globalization*. Urbana: University of Illinois Press.

LeDoan, 2017. 'Tình yêu đồng tính: "Yêu đàn ông khổ thế đấy" (Homosexual love: 'Loving men is so hard').' *Việt nam Mới*, 7 July. https://vietnammoi.vn/tinh-yeu-dong-tinh-yeu-dan-ong-kho-the-day-39293.htm. Accessed 5 December 2024.

Lee, Anri, 2022. 'Zainichi Chōsenjin josei ni totte no kōsasei/fukugō sabetsu o kangaeru koto (Considering intersectionality and compound discrimination for Japan-residing Korean women).' *Buraku kaihō: tokushū. Kōsasei/fukugō sabetsu* (*Buraku* liberation: Special issue on intersectionality and compound discrimination), 830: 37–47.

Lee, Hsien Loong, 2007. 'Full parliamentary speech by PM Lee Hsien Loong in 2007 on Section 377A.' *The Straits Times*, 24 October. https://www.straitstimes.com/politics/full-parliamentary-speech-by-pm-lee-hsien-loong-in-2007-on-section-377a. Accessed 24 November 2024.

Lee, Regina Marie, 2016. 'Traditional values' wear white campaign returning on Pink Dot weekend.' *Today*, 23 May. https://www.todayonline.com/singapore/network-churches-revives-campaign-wear-white-pink-dot-weekend. Accessed 24 November 2024.

Lee, Yu-hsi, 2013. 'Taiwan no daigaku katei ni okeru jendā hōgaku kyōiku no jissen to mondai ten (Practices and problems in gender law education in Taiwan's university courses).' Trans. by Fumiko Sugimoto. *Ritsumeikan hōgaku* (Ritsumeikan Law Review), 2: 291–317.

Legislative Yuan, 1994. *Lifa yuan di 2 jie di 3 huiqi di 4 ci huiyi yi'an guanxi wenshu* (Documents relating to motions in the 4th meeting of the 3rd session of the 2nd legislative term of the Legislative Yuan). Legislative Yuan, Republic of China (Taiwan).

Legislative Yuan, 2004. *Lifa yuan gongbao* (Legislative yuan bulletin), Vol. 93, 33rd term.

Legislative Yuan, 2009. *Lifa yuan di 7 jie di 4 huiqi di 6 ci huiyi yian guanxi wenshu* (Documents relating to motions in the 6th meeting of the 4th session of the 7th legislative term of the Legislative Yuan). Legislative Yuan, Republic of China (Taiwan).

Lembaran Negara Republik Indonesia, 2017. Peraturan Pemerintah Pengganti Undang-undang Republik Indonesia Nomor 2 Tahun 2017 tentang Perubahan atas undang-undang nomor 17 tahun 2013 tentang organisasi kemasyarakatan (Amendment-by-decree of Law No.17/2013 on Mass Organisations: Undang-undang Organisasi Kemayarakatan/UU Ormas).

LGBT Hou Rengou-kai (LGBT Law Coalition) ed. 2019. *Nihon to sekai no LGBT no kadai* (Agenda of LGBT in Japan and around the world). Kyoto: Kamogawa Publishing.

LGBT shien hōritsuka nettowāku, ed., 2016. *Sekushuaru mainoritīzu Q&A* (Q&A on sexual minorities). Tokyo: Koubundou.

Liebermann, Jeffrey A., 2018. *Shurinkusu: daremo shiranakatta seishin igaku no shinjitsu* (Shrinks: The untold story of psychiatry). Trans. by Keiko Yanagisawa and Seiya Miyamoto. Tokyo: Kongō Shuppan.

Lin, Fang-Mei, 1998. 'Dangdai Taiwan fuyun de rentong zhengzhi: yi gongchang cunfei zhengyi wei li (Identity politics and the women's movement in Taiwan: The example of the dispute over retention or abolition of public prostitution).' *Zhongwai Wenxue* (Chungwai literary quarterly), 27(1): 56–87.

Lister, Ruth, 2002. 'Sexual Citizenship.' In F. Isin Engin and Bryan S. Turner eds., *Handbook of Citizenship Studies*. London: Sage.

Listiorini, Dina, 2020. 'Online Hate Speech.' *Inside Indonesia* 139. https://www.insideindonesia.org/online-hate-speech.

Loh, Chee Kong, 2011. 'The Role of the Media: Investigative Journalism in Singapore.' In Terence Chong ed., *The AWARE Saga: Civil Society and Public Morality in Singapore*. Singapore: NUS Press.

Luther, J. Daniel and Jennifer Ung Loh, eds., 2019. *Queer Asia: Decolonising and Reimagining Sexuality and Gender*. London: Zed books.

Lyttleton, Chris, 2008. *Mekong Erotics: Men loving/pleasuring/using men in Lao PDR*. Bangkok: UNESCO Bangkok.

MACSA, 2019. 'Numan must apologise, retract baseless claim on state sponsored violence against LGBTs.' *CENTHRA*, 17 April. https://macsa.com.my/numan-must-apologise-retract-baseless-claim-on-state-sponsored-violence-against-lgbts/. Accessed 21 November 2024.

Madrigal-Borloz, Victor, 2023. 'End of Mission Statement: Visit of the IE SOGI to the Kingdom of Cambodia (January 10–20, 2023).' United Nations. https://www.ohchr.org/sites/default/files/documents/issues/sexualorientation/cfi-visitcambodia/2023-01-19/Cambodia-End-of-mission-statement_IE-SOGI-20Jan2023-EN.docx.

Mahathir, Mohamad, 2018. 'Pendirian Kerajaan Berkaitan Hukuman Sebat.' Facebook Page by Dr. Mahathir bin Mohamad, 6 September. https://www.facebook.com/TunDrMahathir/videos/252306302092283/. Accessed 31 August 2019.

Mahathir, Mohamad, and Shintarō Ishihara, 1994. *"No" to ieru Ajia* (The Asia that can say "no"). Tokyo: Kōbunsha.

Mainichi Shimbun, 2018. 'Sei-teki shoususha: LGBT shuzai "chishiki busoku" kadai o shiteki (Sexual minorities: Problems of LGBT coverage as "insufficient knowledge").' 16 May. https://mainichi.jp/articles/20180515/k00/00m/040/033000c. Accessed 3 March 2024.

Majelis Ulama Indonesia (MUI), 1997. 'Kedudukan Waria (Transgender's position).' *muidigital* http://www.mui.or.id/public/index.php/baca/fatwa/kedudukan-waria. Accessed 17 January 2025.

Makkelo, Ilham Daeng, 2010. *Kota Seribu Gereja: Dinamika Keagamaan dan Penggunaan Ruang di Kota Manado* (The city of a thousand churches: Religious dynamics and space use in the city of Manado). Yogyakarta: Ombak.

Malay Mail Online, 2014. 'Jawi claims rehabilitated almost 2,000 LGBTs into "normal" Muslims.' 12 November. https://www.malaymail.com/news/malaysia/2014/11/12/jawi-claims-rehabilitated-almost-2000-lgbts-into-normal-muslims/781517. Accessed 15 January 2015.

Malaysiakini, 2019. 'Defending LGBTs at Women's March an abuse of democracy-Mujahid.' 9 March. https://www.malaysiakini.com/news/467258. Accessed 15 January 2015.

Manafe, Imanuel Nicolas, 2016. 'Majelis Agama-agama Indonesia Tolak Legalisasi LGBT (Indonesia religious council rejects LGBT legalization).' *Tribunnews.com*, 18 February. www.tribunnews.com/nasional/2016/02/18/majelis-agama-agama-indonesia-tolak-legalisasi-lgbt. Accessed 21 November 2024.

Manalansan IV, Martin F. 2003. *Global Divas: Filipino Gay Men in the Diaspora*. Durham: Duke University Press.

Mann, Susan L., 2015, *Sei kara yomu Chūgoku shi: Danjo kakuri, tensoku, dōseiai* (Chinese history read from sexuality: Segregation of the sexes, foot-binding, and homosexuality). Trans. by Masako Kohama. Tokyo: Heibonsha.

Martel, Frédéric, 2018. *Global Gay: How gay culture is changing the world*. Cambridge: MIT Press.

Martin, Fran, Peter Jackson, Mark McLelland, Audrey Yue, eds., 2010. *AsiaPacifiQueer: Rethinking Genders and Sexualities*. Urbana: University of Illinois Press.

Masaad, Joseph, 2007. *Desiring Arabs*. Chicago: Chicago University Press.

Masaki, Chitose, 2015. 'Haijo to bōkyaku ni sasaerareta gurotesuku na sekentei seiji toshite no Beikoku shuryū "LGBT undō" to dōseikon suishin undō no giman (The US mainstream 'LGBT movement' as a grotesque politics of respectability supported by exclusion and oblivion, and the deception of the movement for same-sex marriage).' *Gendai shisō* (Review of contemporary thought), 43(16): 75–85.

Mastercard, 2018. 'Big Cities, Big Business: Bangkok, London and Paris lead the way in Mastercard's 2018 Global Destination Cities Index.' https://www.mastercard. com/news/press/2018/big-cities-big-business-bangkok-london-and-paris-lead-the-way-in-mastercard-s-2018-global-destination-cities-index/ Accessed 21 November 2024.

McLelland, Mark, 2006. 'A short history of "hentai".' *Intersections: Gender, history and culture in the Asian context*, 12: 1–9.

McLelland, Mark, 2009. 'The role of the "*tōjisha*" in current debates about sexual minority rights in Japan.' *Japanese Studies*, 29(2): 193–207.

McLelland, Mark, Katsuhiko Suganuma and James Welker, eds., 2007. *Queer Voices from Japan: First person narratives from Japan's sexual minorities*. Lanham: Lexington Books.

Media Development Authority, n.d. 'Free-to-Air Television Program Code.' http:// seatca.org/dmdocuments/Singapore%20-%20Free-to-Air%20TV%20Code%20 -%20national.pdf. Accessed 30 August 2017.

Medina, Belen T. G., 2015. *The Filipino Family* (3rd Edition). Quezon City: University of the Philippines Press.

Merdeka, 2016. 'Menkes sebut LGBT adalah masalah kejiwaan dan sumber penyakit (Minister of Health declares LGBT a mental health issue and source of illness).' 22 February. www.merdeka.com/peristiwa/menkes-sebut-lgbt-adalah-masalah-kejiwaan-dan-sumber-penyakit.html. Accessed 21 November 2024.

Meta, Kong and Leonie Kijewski, 2017. 'Rules allowing censorship of depictions of homosexuality criticised.' *The Phnom Penh Post*, 9 May. https://www. phnompenhpost.com/national/rules-allowing-censorship-depictions-homosexuality-criticised. Accessed 3 December 2023.

Millett, Kate, 2000. *Sexual Politics*, 1st paperback ed.. Urbana and Chicago: University of Illinois Press.

Ministry of Education, Taiwan, 2001. '*Liangxing pingdeng jiaoyu fa* cao'*an' yanni jihua qimo baogao* (Final report on research and development of the 'Draft Act on Both-Sexes Equal Education' project).

Mitsuhashi, Junko, 2015. 'LGBT to iu kotoba no kigen ni tsuite (On the origins of the term 'LGBT').' *Tasogare Nikki* (Twilight diary). https://junko-mitsuhashi.blog. ss-blog.jp/2015-04-04-1. Accessed 3 March 2024.

Mitsuhashi, Junko, 2022. *Rekishi no naka no tayō na "sei": Nihon to ajia; hengen suru sekushuariti* (Diverse sexes/genders in history: Japan and Asia; protean sexualities). Tokyo: Iwanami Shoten.

Mitsunari, Miho, 2015. *Dōseiai wo meguru rekishi to hou: songen to shiteno sekushuariti* (The history and law on same-sex love: Sexuality as dignity). Tokyo: Akashi Shoten.

Miyawaki, Satoshi, 2019. *Firipin katorikku kyōkai no seiji kan'yo* (The political involvement of the Philippine Catholic Church). Osaka: Osaka University Press.

Morledge, William R., 2008. 'Grand Prix: Revisiting an Historic Bangkok Bar.' http:// www.bangkokeyes.com/2008nov01.html. Accessed 21 November 2024.

Morris, Rosalind C., 1994. 'Three Sexes and Four Sexualities: Redressing the Discourses on Gender and Sexuality in Contemporary Thailand.' *positions*, 2(1): 15–43.

Muc Tim, 2008. 'Điểm cộng và điểm trừ cho 9X (Pros and Cons for 9X).' *VTC News*, 23 May. https://web.archive.org/web/20080526005212/http://vtc.vn/gioitre/ phongcachtre/180658/index.htm. Accessed 6 December 2024.

Mucciaroni, Gary, 2008. *Same Sex, Different Politics: Success and Failure in the Struggles over Gay Rights*. Chicago: University of Chicago Press.

Muhammad, Husein, Siti Musdah Mulia and Marzuki Wahid, 2011. *Fiqh Seksualitas: Risalah Islam untuk Pemenuhan Hak-Hak Seksualitas* (Fiqh of Sexuality: An Islamic treatise for the fulfillment of sexuality rights). Yogyakarta: PKBI.

Murtagh, Ben, 2013. *Genders and Sexualities in Indonesian Cinema: Constructing gay, lesbi and waria identities on screen*. London: Routledge.

Muthmainnah, Yulianti, 2016. 'LGBT Human Rights in Indonesian Policies.' *Indonesian Feminist Journal*, 4(1): 13–29.

MyJobs Myanmar, 2018. *Myanmar Candidates Salary Survey 2018*. https://www. ccifrance-myanmar.org/sites/ccifrance-myanmar.org/files/resources-documents/ myjobs_myanmar_candidates_salary_survey_june_2018.pdf. Accessed 21 November 2024.

Nagayasu, Shibun, 2017. 'Jiten/jiten no henken kijyutu wo teiseishiteitta jidai (When we corrected the biased entries in dictionaries),' https://www.yomiuri.co.jp/ yomidr/article/20170222-OYTET50022/. Accessed 8 December 2024.

Nakagawa, Shigenori, 2016. 'Jichitai ni okeru dōsei pātonāshippu seido no dōnyū: Dōsei pātonāshippu seido no kongo no kadai (Introduction of the same-sex partnership system in local governments: Future issues for the same-sex partnership system).' In Masayuki Tanamura and Shigenori Nakagawa eds., *Dōsei pātonāshippu seido: Sekai no dōkō, Nihon no jichitai ni okeru dōnyū no jissai to tenbō* (The same-sex partnership system: World trends and the realities of and outlook for introduction in Japanese local government). Tokyo: Nihon kajo shuppan, pp. 210–229.

Nakamura, Usagi, 2003. 'Kotoba ga naku temo watashi wa sonzai suru (Even without words, I exist).' In Noriaki Fushimi, ed., *Hentai (Queer) Nyumon* (Introduction to Queer). Tokyo: Chikuma Shobo, pp. 314–318.

Nambiar, Predeep. 2018. 'Caci LGBT tak bantu usaha pemulihan, kata Jakim.' *Free Malaysia Today*, 29 October. https://www.freemalaysiatoday.com/category/bahasa/2018/10/29/caci-lgbt-tak-bantu-usaha-pemulihan-kata-jakim/. Accessed 31 August 2019.

Nandamālābiwuntha, 2011. *Thawtapan I Bawayokponhlwa* (The form of being of the sotāpan). Yangon: Apyibyi hsainya Hteirawada Bokda Thathanapyu Tekkatho.

Narupon Duangwises and Peter A. Jackson, 2021a. 'A Homoerotic History of Bangkok's Gay Middle Class: Thai Gay Bars and Magazines in the 1980s and 1990s.' *Journal of the Siam Society*, 109(2): 59–77.

Narupon Duangwises and Peter A. Jackson, 2021b. 'Effeminacy and Masculinity in Thai Gay Culture: Language, Contextuality and the Enactment of Gender Plurality.' *Walailak Journal of Social Science*, 4(5): 1–23.

Narupon Duangwises and Peter A. Jackson, 2023. 'Evolving Thai Homoeroticism: Male Nudity and Multiple Masculinities in Gay Magazines Since the 1980s-2010s.' *Asia Social Issues* (Walailak University), 16(2): 1–24.

National AIDS Program, 2014. 'Global AIDS Response Progress Report: Myanmar.' https://www.unaids.org/sites/default/files/country/documents/MMR_narrative_report_2014.pdf. Accessed 14 November 2020.

National Institute of Statistics, 2021. *Statistical Yearbook of Cambodia 2021*. Ministry of Planning. https://www.nis.gov.kh/nis/yearbooks/StatisticalYearbookofCambodia 2021.pdf. Accessed 21 November 2024.

Nattapol Wisuttipat, 2022, *Spicy: Gendered Practices of Queer Men in Thai Classical String Music*. PhD Thesis. University of California, Riverside.

Nautical Inn, 2011. 'Information.' http://www.nauticalinn.co.th/home/index.php?option =com_content&view=article&id=1&Itemid=3&lang=en. Accessed 21 November 2024.

Ng, Yi-Sheng, 2006. *SD21: Singapore Queers in the 21st Century*. Singapore: Ooga-chaga Support Group.

Nguyen Thi Hoai, Chau, 2013. 'Gendai Betonamu toshibu no fukei shinzoku shūdan ni okeru josei yakuwari no hen'yō: Jukyō kihan to no kankei kara (Women's changing roles in patrilineal kin groups in urban Vietnam: From the connection with Confucian norms).' *Okayama daigaku daigakuin shakai bunka kagaku kenkyū kiyō* (Journal of humanities and social sciences, Okayama University), 36: 149–168.

NHK, 2015. 'LGBT tōjisha ankēto chousa: 2600-nin no koe kara (Survey on LGBT people: From the voices of 2,600 people).' NHK, https://www.nhk.or.jp/d-navi/link/lgbt/. Accessed 3 March 2024.

'Nihon ni okeru kuia sutadīzu no kōchiku' kenkyū gurūpu ('Construction of Queer Studies in Japan' Research Group), ed., 2017, *Survey of Policies Related to Sexual Orientation and Gender Identity in Local Governments Nationwide (conducted from April to July 2016) Report*. Japan Society for the Promotion of Science (JSPS) Grants-in-Aid for Scientific Research, adopted research themes for fiscal years 2013-2016 (Grant-in-Aid for Scientific Research (B) No. 25283018 'Construction of Queer Studies in Japan').

Nikkei Business, 2007. 'Kyodai shijō "LGBT" to wa (The Huge 'LGBT' Market).' 26 February.

Nimol, Seoung, 2013. 'PM says no need for legalized same sex marriage, but LGBTQ+ community says otherwise.' *CamboJa News*, 13 July. https://cambojanews.com/pm-says-no-need-for-legalized-same-sex-marriage-but-lgbtq-community-says-otherwise/. Accessed 21 November 2024.

Ning Yin-Bin, 2018. 'Fenshi yu tongxinglian minzu zhuyi zhi hou: yiyi zhiyi yixia de zhishi shengchan (Pinkwashing, homonationalism and the politics of colored people knowledge-production).' *Taiwan: A Radical Quarterly in Social Studies*, 111: 231–248.

Ninomiya, Shūhei, 2019. *Kazoku hō* (Family law), 5th Edition. Tokyo: Shinseisha.

Ninomiya, Shūhei, ed., 2017. *Sei no arikata no tayōsei: hitori hitori no sekushuariti ga taisetsu ni sareru shakai o mezashite* (Diversity in sexuality: Aiming for a society where each individual's sexuality is cherished). Tokyo: Nippon hyōron sha.

Norton, Barley, 2006. '"Effeminate" Men and "Hot-Tempered" Women: The Performance of Music and Gender in Vietnamese Mediumship.' In Karen Fjelstad and Nguyen Thi Hien, eds, *Possessed by the Spirits: Mediumship in Contemporary Vietnamese Communities*. Ithaca, NY: Cornell University Press, pp. 55–75.

Nursyahbani Katjasungkana and Saskia E. Wieringa, 2016. *Kriminalisasi Merayap: Pemetaan Undang-undang Nasional serta Peraturan Daerah di Indonesia yang Melanggar Hak Asasi Perempuan dan Kelompok LGBTIQ* (Encroaching criminalization: Mapping national laws and regional regulations in Indonesia that violate the human rights of women and LGBTIQ groups). New York: Outright Action International.

Oetomo, Dede and Khanis Suvianita, 2016. *Hidup Sebagai LGBT di Asia: Laporan Nasional Indonesia: Tinjauan dan Analisa Partisipatif tentang Lingkungan Hukum dan Sosial bagi Orang dan Masyarakat Madani Lesbian, Gay, Biseksual dan Transgender (LGBT)*. (Living as LGBT in Asia: Indonesia National Report: Participatory review and analysis of the legal and social environment for lesbian, gay, bisexual, and transgender (LGBT) individuals and civil society). USAID and UNDP.

Oetomo, Dede, 2001. *Memberi Suara pada Yang Bisu* (Give a voice to the voiceless). Yogyakarta: Galang Press.

Offord, Baden, 2011. 'Arrested Development! Singapore, Indonesia and Malaysia.' In Manon Tremblay, David Paternotte and Carol Johnson, eds., *The Lesbian and Gay Movement and the State: Comparative Insights into a Transformed Relationship*. London: Ashgate Publishing.

Offord, Baden, 2013. 'Queer Activist Intersections in Southeast Asia: Human Rights and Cultural Studies.' *Asian Studies Review*, 37(3): 335–349.

Ōgata, Satomi, 2019, 'Indoneshia ni okeru LGBT undō o torimaku jōkyō: LGBT undō no tenkai to kinnen no tairitsu no kōzu (The circumstances surrounding the LGBT movement in Indonesia: The development of the LGBT movement and the structure of conflict in recent years).' *Kyūshū kokusai daigaku kokusai/Keizai ronshū* (KIU journal of economics and international studies), 3: 47–78.

Oh, Su-Ann, 2012. *Rohingya or Bengali? Revisiting the politics of labelling*. Institute of Southeast Asian Studies. https://www.iseas.edu.sg/articles-commentaries/iseas-perspective/iseas-perspective-2012/201219-rohingya-or-bengali-revisiting-the-politics-of-labelling/ Accessed 17 January 2025.

Ōizumi, Sayaka, 2019, 'Betonamu ni okeru mukei bunkaisan toshiteno seuboshinkō no hogo to kanri (Protection and management of the Virgin Faith as intangible cultural heritage in Vietnam).' *Tōnan ajia kenkyū* (Journal of Southeast Asian studies), 52(2): 235–266.

Okamoto, Masaaki, 2016a. '"Indoneshia" ni okeru LGBT undō no kasseika kara moraru panikku e (From activation of the LGBT movement to moral panic in Indonesia).' *Indoneshia nyūsuretā* (Indonesia newsletter), 92: 19–36.

Okamoto, Masaaki, 2016b. 'Minshuka shita Indoneshia ni okeru toransujendā no soshikika to seijika: Sono pojitibu na paradokkusu (The systematization and politicization of transgender in democratized Indonesia: Its positive paradox).' *Isurāmu sekai kenkyū* (Kyoto bulletin of Islamic area studies), 9: 231–251.

Okamoto, Masaaki. 2021. 'Han LGBT Undōka suru Indoneshia no seishin-igaku (Psychiatry in the anti-LGBT movement in Indonesia).' In Wataru Kusaka, Tsukasa Iga, Kaoru Aoyama and Keiko Tamura, eds., *Tōnan Ajia to 'LGBT' no seiji* (Southeast Asia and 'LGBT' politics). Tokyo: Akashi Shoten, pp. 86–110.

Okano, Yayo, 2015. 'Byōdō to famirī o motomete: Kea no rinri kara dōseikon o meguru giron o furikaeru (Seeking equality and family: Reflecting on the debate around same-sex marriage from an ethic of care).' *Gendai shisō* (Review of contemporary thought), 43(16): 60–71.

Oosterhoff, Pauline, Tu-Anh Hoang and Trang Thu Quach, 2014. 'Negotiating Public and Legal Spaces: The Emergence of an LGBT Movement in Vietnam.' *IDS Evidence Report 74*. Brighton: Institute of Development Studies. https://www.ids.ac.uk/publications/negotiating-public-and-legal-spaces-the-emergence-of-an-lgbt-movement-in-vietnam/ Accessed 21 November 2024.

Osa, Shizue, 2023. 'Jendā no shiten kara mita rekishi (Nihon) (History from the perspective of gender (Japan)).' In Jendā jiten henshu iinkai (Editorial committee of dictionary of gender) ed. *Jendā jiten* (Dictionary of gender). Tokyo: Maruzen Shuppan, pp. 22–23.

Pakatan Harapan, 2018. *Buku Harapan: Membina Negara Memenuhi Harapan.* (Book of Hope: Building the nation, fulfilling hopes) Pakatan Harapan.

Palansamy, Yiswaree, 2018. 'Don't let "extreme ideas" of LGBT dictate Malaysian life, Mujahid warns.' *Malay Mail Online*, 8 October. https://www.malaymail.com/news/malaysia/2018/10/08/dont-let-extreme-lgbt-dictate-malaysian-life-muhajid-warns/1680470. Accessed 31 August 2019.

Pang, Khee Teik, 2018. 'Political Suicide vs LGBT Suicide.' *Queer Lapis*, 18 August. https://www.queerlapis.com/poltical-suicide-vs-lgbt-suicide/. Accessed 31 August 2019.

Panjimas, 2017. 'Ulama Pewaris Nabi, Gerakan Indonesia Beradab: Hentikan Proses Hukum terhadap Ulama (Islamic scholars are the heirs of the Prophet, says the Civilized Indonesia Movement: Stop the legal process against the Islamic scholars).' 22 February. www.panjimas.com/news/2017/02/22/ulama-pewaris-nabi-gerakan-indonesia-beradab-hentikan-proses-hukum-terhadap-ulama/ Accessed 21 November 2024.

Pattaya Blatt, 2003a. 'Das Pattaya Palace Hotel erwacht zu neuem Leben.' http://www.pattayablatt.com/060/Feuilleton.shtml. Accessed 21 November 2024.

Pattaya Blatt, 2003b. 'Die Legende des Pattaya Palace Hotel.' http://www.pattayablatt.com/060/Feuilleton.shtml. Accessed 21 November 2024.

Pattaya Mail, 1998a. 'Another Pattaya icon passes on.' http://www.pattayamail.com/304/continue.htm. Accessed 21 November 2024.

Pattaya Mail, 1998b. 'BJ Bar – the end of an era.' http://www.pattayamail.com/295/features.htm. Accessed 21 November 2024.

Pattaya Mail, 2017. 'Royal Varuna Yacht Club celebrates 60 years of sailing history and tradition.' http://www.pattayamail.com/ourcommunity/royal-varuna-yacht-club-celebrates-60-years-sailing-history-tradition-193390. Accessed 21 November 2024.

Pattaya Mail, 2019. 'June events commemorate U.S. military's discovery of Pattaya.' https://www.pattayamail.com/news/june-events-commemorate-u-s-militarys-discovery-of-pattaya-251032. Accessed 21 November 2024.

Pattayaone, (n.d.). Selection. http://www.pattayaone.com/thepattayabeachresort.html. Accessed 21 November 2024.

Pearce, Ruth, Sonja Erikainen and Ben Vincent, 2020. 'TERF wars: An introduction.' In Ruth Pearce, Sonja Erikainen and Ben Vincent, eds., *TERF Wars: Feminism and the fight for transgender future*. London: Sage, pp. 4–24.

Peh, Shing Huei, 2007. 'Petition to repeal gay sex law sparks heated debate.' *The Straits Times,* 23 October:3.

Peletz, Michael G., 2006. 'Transgenderism and Gender Pluralism in Southeast Asia since Early Modern Times.' *Current Anthropology*, 47(2): 309–340.

Peletz, Michael G., 2009. *Gender Pluralism: Southeast Asia Since Early Modern Times*. New York and Oxon: Routledge.

Perempuan Berpendidikan Teologi di Indonesia, 2015. *Anggaran Dasar* (Constitution). Perempuan Berpendidikan Teologi di Indonesia.

Perhimpunan Dokter Spesialis Kedokteran Jiwa Indonesia (PDSKJI), 2016. *Pernyataan Sikap Pengurus Pusat Perhimpunan Dokter Spesialis Kedokteran Jiwa Indonesia*. (Statement of Position by the Central Board of the Indonesian Association of Psychiatric Specialists), 21 February. https://www.facebook.com/PBIkatanDokterIndonesia

Perreau, Bruno, 2016. *Queer Theory: The French Response*. Stanford: Stanford University Press.

Persekutuan Gereja-gereja di Indonesia, 2016. *Pernyataan Pastoral PGI tentang LGBT* (PGI Pastoral Statement on LGBT) (No. 360/PGI-XVI/2016). https://pgi.or.id/weblama/pernyataan-pastoral-tentang-lgbt/. Accessed 18 December 2024.

Pew Research Center, 2013. *The Global Divide on Homosexuality: Gender Acceptance in More Secular and Affluent Countries. Pew Research Center Report*. Washington, DC: Pew Research Center. www.pewglobal.org/2013/06/04/the-global-divide-on-homosexuality/. Accessed 21 November 2024.

Pew Research Center, 2023. 'Across Asia, views of same-sex marriage vary widely.' 27 November. https://www.pewresearch.org/short-reads/2023/11/27/across-asia-views-of-same-sex-marriage-vary-widely/. Accessed 30 November 2023.

Phạm, Quỳnh Phương, 2022. 'From "Social Evils" to "Human Beings": Vietnam's LGBT Movement and the Politics of Recognition.' *Journal of Current Southeast Asian Affairs*, 41(3), 422–439.

Phan, Hong Nhung, 2018. 'Rainbow flag movements make inroads in Vietnam.' *Vietnam plus*, 15 May. https://en.vietnamplus.vn/rainbow-flag-movements-make-inroads-in-vietnam-post131088.vnp. Accessed 5 December 2024.

Philippine LGBT Hate Crimes Watch, 2012. Press Release: Manila LGBT Groups Celebrate IDAHO 2012. 13 May. http://thephilippineLGBThatecrimewatch.blogspot.com/2012/05/press-statement-manila-LGBT-groups.html Accessed 10 December 2020.

Phinney, Harriet M., 2008. 'Objects of Affection: Vietnamese Discourses on Love and Emancipation.' *Positions: East Asia Cultures. Critique*, 16(2): 329–358.

Phước Hiệp, 2013. 'Thu hồi quyết định xác định lại giới tính (Revocation of gender reassignment decision).' *Thanh niên*, 22 January. https://thanhnien.vn/thoi-su/thu-hoi-quyet-dinh-xac-dinh-lai-gioi-tinh-477444.html. Accessed 5 December 2024.

Pillay, Suzanna, 2018. 'Mujahid: Meeting with Nisha Ayub does not imply support for LGBT culture.' *New Straits Times*, 11 August.

Pink Dot, 2016. 'Featured News' https://pinkdot.sg. Accessed 24 November 2024.

Pink Dot, 2017. 'Pink Dot 2017 official statement.' https://pinkdot.sg/2017/07/pink-dot-2017-official-statement/. Accessed 24 November 2024.

Poh, Lan, 2014. 'Proposed law to better protect, support families.' *The Straits Times,* 9 July. https://www.straitstimes.com/singapore/proposed-law-to-better-protect-support-families. Accessed 24 November 2024.

Poushter, Jacob and Nicholas Kent, 2020. 'The Global Divide on Homosexuality Persists.' *Pew Research Center.* https://www.pewresearch.org/global/2020/06/25/global-divide-on-homosexuality-persists/.

Presto, Athena Charanne R., 2020. 'Revisiting Intersectional Identities: Voices of Poor Bakla Youth in Rural Philippines.' *Review of Women's Studies*, 29(2): 113–146.

Pride, 2014. Matthew Warchus (director). Pathé, 20th Century Studios, CBS Films.

Proud To Be Us Laos. 2020. 'On the occasion of the 100th birthday anniversary of President Kaysone Phomvihane.' Facebook page by Proud To Be Us Laos, December 13. https://www.facebook.com/proudtobeuslaos/posts/pfbid02rHwMiT jGmfSCdCkiZoCx3Foekp2sQ4xiT6eViJoeJNXS5NRfgLkx2QicFYwAWyY9l. Accessed 24 December 2019.

Puar, Jasbir, 2007. *Terrorist Assemblages: Homonationalism in Queer Times.* Durham: Duke University.

Pyidaunzu Thanmada Myanmar Naingngandaw, 2017. *Lunge Yeiya Muwada* (Youth Policy). Myanmar government.

Quintos, Jomar Jay, 2012. 'A Glimpse into the Asog Experience: A historical study on the homosexual experience in the Philippines.' Trans. by Philip Y. Kimpo Jr.. *Plaridel* 9(2): 155–170.

Reid, Anthony, 2014. 'Patriarchy and Puritanism in Southeast Asia Modernity.' *DORISEA Working Paper Series,* No. 8. Göttingen: DORISEA.

Reid, Anthony, 2015. *A History of Southeast Asia: Critical Crossroad.* Chichester: John Wiley & Sons.

Reja Irfa Widodo, 2016. 'Klasifikasi Pedoman Gangguan Kejiwaan Sedang dalam Proses Revisi (Classification of mental disorders guideline under revision).' *Republika*, 24 March. republika.co.id/berita/o4if9k368/klasifikasi-pedoman-gangguan-kejiwaan-sedang-dalam-proses-revisi.

RFA Burmese, 2022. 'Mandalay activist sentenced to a further 22 years in prison: Sue Sha Shinn Thant has already received a 3-year sentence and faces further charges.' https://www.rfa.org/english/news/myanmar/myanmar-activist-sentenced-12142022054247.html. Accessed 22 July 2023.

RFI, 2013. 'Mass wedding: Symbolic action of LGBT community in Vietnam.' 29 May. https://www.rfi.fr/vi/viet-nam/20130529-dam-cuoi-tap-the-tuong-trung-dau-tien-cua-cong-dong-lgbt-viet-nam. Accessed 5 December 2024.

Richardson, Diane, 1998. 'Sexuality and Citizenship.' *Sociology*, 32(1): 83–100.

Richardson, Diane, 2000. 'Constructing Sexual Citizenship: Theorizing sexual rights.' *Critical Social Policy*, 20(1): 105–135.

Richardson, Diane, 2017. 'Rethinking Sexual Citizenship.' *Sociology*, 51(2): 208–224.

Ritchie, Jason, 2015. 'Pinkwashing, homonationalism, and Israel-Palestine: The conceits of queer theory and the politics of the ordinary.' *Antipode*, 47(3): 616–634.

Rizzo, Domenico, 2009. 'Dainiji taisen igo no kōteki ryōiki to gei no senryaku (Public spheres and gay politics since the Second World War).' In Robert Aldrich ed., *Dōseiai no rekishi* (Gay life and culture: A world history). Trans. by Hideshi Tanaka and Takao Taguchi. Tokyo: Tōyō Shorin, pp. 197–221.

Robinson, Will, 2016. 'Donald Trump Enters Stage to "Les Mis" Theme, Welcomes "Deplorables".' *Entertainment Weekly*. 16 September. https://ew.com/article/2016/09/16/donald-trump-les-mis-deplorables/. Accessed 22 October 2024.

RoCK (Rainbow Community Kampuchea), 2019. '"I married a man to satisfy my parents:" Family violence towards lesbian, bisexual and transgender (LBT) people in Cambodia. June 2019.' https://www.rockcambodia.org/wp-content/uploads/2020/07/Family-Violence-LBT_ENG-19.06.2019.pdf. Accessed 30 September 2024.

Rorty, Richard, 1989. *Contingency, Irony, and Solidarity*. Cambridge: Cambridge University Press.

Rorty, Richard, 2000. *Gūzensei, aironī, rentai: Riberaru yūtopia no kanōsei* (Coincidence, Irony, Solidarity: The Possibility of a Liberal Utopia). Trans. by Junichi Saito, Masahiko Okawa and Ryuichi Yamaoka. Tokyo: Iwanami Shoten.

Sabsay, Leticia, 2012. 'The Emergence of the Other Sexual Citizen: Orientalism and the Modernisation of Sexuality.' *Citizenship Studies*, 16(5–6): 605–623.

Saitō, Jun'ichi, 2000. *Kōkyōsei* (Publicness). Tokyo: Iwanami Shoten.

Saitō, Masami and Tomomi Yamaguchi, 2012. '"Seiteki shikō" o megutte: Miyazaki-ken Miyakonojō-shi no jōrei-zukuri to "Sekai nippō" (On 'sexual orientation': Miyazaki Prefecture's Miyakonojō City's ordinance-making and the '*World Times*').' In Tomomi Yamaguchi, Masami Saitō and Chiki Ogiue eds., *Shakai undō no tomadoi: feminizumu no 'ushinawareta jidai' to kusa-no-ne hoshu undō* (The confusion in social movements: Feminism's 'lost era' and grassroots conservative movements). Tokyo: Keisō Shobō, pp. 147–200.

Saitō, Takuya, 2023. 'Kenta-san (Mr. Kenta).' In Hitoshi Ishida ed., *Yakudou suru gei mubumento* (Dynamism of the gay movement). Tokyo: Akashi Shoten, pp. 340–434.

Sakamoto, Yasuyuki, 1988. *Kanbojiago jiten* (Dictionary of Cambodian). Tokyo: Tokyo University of Foreign Studies.

Sakamoto, Yasuyuki, 2006. *Kanbojiago jiten (I–III)* (Dictionary of Cambodian). Tokyo: Tokyo University of Foreign Studies.

Sakinah Ummu Haniy, 2016. 'UI minta studi klub seksualitas tak gunakan nama dan logo kampus (UI asks sexuality club not to use campus name and logo).' *Rappler,* 21 January. www.rappler.com/world/universitas-indonesia-sgrc-ui-lgbt

Sanders, Douglas, 2015.a 'Myanmar These Gay Days. Proceedings for International Conference on Burma/Myanmar Studies.' *Burma/Myanmar in Transition*. Chiang Mai: Chiang Mai University.

Sanders, Douglas, 2015b. 'Same-Sex Relationships: Moves to Recognition in Vietnam and Thailand.' *Kyoto Review of Southeast Asia*, Issue 18. https://kyotoreview.org/issue-18/same-sex-relationships-vietnam-thailand/. Accessed 5 December 2024.

Sandy, Larissa, 2013. 'International agendas and sex worker rights in Cambodia.' In Michele Ford, ed., *Social Activism in Southeast Asia*. London: Routledge, pp. 154–169.

Sankei shinbun, 2015. 'Hashimoto shi VS Jinken Hakubutsukan (ge) "itsumo no sabetsu, jinken no onparēdo": Rinyūaru 1 nengo, ikinari tsuittā de mō hihan (Mr. Hashimoto VS Osaka Museum of Human Rights (vol. 2) 'on parade of the usual discrimination and human rights': One year after the renewal, suddenly fierce criticism on Twitter).' 5 October.

Sasaki, Manabu, 2015. 'Betonamu hirakareta douseikon (Vietnam opens up to same-sex marriage).' *Asahi Shimbun* morning edition, 5 March.

Satō, Kazumi, 2007. 'Minshintō seiken no "jinken gaikō": Gyakkyō no naka no sofuto pawā gaikō no kokoromi (The DPP Government's 'human rights diplomacy': An attempt at soft power diplomacy in the midst of adversity).' *Nihon taiwan gakkai hō* (Bulletin of the Japan association for Taiwan studies), 9: 131–153.

Sayoni, 2011. 'Report on Discrimination against Women in Singapore based on Sexual Orientation and Gender Identity.' https://www2.ohchr.org/english/bodies/cedaw/docs/ngos/Sayoni_Singapore49.pdf. Accessed 8 August 2024.

Schouten, Maria Johanna C., 1998. *Leadership and social mobility in a Southeast Asian society: Minahasa, 1677–1983*. Leiden: KITLV Press.

Scott, James C., 1985. *Weapons of the Weak: Everyday Forms of Peasant Resistance.* New Haven: Yale University Press.

Scott, Joan Wallach, 1988. *Gender and the Politics of History*, Thirtieth anniversary edition. New York: Columbia University Press.

Seckinelgin, Hakan, 2009. 'Global Activism and Sexualities in the Time of HIV/AIDS.' *Contemporary Politics*, 15(1): 103–18.

Sedgwick, Eve Kosofsky, 1985. *Between Men: English Literature and Male Homosocial Desire*. New York: Columbia University Press.

Seidman, Steven, 2001. 'From Identity to Queer Politics: Shifts in Normative Heterosexuality and the Meaning of Citizenship.' *Citizenship Studies*, 5(3): 321–328.

Shazwan Mustafa Kamal, 2018. 'Wan Azizah: LGBT "practices" must be kept private.' *Malay Mail Online*, 20 August. https://www.malaymail.com/news/malaysia/2018/08/20/wan-azizah-lgbt-fine-as-long-as-kept-in-private-not-glamourised/1664056. Accessed 31 August 2019.

Shen, Hsiu-Hua, 2019. 'Kon'in byōdōka ni okeru Taiwan josei undō no kōken (The contribution of the Taiwanese women's movement in marriage equalization).' Trans. by Ken Suzuki and Zhenhui Liang. *Nihon Taiwan gakkai hō* (Journal of the Japan Association for Taiwan Studies), 21: 97–107.

Shiino, Nobuo, 2017. 'Homosexuality o megutte: Homosekushuaru ga byōki de naku naru made (On homosexuality: Until homosexuals stopped being sick).' *Rikkyō daigaku kokusai gakubu kiyō* (Bulletin of the Rikkyo University Faculty of International Studies), 7(2): 39–47.

Shimizu, Akiko, 2017. 'Daibāshiti kara kenri hoshō e: Toranpu ikō no Beikoku to "LGBT" būmu no Nihon (From diversity to guarantee of rights: The US since Trump, and Japan with its "LGBT boom").' *Sekai* (The world), 895: 134–143.

Shimizu, Akiko, 2021. 'Toransunashonaru na undo toshite no toransufobia (Transphobia as a transnational movement).' Lecture at the International Institute of Language and Culture Studies, Ritsumeikan University, 18 December.

Shimizu, Akiko, 2022. 'Sūpā gurū ni yoru itten kyōtō: Han-jendā undō to toransu haijo (Unity by super glue in a single point of struggle: The antigender movement and trans exclusion).' In Shon Fay ed., *Toransujendā mondai: Giron wa seigi no tame ni* (The transgender issue: debating for justice). Trans. by Yutori Takai. Tokyo: Akashi Shoten, pp. 381–389.

Shin Ajia kazoku hō sangoku kaigi (Tri-party conference on new Asian family law), 2018. *Dōseikon ya dōsei pātonāshippu seido no kanōsei to kadai* (The potential and challenge of same-sex marriage and the same-sex partnership system). Tokyo: Nihon kajo shuppan.

Shingae, Akitomo, 2013. *Nihon no 'gei' to eizu: Komyunitī, kokka, aidentiti* ('Gays' and AIDS in Japan: Community, state, identity). Tokyo: Seikyūsha.

Shingae, Akitomo, 2021. 'Daibāshiti suishin to LGBT/SOGI no yukue: Shijōka sareru shakai undō (The future direction of diversity promotion and LGBT/SOGI: Marketized social movements).' In Kōichi Iwabuchi, ed., *Nihon ni ikiru, Nihon o hiraku* (Living in Japan, opening up Japan). Tokyo: Seikyūsha, pp. 36–58.

Shinohara, Yasuo, 2016. 'Dai 3 shō, Dōsei pātonāshippu seido unyō no jissai: Dai 1, Shibuya-ku no seido shikō to unyō no genjyō (Chapter 3, Actual operation of the same-sex partnership system: Section 1, Current status of enforcement and operation of the system in Shibuya City).' In Masayuki Tanamura and Shigenori Nakagawa eds., *Dōsei pātonāshippu seido: Sekai no dōkō, Nihon no jichitai ni okeru dōnyū no jissai to tenbō* (The same-sex partnership system: World trends [and] the realities of and outlook for introduction in Japanese local government). Tokyo: Nihon kajo shuppan, pp. 232–245.

Sin, Yuen, 2016. 'MHA says foreign sponsors not allowed for Pink Dot, or other events, at Speakers' Corner.' *The Straits Times*, 7 June. https//www.straitstimes. com/singapore/mha-says-foreign-sponsors-not-allowed-for-pink-dot-or-other-events-at-speakers-corner. Accessed 24 November 2024.

Singapore CNN, 2022. 'Singapore's Pink Dot pride rally makes a colourful return.' https:/edition.cnn.com/2022/06/19/asia/singapore-pink-dot-pride-gay-queer-lesbian-rights-intl-hnk/index.html. Accessed 21 June 2022.

Sinnott, Megan, 2004. *Toms and Dees: Transgender Identity and Female Same-Sex Relationships in Thailand*. Honolulu: University of Hawai'i Press.

Sinnott, Megan, 2010. 'Borders, diaspora, and regional connections: Trends in Asian "queer" studies.' *The Journal of Asian Studies*, 69(1):17–31.

Smith, Russell Arthur, 1992. 'Beach Resort Evolution: Implication for Planning.' *Annals of Tourism Research*, 19: 304–322.

Social Weather Stations (SWS), 2008. 'Third Quarter 2008 Social Weather Survey: 76% want family planning education in public schools; 71% favor passage of the Reproductive Health Bill.' http://www.sws.org.ph/pr081016.htm

Social Weather Stations (SWS), 2018. 'First Quarter 2018 Social Weather Survey: 61% of Pinoys oppose, and 22% support, a law that will allow the civil union of two men or two women.' https://www.sws.org.ph/swsmain/artcldisppage/?artcsyscode=ART-20180629215050. Accessed 21 November 2024.

Soll, Bianca M., Rebeca Robles-Garcia, Angelo Brandelli-Costa, Daniel Mori, Andressa Mueller, Anna M. Vaiteses-Fontanari, Dhiordan Cardoso-da-Silva, Karine Schwarz, Maiko Abel-Schneider, Alexandre Saadeh and Maria-Inês-Rodrigues Lobato, 2018. 'Gender Incongruence: A comparative study using ICD-10 and DSM-5 diagnostic criteria.' *Revista Brasileira de Psiquiatria*, 40(2): 174–180. DOI: 10.1590/1516-4446-2016-2224.

Soriano, Cheryll Ruth Reyes, 2014. 'Constructing Collectivity in Diversity: Online Political Mobilization of a National LGBT Political Party.' *Media, Culture & Society*, 36(1): 20–36.

Sri Handayani, 2016. 'Lengkap, Tujuh Permintaan Maaf Fidiansjah Usai Disomasi LBH Jakarta (Complete citation: Fidiansjah's seven apologies after being summoned by the Jakarta Legal Aid Institute).' *Republika.co.id.*, 23 March. republika.co.id/berita/o4hhk7394/lengkap-tujuh-permintaan-maaf-fidiansjah-usai-disomasi-lbh-jakarta.

Statistics Bureau, Taiwan Ministry of Education (*Jiaoyu Bu Tongji Chu*), 2023. *Yisi xiaoyuan xing qinhai, xing saorao ji xing baling tongbao jianshu tongji* (Statistics on incident reports of suspected campus sexual assault, sexual harassment and sexual bullying). https://depart.moe.edu.tw/ED4500/cp.aspx?n=0A95D1021CCA80AE.

Stuart, Elizabeth, 1999. 'Christianity is a queer thing: The development of queer theology.' *The Way*, 39(4): 371–381.

Stuart, Elizabeth, 2015. 'The Theological Study of Sexuality.' In Adrian Thatcher ed., *The Oxford Handbook of Theology, Sexuality, and Gender*. Oxford: Oxford University Press, pp. 18–31.

Su, Chien-Ling, 2001. 'Liangxing pingdeng jiaoyu de huigu yu qianzhan (Review and outlook for both-sexes equal education).' *Liangxing pingdeng jiaoyu jikan* (Both-sexes equal education quarterly), 14: 13–18.

Su, Lung-Chi, 2020. 'Tong yun nüshen liyuan biye. You Meinü chonghui minjian (A goddess from the GLBT movement graduates from the [Legislative] Yuan; You Meinu returns to the general community).' *Central News Agency*, https://www.cna.com.tw/news/firstnews/202001200110.aspx. Accessed 19 February 2021.

Sugiura, Ikuko, 2019. 'Seido to no ōshū ni yoru nīzu ninshiki: Dōsei kappuru no hōteki hoshō nīzu o megutte (Awareness of needs by reciprocation with systems: On same-sex couples' legal guarantee needs).' *Wakō daigaku gendai ningen gakubu kiyō* (Bulletin of the Faculty of Modern Humanities, Wakō University), 12: 61–81.

Sugiura, Ikuko, Aki Nomiya and Chizuka Ōe, 2016. *Pātonāshippu seikatsu to seido: Kekkon, jijitsukon, dōseikon* (The lifestyle and system of partnership: Marriage, common-law marriage, same-sex marriage). Tokyo: Ryokufū shuppan.

Suleeman, Stephen, 2019. 'Mengapa STFT Jakarta Terlibat dalam Isu LGBT? (Why is STFT Jakarta Involved in LGBT Issues?).' In Stephen Suleeman and Amadeo D. Udampoh, eds., *Siapakah Sesamaku? Pergumulan Teologi Dengan Isu-Isu Keadilan Gender* (Who are my fellows? Theological struggle with the issues of gender justice). Jakarta: Sekolah Tinggi Filsafat Teologi, pp. 13–22.

Suryakusuma, Julia I., 2011. *State Ibuism: The Social Construction of Womanhood in New Order Indonesia*. Depok: Komunitas Bambu.

Suvianita, Khanis, 2016. 'Against Hatred: LGBTIQ Movements and Human Rights in Indonesia.' Paper presented at the Seminar at Center for Southeast Asian Studies, Kyoto University, 12 February.

Taipei High Administrative Court, 2021. *Taibei gaodeng xingzheng fayuan xinwen gao* (Taipei High Administrative Court press release). https://tpb.judicial.gov.tw/tw/dl-75304-a88b76711faa4fd89c806f49a92fff05.html. Accessed 24 April 2022.

Taiwan Alliance to Promote Civil Partnership Rights (TAPCPR), 2013. 'Banlü meng kaidao qian ren ban zhuo duoyuan jiating xinren "zhao" guolai (Gathering of a thousand couples at the Ketagalan Boulevard banquet table: Newcomers in diverse families come and 'take photos').' https://www.coolloud.org.tw/node/75523. Accessed 24 December 2020.

Taiwan Gender Equity Education Association (Taiwan Xi-ngbie Pingdeng Jiaoyu Xiehui), 2006. *Yongbao Meigui Shaonian* (Embrace the rose boy). Taipei: Fembooks Publishing.

Tâm Lụa, 2019. 'Gender reassignment rights: 4 years of "suspended" guidance, many consequences arise.' *Tuổi trẻ Cuối tuần*, 13 June. https://tuoitre.vn/quyen-chuyen-doi-gioi-tinh-4-nam-treo-huong-dan-phat-sinh-nhieu-he-luy-1506320. htm. Accessed 5 December 2024.

Tamura-Tsuji, Keiko, 2016. *Shingapōru no kiso chishiki* (Basic knowledge about Singapore). Tokyo: Mekon.

Tamura-Tsuji, Keiko, 2023. 'Jendā to sekushuariti o meguru ajia no seiji (Asian politics around gender and sexuality).' In Yoichi Kibata and Satoshi Nakano, eds., *Sekai rekishi 24: Nijūisseiki no kokusai chitsujo* (World history 24: The international order in the 21st century). Tokyo: Iwanami Shoten, pp. 253–272.

Tan, Chris K. K., 2009. 'But "They are like you and me": Gay civil servants and citizenship in a cosmopolitanizing Singapore.' https://anthrosource.onlinelibrary. wiley.com/doi/abs/10.1111/j.1548-744X.2009.0. Accessed 26 November 2024.

Tan, Chris K. K., 2012. 'Oi. Recruit! Wake Up Your Idea.' In Andrey Yue and Jun Zubillaga-Pow, eds., *Queer Singapore: Illiberal Citizenship and Mediated Culture*. Hong Kong: Hong Kong University Press, pp. 71–81.

Tan, Michael, 1995. 'From Bakla to Gay: Shifting Gender Identities and Sexual Behaviors in the Philippines.' In R. Parker and J. Gagnon, eds., *Conceiving Sexuality: Approaches to Sex Research in a Postmodern World*. New York: Routledge, pp. 85–96.

Tan, Michael, 2001. 'Survival through Pluralism: Emerging Gay Communities in the Philippines.' *Journal of Homosexuality*, 30(3/4): 117–142.

Tan, Paul Kenneth and Jack Jin Garry Lee, 2007. 'Imagining the Gay Community in Singapore.' *Critical Asian Studies*, 39(2): 179–204.

Tan, Phong, 2008. *Ethnography of male-to-male sexuality in Cambodia*. Phnom Penh: UNESCO HIV/AIDS Prevention Programme.

Tan, Roy, 2012. 'A Brief History of Early Gay Venues in Singapore.' In Andrey Yue and Jun Zubillaga-Pow, eds., *Queer Singapore: Illiberal Citizenship and Mediated Cultures*. Hong Kong: Hong Kong University Press, pp. 117–147.

Tang, Shawna, 2017. *Postcolonial Lesbian Identities in Singapore: Re-thinking Global Sexualities*. New York: Routledge.

Taniguchi, Hiroyuki, 2016. 'Nihon ni okeru dōsei kappuru o meguru kenri hoshō undō no tenkai (Development of the movement in Japan for guarantee of rights regarding same-sex couples).' *Nihon jendā kenkyū* (Journal of gender studies Japan), 19: 19–31.

Taniguchi, Hiroyuki, Hitoshi Ishida, Saori Kamano, Kazuya Kawaguchi and Yuri Horie, 2017. *Zenkoku jichitai ni okeru sei jinin sei shikō ni kanren suru shisaku chōsa (2006-nen shigatsu~shichigatsu jisshi) hōkokusho* (Report on the survey of policies related to gender identity and sexual orientation in local governments in Japan (conducted from April to July 2016)), Grant-in-Aid for Scientific Research,

Japan Society for the Promotion of Science (JSPS). Grant-in-Aid for Scientific Research, 2013–2018 (Grant-in-Aid for Scientific Research (B), Project No. 25283018, 'Construction of Queer Studies in Japan').

Taylor, Keeanga-Yamahtta, ed., 2017. *How We Get Free: Black Feminism and the Combahee River Collective*. Chicago: Haymarket Books.

Tempo, 2016. Indikator: Kontroversi LGBT (Indicator: Controversy on LGBT). 6 March. majalah.tempo.co/read/indikator/150172/kontroversi-lgbt. Accessed 21 November 2024.

The Star Online, 2019. 'Women's group disappointed by govt backlash over support for LGBT community during rally.' 10 March. https://www.thestar.com.my/news/nation/2019/03/10/womens-group-disappointed-by-govt-backlash-over-support-for-lgbt-community/. Accessed 15 January 2015.

Thiên Kim, 2012. 'Chấp nhận hôn nhân đồng tính là văn minh! (Accepting same-sex marriage means civilization).' *Người Lao động*, 6 July. https://nld.com.vn/ban-doc/chap-nhan-hon-nhan-dong-tinh-la-van-minh-20120705080835850.htm. Accessed 5 December 2024.

Thoreson, Ryan R., 2011. 'Capability Queer: Exploring the Intersections of Queerness and Poverty in the Urban Philippines.' *Journal of Human Development and Capabilities*, 12(4): 493–510.

Thoreson, Ryan R., 2012. 'Realizing Rights in Manila: Brokers and the Mediation of Sexual Politics in the Philippines.' GLQ: *A Journal of Lesbian and Gay Studies*, 18(4): 529–563.

Thư Viện Pháp Luật a. https://thuvienphapluat.vn/van-ban/quyen-dan-su/Luat-Hon-nhan-va-gia-dinh-1959-2-SL-36857.aspx. Accessed 1 October 2024.

Thư Viện Pháp Luật b. https://thuvienphapluat.vn/van-ban/quyen-dan-su/Luat-Hon-nhan-va-gia-dinh-1986-21-LCT-HDNN7-37246.aspx. Accessed 1 October 2024.

Thư Viện Pháp Luật c. https://thuvienphapluat.vn/van-ban/bo-may-hanh-chinh/Hien-phap-1992-cong-hoa-xa-hoi-chu-nghia-Viet-nam-38238.aspx. Accessed 1 October 2024.

Thư Viện Pháp Luật d. https://thuvienphapluat.vn/van-ban/quyen-dan-su/Luat-Hon-nhan-va-Gia-dinh-2000-22-2000-QH10-46450.aspx. Accessed 1 October 2024.

Thư Viện Pháp Luật e. https://thuvienphapluat.vn/van-ban/Bo-may-hanh-chinh/Hien-phap-nam-2013-215627.aspx. Accessed 1 October 2024.

Thư Viện Pháp Luật f. https://thuvienphapluat.vn/van-ban/quyen-dan-su/Luat-Hon-nhan-va-gia-dinh-2014-238640.aspx. Accessed 1 October 2024.

Tiffany's Show Pattaya, n.d. The Legend: 45th Year Tiffany Show Pattaya. https://www.tiffany-show.co.th/about. Accessed 21 November 2024.

Tilaga, 2017. 'Gender & Sexuality.' In SUARAM ed. *Malaysia Human Rights Report 2016*. Petaling Jaya: Suara Inisiatif Snd Bhd, pp. 150–171.

Tiwon, Sylvia, 1996. 'Models and Maniacs: Articulating the Female in Indonesia.' In Laurie J. Sears, ed., *Fantasizing the Feminine in Indonesia*. Durham: Duke University Press, pp. 47–70.

Togo, Ken, 2002. *Jyoushiki wo koete: Okama no michi 70nen* (Beyond Common Sense: The 70-year journey of an *okama*). Tokyo: Potto Shuppan.

Tolentino, Roland, 2007. 'The Cultural Idioms of Filipino Transvestism.' In T. R Fernandez Tupas, ed., *(Re)Making Society: The Politics of Language, Discourses, and Identity in the Philippines*. Quezon City: University of the Philippine Press, pp. 169–188.

Tonny, 2016. 'Dr. Fidiansjah Plin-plan tentang Isi PPDGJ-III? (Dr. Fidiansjah's flip-flopping on the contents of the third version of Guidelines for the Classification and Diagnosis of Mental Disorders).' *Kompasiana*, 22 February. kompasiana. com/tonny.mustika/56c8387c86afbd6605973829/dr-fidiansjah-plinplan-tentang-isi-ppdgjiii.

Trâm Anh, 2012. 'Chuyện của người đồng tính công khai lớn tuổi nhất Việt Nam (The story of the oldest homosexual person who came out in Vietnam).' *An ninh Thủ đô*, 25 November. https://anninhthudo.vn/chuyen-cua-nguoi-dong-tinh-cong-khai-lon-tuoi-nhat-viet-nam-post154001.antd. Accessed 5 December 2024.

Tran, Quang-Anh Richard, 2011. *From Red Lights to Red Flags: A History of Gender in Colonial and Contemporary Vietnam*. PhD Thesis. University of California, Berkley.

Transgender Punk Activist, Taiwan (Kuaxingbie changyi zhan), 2014. *Taiwan kuaxingbie renshi quanyi CEDAW gongyue yingzi baogao* (Transgender rights in Taiwan: Shadow report on the convention on the elimination of all forms of discrimination against women (CEDAW). https://www.iwomenweb.org.tw/ Upload/UserFiles/files/Transgender-on-CEDAW-CH.pdf. Accessed 1 July 2023.

Tremblay, Manon, David Paternotte and Carol Johnson, eds., 2011. *The Lesbian and Gay Movement and the State: Comparative Insights into a Transformed Relationship*. London: Ashgate Publishing.

Troch, Lieve, 2002. 'A Feminist Dream: Toward a Multicultural, Multi Religious Feminist Liberation Theology.' *Journal of Feminist Studies in Religion*, 18(2): 115–121.

Trung tâm Nghiên cứu Kinh tế và Chiến lược Việt Nam (VESS) and Viện nghiên cứu Xã hội, Kinh tế và Môi trường (iSEE), 2021. Báo cáo Đánh giá Tác động Kinh tế của Hôn nhân Cùng giới tại Việt Nam (Report on the Economic Impact Assessment of Same-sex Marriage in Vietnam). Hà Nội: iSEE and VESS.

Tubeza, Philip C., 2017. 'Duterte favors same-sex marriage.' *Philippine Daily Inquirer*, 18 December. https://newsinfo.inquirer.net/953326/duterte-favors-same-sex-marriage.

Tuoi Tre News, 2013. '8,300 signatures for same-sex marriage in Vietnam.' *Tuoi Tre*, 18 October. https://tuoitrenews.vn/news/lifestyle/20131018/8300-signatures-for-same-sex-marriage-in-vietnam/1215.html. Accessed 5 December 2024.

Turnbull, Mary C., 2009. *A History of Modern Singapore 1819–2005*. Singapore: NUS Press.

Ueyama, Shinichi and Osaka Shiyakusho, 2008. *Gyosei no keiei bunseki: Osakashi no chosen* (Administrative management analysis: The challenge of Osaka City). Tokyo: Jiji Tsushin-sha.

Umpika Sawatwong, 2015. 'Thanon Sukhumwit kap Kankhayaitua khong Kitchakam tang Setthakit nai Phumiphak Tawanok khong Prathet Thai chuang Thotsawat 2480–2520 (Sukhumvit Road and economic growth in Eastern Thailand: 1940s to 1980s).' *The Thammasat Journal of History*, 2(1): 13–63.

Ünaldi, Serhat, 2011. 'Back in the Spotlight: The cinematic regime of representation of *kathoeys* and gay men in Thailand.' In Peter A. Jackson, ed., *Queer Bangkok: 21st Century Markets, Media, and Rights*. Hong Kong: Hong Kong University Press, pp. 59–80.

UNDP, USAID, 2014. *Being LGBT in Asia: Cambodia Country Report*. Bangkok.

United Nations Philippines, 2019. 'The UN stands with Pride.' 15 June. https://philippines.un.org/en/43044-un-stands-pride. Accessed 18 July 2023.

Ủy ban Quốc gia phòng chống AIDS, ma túy, mại dâm, 2012. 'Trưng cầu ý kiến về hôn nhân đồng tính (Referendum on same-sex marriage).' 6 July. http://tiengchuong.vn/Tin-tuc-su-kien/Trung-cau-y-kien-ve-hon-nhan-dong-tinh/7391. vgp. Accessed 5 December 2024.

Vachon, Michelle, 2004. 'King Lends Support to Same Sex Marriages.' February 21. *The Cambodian Daily*. https://english.cambodiadaily.com/news/king-lends-support-to-same-sex-marriages-38377/. Accessed 17 January 2025.

Vania Evan, 2020. 'Tren Ruqyah LGBTQ: Tak Efektif tapi Justru Tambah Populer di Indonesia (Trend of Islamic healing practices for LGBTQ: Not effective but increasingly popular in Indonesia).' *Vice.com.*, 14 February. www.vice.com/id/article/n7j3y7/tren-ruqyah-lgbtq-tak-efektif-tapi-justru-tambah-populer-di-indonesia.

Viet-Jo, 2005. 'Kōkyō no ba ni okeru gonin ijō no shūkai demo koui wo kisei (Regulation of the acts of assembly and demonstration of more than five people in public places).' 6 October. https://www.viet-jo.com/news/politics/051005051427.html.

Vietnam Law & Legal Forum, 2023. 'Legal efforts to better protect human rights of transgender people.' 28 February. https://vietnamlawmagazine.vn/legal-efforts-to-better-protect-human-rights-of-transgender-people-69628.html#:~:text=In%20 Vietnam%2C%20the%20right%20to,to%20the%20reassigned%20gender%20in. Accessed 5 December 2024.

Võ, Văn Thanh, Lê Kiên and Chi Mai, 2013. 'Same-sex marriage: Why is it not yet recognized?' *Tuổi trẻ*, 15 September. https://tuoitre.vn/hon-nhan-dong-tinh-vi-sao-chua-cong-nhan-569132.htm. Accessed 5 December 2024.

Vong, Sokheng, 2007. 'Prime Minister Hun Sen disowns adopted daughter.' *Phnom Penh Post*, 1 November. https://www. phnompenhpost.com/national/prime-minister-hun-sen-disowns-adopted-daughter. Accessed 30 November 2023.

Vũ, Hoàng Hiếu, 2016. 'Lên Đồng: giải phóng ẩn ức và thể hiện bản sắc ở những người thiểu số tính dục trong xã hội Việt Nam đương đại (Len Dong: Liberating repressed emotions and expressing identity among sexual minorities in contemporary Vietnamese society).' *Văn hóa dân gian*, 6(168): 20–27.

Vu, Kon Zao (Vũ, Công Giao), 2015. 'Betonamu ni okeru dōseikon (Same-sex marriage in Vietnam).' In Tomiyuki Ogawa, ed., *Ajia ni okeru dōseikon ni taisuru hōtekitaiō* (Symposium on the present legality of same-sex marriages in Asian countries), Fukuoka University Review of Law, International Symposium Materials, 61(1): 458–477.

Wakabayashi, Masahiro, 2008. *Taiwan no seiji: Chūka minkoku Taiwanka no sengo shi* (Taiwanese politics: The postwar history of the Taiwanization of the Republic of China). Tokyo: The University of Tokyo Press.

Warner, Michael, 2012. 'Queer and Then.' *Chronicle of Higher Education*. https://www.chronicle.com/article/queer-and-then. Accessed 22 October 2024.

Washida, Hidekuni, 2023. 'Voting behaviour after the collapse of a dominant party regime in Malaysia: Ethno-religious backlash or economic grievances?' *The Round Table*, 112(3): 249–272.

Weiss, Meredith, 2019. 'An interview with Malaysia's Foreign Minister, Saifuddin Abdullah.' *New Mandala*, 9 April. https://www.newmandala.org/an-interview-with-malaysias-foreign-minister-saifuddun-abdullah. Accessed 31 August 2019.

Welker, James, ed., 2022. *Queer Transfigurations: Boys Love Media in Asia*. Honolulu: University of Hawaii Press.

West, Candace and Don H. Zimmerman, 1987. 'Doing gender.' *Gender & Society*, 1(2): 125–151.

Wiegele, Katharine L., 2004. *Investing in Miracles: El Shaddai and the Transformation of Popular Catholicism in the Philippines*. Honolulu: University of Hawaii Press.

Wieringa, Saskia, 1998. 'Sexual Metaphors in the Change from Sukarno's Old Order to Suharto's New Order in Indonesia.' *Review of Indonesian and Malaysian Affairs*, 32: 143–178.

Wijaya, Hendri Yulius, 2020. *Intimate Assemblages: The Politics of Queer Identities and Sexualities in Indonesia*. Singapore: Palgrave Macmillan.

Williams, Tennessee, 1975. *Memoirs*. Garden City, NY: Doubleday.

Winter, Sam, 2006. 'Thai Transgenders in Focus: Demographics, Transitions and Identities.' *International Journal of Transgenderism*, 9(1): 15–27.

Wolfgang, Ben, 2016. 'Hillary Clinton seizes upon "nasty woman" as Trump takes verbal self-destruction to new heights.' *The Washington Times*, 26 October. https://www.washingtontimes.com/news/2016/oct/26/hillary-clinton-seizes-upon-nasty-woman-as-trump-t/. Accessed 22 October 2024.

Wong, Andrew and Qing Zhang, 2001. 'The Linguistic Construction of the Tongzhi Community.' *Journal of Linguistic Anthropology*, 10(2): 248–278.

Woods, Chris, 1995. *State of the Queer Nation: Critique of Gay and Lesbian Politics in 1990s Britain*. London and New York: Continuum.

Woods, Eddie, 2013. *Tennessee Williams in Bangkok*. Rhode Island: Inkblot Publications.

World Professional Association for Transgender Health (WPATH), 2012. Standards of Care for the Health of Transsexual, Transgender, and Gender Nonconforming People, Version 7. https://www.wpath.org/media/cms/Documents/SOC%20v7/SOC%20V7_English.pdf. Accessed 21 November 2024.

Yamamoto, Hiroyuki, 2018a. 'Firipin no gei komedi eiga ni tōei sareta kazoku no katachi: Wen Deramasu kantoku no "Bijo to shin'yū" o chūshin ni (Shapes of the family projected in Filipino gay comedy films: Focusing on director Wenn Deramas's "Beauty and Her Best Friend").' In Madoka Fukuoka and Shōta Fukuoka, eds., *Tōnan Ajia no popyurā karuchā: Aidentiti, kokka, gurōbaruka* (Popular culture in Southeast Asia: Identity, nation, and globalization). Tokyo: Style Notes, pp. 230–256.

Yamamoto, Hiroyuki, 2018b. 'Seibo to ningyo: Firipin eiga ni okeru gei kappuru hyōshō (The virgin and the mermaid: The representation of gay couples in Philippine cinema).' In Hiroyuki Yamamoto, ed., *Haha no negai: konsei Ajia eiga kenkyū 2017* (Mother's wish: Hybrid Asian film studies 2017). *CIRAS* (Center for Information Resources of Area Studies) *Discussion Paper*, 77: 34–40.

Yamazaki, Naoya, 2002, 'Taiwan ni okeru kyōiku kaikaku to "kyōiku hondoka": "Kokka nindō" to kōkyōiku o meguru seiji (Education reform and 'indigenization of education' in Taiwan: The politics around 'national identity' and public education).' *Kokusai kyōiku* (International education), 8: 22–43.

Yasui, Hiroshi, 2018. '"Chūtō de mottomo gei furendorī na machi": Isuraeru no seiteki shōsūsha ni kansuru kōhō senden no gensetsu bunseki ('The most gay-friendly city in the Middle East:' Analyses of discourse on gender and sexual minorities in Israeli publicity and propaganda).' *Nihon chūtō gakkai nenpō* (AJAMES), 34(2): 35–70.

Yokoyama, Michifumi, 2007. 'Nihon ni okeru feminizumu to ekorojī no fukou na sougu to ribetsu: Feminizumu to ekorojī no kessetsu-ten nikansuru ichi-kousatsu (Unhappy encounter and separation about feminism and ecology in Japan: A consideration about the juncture between feminism and ecology).' *Yokohama Journal of Technology Management Studies*, 6: 21–33.

Yomiuri Shimbun, 1998 'Hikisakareta dōseiai fūfu (A homosexual couple torn apart).' morning edition, 9 June.

Yomota, Inuhiko, 2017. *Nihon eiga wa shinrai dekiru ka* (Can Japanese cinema be trusted?). Tokyo: Gendai shichōshinsha.

Youngblood, Robert L., 1990. *Marcos Against the Church: Economic Development and Political Repression in the Philippines*. Manila: Ateneo de Manila University Press.

Yu, Ren-Chung, 2018. 'I Don't Support LGBT but am Against Discrimination.' Facebook page by Ren Chung Yu, 7 July. https://www.facebook.com/renchung. yu/posts/10103023690451915. Accessed 31 August 2019.

Zhao, Jing and Shi Tou, 2015. 'Women zai zheli (We are here).' *Nüquan zhi sheng* (Feminist voices). (Genya Fukunaga, trans., 2016. "We are here!": Beijing Women's Association. Documenting the Congress and the Chinese Lesbian Movement, screened at the 10th Kansai Queer Film Festival.)

Zhou, Daguan, 1989. *Shinrō fudoki: Ankōruki no Kanbojia* (*Zhēnlà fēngtǔ jì* (The customs of Cambodia: Cambodia in the Angkor period). Annotations by Hisanori Wada. Tokyo: Heibonsha.

Zurairi, A. R., 2014. 'Jakim's "spiritual camp" tried to "change" us, lament Muslim transgenders.' *Malay Mail Online*, 23 November. https://www.malaymail.com/ news/malaysia/2014/11/23/jakims-spiritual-camp-tried-to-change-us-lament-muslim-transgenders/788375. Accessed 31 August 2019.

Index